BINDING
Vol. II

The binding design on this volume is an authorized facsimile of the original art binding on the official Belgian copy of the Versailles Peace Treaty, which was signed by King Albert and Foreign Minister Hymans, and deposited in the Archives of the Belgian Government.

The Marne
The Forces of General Foch
drive the Germans back across
the Marne at Epernay

Painting by Georges Weiss

SOURCE RECORDS

OF

THE GREAT WAR

A COMPREHENSIVE AND READABLE SOURCE RECORD OF THE
WORLD'S GREAT WAR, EMPHASIZING THE MORE IMPORTANT
EVENTS, AND PRESENTING THESE AS COMPLETE NARRATIVES
IN THE ACTUAL WORDS OF THE CHIEF OFFICIALS AND MOST
EMINENT LEADERS

NON-PARTISAN   NON-SECTIONAL   NON-SECTARIAN

PRESENTING DOCUMENTS FROM GOVERNMENT ARCHIVES AND
OTHER AUTHORITATIVE SOURCES, WITH OUTLINE NARRATIVES,
INDICES, CHRONOLOGIES, AND COURSES OF READING ON SOCIO-
LOGICAL MOVEMENTS AND INDIVIDUAL NATIONAL ACTIVITIES

EDITOR-IN-CHIEF
CHARLES F. HORNE, PH.D.

DIRECTING EDITOR
WALTER F. AUSTIN, LL.M.

With a staff of specialists

VOLUME II

❧ ❧

National Alumni

CONTENTS

VOLUME II—1914

The Red Dawning of "Der Tag"

PAGE

CONTENTS

ILLUSTRATIONS

VOLUME II

1914

THE RED DAWNING OF "DER TAG"

AN OUTLINE NARRATIVE OF

THE FIRST GERMAN DASH FOR WORLD VICTORY AND ITS REPULSE

BY CHARLES F. HORNE

THE chief impression which must ever remain to mankind from the opening months of the Great War, is of the tremendous power and horror of the attack, and the yet more tremendous courage and endurance of the resistance. *"Der Tag,"* the day the German chiefs had so long planned, dawned with a red awfulness of flame and blood such as no man may picture to others, and no future generation can revision from our words. Germany in assault was the most stupendous engine of destruction which has swept over the Earth since the days of ancient, cataclysmic deluge. Yet at first the world of civilization remained blind to the full extent of the threatening annihilation. Mankind took three years to become fully roused, and to gather its full powers into triumphant resistance.

Those who met the first shock of the disaster suffered most. Belgians, Serbians, French and British, the full grief of mourning descended first upon these. Yet they did not break beneath the agony. Even when their suffering was sharpest, they remained firm to fight. That is where Germany miscalculated, where her fell design broke down. She underestimated the heroism of the human soul. She thought men had been weakened by the easy living which civilization had brought, had degenerated as once they did in old pagan days under the Roman "peace." And instead Germany found men had grown strong, unspeakably, unbelievably strong, uplifted by the higher ideals which the Christian civilization had taught.

When the German autocracy thus let loose its tremendous forces against bewildered Europe, the German High Military Staff did but follow plans long and carefully prepared. They had decided to burst upon the world as "supermen," that is, men made superhumanly strong by discarding every other impulse and desire, and concentrating absolutely on their one purpose, victory. They became monsters, unhampered in their trickery by the sense of honor which binds most men to their plighted word, unrestrained in their devastation by those principles of morality which set limits to the brute savagery of ordinary mortals. So far as might be, these self-admired leaders tried to make their soldiers as "hard" as themselves. This explains the sickening horror of those first months of the War, so unbelievable that even now comfortable people who did not personally rush into the struggle and face the actual presence of its brutalities, cannot help a secret feeling that these must have become exaggerated in the telling.

The strategy of any contest consists largely of outreasoning your opponent, of judging correctly the scope of his attack while so organizing your own as to assail him from an unguarded angle. In the mighty strategic contest of the Great War, Germany won the first points, because her opponents had expected that this war would be fought like others of recent days, with at least some outward respect for International Law and Christian doctrine. Germany escaped the entire scope of the Allies' judging, by having cast aside every such restriction. Her leaders attempted to disguise this "superhuman" or super-bestial attitude by raising noisy outcry against their opponents as breakers of the rules of civilized war. They accused the Allies of ignoring not only the established rules but also several others, which Germany invented on the moment and declared the Allies should have followed. But the German rush on Belgium soon made clear, to most of the horrified onlookers, the frenzied savagery of the German attitude, though not as yet the worldwide scope of the German purpose.[1]

[1] See § IV, "Belgium's Agony," by Whitlock, Von Bissing, etc.

What happened was, in its briefest outline, as follows: Germany, France and Great Britain had each guaranteed the neutrality of Belgium. No foreign soldier was to be allowed to march across this supposedly happy little oasis, so nobly sheltered from the storms of war. Hence the French authorities, always anticipating that the German deluge would sweep upon them some day, reckoned that the assault could only come along the border where the two lands actually touched, the long disputed frontier of the Rhine lands, Alsace and Lorraine. To bar this obvious line of attack, France built behind this eastern frontier mighty fortifications at Verdun and elsewhere, adding to these year after year, until she believed her defenses absolutely secure. Her northern border, where Belgium and Luxemburg intervened between herself and Germany, she left unguarded, not wholly, but comparatively so. She did not trust too blindly to Germany's plighted word; what she trusted was Germany's political common sense. A German attack on Belgium was almost openly equivalent to an attack on England, a preparatory step toward crossing the English Channel. Surely Germany, having a war with France on her hands, would not be so reckless as to challenge Britain at the same moment! Yet that is exactly what Germany did. For the sake of seizing the Belgian lands and attacking France from the weakest side, Germany defied Britain. And the whole British public, and the British colonials as well,[1] recognized the challenge. With the sturdiness of the great British brotherhood, they accepted the War as their own.

That unprotected northern frontier, with the tragic ravaging which ensued both in Belgium and in northern France, that was the price France paid for the British alliance. It was the means by which she convinced the world of the Nietzschean character of her foe. The unguarded border led Germany on to a full revelation of the falsity which ruled in her high places, the stupidity which was spreading in the low, and the brutality so ready to leap forth in all.

The German strategists hoped to go through Belgium

[1] See § XX, "Canada Rushes to Britain's Aid," by Aitken.

and then crush France utterly, in such swift time that unready Britain would be unable to interfere, and would then
accept the accomplished fact.   As for Russia, they counted
on her confusion and cumbrous slowness, weaknesses which
their own agents in high Russian office would increase.   They
believed Russia would not have her troops assembled until
after France was broken.   Austria was to crush Serbia in
similar swift fashion; and the triumphant Central Powers
were then to offer peace to their remaining foes, while holding fast to the desolated regions they had made their own.
With the purpose and direction of the first assault thus understood, let us look to the weight of the enormous force
which was to drive the blow.

THE STRENGTH OF THE OPPOSING FORCES

The Great War went back to ancient days in more than
one impressive feature, and most markedly in this, that it
was waged not merely by the small class of professional
fighters, such as had constituted the armies of preceding
centuries.   The German Government from the first, and the
others very rapidly as the necessity compelled, summoned
their entire people to help, if not in fighting, then in making
munitions or in other ways.   This was indeed a "War of
Nations."

Germany possessed over seventy million people, which
meant ultimately an army of perhaps nine million soldiers;
and her leaders had managed to rouse the populace almost
unanimously to a temper most effective for victory.   The
people actually believed their "fatherland" was being attacked.   They also believed themselves to be glorious and
their foes despicable.   They were as confident as they were
angry, fiercely pleased to have been assailed, so that they
could prove their power.   Moreover, they were to show
themselves in the end as stubborn and endurant as they were
fierce and eager.

Their ally, Austria, held sway over fifty million people;
but these were by no means so united or so formidable as
the German millions.   Most of Austria's subjects were of
alien races, some of them more inclined to fight against than

with her. She did her utmost. She drove all her peoples into war work, plunged them into utter starvation, and slaughtered thousands who refused to fight. She raised by violent compulsion some five million troops. But often these had to be employed for police duty at home rather than conquest abroad, and only a few of the most favored regiments showed anything like the German energy and efficiency. Later, from her Turkish alliance, Germany gathered another million and a half of valiant fighters, but she had always to supply them with German officers. From Bulgaria she gained half a million. In all she thus controlled some sixteen million fighting men, half of them being of excellent material, and perhaps five millions being immediately ready to be hurled into the attack.

Opposed to this enormous force, the only country really prepared for war, as Germany and Austria were prepared, was France. France with less than forty million people against Germany's seventy millions! That meant for France an ultimate army of five million, with an immediate fighting force of only about two million. Russia, her military ally most nearly ready for the fray, could perhaps ultimately have raised twelve million fighting men, patriots resolute and valiant enough, man for man, to have matched either French or Germans. But as Russia had never munitions for anything like her numbers, and as she never did succeed in training and bringing forward all her people, her armies were often little better than half-armed mobs, a fair match perhaps for the unwilling Austrians, but wholly outclassed by Germany's well equipped troops. German artillery swept away the helpless Russians by the thousands.

As to France's other allies, the Serbian soldiers were staunch and hardy as any in the world, but there were less than half a million of them all told. Britain's control of the seas was one of the finally decisive factors in the rescue of civilization;[1] but the immediate shock of battle had to be met on land, and Britain had only the relatively tiny army of one hundred thousand men to dispatch to France's aid.

[1] See § II, "Britain Asserts Control of the Seas," by Leyland, Reventlow, etc.

As the years passed she raised from her forty million **British** and Irish population an army of four million, and from her colonies a million more. Belgium from her eight million people might possibly have raised a million men to fight; but Belgium was so immediately stricken down that she probably never put into the field more than two hundred thousand.

Thus for the first phase of the titanic warfare, there were on the Eastern front some two million Austrians and half a million Germans matched against a roughly equal number of Russians and Serbs. On the West, three million Germans hurled themselves against two million Frenchmen supported by some scattered forces of Britons and Belgians. Not all of these multi-millions of humanity could meet in any one engagement. They were spread out along many frontiers and important transport lines. But, though we must thus deduct heavily from our estimate of the numbers meeting in the actual clash of battle, the mighty fact remains that never since earth began have men fought with anything like such giant forces, such destructive engines of death, or such enormous slaughter. Napoleon at his height of power never commanded more than five hundred thousand soldiers and never brought nearly that many into a single battle. Waterloo and Gettysburg were fought by less than a hundred thousand men on either side. Only in the Russo-Japanese war of 1905 did there begin to be any approach to armies such as those of the Great War; and even the masses of 1905 gave but a faint suggestion of the stupendous force with which Germany was to assail the world and with which the desperate world was to rally and hurl her back. "There were giants in those days."

THE OPENING MOVES OF WAR

The actual fighting began in the last days of July. Austria, immediately after declaring war on Serbia, began bombarding the latter's capital, Belgrade. This lay just south of Austria's domains, separated from them by the broad Danube River, across which the powerful Austrian cannon easily hurled their shells. It was an old-fashioned bombard-

ment, slow and rather casual, conveying no hint of how
different and how terrible was to be the later cannonading
of the Great War. To the bombardment the Serbians, being
deficient in artillery, made no adequate reply. Then an Austrian army gathered along the Danube and made some rather
desultory attempts at crossing, scarcely more than feints.
They were easily repulsed.

Obviously this was little more than a pretense of war.
Austria having made good her threat of attacking Serbia,
was waiting to see whether Europe would submit, and especially whether Russia would come to Serbia's aid. If so,
the main Austrian mobilization would have to be, not along
the Danube, but along her own northern and eastern frontiers where the Russians dwelt. She might have to postpone the promised chastisement of Serbia.

Russia did mobilize, and with unexpected rapidity, so that
by mid-August, two weeks after war began, the main Austrian forces were fully occupied against Russia. Perhaps,
therefore, it would have been wiser for the Austrian generals
to have remained merely on the defensive against Serbia.
The Austrian subject nations, however, had been so ve-
hemently assured both of Serbia's guilt and of her approaching punishment, that for political purposes Austria felt
pledged to an invasion. Hence, beginning about August
10th, an army of a quarter of a million Austrian troops,
mainly Hungarians because Hungary was most bitter in its
hatred of Serbia, forced their way across the Serbian border.[1]

Austria's chief military secret in preparing for this war
had been the building of enormous guns, far more powerful than the rest of the world suspected her of possessing.
Hence it was to her artillery that she chiefly trusted throughout. She reckoned now that her Hungarians plus her artillery would more than match any equal number of the sturdy
Serb mountaineers. The latter, however, shrewdly withdrew
into the mountains before the Austrian advance, until the
artillery had become hopelessly mired in Serbian mud; then
the mountaineers swept down upon the foe in repeated
charges, broke them at last, and sent them fleeing back to

[1] See § I, "Austria Devastates Serbia," by Savic, Petrovitch, etc.

Austrian territory. This first great conflict of the Great War is called the Battle of the Jadar (yăd-ăr′) River. It lasted for several days (August 18th-22nd), involved a quarter million men on each side, and ended in a complete Serbian victory—a triumph for the Allies. The Serbs had established beyond question their worth to Allied Europe, their power and courage as a fighting race.

Austria explained matters to her peoples by announcing that she had never intended more than a "punishing expedition" into Serbia, that this punishment had been accomplished, and her armies therefore had withdrawn. She neglected to include the fact that the withdrawal had been in any way hastened by the blows of the Serbian army. As for the punishment, it had been inflicted on the invaded district with even more barbaric savagery than that which at the same time was astounding and horrifying the western world in the German assault on Belgium.

THE RUSH THROUGH BELGIUM

Turn now to that assault on Belgium, the opening of the main campaign of the War. In the east Germany was but passive at first, was only holding back the attack. It was in the west that she had decided to win the contest swiftly by crushing France with all possible haste. Hence the advance upon Belgium was begun even before war was declared upon France. In previous years the Germans had built "strategic" railways which ran straight to Belgium's border and stopped there, railways having very little use in peace but of enormous value for her long-laid war plan. By these roads she hurled great armies into Belgium, crossing the frontier on August 3rd.[1]

For this invasion the German army leaders offered an excuse. They said to the Belgians, France has already sent soldiers into your country, and thus broken the international promise of sparing you; hence we must meet her in the same way. This accusation against France was wholly untrue. As our previous volume has shown, France

[1] See § III, "The Assault on Liege," by Leman, Bethmann-Hollweg, etc.

withheld her troops everywhere at an obvious distance behind her own frontiers.   In fact, the German Chancellor soon uttered a franker statement of the true German view. He announced to his parliament that Germany had deliberately wronged Belgium, because that was the easiest way —indeed, he implied it was the only way—by which Germany could win the war.   Thus spoke the "superman!" Whatever was of value for Germany was to be done, no matter what crimes it involved, what treachery, or what robbery and massacre of the unoffending Belgians.

Of course, not all Germans concurred in this policy of falsehood. The vast majority of the people, and presumably many of the officials themselves, believed religiously every statement issued by their government.   They had worked themselves into that state of emotional hypnosis in which a person can believe anything he wishes to believe.   Their whole course during the first months of the war reveals them as a people who had thus lost their power of reasoning, monomaniacs obsessed with the idea that they were always right and their foes wholly evil and to be destroyed.   It is not possible for other human beings to live with monomaniacs who have thus rejected their human brotherhood and become pledged to self-worship and to slaughter.

The diaries kept by German soldiers at the front form most revealing reading on this point.   Every writer repeats the tales of atrocious and unprovoked assaults by Belgian civilians.   Not one has really encountered such a case himself; all have simply heard and believed the rumors.   Only one or two of the diarists have bothered to investigate individual stories, and they have found these unproven; yet they continue to believe.   Some of the writers regret the horrors everywhere perpetrated by their comrades in revenge, but to not one does it occur that the torture of a friend of yours gives not the slightest reason or justification for your torturing another and quite innocent person, that the two facts are in truth wholly unrelated—except by your own unreasoning fury.

There can be little question to-day that the German Government had deliberately worked its soldiers up to this pitch of frenzy, so as to make them fit instruments for its policy of severity.   The German leaders who seized Belgium meant to keep Belgium, had always planned to do so, and meant to rule the surviving Belgian population as a wholly crushed and submissive peasant people.   Germany did not want another Poland or another Alsace, grumbling in constant protest.   Hence the daring and desperate resistance of the Belgian Government and the Belgian army probably did but little to aggravate the desolation which would in any case have been at some stage inflicted upon the helpless populace.[1]

The first large organized resistance of the Belgian army occurred some twenty miles behind their frontier.   When the invading Germans reached the city of Liege (Lee-ā-zh), the third largest in Belgium, they found its fortifications hastily manned for resistance.   They assailed the line of forts promptly and boldly, rushing forward in masses, just as they had rushed upon and overwhelmed the French in 1870.   Their opening tactics were thus the same as half a century before.   But man's defensive weapons had developed enormously in that half century.   Such a rush of human bodies was impossible against the machine guns and other firearms of to-day.   The Germans learned this slowly and at heavy cost.

They were held back at Liege from August 4th until about August 14th; and they only battered their way onward then because they borrowed the huge guns or "howitzers" made by their Austrian allies.   Liege was supposed to be a fortress of the highest grade; but the new monster guns easily wiped the Belgian forts out of existence.   The Austrian howitzers and the Belgian machine guns thus furnished the first two examples of the increasing deadliness of warfare, of the human insect's increasing physical littleness and helplessness in the midst of his own terrible inventions.

Liege marked the only large or temporarily successful resistance of the Belgian army without French or British assistance.   There were several minor engagements; but

[1] See § VIII, "The Destruction of Louvain," by Essen, Von Jagow, etc.

the main body of the Belgians fell back to their still more celebrated city fortress, Antwerp, the center and citadel of their country. Their capital, Brussels, they abandoned to the Germans, who entered it on August 20th. For the moment the German commanders contented themselves with this. They left northern and western Belgium untouched, while they swept southward along the open road to France.

FRANCE IN HER HOUR OF TRIAL

Meanwhile, what of the French? Their troops had been swiftly marshaled along that eastern or German border where they expected the attack. They were less prompt of mobilization than the Germans, who had planned the moment of assault. Yet the French were marvelously prompt in this enormous work of gathering an entire nation into arms. Within four days they were prepared, and began a tentative invasion into Alsace. They were at first merely feeling out the Germans. Was there a huge force of enemies in Alsace as well as at Liege? Was the German blow to fall upon two sides at once? Finding Alsace but thinly guarded, the advance grew bolder. A considerable portion of the former French provinces of Alsace and Lorraine was reoccupied, amid the rejoicing welcome of the inhabitants. A striking contrast this to the German invasion and destruction in neutral Belgium! In Alsace a populace whose majority were German both by birth and ancestry and who were at least nominally enemies to the French, were treated with every kindness and encouragment.[1]

An increasing rush of German troops soon met and checked this French advance. The first large Franco-German battle of the war was fought here on German territory on August 21st not far from Metz. The Germans call it the battle of Lorraine, though the French have called it the "First Battle of Nancy," taking the name from their own metropolis nearest to the region, the city in which General Joffre (zhof) had established his headquarters. The contest resulted in decided defeat for the Frenchmen. They retreated in disorder, and were only savd from worse by

[1] See § VI, "The French Invade Alsace," by Perris, Steinacker, etc.

the steadiness of one corps thenceforth known as the Ironsides. The commander of this division, who thus first won distinction among French generals, was he who was afterward to win the main distinction of the War, General Foch (Fōsh).

In one way this first battle of Nancy was but a part of the "Battle of the Frontiers," the series of huge engagements waged wherever the advancing French and German armies met.[1] The French were shifting their line of defense rapidly from the east to the threatened north. Some of their troops crossed the Belgian frontier by August 15th, when they helped the Belgians drive the enemy back from the Belgian city of Dinant (Dē-nahn'). The French troops that crossed the border in this region did not, however, advance far before they met the main German forces. Everywhere the French advance guards were pushed back. The opening stroke of this widespread frontier battle may be assigned to August 20th, when the great German howitzers, having been securely planted before Namur (Nă-meer'), began their bombardment of that last Belgian frontier forss.

Namur was a fortified city as powerful as Liege; and the A. had counted considerably on its resistance. But it pro helpless before the mighty guns; and by August 23rd the r ainder of its Belgian garrison retreated into France to esc capture. On August 22nd the general battle began. It hief and decisive moment occurred when the Germans fo d their way across the Meuse (muse) River, flowing fr Dinant to Namur. This compelled a general retreat of t French in the east, and meanwhile they were being forced ack from Charleroi (shăr-lĕ-rwah) in the western area. Ve may well speak of each of these movements as a grea battle in itself. To their number we must add one still fur er west at Mons, where the western extreme of the French defense line was being hurriedly occupied by the first British troops who had hastened to the continent, that "first hundred thousand" under Sir John French. These fell back from Mons on August 24th, being

[1] See § VII, "The Battle of the Frontiers," by Joffre, Steinacker, etc.

the last of the defending line to be withdrawn from Belgium.

Now came the retreat to the Marne. French strategists tell us that General Joffre had never wished to send his troops to the northern frontier. Belgium's heroic resistance had compelled France in honor to hasten to the rescue. Now the rescue had failed, and Joffre resumed his original purpose. He was resolved to retreat until his still gathering forces could be all prepared, and could meet the Germans under the best possible conditions.

Hence ensued wild and terrifying days for Western Europe. The little British force had the farthest to retreat and had been the last to start. Again and again it seemed as though the Britons must be engulfed in the onrushing wave of Germans under General von Kluck. Moreover, the German troops carried into France the same systematic grimness which they had shown in Belgium. They marched, they fought, they rioted with the strength of delirium. They were drunken with the pride of conquest and the plundered liquors of France. The world grew sick with a mingling of disgust and fear.

By September 1st von Kluck's advance was threatening Paris. Must this great metropolis also be abandoned to ravage? The French Government heroically refused to order Joffre to alter his plan of retreat. If Paris must be sacrificed, it must. On September 3rd the Government officially withdrew from the capital and established its masses of clerks and counselors at Bordeaux.[1]

Then came the dramatic moment of the German army's change of direction. If the French could abandon the rich prize of Paris, so also could the Germans. Instead of spending time and men on its besiegement, von Kluck turned suddenly away from the capital and moved eastward to join the other German armies in their pursuit of the still retreating French.

But that retreat now ceased. South of the Marne River, in a great arc swinging from Paris southeast and then northeast till it reached Verdun and then swung southeast again into Alsace, the French nation had turned at bay, to begin

[1] See § XI, "The Abandonment of Paris," by Galliéni, etc.

the mighty Battle of the Marne, the battle that saved France, and so perhaps saved the world.[1]

THE REPULSE OF THE GERMAN RUSH

This stupendous struggle may be best grasped by noting its three successive phases. The first, which is commonly spoken of as a separate battle, occurred along the Alsace frontier beyond Verdun. Here, where the French had been beaten back from German territory in the first battle of Nancy, there gradually increased from about August 25th a second and far greater battle of Nancy. This was an attempt by the Germans, commanded by Prince Rupprecht of Bavaria, to break through the eastern frontier defenses and march in behind the main French army which was retreating from the north. The Germans planned thus to cut off the French army from its supplies and encircle it in a vast destruction, like that in which the French armies in 1870 had been similarly encompassed.

The last week of August was spent around Nancy in partial attack and counter-attack, the grouping of forces for the main assault. Then for another entire week, from September 1st to 7th, the Germans conducted a tremendous artillery attack. Under cover of this they hurled corps after corps of infantry against the French positions, often advancing in dense masses as at Liege. But the French had also a special gun which they had invented for this war, the "75," which worked far more rapidly and more accurately than any other. With the 75's and with the bayonet the French drove back each charge, however desperate. The assailants perished in countless thousands, and in vain; autocracy had never been more spendthrift of its "cannon-fodder." This defense of the hills, called the Grand Couronné of Nancy, was the real turning of the tide, the breaking point of the first great German rush which had so nearly annihilated France.[2]

While the struggle on the Grand Couronné was still at issue, von Kluck made that famous turn aside from Paris, sweeping across the front of its defenders. These, under

---

[1] See § XIV, "The Marne," by Madelin, Reinach, French, etc.
[2] See § XII, "The Turning of the Tide," by Barrès, De Souza, etc.

General Maunoury, attacked him as he passed, and so on September 5th began the second phase of the Marne battle. This phase, from the river which here separated the foes, is often called the Battle of the Ourcq (oork). It was in itself a mighty four-day battle. Von Kluck, caught in flank, reversed his southward march and fought magnificently. He endeavored to flank Maunoury in turn; and he almost succeeded. At a critical moment the troops inside of Paris came pouring out in taxicabs to Maunoury's aid; and again it was von Kluck's flank which was threatened. The British now turned upon him also. By September 7th they had fought their way back across the Marne, retracing the last steps of their stubborn backward battle. By September 9th von Kluck, menaced on three fronts, withdrew from the Ourcq River in hurried retreat.[1]

Meanwhile, on September 6th, General Joffre began the third phase of the Marne battle, the great main struggle of the central armies. Matters were going well for him on either wing, before Nancy and before Paris. But what could victories at both extremes avail, if the main German forces broke through his line in the center? If they thus separated his two wings, they could encircle each and cut off its supplies. Here in the center were massed the armies of the Prussian Crown Prince, the Saxons under von Hausen, the Wurtembergers under their own Duke, and another Prussian army under von Bülow.

For four days the havoc was awful. The French were almost exhausted. In the very center of their line stood an army commanded by General Foch. On September 9th, Foch had used the last of his reserves. He summoned his men for one final effort and—smashed through the German line. It had been weakened even more than his own, weakened partly because von Kluck's retreat in the west had forced the other German armies to spread troops in that direction to protect themselves. So now the German center had given way instead of the French. The troops of Foch and others pushed into the gap. To escape being caught in their own trap, the German armies, still fighting fiercely

[1] See § XIII, "Battle of the Ourcq," by Clergerie, Von Kluck, etc.

both to left and right, were compelled to withdraw. The Crown Prince was the last to give to his own regiments the reluctant order to retreat.

Thus ended the first campaign of the War. It might even, despite all the four terrible years that followed, be called the decisive campaign. The first German plan for victory, the rush which was to have overwhelmed France immediately, had failed. Germany had now to face the consequences of her leaders' policy of falsehood and ferocity. She was a self-convicted criminal, abhorred by the public sentiment of all the world. She was not, and never could be, the victorious dictator she had hoped to become, able to defy with contemptuous arrogance the world sentiment against her.

The French, however, overestimated the victory of the Marne. They hoped to send the foe fleeing in disorder back to Germany. In this they failed. The German colossus was only checked, not overthrown. Its armies withdrew across the Aisne (ān) River, a retreat of over forty miles in some places; but there in a position of great natural strength they turned at bay.[1] The British, pursuing eagerly after von Kluck, had here perhaps their hardest fighting and suffered their severest losses. The French were more cautious; but soon all realized that the German retreat was at an end. To the early hand to hand fighting along the Aisne, there soon succeeded artillery duels. Both sides managed to drag forward their deadliest guns. Then came the digging of trenches for protection, then the raiding of trenches, and then their defense by building wire entanglements. The old style warfare gave place to the new. Generals had learned at awful cost the impossibility of a direct frontal attack as against modern firearms.

The strategic movements which next followed have been well called the "Race to the Sea," though it was at first an unconscious race. Hopeless of driving the Germans from the Aisne by direct assault, Joffre drew troops away from that eastern line where the Germans had been so easily held back at the Grand Couronné; and the soldiers thus gath-

[1] See § XV, "The German Rally on the Aisne," by Swinton, etc.

ered he sent to the west end of his line, planning to turn the German flank. The Germans responded with a similar movement to outflank this new French force. Another army of French was then sent to flank these Germans and another German army followed in its turn. Battle after battle ensued; and the trench line, which already extended east and west from Alsace almost to Paris, now began to push northward from near Paris, reaching ever onward toward the northern sea. Marching troops covered in reverse order almost exactly the course which the British and von Kluck had followed in the retreat on Paris.

GERMANY BEGINS A NEW CAMPAIGN

This opened the second phase of the Great War in the west. Foiled in her first rush, Germany now planned to seize all the northern coast of France and Belgium and thus keep the British out of the land war, locked in their island home, while southern France could be crushed in a more leisurely grip. Here again the German effort was stupendous and almost successful. And here again the resistance was brilliant, desperate, and at its very last extremity was just sufficient to hold off the exhausted foe.

The Germans first turned their attention once more to helpless Belgium. They set themselves to seize such portions of the land as they had before passed by. This of course was a second and more open breaking of their assurance that they only sought a passageway through Belgium, and would afterward "right the wrong" thus done her. Frankly as conquerors now, they brought up their huge guns against Antwerp. With ridiculous ease they battered to pieces its celebrated, but in our day hopelessly outclassed, fortifications. They soon captured the city; and its fall made them masters of all northern Belgium.[1]

Only a little strip of seacoast, extending from the west of Antwerp to the French border, remained outside their possession. Along this the little remnant of the Belgian army retreated, still fighting, until close to the French border at the mouth of the Yser (ē-ser) River they met the French

[1] See § XVII, "Capture of Antwerp," by Doyle, Falkenhayn, etc

and British troops, who were once more advancing to aid them. Here was fought the Battle of the Yser, a strange, weird conflict, amid sand dunes and flowing tides, with the British warships scraping along the beaches to join in the fight. It ended only when the Belgians threw open their dykes and flooded the Yser plain, turning it to an inland gulf upon whose shallow waters tossed the dead bodies of uncounted thousands of the contestants.[1]

Human life was held cheap indeed in those desperate days, unthinkably cheap. Autocracy wrung from its subjects all they had; and Democracy gave as copiously of its best. The richest blood of all the world, the blood of young manhood glorious in its fire and strength, was poured out in torrents. And Europe pays! Pays in that she must plod on now in later generations with the labor and the guidance chiefly of the "second-rates," those who through some weakness were not strong enough to fight.

The toll of lives was at its heaviest further southward along the Yser, where French and British fought against the invaders the first great Battle of Ypres (eep'r). In the course of the "race for the sea" the little British army of General French had been withdrawn from its trenches along the Aisne and sent back to the north to fight, almost where it had begun its campaign, on the Belgian border. It now filled the last gap in the defenses which stretched from Paris to the northern sea; and its defense centered around Ypres, the only Belgian city of any size that was still uncaptured. After Ypres had been destroyed by German guns, the only town remaining in the tiny unconquered corner of Belgium behind the Yser was Furnes (feern), a little place of about six thousand inhabitants. The Germans tauntingly called the Belgian ruler "the king of Furnes." But their utmost efforts never succeeded in depriving the Belgians of the solace of holding that one free strip of their otherwise captured land.

Ypres had now to bear the main brunt of this second great German effort for victory. For over a month, from late October until late November, the battle continued with

[1] See § XVIII, "Battle of the Yser," by De Wiart and Joffre.

endless cannonade and almost daily assaults. On October 31st both the British and French lines were on the verge of giving way. All their reserves had been exhausted; and the story is told of a mad scraping together of a last force of "irregulars," of cooks and clerks and wagon-drivers and staff officers, who were rushed forward together in one final effort at resistance. But again as at the Marne, the Germans, even more exhausted than their foes, were the first to give way. Again, as at the Marne, the world was saved by a margin so narrow that the victory must be accounted as the work of God rather than of men.[1]

After that the Allies' line was strengthened by new troops, and grew ever stronger. The repeated German assaults were more and more hopeless and more reckless, and frightfully costly of German life. In the main assault on the Grand Couronné at Nancy and now again at Ypres, the German Emperor is said to have come in person to witness and encourage his soldiers in the great final advance which was to mark the day of Germany's decisive victory. But on both occasions he had to witness instead the terrible miseries of defeat. Germany had indeed conquered harmless Belgium, and she held about one-tenth the territory of France; but in all its main purposes her carefully prepared assault on western Europe in 1914 had resulted in complete failure, had been as costly to her in human life as it was morally disgraceful.

GERMAN SUCCESSES IN THE EAST

On Germany's eastern frontier, on the contrary, she accomplished her purpose, though that purpose, as we have already seen, was merely defensive. She meant to hold Russia in check while concentrating her own strength in the west. This she accomplished by leaving the eastern war mainly to Austria; and she thereby achieved a further and ultimately larger profit. Austria, in her straining effort at a task far beyond her muddled strength, broke down so completely that she became thereafter, as the German leaders had expected, their helpless vassal. She was dependent

[1] See § XIX, "Ypres: the Struggle for the Channel Ports," by Hilditch, etc.

on them for her very existence, a mere tool in their crafty hands, to be wielded for their profit, at their will.[1]

At first, however, Russia gave Germany some uneasy moments. Her mobilization, so much more rapid than had been expected, was followed by a prompt invasion of Germany's border province, East Prussia. This advance was made on no such vast scale as the struggle in the west; perhaps four hundred thousand poorly-armed Russians were engaged. Russia thus began vigorously an old-fashioned war such as Russia understood. But the Germans, being unready, could not resist even this inefficient force. The small defensive armies of Prussians fell back defeated; and a fugitive populace began streaming toward Berlin.

One cannot but admire the steadiness of the German rulers under this shock to their excited and overconfident people. There was much talk in early days of the Germans having met this Russian invasion by a hurried shifting of troops from the western front, thus weakening their forces there so as to cause the western defeat. We know now that they did nothing of the sort. They sternly entrusted the east to its own defenders, gathered for it a few more troops, never so numerous as the Russians, and then took their most important step by sending to command in the east a retired general disliked by the authorities, but known to be a master of his art, von Hindenburg, a typical German commander, strong, patient, merciless.

The Russians were advancing in two armies. Von Hindenburg outmaneuvered the first one, defeated and utterly annihilated it in the Battle of Tannenberg.[2] The second he drove in retreat back across the frontier. Later, when another Russian invasion was attempted, he defeated this almost as completely in the Battle of the Mazurian Lakes.

AUSTRIA IN TROUBLE

Much as these East Prussian invasions startled the populace of Berlin, and much as their defeat uplifted the repute of von Hindenburg, they were by no means the principal

[1] See § X, "Russia Crushes the Austrians," by Vizetelly and Radziwill.
[2] See § IX, "Tannenberg, Russia's First Disaster," by Hanotaux, etc.

movements on the eastern front. The main Russian army was engaged not upon the German but upon the Austrian border. Here, where the Russian possessions in Poland joined those of the Austrians in Galicia, armies amounting to two million men on either side engaged in a widespread campaign. In numbers this huge contest probably equaled that in the west, but not in the power of the fighting forces. The Austrian attack was sharp at first, but was soon flung back; and the Russians were invading Galicia. There was a series of battles culminating September 2nd at Lemberg, the Galician capital. Here the Austrian resistance broke utterly. The main army was put to flight, and all of Galicia except the strong fortress city of Przemysl (prä-meel) was abandoned to the Russians. Przemysl was left isolated to withstand a siege, though the Russians had no such guns as had made the Belgian fortresses crumble before the Germans, so the siege promised to be one of the olden style, lasting as these sometimes did for months or years.

Except for the defense of Przemysl, Austria's rout was complete. Her main armies did not halt until they reached the security of the Carpathian Mountains, a huge barrier of rocky, snow-crowned peaks which separated the eastern Austrian province of Galicia from the more central domain of Hungary.

Now it was that Germany came to the aid of sore-stricken Austria. Von Hindenburg, having achieved his first victory at Tannenberg, made a sudden attack upon Russian Poland. So boldly and swiftly did he advance that he soon threatened the capital, Warsaw; and the ravage inflicted by his troops in Poland was far more widespread than any the Russians had visited upon East Prussia. The German advance accomplished its object. The Russian armies, abandoning their further invasion of Austria, hurried back to defend their own land from the terrible Hindenburg.

The first invasion was little more than a raid, from which Hindenburg hastily retreated. In late November, however, he came on again.[1] The battle of Ypres was over in the

[1] See § XXIV, "Failure of the German Advance on Warsaw," by Fortescue, Hindenburg, etc.

west; Germany had abandoned all hope of victory there. Her faith now turned to the east. What could the great Hindenburg accomplish for her there? The ever-gathering new troops were now sent to him until he had an army indeed. Slowly, heavily Hindenburg battered his way through the now assembled and multitudinous armies of the Russians. He drew their entire attention, giving Austria opportunity to rally, and even to attempt another Serbian campaign. Throughout November and far into December the Germans fought on in Poland, facing a winter cold more terrible than the foe. We speak of winter conditions in the trenches of the west as having been almost too painful and exhaustive for human beings to endure. But bad as were the western winter trenches, the sufferings in the east were still worse—and the German forces resisted them. The Russians were somewhat more inured against the cold. At length even Hindenburg admitted that the limit of human power had been passed. He withdrew a grimly depleted army from this first assault on Warsaw.

Austria had also failed in her repeated attack on Serbia, being badly defeated at Kragujevatz.[1] So that the first six months of the war now ended in a sort of general lull. The depth of winter rendered any large campaigning well-nigh impossible. Both sides could rest and take stock of the past, while straining every effort to gather fresh forces for the coming spring.

Germany had won one decisive battle at Tannenberg and she had won control of Belgium, of a considerable section of France and of a part of ravaged Poland. But she had lost an enormous number of her best troops; she had seen her plan of conquest completely checked by the Allies in the great defensive battles of the Marne and Ypres and Warsaw; and her ally Austria had been beaten to the earth at Lemberg, as also by the despised Serbians at the Jadar and Kragujevatz.

[1] See § XXV, "Kragujevatz, Serbia's Last Victory," by Laffan, Marincovich, etc.

THE SPREADING OF THE WAR

To offset these heavy blows, Germany had secured another and a useful ally, Turkey, which formally entered the war upon her side in November.[1] German intrigue had ensnared Turkey in this war in which she had no real interest, and in which, as her wiser leaders foresaw, she would become the victim whether Germany won or lost.[2] The aid of Turkey enabled the Germans to strike their first great blow for the throttling of Russia. She was now cut off from receiving supplies by either the Black Sea or the Baltic, the south or the north. Only the bleak Arctic port of Archangel remained open to her in Europe. Her sore-pressed allies could lend her little help; and Russia had shown no aptitude for creating her own munitions of war. Her armies, always inclined to degenerate into excited mobs, were soon to become wholly of this type, patriotic but incapable.

In the world beyond Europe, affairs had gone far worse for Germany. But this she had expected. Even before Turkey joined her, Japan had joined the Allies.[3] Japan lent her friends none of the land forces they so sorely needed for the European fight; but her navy, added to that of Britain, completed the Ally supremacy over all the oceans, islands and far unpeopled coast lines of the world. Japan promptly besieged and captured the German territory in China, and then the Japanese ships seized one by one the German island colonies in the Pacific. Australia also did her part in capturing these.

In Africa also there was genuine and at times bitter war, the British and French colonies against the German.[4] The Germans could get no help from home; the Allies could count on it to an ever-increasing extent. South Africa with its Dutch Boers, where Germany had hoped for a rebellion in her favor, remained loyal to Britain. A few embers of revolt were soon stamped out; and before the end of the year Germany's only remaining colony was East Africa.

[1] See § XXII, "Turkey Declares War," by Sultan Mehmed, etc.
[2] See § V, "Turkey Lends Germany Support," by Morgenthau, etc.
[3] See § XXIII, "Capture of Tsing-tau," by Okuma, Schlieper, etc.
[4] See § XXI, "Germany Loses African Possessions," by Karstedt, etc.

There the jungle depths enabled the Germans and their negro subjects to continue resistance for more than two years, but never with any prospect of ultimate success. They only hoped to hold out until the European War was over; and in this they failed.

On the oceans, as we have already seen, Britain's prompt gathering of her fleets had given her command. A few German commerce raiders managed to slip out from this port or that, and plunder Allied shipping for a while. But each raider sooner or later was run to earth by the keen British pursuit. Even Germany's war-fleet in Asiatic waters could lend only a momentary spectacular interest to the one-sided struggle.[1] This fleet, cutting away from its Asiatic base and threatened destruction by Japan, fled to the coast of South America. Here, off the Chilian shore, it attacked and destroyed two smaller British warships. Next, however, it stumbled on a British squadron which far outclassed it; and so it too perished. Its defeat was called the battle of the Falkland Islands.

In European waters Germany kept her main fleet safe in harbor and fell back, for vengeance, on her submarines. With these she achieved one startling success, when a single U-boat sank three British warships in one brief attack.[2] But here, as in the land war, new weapons of attack were soon met by new methods of defense. The submarines never again achieved so startling a success; and the battleships continued as of old the masters of the ocean. Not until a later period did Germany in her desperation find a new way of breaking international law by directing her U-boats to the destruction of unarmed merchant ships and neutrals. Thereby she opened a new era of the War. But during 1914 she accepted her defeat at sea. She was accustomed to waiting for time to ripen her revenges; and she hoped to settle her accounts with Britain fully, when the German victory had been won on land.

[1] See § XXVI, "The Sea-Fights in the Southern Ocean," by Dixon and Admiral Foss.
[2] See § XVI, "The Submarine's First Triumph," by Weddigen, etc.

AUSTRIA DEVASTATES SERBIA

THE SERB VICTORY OF THE JADAR

JULY 29TH-AUGUST 23RD

VLADISLAV SAVIC   WOISLAV PETROVITCH
PROF. R. A. REISS   GENERAL KROBATIN

The first actual breaking of the world's peace in the Great War began on the Austrian frontier. Having declared war on Serbia on July 28th, the Austrians next day began an immediate though not very severe bombardment of the Serbian capital, Belgrade. This ancient fortress city has been famous for centuries, in song and story, as civilization's outpost against the invading Turks. It was, however, wholly unfitted to resist an assault from the North and West, the Christian regions which it had so long defended. Especially was it helpless against the huge modern artillery in which Austria had specialized. Hence the Serbs promptly removed their seat of government to the more sheltered city of Nish, deep in the heart of the country.

Along the northern frontier Serbia was separated from the many Austro-Hungarian lands by the great Danube River; and along this for a week there continued a sort of casual fighting. Shots were fired from either bank; small expeditions dashed across and hastily withdrew. Then, about the tenth of August, the Austrians began a determined invasion in force, not along the Danube, but on Serbia's northwestern frontier, separated from the Austrian lands by two lesser rivers, the Drina and the Save, tributaries of the mighty Danube.

In this wild and mountainous Serbian region, there followed the first great pitched battle of the war between equal forces, one of those stupendous battles continued day after day along lines so extended that defeat on one field might well be counterbalanced by victory on another, many miles away. The Serbians finally crushed the center of the Austrian front and drove it into flight down the Jadar River, a little stream flowing from the heart of Serbia through the huge Tzer Mountain ridge and on down to the Drina River on the boundary. The contending armies in this first of the decisive monster battles of the war numbered at least a quarter million on either side.

The first Austrian invasion thus ended in complete defeat, a great triumph for the Serbs. Their chant of joy is here voiced by two of their best known patriotic writers, Savic, the soldier and scholar, who took part in the fighting, and Petrovitch, the diplomatic representative of Serbia in Britain. The official Austrian view of the defeat is given by the Austrian Minister of War.

Unhappily a grimmer thing remains to tell, for which we draw upon the pen of a neutral, Prof. Reiss of the Swiss university of Lausanne. War in the East has ever been a thing of hideous brutalities; but the savageries with which the Central Powers made the Great War so horrible in its opening phases were encouraged by an officially .manufactured hatred for which we know no parallel. The Austro-Hungarian authorities here commanded, and the Hungarian troops inflicted torture and shame and death upon the unresisting. They called their attack a "punishing" expedition; and they "punished" with no regard to age or sex or guilt. This is not a "war-propaganda" statement. It is what the sober voice of History must say for all the future. Read here the evidence, presented in its mildest form and practically uncontroverted from Austrian sources.   C. F. H.

BY VLADISLAV SAVIC

AUSTRIA-HUNGARY declared war, but hesitated to open hostilities. She was unprepared or unable to imitate the example of Germany in her violent advance into Belgium, and thus she lost some precious moments which perhaps compromised her whole Serbian campaign. Blinded by their overwhelming conceit, the Austro-Hungarian generals could not imagine that Serbia would dare to resist. They planned to occupy Belgrade, to hang a few hundred influential citizens, and thus quench their thirst for revenge by inflicting upon Serbia a moral and material punishment. They expected vaguely that the war might end in this way. It was this that saved Serbia for the moment.

Had Austria-Hungary attempted to imitate the German onrush through Belgium, Serbia's position would have been seriously compromised, for her greatest danger would have been a quick, resolute advance of the Austro-Hungarian troops already massed on her frontiers.

Fortunately, nothing of the kind happened. During the first week, the Austro-Hungarian forces confined themselves to incessant but irresolute and feeble attempts to cross the Save and take Belgrade, but every time they were repulsed with great losses. This gave time and instilled new courage into the whole Serbian army. Within two weeks, the Serbian army was concentrated, full of confidence, ready to fight an army half a million strong.

The Serbian army consisted of troops of the first ban, men from 20 to 30 years of age, the second ban from 31 to

37 years, the third ban from 38 to 45, and, lastly, the troops of the national defense, men from 45 to 55 and from 17 to 20 years of age. The mobilizing being general, Serbia was able to meet Austria at once with an active army 350,000 strong. The number of available men was greater, but Serbia was short of rifles, and many thousands of troops were armed and included in the active army some weeks later after some 120,000 rifles had been sent from Russia.

The newly annexed provinces were represented by some thousands of young recruits who had only had about five months of military service when war broke out, but who immediately gave proof of their valor and dashing bravery.

Two weeks later, exasperated by the Serbian stubbornness at Belgrade, the Austro-Hungarian generals quite abandoned the idea of taking Belgrade by costly frontal attacks, and so they concentrated large forces, 250,000 strong, in the northwest corner of Serbia. They crossed simultaneously the rivers Drina and Save, and spread their army over a front sixty miles long. They advanced proudly into Serbia, confident that the occupation of that country was a matter of two weeks. But already some serious and bitter fighting had taken place round Shabatz, with the troops who were defending that town and the passage of the Save. The Serbians withdrew, and, rallying their forces, met the enemy on the eastern slopes of the Tzer Mountain. The Austro-Hungarian left wing resting on the river Save and the right wing on the Drina could not be turned, but the Serbs made a fine coup, by dashing with unexpected impetuosity against the center. In a very hot battle lasting several days (the 18th to the 22nd of August) they beat the Austro-Hungarian center and occupied the ridge of the Tzer Mountain. A wedge was driven into the Austro-Hungarian forces cutting them into two parts, which were beaten one after another in engagements lasting ten days. This Serbian victory, known as the Battle of the Jadar River, was the first serious defeat of the Teutonic armies, and marked the turning point in checking the tide of German militarism. This victory was due to General Stepanovic, who is known in the Serbian army as "one who never lost a battle."

The advantages of this victory were twofold. The Serbians were able to hold on their frontiers large Austrian forces which could have been employed more advantageously elsewhere, and the moral effect of the victory was enormous. This little Serbia, of which Austro-Hungarians spoke with contempt, won the first general battle on a European front; and her success, thrilling through the hearts of the soldiers of the Allies, contributed to the Russian advance in Galicia, and set a fine example and was a good augury for the brave men who won the battle of the Marne.

BY WOISLAV PETROVITCH

When on the evening of July 25th the Crown Prince Alexander, acting as Prince Regent, signed the order for mobilization, Serbia was as entirely unprepared for war in every respect, save actual experience of warfare, as any country that has ever been summoned to take the field in self-defense. Little or none of the recent wastage had as yet been made good. The orders placed abroad for cannon, rifles, ammunition, clothing, and stores had not yet been carried out; heavy guns, automobiles, flying machines were lacking. During the campaign which followed, it frequently happened that a regiment went into the firing line with one rifle for every two men, those who were unarmed taking both the place and the weapons of those who fell.

The declaration of war on the 28th was followed on July 30th by a desultory bombardment of the unfortified Serbian capital from batteries on the opposite shore and monitors on the river. This, however, was the only action taken during the first few days, and Austria's failure to strike while Belgrade lay defenseless and open to easy occupation is significant testimony to her alarm at the European situation and anxiety to compromise.

It was impossible for the Serbian armies to line the Austro-Serbian frontier, which extends to 340 miles, especially as in summer the Save and the Drina are easily forded at numerous points. Voyvoda [Field Marshal] Putnik therefore fell back upon the traditional lines of defense, and, while the Government withdrew from Belgrade to Nish, he grouped the main armies in the Shumadija, whence they could rapidly move either north or west. Strong detachments were posted at Valyevo and Uzhitse, and outposts stationed at every important point on the frontier, after which all the General Staff could do was to wait till the enemy's plan of invasion materialized.

At the beginning of August, Belgrade, Semendria, and Gradishte were subjected to a more vigorous bombardment, and a number of attempts to cross the Danube were made and repulsed with heavy losses. One Austrian regiment was practically wiped out. The Serbian staff knew, however, that several army corps were stationed in Bosnia, and refused to be misled by these feints on the Danube. Attempts followed to cross the Drina at Lubovia and Ratsha, and the Save at Shabatz, and these were looked upon as more significant. Desultory fighting round places as far apart as Obrenovats and Vishegrad continued until August 12th, when the first penetration of Austrian troops into Serbia was signaled from Losnitsa. At that town and at Leshnitsa the Thirteenth Army Corps effected a crossing, while on the same day the Fourth Army Corps crossed the Save to the north of Shabatz, and other troops the Drina. By the 14th, over a front of about one hundred miles, six great columns had crossed the rivers and were converging on Valyevo.

The great bulk of the invaders had entered by the valley of the Jadar; the Third Serbian Army and part of the Second Army now advanced with all possible speed to meet them; meanwhile the remainder of the Second Army was ordered to block the advance from Shabatz. The Austrian plan was obviously to isolate and overwhelm the Second and Third Serbian Armies in the wedge of land between the Save, the Drina, and the Jadar; this object once attained, the road to Valyevo and Kragujevatz lay open, and Serbia was at the mercy of the invader.

On the 14th the Austrians were brought to a temporary halt by the Serbian detachments retreating from Losnitza, who dug themselves in across the Jadar Valley at Jarebitsa, and gave the main armies time to hasten westward by forced marches; but the first real shock of battle came on the 16th, when the Austrian column of almost 80,000 men, advancing from Leshnitsa to the north of the Tzer Mountain, was heavily defeated and routed at Belikamen, two regiments having been annihilated. Pursuing their advantage, the Serbians drove in a wedge between the Austrian forces advancing from Shabatz and those operating south of the Tzer Mountain along the Jadar. From this moment the Shabatz and the Jadar campaign became distinct operations.

At the same time, south of the Tzer, a violent and indecisive action had taken place, and the Serbians were at length compelled to evacuate Jarebitsa on finding their left wing threatened by a force advancing, in hitherto unsuspected strength, from Krupani. The retirement was completed by the morning of the 17th.

On August 18th the Crown Prince Alexander, having thrown the Austrians back upon Shabatz and brought up re-enforcements south of the Tzer, deployed his army on a front of thirty-five miles, extending from Leshnitsa to the neighborhood of Lubovia. Inspired with memories of Kumanovo and Prilip, the Serbians gradually forced their way westward, along the Tzer and Iverak ranges, and down each bank of the Jadar, throwing the enemy back upon Leshnitsa and Losnitza.

August 19th was the decisive day of the struggle; the Austrians gave way at every point; their retreat along the valleys was shelled by the Serbian guns advancing along the intervening heights, and gradually converted into a rout, in which rifle and bayonet completed the work of the guns. By the 23rd the Serbian armies, after taking quantities of prisoners and artillery, had hurled what was left of the Austrians back across the Drina. Thus ended the five days' engagement which will be known as the battle of the Jadar.

In the meantime strong Serbian forces had crossed the Dobrava Valley and advanced on Shabatz, round which the Austrians had fortified a wide circle. Violent fighting took place on the 21st and 22nd, on which day the Serbian troops worked their way round to the western approaches of the town. They tightened their cordon on the 23rd, and during the night brought up siege artillery. When the bombardment had begun on the morning of the 24th, it was discovered that the Austrians had decamped, after murdering in cold blood fifty-eight prisoners from the Thirteenth and Fourteenth Serbian Regiments, whose bodies were found piled up in three rows in a private house. By 4 p. m. the Serbians had reached the banks of the Save, and the first invasion of Serbia was at an end. The Austrians' explanation of their retreat, after the "successful accomplishment" of their incursion into the enemy's territory, on account of "more important operations at other points," is still fresh in public memory.

As a result of their attempt to "execute" Serbia, the Austrians had lost 8,000 dead, 4,000 prisoners, and about 30,000 wounded; forty-six cannon, thirty machine guns, and 140 ammunition wagons, besides an enormous mass of stores and transport. The Serbian troops had lost 3,000 dead and 15,000 wounded.

As for the civilians of the districts invaded, they were treated with a disregard of every law of civilized warfare, and a fiendish refinement of cruelty and malice, probably without parallel in modern history. The instructions issued to the Austrian troops, in the form of leaflets, began with the words: "You are going into a hostile country, the population of which is animated by fanatical hatred, and in which murder is rife in all classes of society. . . . Toward such a population there is room for no feeling of humanity or generosity." The procedure adopted was, on entering any town or village, to shoot out of hand either the Mayor or a number of selected inhabitants (amounting to fifty at Leshnitsa), in order to "inspire terror"; to secure hostages among those that remained, and to take prisoners and remove to Austria the youths under military age, "in order that King Peter might remain without soldiers for some years."

At the same time the troops were given to understand that the campaign was an execution, and that they might not only loot and burn and ruin, but murder, violate and torture at will, "because these people were Serbians." The pent-up hatred and natural instinct of the Magyar found expression in deeds which could not, without offense, be described here; as a mild example we may cite the case of a man who in the village of Dvorska was tied to a mill-wheel; knifing him as he was whirled round was then engaged in by the soldiers as a game of skill.

Extortion of money from a woman by the threat to kill her babe was common, and generally followed by the murder of both; wanton mutilation was commoner still; and this during the invasion. The record of the Austrian retreat is probably one of the blackest chapters in the history of mankind; whole families were burned alive, or systematically bayoneted and laid out in rows by the roadside; the treatment of the female population can only be hinted at; in their case the final act of murder must be looked on as a crowning mercy.

In the track of the army that fell back on Losnitza followed a small group of doctors, officials, and engineers of Serbian, Dutch, and Swiss nationality, who reported circumstantially, and photographed, what they found. A day will come when the indictment thus constituted must be met by the Magyar race at the bar of public opinion.

BY R. A. REISS

Very shortly after the beginning of the war Serbia cried out in horror at the abominable excesses of which she accused the invading Austro-Hungarian army; but the public, at least in neutral countries, remained skeptical. I confess that I was myself not convinced by reading the Serbian complaints. However, when I received the invitation of the Serbian Government, I believed it to be my duty to accept it. Is it not the duty of an honest man, if cruelties have really been committed, emphatically to denounce them, and if only isolated cases of atrocities have occurred, to point out that a whole army cannot be made responsible for the misdeeds of a few hooligans such as are found among all nations?

I therefore started for Serbia, and I conducted my inquiry with every necessary precaution. I did not limit myself to interrogating hundreds of Austrian prisoners and hundreds of eye-witnesses; I went to the spot, sometimes with shells bursting around me, to inform myself of everything that it was possible to investigate. I opened graves; I examined the dead and wounded; I visited bombarded towns; I went into houses and I carried on there a scientific inquiry, using the most scrupulous methods; in short, I did my utmost to investigate and verify the facts which I report in this work. I will not add to it any useless comments, I will leave my witnesses to tell their own story, and will merely state the facts that I have established. The reader will form his opinion for himself.

I. *Explosive bullets.*—After the Austrian defeats on the Jadar and the Tzer, Serbian soldiers returning from the front stated that when the enemy fired at them two explosions were heard; the sharp report of the rifle as it was fired, and a second explosion which seemed to occur sometimes behind them and sometimes in front. The explanation of this mystery was soon discovered in the bandoliers of Austrian prisoners of war. Cartridges were there found which were outwardly exactly like ordinary cartridges, except that they had a black or red ring round the case near the shoulder. On opening these cartridges it was ascertained that they were really explosive bullets, use of which is forbidden by the rules of war and international conventions.

Later on the Serbian army not only found cartridges of this nature on prisoners; they also seized whole boxes full of them. In addition the belts of machine guns were found wholly or partly equipped with cartridges with explosive bullets.

The boxes containing the clips which were stocked with these cartridges were labeled with the word *Einschusspatronen* or 10 *Stück scharfe Uebungspatronen.* The cartridges came from the State manufactory of Wellersdorf near Vienna and the base of their case bore the date 1912 and the double headed Austrian eagle.

If the bullet in its flight is stopped by some obstacle (bone, wood, etc.) the striker, driven forward by its own momentum, strikes the cap, and thus produces the explosion of the powder which in its turn explodes the bullet. This bullet, therefore, has precisely the characteristics of explosive bullets such as have been used up to now only for shooting pachydermatous animals.

I saw a very great number of wounds which had been produced by the *Einschusspatronen,* in hospitals, in the advanced ambulances and even on the field of battle. In general, the orifice of entry is normal and small. The orifice of exit from the body on the other hand is enormous and the flesh is often protruded in the form of a mushroom. The inside of the wound is shattered and the bones which have been struck are broken into small splinters. The bullet on exploding inside the body is broken up and its fragments act like shrapnel. To this must be added the effect of the gases. The wounds are therefore very serious. A limb which has been struck by an explosive bullet is almost always lost; a wound in the head or the trunk is inevitably fatal.

Ordinary bullets fired at a very short range may also produce wounds whose orifice is normal at the point of entry and very large at the point of leaving the body; but these wounds, of which I have seen a very great number, do not tear so large a channel through the body as wounds made by explosive bullets. Besides we have often extracted from the wounds shattered fragments of explosive bullets. There is therefore no doubt that these explosive Austrian bullets were used against Serbian soldiers. The number of persons so wounded proves that their use was very frequent. Surgeon-major Lioubischa Voulovitch for example has placed on record 117 cases of wounds caused by explosive bullets at the sixth reserve hospital of Valievo in nine days.

I questioned a large number of Austro-Hungarian prisoners on the use of the *Einschusspatronen,* and their replies led me to put the following facts on record:

1. Cartridges with explosive bullets were used in regiments Nos. 16, 26, 27 (Hungarian), 28, 78, 96 and 100.

2. They were only distributed to the troops towards the middle of December, that is to say after the defeat on the Jadar and Tzer.

3. The soldiers had no knowledge of them before the war: "They were always shut up in time of peace and their

use is reserved exclusively for war," said the witness, number 27, to me.

4.   Several soldiers were told that these cartridges were intended to be used for the purpose of ascertaining the range.

5.   An admission was made to many others that they were explosive bullets which produced very serious wounds.

6.   Good marksmen and non-commissioned officers received from five to thirty of these cartridges.

When this use of explosive bullets against the Serbians was denounced, the Austrians at first denied the fact but later they confessed that they used special cartridges to get the range.   The *Einschusspatronen* were intended to allow of the observation of the range by smoke during the day and fire by night, smoke and fire being produced by the explosion of the mixture of powder and aluminium contained in the interior chamber of the bullet.

I have made experiments with these cartridges and I believe it to be impossible in reality to get the range by means of the smoke or flame.   So far as concerns the smoke, the amount of it is relatively small and it cannot be seen distinctly at a great distance.   Moreover, just as in the case of the explosive mixtures of aluminium or magnesium employed in photography, the smoke is forced immediately by the explosion of the gases to a height which is more or less great, and the cloud of smoke is only formed at a very considerable distance from the place of the explosion.   It is therefore impossible that the smoke could show whether the target has really been hit.

The flame is well seen at night, but how can any one know whether it rises from the target aimed at or not?   Even when one sees a small fixed light burning in the night it is almost impossible to gauge its distance since the elements for comparison are absent.   How, therefore, can one gauge a distance with the aid of a light which only lasts an instant?

The Austro-Hungarians have also used expanding bullets (dum-dum) made in 1914.   I have in my possession specimens of these cartridges with expanding bullets, much less dangerous than the cartridges with explosive bullets, which were found in boxes on the battlefields of Crnabara and Paraschnitza.

II. Bombardment of open towns also entered into the program of the *Strafexpedition*—the Punitive-expedition—as the Austro-Hungarians called it. Thus the towns of Belgrade, Shabatz and Losnitza were bombarded.

I visited these three towns during the bombardment, and I there ascertained the following facts:

Belgrade. I was at Belgrade from October 2-4, 1914. At this date the Austrians had bombarded the town for 36 days and nights. Belgrade is an open town, for its ancient Turkish fortress cannot be regarded as a work of modern defense. It is an interesting historical monument and nothing more. This, however, did not prevent the Austro-Hungarians from bombarding it freely.

The shells were aimed at private houses, Government buildings and factories without any distinction. Thus the University has been almost wholly destroyed, the Serbian national museum exists no longer, the old royal palace is damaged, as are also the Hotel de la Loterie and the railway station. The State tobacco manufactory was burned to the ground by incendiary shells. Austrian shells struck the Russian and British Legations in spite of the Spanish flag which was flying above them, and the Austrian gunners sent two shots through their own Legation.

I made an examination to see whether the private houses which were damaged or destroyed by the bombardment were situated near the Government buildings, and I have ascertained that for the most part this was not the case. We must conclude that the Austrians were trying to destroy these houses. Sixty State buildings and 640 private houses were struck by projectiles.

Even the hospitals were struck. Thus the State General Hospital was bombarded four times; the private residence of the governor of the hospital, the operating theater of the surgical section, which is situated in the courtyard in a special building, and the lunatic asylum were damaged.

I draw the attention of my readers to the bombardment of the university, the national museum and the hospital. The

Hague Convention, signed by Austria-Hungary, contains the express stipulation that buildings devoted to science, the arts, and charity must be preserved if they do not serve any military end. These buildings were not being used for any military purposes, and they are not situated in the neighborhood of buildings whose destruction was necessary for strategical reasons.

I have also discovered some evidence of bombardment by shrapnel shells; in particular the university and its lecture halls are riddled with bullets which have come from these projectiles; I have kept a certain number of them as pieces of evidence. Normally shrapnel is only used in war against enemy forces and never for the bombardment of open towns. The use of such deadly weapons proves that the Austro-Hungarians sought to destroy the civil population of Belgrade.

At the time of my inquiry at Belgrade 25 civilians had been killed and 126 wounded by the bombardment. Among these latter 37 were struck by shrapnel and 87 by shells.

Shabatz. I was at Shabatz from October 22-24, 1914. Shabatz is one of the richest towns in Serbia. At the time of my visit it had already been subjected to an invasion by the Austrians, who were driven out after their defeat on the Jadar and Tzer. Since the commencement of the war this town has been bombarded almost daily, and very few civilians have remained in it. The center of the town had been almost entirely destroyed by ordinary shells and incendiary projectiles. Of the greater part of the houses there remained nothing but the façades blackened by fire. In all, 486 houses had been destroyed or damaged. The bombardment of this open town served no strategic object, for the Serbian positions were outside it.

Losnitza. I found at Losnitza the same rage for destruction which had already struck me at Shabatz. I was in this town at a time when there were neither soldiers nor civilians in it, but nevertheless shells, incendiary or otherwise, continued to rain upon it.

The number of houses burnt by the soldiers of the army of invasion is incalculable. Both in town and in country, houses have been burnt without any necessity. At the time of my inquiry in the four divisions of the district of Shabatz alone 1,658 houses had been burnt; namely, Potzerski division, 232; Matchvanski division, 457; Asboukavatzki division, 228; Iadranski division, 741. It must be observed that these divisions are agricultural divisions, and that the 1,658 houses burnt are village houses. In consequence of this burning 1,748 families of the four divisions are homeless.

The deposition of the Mayor of Petkovitza, Pantelia Maritch, proves that this burning was deliberately organized by the invading army. He declares that the Austro-Hungarian soldiers had with them little tin pots. They painted with the contents of these pots the houses which they wished to set on fire and then set a light to them with matches. Similar information was given to me in other places.

III. *Massacres of prisoners and wounded soldiers.*— The Austro-Hungarian army have frequently massacred Serbian soldiers who have been made prisoners. This statement is proved by the evidence of Austrian prisoners, by the official reports of the Serbian military authorities, by the depositions of eye-witnesses, and finally by photographs taken on the spot. I publish below some of these depositions, in which I substitute fictitious initials for the names of my Austro-Hungarian witnesses to avoid the disagreeable consequences which would otherwise ensue when they return to their own country.

A. X., of the 16th *regiment of infantry,* saw in a little wood at Preglevska Tzerkva eleven or twelve Serbian wounded asking for help. Lieutenant Nagj, of the 37th Hungarian Regiment, ordered that they should not be helped and even threatened those who wished to help them with his revolver. The Hungarian soldiers cut the throats of the wounded with their knives and bayonets.

B. X., of the 28th *regiment of the line,* states that not far from Kroupani a wounded Serbian was groaning under a tree. An Austrian soldier of the 27th regiment killed him with a revolver shot.

C. X., of the 78th *regiment of infantry,* saw at Shabatz three Hungarian soldiers (a Corporal and two soldiers) leading away a Serbian soldier who was a prisoner to shoot him.

E. X., of the 28th *regiment of infantry.* After an engagement near Kroupani E. X. went over the battlefield accompanied by hospital orderlies and found two wounded Serbian soldiers. He wished to take them to the Hülfsplatz (advance ambulance), but the Austrian soldiers refused to bring help to them, and a formal order was necessary to compel them to obey. E. X. accompanied the two wounded. When they passed by the 78th Hungarian regiment, the soldiers of this regiment struck the wounded with their fists; and suddenly a regular tumult broke out because the Hungarians wished to finish off the Serbian wounded with their bayonets. E. X. asked for help from the officers, who helped him to carry his protégés to the ambulance.

Mladen Simitch, native of Bobova, Serbian soldier of the 17th *regiment of infantry, second company, second battalion.* He was in the trenches with many other killed and wounded when the Austrians arrived. They finished off the wounded. Simitch feigned death, and afterwards succeeded in crawling away and escaping; but the Austrians saw him and fired on him.

The Commander of the first regiment of Serbian infantry reports (under date of October 13, 1914, Acte O, No. 280) : Near the Schtipliane river, the Austrians took prisoners about 10 wounded men of the 3rd supernumerary regiment. The wounds of these men were dressed. When the Austrians found themselves obliged to leave their positions in consequence of the attack of the 2nd battalion of the 3rd Serbian regiment, they shot the wounded in order not to let them be retaken alive by the Serbs. The wounded men were found with their wounds dressed, but dead.

At Iovanovatz near Shabatz, about 50 soldiers of the 2nd *Ban* belonging to the 13th and 14th regiments, Timok division, surrendered to the Austrians and gave up their arms to them. They were, however, all massacred by the Austro-Hungarian soldiers inside a house. A little time afterwards the Serbs on recapturing Shabatz found a heap of corpses in the farm of Iovanovatz. Photographs were taken and will form a permanent record of this contravention of all the laws of war.

Sometimes the bodies of wounded soldiers were mutilated before or after their death. Photographs in the possession of the Serbian Government bear witness to this. For example, Captain J. Savitch on August 11-24, 1914, photographed the body of a young Serbian soldier from which the Austrians had torn off the skin of the lower jaw.

IV. *Massacres of civilians. Depositions of Austro-Hungarian prisoners.*—*A. X., of the 26th Regiment,* deposes as follows: He was ordered, and the order was read to the regiment, to kill and burn everybody and everything met with in the course of the campaign and to destroy everything Serbian. Commandant Stanzer and Captain Irketitch gave orders to attack the Serbian population. Before the second invasion orders were given at Yanja on September 10th to conquer and destroy the country. The civilian population were to be taken prisoners. A peasant who showed the way to the troops was shot by Commandant Stanzer and his soldiers, who fired at him five times. On another occasion a Croatian soldier named Dochan boasted of having killed a woman, a child and two old men, and invited his comrades to come with him to see his victims.

B. X., of the 78th Regiment, states that his superiors gave orders that no one should be spared. First Lieutenant Fojtek, of the 2nd Company, said at Esseg (the garrison town of the 78th Regiment) that it was necessary to show the Serbs what Austrians are. Nothing must be spared and every one killed.

C. X., of the 78th Regiment, states that First Lieutenant Bernhard said that everything found living must be killed. Major Belina gave permission to his men to pillage and steal everything they could find.

Corporal D. X., of the 28th Regiment of Landwehr, deposes: At Shabatz the Austrians killed near the church more than 60 civilians who had been previously shut up there. They were massacred with the bayonet to economize ammunition. The work was done by eight Hungarian soldiers. D. X. could not bear to see this sight and left the spot.

The corpses remained on the spot for two days before being buried. Among the victims were old men and children. The order for the massacre was given by the General and Officers.

E. X., *of the* 6th *Regiment of Infantry.* The Hungarian Captain Bosnai gave orders, before crossing the frontier, that everything living should be killed from children of five to the oldest men. When the frontier had been crossed and the troops arrived at the first Serbian village, the Captain gave orders that two houses should be burned and every one killed, even the children in the cradle. About 30 women, children and old men were taken prisoners and driven before the troops during the fight. E. X. saw these civilians wounded or killed by the bullets of the two opposing forces. This happened at Okolischte.

F. X., *of the* 2nd *Bosnian Regiment.* His regiment marching from Lioubovia found at the third village some peasants burnt on the hay by the 100th regiment. The order for this massacre was given by Lieutenant-Colonel Krebs, of the last named regiment.

First Lieutenant Stibitch, of the 2nd regiment, made observations on the subject to Krebs and asked him the cause of this barbarous execution. Krebs replied that they were comitadjis, and that besides it had nothing to do with him.

G. X., *of the* 28th *Regiment of Infantry,* deposes that during the first invasion the Austrian troops killed all the inhabitants and the wounded. Lieutenant Iekete captured 23 peasants and brought them before his captain. The latter drew them up in a line and kicked each of them. If they cried out they were shot at once.

H. X., *of the* 28th *of the Line,* states that the Hungarians devastated all the Serbian villages in Sirmia. Captain Eisenhut gave orders to strike down everything living in Serbia. Mussulman peasants from Bosnia always followed the supply train to pillage.

I. X., *of the* 3rd *Regiment of Bosnian Infantry.* When his regiment arrived at Zvornik there were some civilian Serbian prisoners, women and children. I. X. gave them some bread, but a corporal saw him and tied him up to a tree for two hours. At Tousla there were also many Serbian civilian

prisoners, especially women and children. When these
women went through the town the Croatian soldiers spat in
their faces. On September 29th at ten in the evening, 150
fresh civilian prisoners arrived. They were old men, women
and children. The women could not drag themselves along
any further, and the soldiers drove them on with blows
from the butts of their rifles. The soldiers of the 60th Regiment had taken prisoner a young man of eighteen whom they
hanged on a tree.

K. X., of the 16th *Regiment of Infantry.* At Dobritch,
on August 16th or 17th, K. X. saw soldiers of the 37th Hungarian Regiment kill eleven or twelve children from 6 to 12
years of age with their bayonets. The order for the massacre was given by First Lieutenant Nagj.

In my collection I have also a series of depositions by
other Austro-Hungarian soldiers, who had been taken prisoner by the Serbs, which recount massacres and atrocities
committed on the civilian population of the invaded districts,
but I believe that these few samples are enough to prove to
my readers that even the Austro-Hungarian soldiers confess
the crimes that have been committed by a certain number of
their comrades, and, what is more important, that in the
majority of cases these crimes were committed in obedience
to orders given by their leaders.

I draw special attention to the testimony of H. X. of the
28th Line, who says that the Hungarians devastated all the
Serbian villages in Sirmia, that is to say in their own territory. Other witnesses confirmed H. X.'s statements, and it
appears that the Austro-Hungarian army also committed
many excesses in Bosnia. In addition the following document, which was found by the 4th Supernumerary Regiment
of Infantry and sent on August 23rd (old style) to the Commander of the 1st Serbian army by the Divisional Staff of
the Timok Division (second Ban), proves what I have said.

By order of A. O. K. Op. Kr. 259.
In consequence of the hostile attitude of the population
of Klenak [1] and Shabatz, hostages will again be taken in

[1] Klenak is in Hungarian territory.

all the Serbian villages, etc., even those situated on this side of the frontier, which are or will be occupied by the troops. These hostages are to be killed at once in case of any crime being committed by the inhabitants against the armed forces (treason) and the enemy villages are to be burnt. The Commander of the Army Corps reserves the power to burn the villages on our own territory.

This order is to be communicated without delay to the population by the civil authorities.

HORTSTEIN, general.

BY GENERAL KROBATIN

Official Announcement from the Austrian Ministry of War

Since, owing to the intervention of Russia into our dispute with Serbia, we find it necessary to concentrate our entire force for the great combat in the north, the war against Serbia must be considered only as a "Strafexpedition" (punitive expedition) which, for the same reason, has become a matter of secondary interest. In spite of that, and both in view of the general situation and of the false news which has been circulated by the enemy, an offensive action had been judged opportune. Yet, also for the above-mentioned reason, this operation was limited to a short incursion into the enemy's territory, after the successful accomplishment of which it was necessary to return to an attitude of expectancy, in adjourning the offensive to a more favorable occasion.

The offensive executed by part of our troops was an action replete with bravery and heroism. Its effect was to draw upon us the entire Serbian army, the attacks of which, despite a great numerical superiority, had no result, thanks to the heroism of our troops. The fact that our troops in part suffered heavy losses should not astonish us, for our enemy possessed a numerical superiority and was, in addition, fighting for his existence. Thus when our troops, who had penetrated a long way into Serbian territory, received the order to regain their positions on the Drina and on the Save, they left an enemy completely enfeebled on the field of battle.

BRITAIN ASSERTS CONTROL OF THE SEAS

FIRST NAVAL MOVES, AND THE BLOCKING OF GERMAN COMMERCE

JULY 29TH

JOHN LEYLAND   COUNT ERNST ZU REVENTLOW
M. SAINT-BRICE

No one who studies carefully the history of the Great War will ever believe that Britain either wanted the contest or was prepared for it. The blow struck her statesmen with almost the same amaze as it gave to America. The only one coincidence which told in Britain's favor or seemed to suggest preparation was the fortunate marshaling of her Battle Fleet. Had this at the opening of the War been scattered as usual, broad over the oceans of the world, the great German fleet, second only to that of Britain, might have rushed forth from its sheltering forts. It might have wrought upon the ports and ships of France and Britain such a destruction as would have turned the evenly balanced scales of war. But the British navy was gathered in its fullest strength in the North Sea at the very mouth of the German harbors; and the German fleet was "bottled" from the start.

The British ships had been thus assembled for practice maneuvers; and an order had been issued that they were to demobilize. That order was canceled on July 26th, and the entire tremendous fleet remained in battle trim just where it was needed. Mr. Leyland, Britain's authoritative naval writer, editor of her "Navy Gazette," well points out that the seizure of the control of the North Sea by this fleet should be regarded as scoring one most decisive point in the great struggle. The order accomplishing this was issued on July 29th.

Rumor, ever eager to dramatize the striking incident, tells us that the expected demobilization of the fleet was countermanded because of a single indiscreet remark let fall by a high German official at an international naval banquet. The British officers present at the "love feast" caught the remark and rightly interpreted it as a presage of immediate war. Surely, however, no such warning was needed on July 26th. To have disarmed at that moment, with Austria's ultimatum issued and Germany upholding her, would have been a folly incalculable.

Germany's protest against the British view, her denial that her ships were helpless against the Britons, is here voiced by Count Reventlow, the most vehement of her literary supporters, the most enthusiastic of Pan-Germans. He bases his assertions mainly of course upon the work of the submarine. The fact of Germany's naval downfall, however, refuses to be set aside by argument.

The further course of the British blockade, its extension into an international blockade, and its ultimate effect upon the War, these points are then elucidated by M. Saint-Brice, official writer for the French Government. Germany's official views as to the illegality and injustice of the blockade have been already presented in the preceding volume of this series.

C. F. H.

BY JOHN LEYLAND

WHEN King George returned from the visit he paid to the Grand Fleet in June, 1917, he sent a message to Admiral Sir David Beatty, who had succeeded Sir John Jellicoe in the command, in which he said that "never had the British Navy stood higher in the estimation of friend or foe." It is, however, true that the work of the Sea Service during this unparalleled war has never been properly appreciated by many of those who have benefited by it most. The silent Navy does its work unobserved. The record of its heroism and the services it renders pass unobserved by the multitude. Sometimes it emerges to strike a blow, engage in a "scrap," or, it may be, to fight a battle, and then it retires into obscurity again. Its achievements are forgotten. Only the bombardment of a coast town or the torpedoing of a big ship, which the Navy did not frustrate, is remembered.

Who can wonder that people in the Allied countries are still less able to realize that behind all the fighting of their own armies lies the influence of sea-power, exercised by the British Fleet and the fleets that came one after another into coöperation with it? Without this power of the sea there could have been no hope of success in the war.

On the first day of hostilities the British Navy laid hold upon the road that would lead to victory. There is no hyperbole in saying that the Grand Fleet, in its northern anchorages, from the very beginning, influenced the military situation throughout the world, and made possible many of the operations of the armies, which could neither have been successfully initiated nor continued without it. But in the early days of August, 1914, when, from the war cloud which had overshadowed Europe, broke forth the lurid horrors of the conflict, the situation was extremely critical. What was required to be done had to be done quickly and unhesitatingly, lest the enemy should strike an unforeseen blow. Happily, with faultless knowledge, the strategy of the emergency was realized, and with unerring instinct and sagacity it was applied. The foresight of great naval administrators, and chiefly of Lord Fisher, who had brought about the regeneration of the British Navy, shaping it for modern conditions, was justified a thousandfold.

Never was the need of exerting sea command more urgent than at the outbreak of war. Everything that Englishmen had won in all the centuries of the storied past was involved in the quarrel. Only by mastery of the sea could the country be made secure. Its soil had never been trodden by an invader since Norman William came in 1066. The very food that was eaten and the things by which the industries and commerce of the country existed demanded control at sea. If the British Empire was to be safe from aggression it must be safeguarded on every sea. If England was to set armies in any foreign field of operations, and to retain and maintain them there, with the gigantic supplies they would require; if she was to render help to her Allies in men or munitions or anything else, whether they came from England, or the United States, or any other country, and were landed in France, Russia, Italy, or Greece, or in Egypt, Mesopotamia, or East or West Africa, for the defeat of the enemy, that must be done by virtue of power at sea. Therefore, in this war, as John Hollond, writing his "Discourse of the Navy" in 1638, said of the wars of his time: "The naval part is the thread that runs through the whole wooft, the burden of the song, the scope of the text."

The moment when the First Fleet, as it was then called, slipped away from its anchorage at Portland on the morning of Wednesday, July 29, 1914, will yet be regarded as one of the decisive moments of history. The initiative had been seized, and all real initiative was thenceforward denied to the enemy. The gauge of victory had been won. "Time is everything; five minutes makes the difference between a victory and a defeat," said Nelson. "The advantage and gain of time and place will be the only and chief means for our good," Drake had said before him. By a fortunate circumstance, which should have arrested the imagination as with a presage of victory—a circumstance arranged five months before, as the result of a series of most intricate preparations—time and place were both on the British side.

The First, Second, and Third Fleets, and the flotillas attached to them, had been mobilized as a test operation, and inspected at Spithead by King George, on July 20th. The First Fleet had returned to Portland and the other fleets to their home ports, where the surplus or "balance" crews of the Naval Reserves were to be sent on shore. Then had come the now famous order to "stand fast," issued on the night of Sunday, July 26th, which had stopped the process of demobilization. Dark clouds had shadowed the international horizon. Austria-Hungary had presented her ultimatum to Serbia. She declared war on the 28th. The Second Fleet remained, therefore, in proximity to its reserves of men, and the men were ready to be reëmbarked in the Third Fleet.

Few people realized at the time the immense significance of the memorable eastward movement of the squadrons from Portland Roads, or of the assembly of those powerful forces at their northern strategic anchorages. Those forces became the Grand Fleet, that unexampled organization of fighting force, under command of that fine sea officer, Admiral Sir John Jellicoe. War was declared by Great Britain on August 4th. Successive steps of supreme importance were taken, which, in very truth, saved the cause of the Allies. Disaster and surprise attack were forestalled. The Fleet, fully mobilized, and growing daily in strength, was already exerting command of the sea, and the safe transport of the Expeditionary Force to France was assured. Coöperation with the French Fleet was immediately established—its cruiser squadron in the Channel and its battle squadrons in the Mediterranean.

Of all the theaters of the war, on sea or land, the North Sea is the most important. It is vital to all the operations of the Allies. Command of its waters and its outlets is the thing that matters most. In that sea is the center of naval influence. It is the key of all the hostilities. From either side of it the great protagonists in the struggle look at one another. There the great constriction of the blockade is exerted upon Germany. It is the *mare clausum* against which she protests. Geography is there in the scales against her. She rebels against British sea supremacy. The "freedom of the seas" is, therefore, her claim—though she is endeavoring to qualify to be the tyrant of them. Her only outlook towards the outer seas is from the Bight of Heligoland and the fringe of coast behind the East Frisian Islands, or from the Baltic, if her ships pass the Sound or the Belt, issuing into the North Sea through the Skager-Rak. But they cannot reach the ocean, except through the North Passage, where the Grand Fleet holds the guard. Only isolated raiders, bent upon predatory enterprise, have stealthily gone that way after nightfall. At the southern gate of the North Sea, through the Straits of Dover and in the Channel, the way is barred. The guns of Dover, the Dover Patrol, and certain other deterrents forbid the enemy to adventure in that direction.

The new engines of naval warfare—the mine, submarine, airship, and aëroplane—found their first and greatest use in the North Sea; and only by employing craft which hide beneath the water, and, on rare occasions, by destroyers which seek the cover of darkness for local forays, have the Germans been able to exert their efforts in any waters outside the North Sea. At the beginning of the war they had raiding cruisers in the Pacific and Atlantic, and a detached squadron in the Far East; but the British Fleet reached out to those regions, and, aided by the warships of Japan and France, it drove every vestige of German naval power from the oceans.

The situation in the North Sea is, therefore, of absorbing interest. It may be studied chiefly from the two points of view of the strategy of the opposing fleets and the exercise of the blockade. There is a peculiarity in naval warfare, which is not found in warfare upon land, that a belligerent can withdraw his naval forces entirely from the theater of war by retaining them, as with a threat, or in a position of weakness, behind the guns of his shore defenses. Nothing of the kind is possible with land armies. A general can always find his enemy, and attack or invest him, and, if successful, drive him back, or cause him to surrender, and occupy the territory he has held. The Germans have chosen the reticent strategy of the sea. They have never come out to make a fight to a finish, to put the matter to the touch, "to gain or lose it all." The *animus pugnandi* is wanting to their fleet. It was necessary that they should do something. They could not lie forever stagnant at Kiel and Wilhelmshaven. They could keep their officers and men in training by making brief cruises in and outside the Bight of Heligoland. They might, with luck, meet some portion of the Grand Fleet detached and at a disadvantage.

In any case, they were bold enough to take their chance on occasions, always with their fortified ports and mined waters and their submarines under their lee. They might succeed in reducing British superiority by the "attrition" of some encounters. Such was the genesis of the Dogger Bank battle of January 24, 1915, when that gallant officer, Sir David Beatty, inflicted a severe defeat upon Admiral Hipper, and drove him back in flight, with the loss of the *Blücher* and much other injury. The same causes brought the German High Sea Fleet, under Admiral Scheer, into the great conflict, first with Sir David Beatty, and then with the main force of the Grand Fleet, under command of Sir John Jellicoe, on May 31, 1916.

The mine and the submarine have put an end to the system of naval blockade as practiced by St. Vincent and Cornwallis. No fleet can now lie off, or within striking range of, an enemy's port. Battleships cannot be risked against submarines, acting either as torpedo craft or mine-layers, nor against swift destroyers at night. That is the explanation of the situation in the North Sea. The blockade was necessarily of a distant kind. There are no places on the British coasts where the Grand Fleet could be located, except those in which it lies and from which it issues to sweep the North Sea periodically. The first essential is to control the enemy's communications, which is done effectively at the North

Passage—between the Orkneys and Shetlands, and the Nor-
wegian coast—and at the Straits of Dover. If the enemy
desired a final struggle for supremacy at sea, with all its
tremendous consequences, he could have it. But he can be
attacked only when he is accessible. "There shall be neither
sickness nor death which shall make us yield until this service
be ended," wrote Howard in 1588. That is the spirit of
the British Navy to-day. But, then, the Spanish Armada
was at sea. It was not hiding behind its shore defenses. Be
it noted that the Germans, thus hiding themselves, enjoy a
certain opportunity of undertaking raiding operations in the
North Sea. It is not a difficult thing to rush a force of destroyers on a dark night against some point in an extended
line of patrols and effect a little damage somewhere.

The magnificence of the work of the British patrol flotillas and the auxiliary patrols must be recognized. In the
North Sea these are subsidiary services of the Grand Fleet.
Day and night, in every weather—in summer heats and
winter blasts and blizzards, when icy seas wash the boats
from stem to stern and the cold penetrates to the bone—these
patrols are at work. The records of heroism at sea in these
services have never been surpassed, and England owes a
very great deal to the men who came to her service. The
mercantile marine has given its vessels to the State, from
the luxurious liner to the fishing trawler, and officers and
men have come in who have rendered priceless services. The
trawlers have carried on their perilous work of bringing up
the strange harvest of horned mines by the score. The
patrol boats have examined suspicious vessels, controlled
sea traffic, and watched the sea passages. The destroyer
flotillas have been constantly at work and ready at any time
to bring raiding enemy forces to action. The Royal Naval
Air Service has never relaxed its activity and has engaged
in countless combats.

Such is the magnificent work of the British Navy in
blockading the German Fleet, molesting the enemy's coast
positions, and controlling his communications with the
oceans.

The commercial blockade, by which the enemy's supplies

and commodities are cut off and his exports paralyzed, is too large a subject to be dealt with here. The object is to bring the full measure of sea-power to bear in crushing the national life of the enemy. It is vital but "silent" work of the Navy, and does not lend itself to discussion or description. Questions of contraband and the right and method of search, which arise from the blockade, caused discussions with the United States before the States came into the war. The only object of the British Navy and the Foreign Office was to put an end to the transit of the enemy's commodities, and to do so with the utmost consideration for the interests of neutrals, and complete protection for the lives of the officers and crews in their ships and in the examining ships. For these reasons neutral vessels were taken into port for examination, safe from the attentions of the enemy's submarines. One great hope of the Germans was that the neutrals would become more and more exasperated with England. They remembered that the war of 1812 arose from this very cause. But they were completely disappointed in all such hopes, and they themselves, by interfering with the free navigation of other countries, brought the United States into the war against them.

The blockade work of the examination service and of the armed boarding steamers has been extremely hazardous. It has called for the greatest qualities of seamanship, because conducted in every condition of weather and when storm and fog have made it extremely perilous to approach the neutral vessels—which, moreover, have sometimes proved to be armed enemies in disguise. Hundreds of vessels have been brought into port by the Navy in those northern waters. Sleepless vigilance has been required and the highest skill of the sea in every possible condition of the service, while the seaman has become a statesman in his dealings with the neutral shipmaster. It has been for the Navy to bring the ships into port, and for other authorities to inquire into their status and to take them before the Prize Court if required.

The German High Sea Fleet having failed, the submarine campaign was instituted, and began chiefly in the North Sea. It has never answered the expectations of its authors.

It has not changed the strategic situation in any degree whatever. Great damage has been inflicted upon British interests,
and valuable ships and cargoes have been sunk, and officers
and men cast adrift in situations of ruthless hardship. The
tale of the sea has never had a more terrible record, nor
one lighted by so much noble self-sacrifice and unfailing
courage.

BY COUNT ERNST ZU REVENTLOW

When the German Fleet entered the great contest, it was
not in a state of completion, as many persons abroad believe
it to have been. At that time the German Fleet had been
for some 15 years in the process of being regularly built up,
for the big Navy Bill had not become a law until the summer
of 1900. In that year the German Navy contained only two
somewhat modern battleships. It was calculated at that time
that the rebuilding of the Fleet would be completed in 1920.
In 1906, however, came the great Dreadnought revolution
in shipbuilding which quickly rendered worthless all ships
built before that time (pre-Dreadnoughts), and compelled
tremendous enlargements of wharves, harbors and canals,
gigantic extension of organization, etc. The work of com-
pleting the German Fleet would have extended itself far
beyond the year 1920 under these conditions. If one furthermore takes into consideration that, as the authorities of
all lands acknowledge, experience shows that it requires not
15 but 30 years to build up a fleet with everything that belongs thereto, on water and on land, it is clear that the German Fleet was far from being ready in the summer of 1914.

To this must be added a fact that has been overlooked.
In 1900, when the strength of the German Fleet was decided on, the relations of England to France and to Russia
were bad. England had to maintain strong fleets in the
Mediterranean and in East Asia. The alliance with Japan
was not yet in existence. If these conditions had persisted,
Great Britain could have used only a part of its fleet in a
war with Germany. Since, however, Great Britain desired
to attack Germany when the proper time came, it allied itself
at the right moment with Russia, France, and Japan, and

was thus able to use its entire fleet against Germany and
Germany's allies from August, 1914, on. Then, in the course
of the war, Italy came in with its considerable fleet. The
allies of Great Britain also employed their fleets in the home
waters and on the seas against Germany and its allies. And
since, as is well known, the fleets of Austria-Hungary and
Turkey are very small, the German Fleet had to battle
against an extraordinarily superior might. What has the
German Fleet achieved, according to what plan has it
fought?

Let us begin with the last question: According to what
plan has the German Fleet fought? In the home waters two
enemies were to be considered—Russia in the Baltic, Great
Britain in and beyond the North Sea. In view of the number
of Russian ships in Baltic harbors, the Russian Fleet could
by no means be taken lightly. In the fall of 1914 a half
dozen English submarines were stationed in the Baltic.
Therefore it was necessary to leave a portion of the German
Fleet there, and to be steadily prepared to employ still more
forces in the Baltic should occasion arise. The greatest part
of the German Fleet lay, of course, in the North Sea.

It was from the beginning impossible to prevent the isolation of Germany from the oceans; for, on the one hand,
the German North Sea harbors, above all, the basis of operations of the German Fleet, are too far distant from the English Channel and the northern passage from the North Sea,
to make it possible to keep these open, and, on the other
hand, the German Fleet was much too small. At the beginning of the war, and especially after Great Britain had
taken over the warships being built in British shipyards for
other nations, the German Fleet was hardly half as strong
as the British. The British Isles lie like a long mole before
the North Sea, and for this reason the command of the outlets of the North Sea is very easy for them. The British
ships are at all times near their bases of operations, and in
the case of the English Channel there exists the further fact
that the opposite coast belongs to the ally, France. The commercial blockade could be easily carried out by armed mer-
chantmen, older cruisers and battleships, light cruisers and

torpedo boats, so that the main British Fleet with its great battleships retained complete strategic freedom of action. Therein lay the danger for the small German Fleet, and therein lay also the military necessity of employing a strategy of reserve, so far as favorable opportunities did not present themselves. In view of the unfortunate geographic position of the North Sea, the cutting off of overseas traffic could not be prevented.

It was also the intention of the British Fleet in the first days of the war to carry on a strategy of reserve in the North Sea, to employ good opportunities for making sallies, and also to attempt surprises. The cruiser battle in the Bay of Heligoland on August 28, 1914, was to be a surprise of this nature. It cost us some small cruisers, and it cost the attacking English squadron heavy damage, despite its great superiority. This battle was without any significance so far as the course of the war was concerned. It demonstrated again, however, the unfortunate geographical position of the German coasts; the English knew that the German Fleet could always be found in the so-called Bay of Heligoland, since we have no other harbors there. The British Fleet, on the other hand, which had before then frequently enough been hunted for by our torpedo-boats, was not tied to any definite place, but lay at some point on the coasts of Great Britain. It is highly probable that the leaders of Great Britain's campaign would have carried on a strategy of sorties alternating with one of holding back, in order, on the one side continuously to weaken the German Fleet without running any serious risk to themselves, and on the other, in order so to disorganize and provoke it that it would let itself be induced to enter a great deciding battle under unfavorable conditions and in an unfavorable position. These plans came to nought because of the entry into the naval warfare of a factor which the British Admiralty had not anticipated. This was the German submarine warfare—the war with mines and with submarines.

Through the systematic stragetic employment of mines and submarines the German naval leaders in a short time succeeded in making a continuous stay in the North Sea impossible for the British main Fleet. Only occasionally did detachments of the main English Fleet make short, rapid sorties into the North Sea, only to return immediately to the Irish Sea or to the waters west and north of Scotland. This meant a shattering of all English plans of a military blockade of the German coasts, and of shutting the German naval forces up in the German harbors. The main British Fleet saw itself unable to command the North Sea. Even the mercantile blockade by British warships could not be maintained, since the German submarines had become too dangerous for the large British cruisers and other warships. Therefore the British Admiralty established a gigantic mine-field at the entrance to the North Sea from the English Channel, and proclaimed other portions of the North Sea a military zone which could be traversed by neutral ships only at their own risk.

This was a violation of the rights of neutral shipping unheard of in history; the neutrals have endured it. The British Government simultaneously presented as the chief means of their campaign the starving out of the German people, and by doing so drove Germany to its submarine warfare on British commerce. The submarine warfare had a growing influence upon the whole economic life of Great Britain. No one would have considered possible the things that the German submarines accomplished. It stands without example. Nevertheless, Germany would certainly have gladly stopped this submarine war against commerce if, in return, the freedom and safety of all floating property at sea had been guaranteed.

It was plainly the standpoint of the British Admiralty to avoid serious encounter with the German Fleet except under especially favorable conditions. It feared that it would otherwise have too few ships left, and would be weaker at sea than the United States, after the war. One can say that the motives for holding back the main fleets on both sides were similar, despite the great inequality of the two fleets. In any event, it is correct to say that the great armored ships did not come and fight for fear of the submarines; but there are many other reasons to be considered.

We did not, it is true, command the North Sea without submarines, but we did through them make it impossible for the British Fleet to command the North Sea. That is the great, historically new event of this naval war. The German submarines have everywhere given astounding examples of their military powers. They even voyaged from the North Sea to the Dardanelles, and destroyed a number of English warships there. The two German cruisers *Goeben* and *Breslau* at the beginning of the war were in the Western Mediterranean, and they succeeded in getting through the whole French Fleet from Messina to the Dardanelles. In the Black Sea these two cruisers, in conjunction with the Turkish Fleet, repeatedly fought successfully against the Russian Black Sea Fleet, and the latter, despite its superior might, never dared make an earnest attack in the Turkish waters of the Black Sea.

The cruiser warfare on the seas was conducted independently of all actions. The few German cruisers were from the start on a lost post. They had no supporting bases, and found themselves facing a tremendously superior force of British, French, Japanese, and Russian warships. Mr. Churchill has declared in the House of Commons that there were in all about 90 warships of every description hunting for the few German cruisers. Their situation was, therefore, extremely difficult, and their destruction earlier or later was assured. Their actions could, indeed, damage the enemy, but they could have no influence on the course of the war. Nevertheless, Count Spee succeeded with his squadron in destroying an English cruiser squadron on the Chilian coast. Spee's squadron was then destroyed by a tremendously superior enemy force in the battle off the Falkland Islands. An end was also put to the glorious career of the cruiser *Emden*. Well-informed persons in Germany, as has been said, had never based any hopes on this cruiser warfare, for they knew that the forces were lacking to carry it out on a large scale, and for any long time. But the glory which the German sea-fighters won for themselves on the oceans constitutes a lasting success and a gain which cannot be lost. In every contest they demonstrated that they can be destroyed only by superior English forces, and that, ship for ship, they are superior to the English.

The losses of the German Fleet in the first year of the war were very small. It lost not a single ship of the first class, but only a few submarines and torpedo boats, some small cruisers and a few older cruisers. The German Fleet repeatedly showed that it possessed full freedom of action in the North Sea. The German Fleet coursed about in the North Sea a great number of times, and at times even advanced to the English coasts in order to bombard English coast defenses and marine stations.

The war demonstrated that the days of absolute British supremacy are at an end. Ten years ago the Civil Lord of the British Admiralty, Mr. Lee, declared that the British Dreadnoughts would be on the German coasts before the news of the breaking out of war appeared in the German papers. The war has shown that Mr. Lee was a bad prophet.

BY M. SAINT-BRICE
Official Announcement by the French Government

England and France decided on October 18, 1917, to place an embargo on commerce destined for the neutral kingdoms of Northern Europe—in other words, to forbid all exports except those specially authorized. A similar step had been taken by President Wilson on July 9th with regard to all neutrals. That was a final step, and a decisive date in the evolution of the economic war.

Many persons imagine that the infinitely complex mechanism intended to strangle our enemies was invented at a single stroke and that it remains, with the perfection of a few details, practically the same as it was in the beginning. On the contrary, few instruments of war have been transformed more radically or by a more continuous progression than the affair of wheels within wheels which we call, for lack of a better name, the blockade. The blockade of 1917 no more resembles that of 1914 than the battle of Flanders resembles the battle of the Marne. In the one realm, as in the other, the Allies have been wise enough to

profit from the teachings of half successes and even of reverses.

At first the lists of contraband articles were lengthened.
Remember that in the beginning these lists neglected articles as interesting as rubber, lubricating oil, and fodder. I
will merely mention cotton, which waited nearly two years
for the order forbidding its export—out of consideration
for American interests.   Direct shipments to Germany were
stopped promptly enough.   On the other hand, exportations
out of Germany, bolstering her credit and increasing her war
fund, might have continued freely for a long time if she
had not committed the imprudence of tearing international
law to shreds and proclaiming ruthless submarine war in
British waters (February 3, 1915).   The Allies replied on
March 1, 1915, by interdicting all traffic either going to or
coming from the enemy countries.

Finally, on July 7, 1916, France and England formally
freed themselves from the provisions of the London Convention, which had arranged for lists of absolute and con-
ditional contraband, and had even sought to free a certain
number of articles entirely from war risks.   Thenceforth,
it was admitted that all trade would be held under suspicion,
except when proofs of its innocence were forthcoming.
Thus the burden of proof was reversed.   Until then it was
up to the captor to establish the validity of the seizure by
proving the enemy destination of the cargo.   Since July 7,
1916, it is the seized cargo that has to establish its innocence
as to destination.

As to putting a stop to enemy trading by firms in belligerent countries, it was thought at first that a few simple
measures would be sufficient, such as prohibiting the departure of goods from port and laying heavy penalties on
suspected traffic.   Soon it was realized that even this aspect
of the problem was not simple.   The idea of nationality
varies enormously in the laws of different nations.   Strange
as it may seem, the English law did not permit Germans
and Austrians in neutral countries to be treated as enemies.
To this was added the incredible confusion of interests in
great international enterprises.   The Allies found them-

selves compelled on February 25, 1916, to resort to black-lists formally proscribing houses connected more or less closely with the enemy.

It remained to hinder supplies from reaching the enemy through neutrals. That was the stumbling block. It was difficult to stop the transit of shipments often seemingly honest; still more difficult was it to keep non-belligerents from furnishing the products of their soil and industry impartially to both sides.

For indirect commerce the Allies still had one means of action, since they controlled the ways of access. Besides, they possessed a basis of computation in the statistics of before-the-war trade. Thus they could, almost mathematically, fix the necessary allowance of each commodity for each neutral country, as based on production and imports. But all this was purely theoretical. Practically, nothing is more unreliable than figures. It would have been necessary to know the existing stocks of each commodity, and the changes of demand caused by the war. Let us not forget the consideration which the western powers tried to show, as far as possible, toward trusted nations, up to the time when German methods compelled them to push things to extremes.

Very rapidly the principles of the solution took shape. In November, 1914, there was organized in Holland the Netherlands Oversea Trust, a group destined to become a permanent intermediary between Dutch commerce and the blockade authorities. In October, 1915, the Swiss Surveillance Society was established on similar lines. In Norway and Denmark another system was followed, that of private agreements with commercial houses. Sweden alone resisted all arrangements. The basis of the agreement in every case was to fix upon the amount of contingent importations and to obtain guarantees against reëxportation. On the latter point the results have been most satisfactory. Errors in statistics have been more frequent.

When all is said, the machine would have been very effective if the neutral countries had not disposed freely of their own products. The word freely is, perhaps, out of place when one knows the war methods used by Germany to impose her will upon her smaller neighbors. Her principal argument is not force of arms. Our enemies, who alone are in position to furnish the neutrals with certain essential articles—such as coal and iron—did not have to resort to that method of blackmail. The world knows the methods used by Berlin to compel Switzerland to furnish supplies of cattle and metals in return for bank credits. Holland has found her potatoes and fish in a sense requisitioned; Denmark her farm products. To combat this intensive drain the Allies long were without other resource than that of competition. To buy up all the supplies in neutral markets is expensive. It is a burdensome method and one that cannot always be pushed to its logical end.

There is only one way to stop this enemy traffic, and that is to place the neutrals face to face with a situation in which they will no longer be able to pass along their own products —to kill speculation with want. All the small neutral States are dependent upon foreign trade; their food supply, therefore, depends upon the masters of the sea. But it depends still more upon the United States, the only great country outside of Europe committed to the arbitrament of arms. That is why the American flag was almost like an enemy flag as long as the great transatlantic Republic remained in the neutral camp. From the day America entered the war it became wholly one of the Allies. The Americans, with their business lucidity and the light of two years' experience, perceived the gap in the blockade. That is why President Wilson did not rest until he had all exports under his control. Henceforth the neutrals will have their food imports strictly controlled. They will receive only what is truly required for their needs after their stocks have been greatly reduced and after they have proved the exhaustion of their resources. Under these conditions it becomes practically impossible for them to share their supplies with their neighbors.

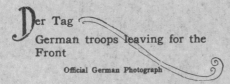

Der Tag
German troops leaving for the
Front

Official German Photograph

THE ASSAULT ON LIEGE

BELGIUM AMAZES THE WORLD BY HER RESOLUTE RESISTANCE

AUGUST 4TH-15TH

EVERARD WYRALL   GENERAL LEMAN
GERMAN AND BELGIAN SOLDIERS' NARRATIVES
VON BETHMANN-HOLLWEG

Historians may never agree as to the precise military value of the check to the first great German onrush which was caused by the determined resistance of the forts surrounding Liege. To some it has seemed that but for this unexpected barrier, the German armies would have swept down on France before she could have organized any effective opposition, that she would have been beaten without ever having the opportunity to fight.

French military critics, however, reject this condemnation of their army staff. They maintain that they could have fought the Battle of the Marne as well and perhaps better at an earlier date, if they had been released from the difficult task of hurrying their troops to the frontier to aid Belgium, and then having to fall back again to the Marne. There are even strategists who believe that the German Staff deliberately planned to lure the reckless Frenchmen into Belgium, where they could be more surely and more crushingly defeated.

But putting aside the question of the military value of Liege's resistance, of its high moral and spiritual value there can be no dispute. The heroism of the little Belgian army and of the firm-hearted Belgian people roused the whole world. Independence was shown to be still treasured, a treasure worth the dying for. Honor was proven to be other than the empty word the German Government had declared it. Amid all the good and noble things which sprang into existence under the tragic pressure of the Great War, there was none larger in spiritual value than this, that the little Belgian army at Liege resisted "to the uttermost."

The city of Liege, the once wealthy metropolis of southeastern Belgium, stands in a broad river valley, the most obvious and easy road by which an army could pass from northern Germany to France. Hence the German plans had long since been laid for an invasion by this road. At least as early as August 3rd her troops were crossing the Belgian border, were seizing little frontier towns like Visé, and clashing with the Belgian outposts. On the morning of August 4th the invaders appeared before Liege; and by that evening, having been refused the city's surrender, they were ready for their assault in force.

37

Thus even before Serbia had been seriously assailed, Belgium found herself at desperate grip with her terrible opponent.

We give here, first, the enthusiastic appreciation of the Belgian struggle written by a well-known British author, then the more exact official statement of the Belgian commander, the hero of the struggle, General Leman. These are followed by individual pictures selected from the letters of both German and Belgian fighters. Then comes the official summary by the German statesman most deeply involved, the Imperial Chancellor, Von Bethmann-Hollweg. The reader may thus appreciate the unequal conflict as it appeared from every side.

C. F. H.

BY EVERARD WYRALL

THE story of the defense and fall of Liege will forever remain in history as one of the epics of the Great War. Not only did the Belgian Army in and about the forts surrounding the city cover itself with imperishable glory, but, by its heroic resistance, changed the whole course of the early period of the war, if not the entire campaign, in France and Belgium. For the Belgians completely broke the first German onslaught, thereby delaying the advance of the Kaiser's Army through Belgium to France, and entirely disorganizing the initial plans of the German General Staff. Numerous, indeed, were the grim and picturesque stories and reports published at the time of the terrible slaughter inflicted upon the German hordes by the gallant soldiers of King Albert, but much will never be known which otherwise might have formed the connecting links of a broken yet glorious story.

Whilst a portion of the German Army enveloped and attacked Visé, the 7th Army Corps under General von Emmich had concentrated upon the plains about Herve prior to an attack upon Forts Barchon, Evegnée, and Fléron. These forts were three of twelve which surrounded the city of Liege, forming a circle thirty-three miles in circumference. Six—Pontisse, Barchon, Fléron, Boncelles, Flémalle, and Loncin—were large forts. The other six—Evegnée, Chaudfontaine, Embourg, Hollogne, Loncin, and Liers were smaller. Situated on the heights, six miles from the center of Liege, and from two to three miles of one another, they commanded the river and all the railways and approaches to Liege. Each fort was armed with eight heavy guns and mortars, and four quick-firing guns. The main armaments were in cupolas, and all had been designed by the great Belgian military engineer, General Brialmont, and built under the direct supervision of Belgian engineers by a French firm. Each large fort was built for a garrison of 200 men, and each small fort to hold 169 men. Between the forts were trenches constructed so as to form a connected chain of fortifications. The forts were considered impregnable against all *known* artillery, and even against very heavy siege guns they could have held out for many weeks. In shape the forts were triangular, each built of concrete, with revolving and disappearing steel turrets or (as they were popularly called) cupolas. Such were the defenses about Liege which the Germans had to capture or batter to pieces ere they could hope to gain a permanent hold upon Belgium.

As to the defenders, the forts and connecting trenches were held by approximately 22,000 Belgian troops under the command of that most gallant soldier, General Leman. For its adequate defense Liege should have had at least 50,000 troops, but the advance of the Germans had been so rapid that the Belgian forces, being largely composed of militia, could not send two-thirds of the necessary force to meet the 7th German Army Corps,[1] which was flung against the three most easterly forts—Barchon, Evegnée, and Fléron. The Germans, indeed, did not anticipate the least difficulty in taking these forts, for they were under the impression that most of the Belgian forces were even then collected some miles northwest of Liege, viz., at Diest. Moreover, they were so confident that the Belgians would only offer a feeble resistance that they had prepared a time-table by which they intended taking Brussels on August 3rd, and Lille on August 5th. The time they should have been in Brussels had already expired when they began to attack Liege.

On the night of Tuesday, August 4th, the 7th German

---

[1] An army Corps of 1914 may be roughly figured as containing forty thousand men, a Division contained half as many, and a Regiment about 3,500. In later years the numbers were much smaller.

Army Corps massed opposite the spaces between the three forts, advanced to the attack. Previously, according to the German theory of war, their artillery had shelled the forts, an operation which had not the slightest effect upon either the defenses or the defenders, for the shells were badly timed, and those which struck the steel cupolas or solid concrete surroundings exploded without doing serious damage. But the Germans advanced, confident that their "terrible artillery" had successfully prepared the way for an infantry attack.

They advanced in close formation, shoulder to shoulder, their rifles at their hips as if on the parade ground at Potsdam. Destruction overtook some of them even before they were ready to advance, for, in forming up, the 3rd Battalion of the 125th Regiment approached too close to the entrenched Belgians and was cut to pieces, not more than thirty surviving the withering rifle fire poured upon them. The special points of attack were the two spaces between the three forts. Here, however, the Belgians were most strongly entrenched, and when the advancing hordes at last came within rifle range, a hurricane of shot and shell swept away the front ranks, impeding the advance of the rear ranks, who stumbled over hundreds of their mangled comrades in a vain effort to reach the Belgian position. To make matters worse, the forts threw powerful searchlights on to the advancing columns, and soon the air was rent with the shrieks and groans of the wounded as they fell in masses before the terrible fire of the Belgian field guns, machine guns, and rifles. Not one German got within fifty yards of the Belgian trenches, and when at last the shattered remnants of the army wavered and fell back, the victorious defenders leapt from their trenches and charged the battered enemy, chasing them far into the dark night, taking hundreds of prisoners. Thus the first German attack upon Liege had failed—and failed ignominiously. So terrible were the German losses that Von Emmich was compelled to ask for an armistice in which to bury his dead—a request which was rightly refused, the Belgians fearing the enemy would make other uses of the momentary cessation of hostilities.

The following morning, August 5th, saw the opening of an artillery duel between the guns of the forts and those of the Germans, in which the latter were outranged and beaten; the Belgians destroyed two guns and badly damaged others. The invaders had been so sure of easily overpowering the Belgians that they had not brought their heavy guns, or even as it transpired later, sufficient commissariat. They found themselves therefore faced by the necessity for sending hurriedly for their siege howitzers, and in the meantime they endeavored once more to gain possession of the forts on the eastern banks of the Meuse, or to penetrate between them and force their way into the city of Liege. To effect this end General von Emmich brought up two additional Army Corps, the 9th and 10th, and extended his attack southwards between Forts Flémalle, Boncelles, and Embourg, as well as on Fléron, Evegnée, and Barchon and the spaces between them. And now General Leman, the gallant Belgian commander, found himself in difficulties. With so small a force at his disposal he could not hope to hold three German Army Corps perpetually at bay, but for the moment he could only bring a portion of his forces from their first position and extend them over the defenses in and about Forts Flémalle, Boncelles, and Embourg.

On the morning of August 5th, therefore, after the usual preliminary bombardment, Von Emmich, having first demanded the surrender of the city of Liege under threat of bombardment, again flung his forces against the openings between the forts in an endeavor to force his way through. Again a perfect hurricane of bullets and shells swept away his advancing columns, covering the ground with dead and wounded in one horrible mangled mass of groaning, writhing soldiery, and in places piling up the dead and wounded to a height of three feet. The German casualties were enormous; they admitted a loss of 25,000 men, though these figures were subsequently revised. But the fact remains that they suffered terrible losses out of all proportion to the casualties sustained by the brave Belgians. All day long the attacks continued. With useless valor the German commander threw battalion after battalion against the extended

Belgian position and forts, but they were flung back each time in broken and disordered masses.

By the morning of August 6th, however, the German big guns had arrived, and, having been placed in position, opened fire upon the city as well as upon the forts. In the former panic reigned, for, with an interval of only one hour, the Germans for seven hours poured shells into the city. One completely wrecked the roof of the cathedral, and the university was destroyed. Many people were killed and numbers wounded, and the effect was so terrible that further resistance was folly. The city was therefore surrendered, though the forts remained intact. Before the Germans marched into Liege, General Leman, with admirable strategy, had withdrawn the bulk of his field troops beyond the banks of the Meuse, leaving the forts garrisoned and well able to protect themselves against any attacks made upon them. A peculiar position thus presented itself—Liege, so far as the civilian population was concerned, was in the hands of the enemy, but Liege in the military sense, the forts and their garrisons, were still intact, and doing terrible execution upon the enemy whenever he came within range of the guns and rifles of the entrenched Belgian troops.

The German forces marched into Liege in parade order, singing patriotic songs and performing their ridiculous goose step as if passing in review order before the Kaiser. Immediately their commander gave orders that, if a single shot was fired in the city, the whole place would be devastated. But beyond the city the Germans held no sway, for the forts still held out and their guns dominated the roads by which alone fresh German forces could advance. To the northeast of Liege, beyond the circle of the forts, the main Belgian field force and general staff were advancing from Louvain in order to repel any attempted invasion of the right banks of the Meuse, upon which, so far, the Germans had entirely failed to set foot. They held Liege with 120,000 men, but were in a most perilous position, for, encompassed as they were, by the forts, it was impossible for them to move out of the city in any considerable force, and only at night was it possible for them to pass in and out between the intervals of the fortifications in small parties. North and south of Liege the Belgians had blown up the bridges over the Meuse, and time after time, as the Germans endeavored to push their pontoons across the river, they were swept away by the artillery fire from the forts.

It was evident, therefore, to the German Staff that, before any advance could be made, the capture or demolition of the forts must be accomplished. Accordingly huge siege howitzers were brought up, and systematically the forts were bombarded and smashed to atoms. In the case of one fort, Loncin, a vivid account of the terrible bombardment to which it was subjected before being blown into the air, was supplied by an officer of the Belgian Army:—"It was impossible for the Germans to take our forts by frontal attacks; they therefore resolved to bring up their siege material, and put our forts out of action by a violent bombardment. By a gradual approach their infantry invested the forts from a distance, isolating them one from another. Once master of the intervals between the forts, they managed to introduce into the city by night several of their most powerful batteries. They were thus able to attack from behind forts which had not been constructed to resist artillery fire from this direction. Soon the fort of Loncin was completely isolated. Day and night, however, in this mighty hive of iron and concrete, each man went about his business calmly and courageously. There was no respite in the bombardment. The shells which struck the fort burst with a terrific report, but caused little damage. All the same, life inside became daily more terrible. The galleries were dark at night, for the electric generators had been destroyed. Gradually the air became heavier, charged with the acrid scent of powder. On August 14th, at four o'clock in the afternoon, invisible siege artillery opened fire on the fort. The bombardment lasted twenty-four hours. Every minute two, three, or four shells burst on the cupola with a noise of thunder. Tongues of flame and puffs of thick smoke entered by every crack. As we did not know the position of the enemy's guns, our cannon remained silent. The whole garrison concentrated in the vast central gallery, where they were in safety, for the galleries toward the front were no longer tenable. During the night, when the bombardment had relaxed, General Leman sent men to examine the state of the cupolas. Most of them had suffered but little damage. At dawn, firing began again fiercer than ever. The garrison busied itself with extinguishing the beginnings of the conflagration at points where the woodwork had taken fire. We were still perfectly confident and calm, although we suffered a little from being penned up in the central gallery, which was filled with smoke. We were all of us ready to run to our posts, for an attack was anticipated for that night. Suddenly, at five o'clock in the afternoon, a terrible explosion shook the whole fort. It was the powder magazine which had blown up, perhaps as the result of the sudden outbreak of a fire which had been smoldering unperceived. It is impossible to describe in words the awful effect of this explosion. The center of the fort collapsed in a cloud of flame and dust and smoke. It was a scene of indescribable devastation. A broken cataract of blocks of stone, of concrete, of fragments of cupolas, which crushed beneath it almost the whole garrison, which had already been decimated by the violence of the explosion. The explosion was succeeded by a silence as of death. The enemy's artillery no longer fired. Then suddenly those who still lived saw German infantry running up from all sides, threading their way through the ruins of the fort, and with infinite precautions searching for the survivors. They had extricated several wounded from the débris, when they came upon the body of General Leman. The heroic defender of Liege lay unconscious but still breathing. He was placed on a stretcher and was carried from the fort. Meanwhile another party of the enemy were searching the ruins by the light of lanterns. Suddenly, from one of the galleries which had resisted the explosion, came the sound of shots. The Germans stopped in their advance. By the light of their torches they saw, massed at the end of the corridor, all that was left of the garrison of the fort. Black with powder, their faces streaked with blood, their clothes in ribbons, their hands grasping rifles, the heroic twenty-five still sought to resist. Touched to nobility by such splendid heroism, the Germans made no attempt to attack. Instead, they flung aside their weapons and ran to the aid of the brave Belgian soldiers, who were already half-asphyxiated by the poisonous gases set free by the explosion. Of the 500 men who formed the garrison of Fort Loncin, 350 are dead, and more than 100 severely wounded."

In commemoration of the gallant defense of Liege the French nation subsequently conferred the Legion of Honor upon the city.

BY GENERAL LEMAN
Diary from His German Prison at Magdeburg

On the 11th the Germans started bombarding us with 7 and 10 centimeter cannon. On the 12th and 13th they brought their 21 centimeter guns into action. But it was not until the 14th that they opened their heaviest fire and began their destruction of the outer works. On that day, at 4 o'clock in the afternoon, a German officer approached to within 200 yards of the fort with a signaling flag in his hand; and shortly afterwards, the siege gunners, having adjusted their range, began a fearful firing, that lasted a couple of hours. The battery on the left slope was destroyed, the enemy keeping on pounding away exclusively with their 21-centimeter cannons.

The third phase of the bombardment began at 5 o'clock in the morning of the 15th, firing being kept up without a break until two in the afternoon. A grenade wrecked the arcade under which the general staff were sheltering. All light was extinguished by the force of the explosion, and the officers ran the risk of asphyxiation by the horrible gases emitted from the shell. When firing ceased, I ventured out on a tour of inspection on the external slopes, which I found had been reduced to a rubble heap. A few minutes later, the bombardment was resumed. It seemed as though all the German batteries were together firing salvoes. Nobody will ever be able to form any adequate idea of what the reality was like. I have only learned since that when the big siege mortars entered into action they hurled against us shells

weighing 1,000 kilos (nearly a ton), the explosive force of
which surpasses anything known hitherto.   Their approach
was to be heard in an acute buzzing; and they burst with a
thunderous roar, raising clouds of missiles, stones, and dust.

After some time passed amid these horrors, I wished to
return to my observation tower; but I had hardly advanced
a few feet into the gallery when a great blast passed by, and
I was thrown violently to the ground. I managed to rise,
and continued my way, only to be stopped by a choking cloud
of poisonous gas. It was a mixture of the gas from an explosion and the smoke of a fire in the troop quarters. We
were driven back, half-suffocated. Looking out of a peep-
hole, I saw to my horror that the fort had fallen, slopes and
counter-slopes being a chaos of rubbish, while huge tongues
of flame were shooting forth from the throat of the fortress.
My first and last thought was to try and save the remnant
of the garrison. I rushed out to give orders, and saw some
soldiers, whom I mistook for Belgian gendarmes. I called
them, then fell again. Poisonous gases seemed to grip my
throat as in a vise.

On recovering consciousness, I found my aide-de-camp,
Captain Colland, standing over me, also a German officer,
who offered me a glass of water. They told me I had
swooned, and that the soldiery I had taken for Belgian
gendarmes were, in fact, the first band of German troops
who had set foot inside the forts. In recognition of our
courage, the Germans allowed me to retain my sword.

Gen. Leman's Letter to the Belgian King

Sir,—After honorable engagements on August 4th, 5th
and 6th, I considered that the forts of Liege could only play
the *rôle* of *forts d'arrêt*. I nevertheless maintained military
government in order to coördinate the defense as much as
possible, and to exercise moral influence upon the garrison.

Your Majesty is not ignorant that I was at Fort Loncin
on August 6th at noon. You will learn with grief that the
fort was blown up yesterday at 5.20 p. m., the greater part
of the garrison being buried under the ruins.   That I did

not lose my life in that catastrophe is due to the fact that my escort, Commandant Collard, a sub-officer of infantry who unfortunately perished, the gendarme Thevenim and my two orderlies, Vanden Bossche and Jos Lecocq, drew me from a position of danger, where I was being asphyxiated by gas from the exploded powder. I was carried into a trench, where a German captain named Guson gave me a drink, after which I was made prisoner and taken to Liege in an ambulance. I am convinced that the honor of our arms has been sustained. I have not surrendered either the fortress or the forts. Deign, Sire, to pardon my defects in this letter. I am physically shattered by the explosion of Loncin. In Germany, whither I am proceeding, my thoughts will be, as they have ever been, of Belgium and the King. I would willingly have given my life the better to serve them, but death was denied me.

GERMAN LETTER FROM AN OFFICER IN THE ASSAULT

General Leman's defense of Liege combined all that is noble, all that is tragic. The commander of one fort, at the moment when the bombardment was heaviest, went mad, and shot his own men. He was disarmed and bound. The cupola of another fort was destroyed by a bomb from a Zeppelin. Other forts were swept away like sand castles on the seashore before the relentless waves of the oncoming tide.

As long as possible General Leman inspected the forts daily to see that everything was in order. By a piece of falling masonry, dislodged by our guns, both General Leman's legs were crushed. Undaunted, he visited the forts in an automobile. Fort Chaudfontein was destroyed by a German shell dropping in the magazine. In the strong Fort Loncin General Leman decided to hold his ground or die.

When the end was inevitable the Belgians disabled the last three guns and exploded the supply of shells kept by the guns in readiness. Before this, General Leman destroyed all plans, maps and papers relating to the defenses. The food supplies were also destroyed. With about 100 men,

General Leman attempted to retire to another fort, but we had cut off their retreat. By this time our heaviest guns were in position, and a well-placed shell tore through the cracked and battered masonry and exploded in the main magazine. With a thunderous crash the mighty walls of the fort fell. Pieces of stone and concrete twenty-five cubic meters in size were hurled into the air. When the dust and fumes passed away, we stormed the fort across ground literally strewn with the bodies of the troops who had gone out to storm the fort and never returned. All the men in the fort were wounded, and most were unconscious. A corporal with one arm shattered valiantly tried to drive us back by firing his rifle. Buried in the débris and pinned beneath a massive beam was General Leman.

"*Respectez le general, il est mort,*" said an aide-de-camp.

With gentleness and care, which showed they respected the man who had resisted them so valiantly and stubbornly, our infantry released the general's wounded form and carried him away. We thought him dead, but he recovered consciousness, and, looking around, said, "It is as it is. The men fought valiantly," and then, turning to us, added: "Put in your dispatches that I was unconscious."

We brought him to our commander, General von Emmich, and the two generals saluted. We tried to speak words of comfort, but he was silent—he is known as the silent general. "I was unconscious. Be sure and put that in your dispatches." More he would not say.

Extending his hand, our commander said: "General, you have gallantly and nobly held your forts." General Leman replied: "I thank you. Our troops have lived up to their reputations." With a smile he added: "War is not like maneuvers"—a reference to the fact that General von Emmich was recently with General Leman during the Belgian maneuvers. Then, unbuckling his sword, General Leman tendered it to General von Emmich. "No," replied the German commander, with a bow, "keep your sword. To have crossed swords with you has been an honor," and the fire in General Leman's eye was dimmed by a tear.

LETTER FROM A BELGIAN OFFICER IN THE TRENCH ATTACK

Some of us late arrivals only managed to get to our posts when the German attack began. It was night time. We replied sharply with our guns. Until the dawn came we had no very distinct idea of what our practice was. Then we noticed heaps of slain Germans in a semicircle at the foot of our fort. The German guns must have been much less successful, because they rarely hit us that night. They did better at daybreak. We did better still.

As line after line of the German infantry advanced, we simply mowed them down. It was terribly easy, monsieur, and I turned to a brother officer of mine more than once and said, "Voila! They are coming on again, in a dense, close formation! They must be mad!" They made no attempt at deploying, but came on, line after line, almost shoulder to shoulder, until, as we shot them down, the fallen were heaped one on top of the other, in an awful barricade of dead and wounded men that threatened to mask our guns and cause us trouble. I thought of Napoleon's saying—if he said it, monsieur; and I doubt it, for he had no care of human life! —"C'est magnifique, mais ce n'est pas la guerre!" No, it was slaughter, just slaughter!

So high became the barricade of the dead and wounded that we did not know whether to fire through it or to go out and clear openings with our hands. We would have liked to extricate some of the wounded from the dead, but we dared not. A stiff wind carried away the smoke of the guns quickly, and we could see some of the wounded men trying to release themselves from their terrible position. I will confess I crossed myself, and could have wished that the smoke had remained.

But would you believe it, this veritable wall of dead and dying actually enabled those wonderful Germans to creep closer, and actually charge up the glacis? Of course, they got no further than halfway, for our maxims and rifles swept them back. Naturally, we had our own losses, but they were slight compared with the carnage inflicted upon our enemies.

BY VON BETHMANN-HOLLWEG, GERMAN CHANCELLOR
Official Address to the Belgian Government

The Fortress of Liege has been taken by assault after a gallant defense. The Government deeply regrets that the attitude of the Belgian Government towards Germany has led to sanguinary encounters. Germany does not come to Belgium as an enemy. It was only when it had been forced by circumstances and in presence of military dispositions made by France that the German Government was obliged to take the grave step of penetrating into Belgium and of occupying Liege as a *point d'appui* for further military operations.

The Belgian Army having preserved in the most brilliant fashion the honor of its armies by its heroic resistance against a greatly superior force, the German Government now asks H.M. the King and the Belgian Government to spare Belgium the continuation of the horrors of war. The German Government is ready to enter into any kind of convention with Belgium which can in any way be made compatible with the differences between itself and France. Germany reaffirms in the most solemn manner that she has not been actuated by any intention to appropriate Belgian territory; such an intention is entirely foreign to her. Germany is still always ready immediately to evacuate the kingdom of Belgium as soon as the situation in the theater of war permits her to do so.

THE BELGIAN GOVERNMENT'S REPLY

The proposition which has been submitted to us repeats the demand formulated in the ultimatum of August 2nd. Faithful to her international obligations, Belgium can only repeat her answer to that ultimatum, especially seeing that since August 3rd her neutrality has been violated, a lamentable war has been waged on her soil, and the guaranteeing Powers have immediately and loyally responded to her appeal for help.

BELGIUM'S AGONY

GERMANY OFFICIALLY ADOPTS THE POLICY OF SUPPRESSION

AUGUST-SEPTEMBER

BRAND WHITLOCK   GENERAL BARON VON BISSING
EMPEROR WILLIAM II.   JOHANNES JORGENSEN
MAJOR-GENERAL DISFORTH
A GERMAN SOCIALIST DESERTER

Germany's apologists, both within the ancient empire and in other lands, have gone to reckless extremes in defending the fatherland against the awful charges of wholesale and official massacre in Belgium. For example, according to the amazing document of the Ninety-three leaders of German thought, here to be quoted, German hands and hearts remained white as snow through all the heroic process of conquering neutral Belgium.

For the fair-minded but bewildered reader, therefore, it becomes the absolute duty of the historian to speak in the plainest and most unmistakable words in declaring that the bulk of charges against Germany have been proven completely by every form of legal evidence, including confession and admission of the commanding German officials themselves. On the other hand, the feeble counter-charges made by the Germans in partial extenuation of their guilt have never been judicially established; have, in cases where investigation remained possible, been wholly disproven and withdrawn; and would, even if true, have been neither answer nor excuse for the awful German barbarity.

The full evidence of these conclusions is easily accessible. It is presented here in compacted form. First comes the official statement of Brand Whitlock, the United States Minister to Belgium throughout the disaster. This final report was issued after the United States had entered the War, but it is only a summarizing of Mr. Whitlock's individual reports delivered during 1914 and the following years. Then he had spoken as a neutral, but as a neutral overcome with horror and disgust at what he personally had seen and faced. He remains the chief neutral witness in the case.

But are neutral witnesses needed? Read what follows: the official proclamations of the German governor in supreme command, General Von Bissing. He was dismissed from office in the later years of Belgian occupancy, and a more severe ruler appointed in his stead. Consider especially Von Bissing's order as to the treatment of prisoners, prisoners who had been collected in crowds without any charge against specific individuals, without trial, often without hearing, and shipped by carloads into Germany. Think what the rising generation of Germans had been trained to become under rulers such as Von Bissing, and then try to think of the agony to be inflicted by a governor yet more severe.

Next we present here the Kaiser's notorious telegram to the United States Government accusing the Belgians. The Kaiser, in this letter, backs up Von Bissing. He makes extravagant and hysterical charges, which are false, and in this extreme form false to the point of obvious absurdity, but which the self-righteous monarch never withdrew. Moreover, as late as 1919, the German chief of staff, General Ludendorff, in his noted book upon the war referred to the Kaiser's letter as though its falsities were facts, regretting the failure of its "appeal to the American sense of justice" as against "the Belgian atrocities."

Were these chief German leaders deceived or deceiving? With Ludendorff there can be no question. To the impartial reader the purpose of his book stands immediately revealed in that evil phrase. He had in his hands the full information necessary for honesty and he preferred dishonesty. He persisted in the foul system in which he had been trained, the repeating of a falsehood constantly and boldly until men shall become doubtful as to where truth really lies, shall see neither black nor white but confuse all things as gray. So may a Ludendorff hope to appear no worse than others.

It was under this policy that the German Government attempted in 1914 to shift upon the Belgian Government, or at least to throw into gray confusion, the responsibility for the entire invasion of Belgium. The conquerors took from the Belgian Government archives some perfectly harmless, routine documents. These were military reports working out a theoretical problem as to how, if Belgium and Britain were allied, and if Germany attacked them, their forces might best co-operate. Similar military reports assuming every conceivable alliance and combination existed under every government of Europe. They were an obvious part of military training and of statesmen's meditations. Germany deliberately distorted these documents, and then published the falsified forms as "proofs" of a secret and treacherous Belgian-British compact or alliance against Germany. The deceit of this shallow trick was at once revealed; yet thereafter all German officials and publications always referred to the Belgian-British compact as a proven fact. Ordinary Germans presumably believe in it to this day. Great is the ancient power of falsehood; and greater still was the old German Government's belief in it.

As to the Kaiser's own belief in his own letter at the time of writing it, perhaps it was sincere. The German Military Staff may have placed the Belgian charges before him in a misleading and convincing light. The question has no value except for those who would seek to study the inner character of the human being raised by lot to the awful eminence and responsibility for the German cataclysm.

After the Kaiser's letter we present the estimate of another neutral, not of an eye-witness now but of a judge, the noted Danish writer, Jorgensen. He weighs the evidence on either side, quotes its more striking passages, and gives the decision of the world. Would Germany still reopen the case? A chance is given her. One of her higher generals, Disforth, is quoted, to show what has seemed to most of us the real German attitude, the only real explanation of all the crimes of 1914. Germans had indeed adopted the faith that they are a "super-race" who should dominate the world at any cost.

Last comes the voice of unofficial Germany, the socialist, helpless, anonymous even, forced into the ranks as "cannon-fodder," and revealing with dramatic clearness what the cannon-fodder thought of it all. There is no human document of the ages more well worth reading than this particular German's human story.

C. F. H.

BY BRAND WHITLOCK
Condensed from his official report of September 12, 1917, to the
U. S. Secretary of State

OVER all this area, that is in the country lying about Visé, Liege, Dinant, Namur, Louvain, Vilverde, Malines, and Aerschot, a rich agricultural region dotted with innumerable towns, villages and hamlets, a land of contented peace and plenty, during all that month of August there were inflicted on the civilian population by the hordes that overran it deeds of such ruthless cruelty and unspeakable outrage that one must search history in vain for others like them committed on such a prodigious scale. Towns were sacked and burned, homes were pillaged; in many places portions of the population, men, women, and children, were massed in public squares and mowed down by *mitrailleuses,* and there were countless individual instances of an amazing and shameless brutality. The stories of these deeds gradually filtered into Brussels in ever increasing numbers as the days went by, brought by the refugees, who, in crowds, fled the stricken region in terror. It was difficult at first to believe them; but the stories persisted, and were told with such detail and on such authority that one could no longer doubt their essential truth. They became a matter of common knowledge and public notoriety; and they saturated the general mind with their horror.

Take, for example, the following cases: Battice, in the province of Liege, is about five kilometers from Bligny. It was pillaged and burned on the 6th of August by Germans who had been repulsed before the forts of Liege. Thirty-six persons, including three women, were massacred, the village methodically burned, and the church destroyed.

The Germans entered Aerschot on August 19th. The greater part of the inhabitants who had remained in the town were shut up in the church for several days, receiving hardly any nourishment. On August 28th they were marched to Louvain. Upon their arrival there they were let loose and were fired upon by German soldiers. The following day they were marched back to Aerschot, the men being again shut up in the church and the women were put in a building belonging to a Mr. Fontaine. Many women and young girls, it is said, were raped by the German soldiers. Upon one occasion seventy-eight men were taken outside the town and were made to pass before German gendarmes who struck them with the butts of their revolvers. Of these seventy-eight men only three escaped death. At another time a number of men were put in rows of three, the Germans shooting the third man in each row. The Germans killed over one hundred and fifty of the inhabitants of Aerschot, and among this number were eight women and several children. The pillage and firing of houses continued for several days, and a great quantity of furniture and objects of art were sent to Germany. On the 6th of September, three hundred of the inhabitants were carted off in wagons to Germany. In the seven small villages surrounding Aerschot, forty-two persons were killed, four hundred and sixty-two were sent to Germany, one hundred and fifteen houses were burned and eight hundred and twenty-three were pillaged.

One of the most sorely tried communities was that of the little village of Tamines, down in what is known as the Borinage, the coal fields near Charleroi. Tamines is a mining village in the Sambre; it is a collection of small cottages sheltering about 5,000 inhabitants, mostly all poor laborers.

The little graveyard in which the church stands bears its mute testimony to the horror of the event. There are hundreds of new-made graves, each with its small wooden cross and its bit of flowers; the crosses are so closely huddled that there is scarcely room to walk between them. The crosses are alike and all bear the same date, the sinister date of August 22, 1914.

Whether their hands were cut off or not, whether they

were impaled on bayonets or not, children were shot down, by military order, in cold blood. In the awful crime of the Rock of Bayard, there overlooking the Meuse below Dinant, infants in their mothers' arms were shot down without mercy. The deed, never surpassed in cruelty by any band of savages, is described by the Bishop of Namur himself:

This scene surpasses in horror all others; the fusillade of the Rock Bayard near Dinant. It appears to have been ordered by Colonel Meister. This fusillade made many victims among the nearby parishes, especially those of des Rivages and Neffe. It caused the death of nearly 90 persons, without distinction of age or sex. Among the victims were babies in arms, boys and girls, fathers and mothers of families, even old men.

It was there that 12 children under the age of 6 perished from the fire of the executioners, 6 of them as they lay in their mothers' arms: the child Fiévet, 3 weeks old; Maurice Bétemps, 11 months old; Nelly Pollet, 11 months old; Gilda Genon, 18 months old; Gilda Marchot, 2 years old; Clara Struvay, 2 years and 6 months.

The pile of bodies comprised also many children from 6 to 14 years. Eight large families have entirely disappeared. Four have but one survivor. Those men that escaped death —and many of whom were riddled with bullets—were obliged to bury in a summary and hasty fashion their fathers, mothers, brothers, or sisters; then after having been relieved of their money and being placed in chains they were sent to Cassel [Prussia].

Monceau-sur-Sambre (Charleroi) was pillaged and sacked on the 22nd of August. Twelve inhabitants were shot by firing squads and twenty-eight as they emerged from their burning houses. Thirty of all ages and both sexes were wounded under similar conditions. Sixty-two houses were looted and two hundred and fifty burned. French soldiers were holding a bridge on the Sambre with machine guns and rifles and had received the Germans with a short but spirited fusillade.

Gougnies, in the province of Hainaut, was sacked on the 23rd of August. No fighting had taken place there and the

first troops had passed through quietly.   On Sunday, the
23rd, claiming that civilians had fired on their troops, the
Germans set fire to various parts of the village.   Seventeen
houses were burned, and among those one in which Mr.
Piret, provincial councilor for the Hainaut, had established
a hospital.   Ten wounded French soldiers therein were
burned alive.   Mr. Piret in spite of his great age was taken
out and shot the next day at Le Roux.   Two other inhabitants of Gougnies, Messrs. Thiry, aged 83, and Gre-
goire, 56, were also shot.

It is interesting to note that near Louvain at Heverle is
the château of the Duc d'Arenberg, a German; many of the
houses in the village belonged to him; on these houses there
were posted little cards, one of which I attach to this report; they read:

"This house must be protected.   It is strictly forbidden to
enter the houses or to burn them without the consent of
the Kommandantur."

Certain houses were marked, in chalk: *"Nicht plün-
dern."* [Do not pillage.]

During the whole of that terrible month of August
[1914], and during a part of September, eastern Belgium
was the scene of such happenings, from the deliberate and
systematic organized massacres of civil populations, with
isolated murders and outrages, violations of women, and
those nameless deeds one cannot bring oneself to mention
and yet somehow hears; down to the sack of wine cellars by
drunken soldiers. . . .

There is little doubt that the German soldiers often
fired because of the fear of francs-tireurs, but there is no
convincing evidence that they were actually fired upon; indeed, no serious effort seems to have been made judicially
to establish the fact.   As to have a town given over to fire
and sword, it sufficed simply for a German soldier to cry:
"Man hat geschossen" [Some one fired a shot], so it seems
now to suffice, when justification is attempted, to say: "The
Belgians fired on us." . . .

The Bishop of Namur writes to the Governor-General
in Belgium, subjecting the [German] "White Book" to an

examination that is without mercy in its logic. After having gone over the different charges of the Germans concerning the firing by civilians, he points out to the Governor-General that, in the "White Book," there is not a word concerning the tragedy at Tamines, not a word about Surice, not a word about Spontin, not a word about Namur, not a word about Fehe, not a word about Gommeries, not a word about Latour, not a word, in short, about sixty-five other places where there was pillage and massacre and incendiarism.

The Bishop shows, in the appendix devoted to Dinant, that almost three hundred times the [German] "White Book" contented itself with repeating the unsupported allegation, "They have fired on us"; and he adds, with perfect comprehension of the German psychology, when this is denied, when the Germans are challenged to produce proof—proof, they reply, simply: "You cannot deny this; a German soldier said so."

It may be that there were instances where Belgian housewives threw boiling water on the soldiers, it would not have been surprising if they had, though it seems somewhat less likely in the case of boiling tar, as housewives are not generally in the habit of keeping boiling tar available as means of defense, and it is not stated how the German soldiers were roasted. But it would seem that there could not have been enough boiling water in all Belgium, even had it all been flung at German soldiers, to make it a military necessity to burn, to slay, to sack and to pillage on such a scale.

BY GENERAL BARON VON BISSING

As German Military Governor of Belgium he issued a Proclamation, dated August 29, 1914, which said in part:

If a blinded and maddened population treacherously attacks and slaughters without pity the brave sons of our people who are facing death for their country, as well as the wounded, doctors and hospital nurses [1]—if bands of men

[1] The leading Berlin Socialistic newspaper, under date of October 22, 1914, said:

"We have already been able to establish the falseness of a great number of assertions which have been made with great precision and published everywhere in the press, concerning alleged cruelties com-

endanger the safety of the lines of communication of the armies, self-preservation requires that extreme measures should immediately be adopted against them. Indeed, it is a sacred duty of the military commanders to take such measures. In such a case the innocent will have to suffer with the guilty. The repeated instructions of the command of our army have allowed no doubt to subsist as to this matter. It is no doubt to be regretted that in repressing these infamous acts it should be impossible to spare human lives, and that isolated houses as well as flourishing villages, and even entire towns, should be annihilated, but this should not provoke misplaced sentimentality. All that we may destroy is, in

mitted by the populations of the countries with which Germany is at war upon German soldiers and civilians. We are now in a position to silence two others of these fantastic stories.

"The War Correspondent of the *Berliner Tageblatt* spoke a few weeks ago of cigars and cigarettes filled with powder alleged to have been given out or sold to our soldiers with diabolical intent. He even pretended to have seen with his own eyes hundreds of this kind of cigarettes. We learn from an authentic source that this story of cigars and cigarettes is nothing but a brazen invention. Stories of soldiers whose eyes are alleged to have been torn out by francs-tireurs are circulated throughout Germany. Not a single case of this kind has been officially established. In every instance where it has been possible to verify the story its inaccuracy has been demonstrated.

"It matters little that reports of this nature bear an appearance of positive certitude, or are even vouched by eye-witnesses. The desire for notoriety, the absence of criticism, and personal error play an unfortunate part in the days in which we are living. Every nose shot off or simply bound up, every eye removed, is immediately transformed into a nose or eye torn off by the francs-tireurs. Already the *Popular Gazette of Cologne* has been able, contrary to the very categorical assertions of Aix-la-Chapelle, to prove that there was no soldier with his eyes torn out in the field ambulance at this town. It was said, also, that people wounded in this way were under treatment in the neighborhood of Berlin, but whatever inquiries have been made in regard to these reports, their absolute falsity has been demonstrated. At length these reports were concentrated at Gross Lichterfeld. A newspaper published at noon, and widely circulated in Berlin, printed a few days ago in large type the news that at the Lazaretto of Lichterfeld alone there were 'ten German soldiers, only slightly wounded, whose eyes had been wickedly torn out.' But to a request for information by comrade Liebknecht the following written reply was sent by the chief medical officer of the above-mentioned field hospital, dated the 18th of the month:—'Sir: Happily there is no truth whatever in these stories. Yours obediently, PROFESSOR RAUTENBERG.'"

our eyes, less in value than the life of a single one of our brave soldiers. That is self-evident, and indeed, properly speaking, it is not necessary to mention it.

Whoever speaks here of barbarity commits a crime. Rigorously to carry out a duty is to obey a mandate of a high civilization [Kultur], and in that matter the population of the enemy's country has only to take a lesson from our army.

A similar Proclamation of December, 1914

In an order of the day, I recently appealed to the public not to display false and misplaced sentiments of sympathy towards the prisoners of war. You should show more of a German conscience.

Must I again repeat this remonstrance? It would seem so. According to the reports which have been submitted to me, all kinds of dainties, and in particular chocolates, have again been offered to the prisoners in spite of the prohibitions which have been issued, and that at Munster as well as elsewhere. Are you so full of pity for others and so anti-German in spirit that you do not hear the cries of distress of our own prisoners in France? You may be sure that they are not offered chocolate there. Unfortunately, it is not possible completely to isolate from the outside world the prisoners of my district. I have, therefore, been obliged to put an end to the commerce in provisions and dainties which has been established in the encampments without my authority. It is mostly children and young people, and in particular little girls, who crowd round the prisoners unceasingly. They are entirely wanting in good breeding. It is for their relatives and the schools to alter this state of things.

If these warnings should remain without result, recourse will be had to exemplary punishment in order to put a stop to this anti-German conduct. It is on the sentiment of the young generation that the future of our country depends.

The General Commanding,

VON BISSING.

BY EMPEROR WILLIAM II.

This was sent as a telegram to the President of the United States, under date of September 7, 1914

I feel it my duty, Mr. President, to inform you as the most prominent representative of principles of humanity, that after taking the French fortress of Longwy, my troops discovered there thousands of dumdum cartridges made by special government machinery. The same kind of ammunition was found on killed and wounded troops and prisoners, also on the British troops. You know what terrible wounds and suffering these bullets inflict and that their use is strictly forbidden by the established rules of international law. I therefore address a solemn protest to you against this kind of warfare, which, owing to the methods of our adversaries, has become one of the most barbarous known in history.

Not only have they employed these atrocious weapons, but the Belgian Government has openly [2] encouraged and, since long, carefully prepared the participation of the Belgian civil population in the fighting. The atrocities committed even by women and priests in this guerilla warfare, also on wounded soldiers, medical staff and nurses, doctors killed, hospitals attacked by rifle fire, were such that my generals finally were compelled to take the most drastic measures in order to punish the guilty and to frighten the bloodthirsty population from continuing their work of vile murder and horror.

Some villages and even the old town of Loewen [Louvain], excepting the fine hôtel de ville, had to be destroyed in self-defense and for the protection of my troops. My heart bleeds when I see that such measures have become unavoidable and when I think of the numerous innocent peo-

---

[2] As this word "openly" reaches the apex of these extravagant charges and should be the point most easily proven, let us assure the reader that it is flatly not so. The Belgian Government fairly flooded the land with proclamations and warnings by various local authorities, forbidding the civil population to take any part in the warfare, cautioning them of the awful consequences that would ensue.

ple who lose their home and property as a consequence of
the barbarous behavior of those criminals.[3]

Signed,

WILLIAM, EMPEROR AND KING.

BY JOHANNES JORGENSEN

[Early in the War two official pamphlets were issued in
Germany, circumstantially denying all charges of falsehood
or brutality. The neutral scholar Jorgensen quotes these
and then proceeds to analyze them. The one was called "The
Truth about the War," the other "The Voice of Truth."
The latter and more astounding one was signed by ninety-
three of the leading authors, artists and scholars of Germany. No document could possibly be more representative
of the German race. It begins as follows:]

"We, as leaders of German Learning and Art, send forth
to the united World of Culture a protest against the Lies
and Slanders with which our enemies endeavor to befoul
Germany's spotless Cause in the hard struggle for existence
which has been forced upon her. The immovable witness of
events has exposed the fables of German defeats. With
still greater ardor they endeavor to falsify the character of
facts and to bring suspicion upon us. Against these machi-

---

[3] Commenting on this telegram the German scientist, Lorenz Muller,
wrote in prominent type in a scientific review in Germany:

"Officially, no instance has been proved of persons having fired,
with the help of priests, from the towers of churches. All that has
been made known up to the present, and that has been made the object of inquiry, concerning alleged atrocities attributed to Catholic
priests during this war, has been shown to be false and altogether
imaginary, without any exception. Our Emperor telegraphed to the
President of the United States of America that even women and
priests had committed atrocities during this guerilla warfare on
wounded soldiers, doctors and nurses attached to the field ambulances.
How this telegram can be reconciled with the fact stated above (that
there is nothing against the priests) we shall not be able to learn
until after the war." Here is truthfulness combined with a most
typically German trustfulness in the Kaiser.

As to the charges about "dumdum" bullets, these have never been
reënforced by any evidence, such as, for example, the simple method of
exhibiting a few of the "thousands of cartridges" with the proofs
that they were made by French "government machinery." After the
Peace Treaty a German government bulletin withdrew the charges.

nations we raise our voice in protestation. This voice shall be the herald of Truth.

"*Est ist nicht wahr*" [It is not true] that Germany is guilty of this war! . . .

"It is not true that our soldiers have attacked the life or property of a single Belgian citizen without the utmost provocation. Over and over again, in spite of all appeals, the populace have shot from ambush, have mutilated the wounded, and murdered the doctors whilst carrying on their work of mercy. There could be no more infamous deception than to try to shelter these criminals and to represent their just punishment by the Germans as a crime."

The Ninety-three representatives of German Culture are here in perfect agreement with the German Emperor. With his hand and seal, with his full signature: WILHELM II. R., the Kaiser wrote to President Wilson, laying before him his solemn indictment and protest, not only against his opponents' "barbaric methods in war" (that was before the poisonous gases were used), but against the fact that the "Belgian Government had not only *encouraged* but had, *long previously, prepared* the Belgian civilian population to participate in the fighting." [4]

In accord with this "The Truth about the War" contains a chapter with the title: "Louvain and Belgian atrocities." It shows how cruelly the Belgians had behaved towards the Germans, and since the world has hitherto heard so much to the contrary it is interesting to read the German accusation against Belgium.

The chapter begins with a comparison between Luxemburg and Belgium, to the advantage of Luxemburg. "In Luxemburg the Government and people bowed reasonably before the military necessity." Yes, that I can believe. I remember an evening in the capital of the Grand Duchy when some good friends jestingly proposed that I should make a speech next morning to the Army of Luxemburg. "It is not too large to fill the space outside your window, and you could begin by 'Dear Army.'" Luxemburg has a

[4] The words in italics were underlined by the German Emperor himself.

quarter of a million inhabitants, whilst Belgium has eight and a half. Luxemburg was necessarily restricted to a verbal protest against the German invasion which was, in fact, made by the President of the Council, Monsieur Eyschen.

"They were blinded in Belgium," says the German Protest; "they seemed to have forgotten how their country had suffered under the ambition and rapacity of the French and the selfishness and faithlessness of England." What an argument! Because in 1792 the French had plundered Belgium, the Belgian Government in 1914 should not keep its faith as a neutral State.

"The Belgians are to be pitied. For years they have given themselves over to a fanatical hatred of the German Kingdom and its people. They believed blindly all that was said by the newspapers of Paris, and by the Belgian papers in imitation; and all that French plays, French films, French cabarets and such like created in the way of suspicion, slander and abuse against Germany. They described German officers as spies and rapers of women (*Frauenvergewaltiger*, I translate the word as I can); German soldiers as beasts in the form of men, the German Kingdom as warloving, as the 'German polypus,' with monstrous tentacles, and as a land of reaction, arrogance, and barbarity. The Belgian Press joined in the slanderous campaign of France contrary to its neutrality. What was thus sown in hate and contempt was harvested in horror."

These are simply the tactics of the wolf with the lamb that the Germans are using. The blame for what was done in Belgium must indisputably, undeniably, be laid on the shoulders of the Belgians. Any one who has traveled in Belgium in the last ten years (my first visit there was fifteen years ago) knows how untrue this tale is of hatred of the Belgians for Germany. The fact cannot be concealed that the French element and French influence in Belgium was diminishing very much, and that the Flemish national movement leant strongly towards the Germanic character and origin of the population. Germany had already made great progress in the pacific conquest of Belgium. German beer, German newspapers, German industries, as well as German music, German books, German science and German art were to be found everywhere. As for the Press campaign against Prussia described above, the present writer for months together has read daily two and three Belgian papers (*Vingtième Sicèle, Métropole, Soir*), and has never seen a trace of this campaign. And of what "neutrality-breaking agreement with France" has the Belgian Government been guilty? When and where had the Belgian Government before or during the ministry of de Broqueville been guilty of a Press campaign against Germany?

But this chapter is only written to make it seem probable and explicable that the Belgian people consists of assassins, as the Ninety-three express it. Hence the pathetic change of key: "What was then sown in hatred and contempt was harvested in horror." One trembles for the lives of the Germans.

What one cannot understand (I say it in parenthesis), is that since the Germans knew of this anti-German agitation in Belgium, why did they not try to work against it in time? A couple of well-written periodicals in French or Flemish, published in Antwerp, for example, the center of Germanism in Belgium, would have done great service and prevented the growth of the "harvest of horror."

Another point for consideration is this: and it is not in parenthesis, but in large type: *"What right have the Germans to demand that they should not be hated and despised?"* Because some one in a non-German country (and Belgium is not a German country and *never was* a German country) —because in such a country one forms the opinion that Germany is a "polypus" which has Europe in its grasp from the Adriatic to Cape Skagen, or that the German Empire is in reality reactionary, arrogant and barbarous, is it, then, a crime if they express that opinion? If Germany is in truth no polypus, but a little peaceful garden snail, it is easy to prove it. If Germany is the home of political progress, of sound self-knowledge and gentle manners, then this impression must without fail be conveyed to all who visit, or come in contact with, the inhabitants of the country. Why do we speak of "French courtesy," of the "English gentleman," of

"Spanish pride," if it is not that these qualities describe the impression that generation after generation has received of those nations? We speak of "German *Gemüthlichkeit,*" and this is certainly the most striking quality in the great *Vaterland.* It is a quality of private life which is to be seen at its best in a cheerful gathering round a "bock" of Munich beer or a bottle of sparkling Moselle. But the *Gemüthlich* over his bottle of wine can quite as well be a political reactionary, and it does not preclude his being brutal and over-bearing as an officer or civilian to his subordinates, to those who have no redress.

Let me return to *"Die Wahrheit über den Krieg."*

In the middle of the month of August the German Government sent the following proclamation to the Belgian Government :—

"The Royal Belgian Government has rejected Germany's benignant offer to spare their land from the horrors of war. It has raised itself in armed opposition against the passage of troops necessitated by the enemies of Germany. It has chosen war. In spite of the Note of August 8th, in which the Belgian Government declared that, according to its agreement, it would only make war upon troops in uniform, in the fighting round Liege numbers of people have taken part in the combat under the protection of civilian dress. They have not only fired on German troops; they have cruelly killed the wounded and shot down doctors at their work. At the same time the population of Antwerp has destroyed German property in the most barbarous manner and brutally cut down women and children with the sword. Germany calls upon the civilized world to witness the shedding of this innocent blood, and the way in which Belgium has made war in the face of all civilization. If, henceforward, the war assumes a cruel character, Belgium bears the blame. To protect our German troops from the unbridled fury of the people, we shall, in future, treat every one not in uniform, who cannot justify his participation in the fighting by some outward mark or sign, as an outlaw, inasmuch as, sharing in the fighting, he injures German lines of communication, cuts telegraph wires, causes explosions, and takes an unlawful part in the perpetration of warfare. He will be treated as a sniper, and be shot at once under martial law."

"So," the simple man might say, "when a robber breaks into my house and I leap from my bed and defend myself with anything that I can lay my hand upon—a poker or a candlestick—and I succeed in giving my robber a few bruises, he has the right to go out into the street and complain loudly that I have not defended myself with a Browning revolver or any other regular weapon. And he, the robber, who has no business at all in my house, shall stand forth before the civilized world's judgment and call me a brute, me, whom he has attacked.

"He may, to crown his hypocritical insolence, call me to reckoning for the innocent blood that has been spilled—the blood that never would have been shed if he had not broken into my house!"

But a man must be very simple to waste any surprise upon such a situation. *It is, of course, the lamb's fault if it does not lie still while the wolf eats it.*

Having written these words I can no longer treat these things with irony. It is unbelievable what calumnies and slander German writers—official and other—have allowed themselves to use to blacken and slander a people who at the worst have fought a tragic and bitter fight for hearth and home against an overwhelming and aggressive power.

What were Andreas Hofer and his Tyrolese other than sharpshooters—a people in arms in self-defense, for life or for death? Their name is held in honor—Hofer is a hero, whilst the Belgians, who do as the Tyrolese did a hundred years ago, are called "assassins" and "brutes."

But it is not even certain that these things were done at all. Let us look at the German evidence. It has throughout one common characteristic. It is all vague and indeterminate. It never, or rarely, gives names of places or people. We read, for example, in one of the documents the narrative of a military doctor: "In a village near Verviers we found a soldier with his hands tied behind him and his eyes put out." What village? What was the name of the soldier?

Where was he found? Under what circumstances? Where is the evidence of the person who saw him?

The military doctor continues: "In one village a young woman stepped up to a military automobile, held a revolver to the head of the chauffeur and shot him."

Again the same vagueness. Which village? What was the name of the chauffeur?

We have to believe the German *"Es ist wahr"* (It is true), as we are obliged to believe the German *"Es ist nicht wahr"* (It is not true). It is an exception that we *find the name of the place given*. These two occurrences are mentioned as happening in the village of Gammenich, near the frontier. Here a "gentleman from Aachen" (Name? Profession? Age?) was killed, having left his automobile for a moment. An ambulance was shot at from a house (What ambulance? What were the names of the doctors? Where is the evidence of the hospital orderlies?) There is no evidence brought of the truth of their statements. We need something more.

A military doctor appeals to our sympathy for a soldier "who was shot from behind a hedge in such a manner that his skin was still full of powder." And thereupon he gives vent to his feelings, plays on all the stops of German pathos which now swell into the full tones of an organ fugue. "Is this the way the civilized Belgians make war? How should the blood not roar in our ears and rage in one's heart! And then the Belgians wonder that we proceed ruthlessly against a civil population suspected of such crimes! One's heart swells in one's breast and *civis Germanicus sum* has become the expression of pride when we see the proud attitude of our magnificent Army. But it bleeds to see our poor boys shed their blood beneath the peasant's pitchfork or the kitchen knife of a fanatical Belgian woman. Who can wonder that we level to the earth the villages where our men are attacked!"

We find the same inconceivable distortion of moral values in all the published documents. There is never a moment's doubt of Germany's right, first to invade a country and then to decree how it shall fight, and lastly to judge and punish all that oppose themselves to German rule. We have in this attitude the true German mentality. He has no feeling for the right or for justice (for that does not exist— a treaty is "only a scrap of paper") but only for outward order and correctness.

Thus a German soldier relates in a technical and cold-blooded manner how they set fire to a house in Louvain from which they had shot at the troops. "As the inhabitants came out one by one they were shot to pieces (*abgeschossen*—I cannot translate into another language the calm stolidity of that word *abgeschossen*. It implies a methodical, almost mechanical proceeding, like that of stamping letters).

The evidence of the above assertion appeared in September, 1914, in the *Hamburger Nachrichten,* and has the honor of being quoted in *"Die Wahrheit über den Krieg."* It is by this fount of truth that I am illuminated.

A captain in the German Army writes:—

"A civilized people can have no conception of the behavior of the inhabitants. I believe I have proof that the Belgians have been officially encouraged by the French to perpetrate this monstrous guerilla warfare. This must be the case, for all the houses behind my position—about ten in all—which I have visited, have been for some time prepared with this object. The roofs are pierced with gun holes. Iron pipes are placed in the walls with a steel flap which opens outwards. When the rifle is thrust out to shoot, the flap is raised. The gun being withdrawn, the flap falls down again. I found this arrangement in several houses. I have visited them all personally with my platoon commander. From outside, these contrivances have the appearance of ornaments; in the center is a support, cemented from without, which must have been prepared before the war, and it is my opinion that the Belgians systematically prepared all this.

"In the house where we are living—a villa belonging to well-to-do people—the steel flaps are all numbered '3350.' The articles seem to have been made in a manufactory and numbered after the houses to which they were delivered."

This is so ridiculous that one does not know whether to

laugh or to cry. As every one who has lived in Belgium knows (and as the German captain could have known had he asked), these iron-covered holes are used for fixing up the scaffolding for repairs to prevent damage to the façade. In the same way in Denmark we put shelves in the walls for scaffoldings. These pipes are found particularly in well-to-do houses, and in such a house the captain was living. They *are* made in a manufactory, but that is the only part of the German hypothesis that is correct. The outer flaps that seem to the captain so dreadfully suspicious are, as one might think, to prevent the draught through the pipes. Thus a whole theory is based upon a misstatement such as this, which establishes an understanding with France for the preparation of a guerilla warfare. How could they foresee, for instance, that the Germans would come to Louvain? And this foolishness is spread about and printed and made to serve as proof against Belgium. There is no greater sign of the weakness of the German cause than that she uses such feeble defenses.

All through the war, but especially in those first months, the accusations of the Germans were always directed to the blackening of Belgium in order that Germany should appear less black herself. Germany has no hope of ever appearing white with the whiteness of innocence; the conviction that tigers eat men is a difficult one to uproot, says the Mother Tigress in *Hitopadeça*. But Germany might become gray—"gray from battle"—that would satisfy her quite. She does not seek acquittal either from God or man, she only desires "extenuating circumstances." So long as she escapes hell she is ready to endure purgatory till the end of the world.

The whole newspaper campaign against Belgium is easily understood when once this rather troubled state of mind is admitted. If one cannot use truthful statements, "misrepresentations and suspicions," to quote the words of the Ninety-three, must serve instead.

We will only quote two more of their accusations. New ones are forever appearing. They are like the soap-bubbles that children blow. They glitter for a moment, blown out into a ball of glowing colors, then they burst and become once more a drop of the dirty water of which they were made.

(1) "The Belgian Government openly encouraged the civil population to take part in the fighting and had carefully prepared this participation beforehand. This was especially the case in the fighting at Liege." The German illustrated papers tried to prove this assertion by publishing photographs of the Belgian snipers. It is clear that these snipers were soldiers of the Belgian *Garde Civique,* answering to the *German Landsturm.* The *Belgian Landsturm* was constituted in accordance with the stipulations of the Hague Convention. It is a regular corps, fighting in its own uniform, and called up by the Belgian Government at the outbreak of the war. Since August 8th the German Government had been informed by the Belgian Government through the Spanish Minister in Brussels that the *Garde Civique* would fight with the army.[5]

Can we, then, say that the Belgians never did carry on anything like guerilla warfare against the enemy that invaded their land, or similar to that which the Spaniards carried on against Napoleon? Emil Waxweiler, Director of the Solvay Institute in Brussels, a man known and honored by all the world, was asked this question. His answer is: "These attacks were undoubtedly isolated and exceptional."

Responsible friends told him that snipers shot upon German troops in two places. "That," he says, "may also have happened elsewhere." But directly afterwards he says: "I find a mass of misstatements." He quotes a few:—

"A German train was standing in the station of Jurbise between Mons and Brussels in September, 1914, when a rifle shot was fired. The German soldiers in the train heard the explosion and thought that they were attacked by civilians.

[5] The conditions of the Hague Convention, which were all complied with by the Belgian *Garde Civique,* are (1) to have a person at the head of things who is responsible for his subordinates, (2) to maintain a decided distinction and one easily to be recognized at a distance, (3) to bear weapons without concealment, (4) to fulfill all the rules and customs of war.

They seized some peasants who were working near by and shot them. Later on the mistake was explained: the soldiers expressed their regret and went on their way."

In the little Flemish village of Waereghem, some Belgian infantry were lying in ambush at the back of some farmhouses and fired on some passing German troops. It was said to be a civilian attack and the farms were burnt down as a reprisal.

In a Walloon village a German officer was shot. The Mayor was taken prisoner and was sentenced to punishment (according to the German system of punishing the baker for the blacksmith's fault, which, as a matter of principle, and in the most bloody manner, has been carried out all over Belgium). "Shoot me, if you will," replied the Mayor, "but first have an autopsy of the officer who has been killed." This was done, and it was discovered that he was the victim of a German bullet. Here, as in many other cases, an accidental shot was construed into an attempt at murder. But this point will be treated of further.

(2) "Belgian girls put out the eyes of defenseless wounded on the battlefield."

It is no less a person than the Imperial Chancellor himself who makes this accusation. It was repeated over and over again in the German and pro-German Press. And, in an article by Crispi in the now suppressed Roman paper, *Concordia,* he is not ashamed to write: "The chaste daughters of Belgium shut German soldiers in their houses and mutilated them as they slept."

In the *Vorwärts* on October 22nd of last year an inquiry was conducted, and, later on, by two official commissions held in Germany, it was proved that there was absolutely nothing to justify such a horrible accusation, that it was pure invention: "the legend of the put-out eyes," a social democrat paper rightly called it. The story, thinks Waxweiler, probably arose from the fact that many wounded have lost their eyes from splinters of shrapnel bombs which exploded round their heads. It is time that His Excellency Bethmann-Hollweg made his apologies to the young Belgian women.

"Mais revenons à nos moutons": a suitable appellation. Let us return to our German lambs and the martyrdom they suffered at the hands of the Belgian "jackals"—(this charming name has been invented by the German playwright Herbert Eulenberg, and illustrates the proverb: "Shame follows injury.") Let us return to the "Voice of Truth" of the Ninety-three: "It is not true that a single Belgian citizen's life or property has been touched by our soldiers except under the utmost compulsion." Notice two phrases—"not one single" and "the utmost compulsion." "We answer for this with our name and honor."

Now let us listen to a commentary of truth and of reality, calm, simple, unboasting and unpretentious, therefore, the more heart-rending and awful, like the wail of a Stabat Mater through which moans a Dies Iræ. It is one of the hundreds and hundreds of reports received by the Belgian Government. A Committee was appointed on August 7, 1914, and was composed of the Judge of the Belgian High Court, M. van Izeghem (President); M. Cattier, a Professor of the Brussels University; M. Nys, Assessor of the High Court, Professor of International Law; M. Verhagen, Assessor of the High Court; M. Wodon, Professor of the University of Brussels; M. Medlemmer, as its members, and M. Gillard, Chief of Department of the Ministry of Justice, as Secretary.

Another section of the Committee was afterwards constituted in Antwerp under the leadership of the Belgian Judge, M. Cooreman. Among the members is a former leader in the Belgian Senate, Count Goblet d'Alviella.

The inquiry was conducted by two members of the Committee, who visited the districts occupied by the Germans and inquired into the events upon the scene itself. The reports are distinguished by the most careful minuteness as to details of time, place, and so on. If any historical documents are of value, these are valuable.

From the whole *dossier* I shall select one report only.

It is from the Committee's Summary of their meeting on December 18, 1914. It is given by an eye-witness, Mdlle.

Aline Diericx, and describes the events in the village of Surice on August 24, 1914. It runs as follows:—

"Surice was a small village of a little over six hundred inhabitants in the Commune of Florennes. It was off the high road and it was crossed only by the roads running from Rosée to Mariembourg, through Romedenne, Romerie, and Matagne, and from Franchimont to Soulme and Gochenée. The population were very peaceful people, mostly agricultural laborers. The village was clean, the houses well-kept, and all breathed prosperity. Since the month of June I had been in the country with my sister, Madame de Gaiffier. Our niece, Marie Louise, our brother Ernest's daughter, a young girl of fifteen, lived with us. In front of our house, in a fairly large farm, lived the young girl's father and mother, and another young girl, Marguerite, seventeen years old.

"About the 14th of August, a French battalion had been quartered at Surice. During the 23rd, which was Sunday, there arrived a regular procession of peasants from Egnen, near Dinant, from Onhaye and further away. In the evening we saw flames on the horizon in that direction. That same evening Dr. Jacques arrived from Anthée to seek shelter with us, with his wife and five children. They brought with them several other people, amongst whom were M. Piret, the parish priest in Anthée, the parish priest of Onhaye, and M. Palande's maid from Miavoye. They reassured us somewhat, saying they believed that Surice would escape danger on account of its situation. Nevertheless we were alarmed late that evening by the arrival of two automobiles. In the one was our cook's husband, chauffeur to the Comte de Beaufort of Loyers, who had come to fetch his wife. In the other car was a Captain of Engineers and another officer, accompanied by his wife and his sons, who were army cadets. They gave us a horrible description of what was happening in Namur, and then continued their journey in the direction of Chimay.

"The next morning many of the refugees decided to go on further and disappeared in the direction of Romedenne. In their place there arrived a Professor from the College

of Bellevue in Dinant, Pastor Gaspiard. He told us that
he had been on the point of being shot. He had been arrested, together with the head master of the school, Pastor
Nicolas, and other teachers. They had made them stand
up before the guns, but had afterwards let them go, and
they had escaped through the woods. He was accompanied
by two friends, parish priests in Ostemree, Pastor Capelle,
and the parish priest from Marville, M. Debatty. These
two, however, did not remain long, but decided to go on to
a more safe refuge.

"In the afternoon my sister went to see some French
wounded who were in the ambulance established by the
Fathers of the Holy Family higher up in the village. She
met some French officers, who said that we should be quiet
at least for that night. They were going towards Romedenne, from whence they were reconnoitering the road to
Soulme.

"When she came back from the village about six o'clock
she heard firing. French *mitrailleuses* were being fired from
the churchyard on the high ground between Surice and
Romedenne upon the Germans who were coming from
Soulme.

"We heard the firing from our house too. The refugees
left the garden to hide themselves in a barn, where they
thought they would be in greater safety. It lasted a good
hour. The French retired, and it was said they had killed
a number of Germans. At seven o'clock we closed the shutters and went down into the cellars. About nine the *mitrailleuses* began to fire again, and big guns bombarded the village. Then the Germans established their guns in the yard
next door. My brother hastened to fly. About eleven o'clock
we smelt smoke, and Dr. Jacques and my sister went up to
the first floor, and to their horror saw the whole village in
flames, and our farmyard too. The buildings were in full
blaze and already falling in. So they came down to us and
said it was burning on all sides and that we had better come
out. We went out by the front door, down the steps. All
around were burning houses, Cogniaux's, Tonne's, Mathieu
Chabot's, and others. Later we heard that the inhabitants of

these houses had also sought shelter in their cellars, but had been chased out by the Germans and had fled from the village. More dead than alive, we went back into the hall of the house to wait upon events. We could not sleep, or very little. We all prayed and prepared ourselves. On Tuesday, August 25th, at about six in the morning we heard the sound of hoofs. German officers with revolvers in their hands were exploring the shrubberies of our garden in search of hidden fugitives. They were followed by soldiers, and we heard some one shouting at our door, 'Open!' but at the same moment before we could open it, the door was broken into splinters and forced open. These soldiers were in gray with a covering on their helmets; I did not see their number, my agitation and anguish were too great. With their bayonets fixed they drove us out. I wanted to carry away a little package; a soldier struck me on the arm and would not permit me. They pushed and thrust at my sister; her skirt was torn by bayonets, but she was not wounded. Then came forward the three priests, the parish priests from Anthée and Onhaye, and Pastor Gaspiard; at the sight of them the soldiers ground their teeth, shook their fists in their faces and put their bayonets to their breasts. At the same moment a German covered me with his revolver. Whilst this scene was enacting indoors the outbuildings of our house and the garden were set fire to. We were made to stand in a row and believed our last hour had come. We were marshaled round the house, and as we passed the windows of the hall the soldiers broke them in with the butt end of their rifles. We were then driven out on the road towards the church; several others joined us, and people kept coming out of the houses that were still standing, driven out by the soldiers. At this moment our parish priest, Monsieur Poskin, appeared with his old mother of eighty, his sister, Mademoiselle Thérèse, and his other sister, Marie and her husband, the school inspector, M. Schmidt from Gerpennes, and their four children—they had come over to Surice the day before to seek refuge. The soldiers continued their cruelties. They shot at the helpless old people; our old chorister, Charles Colet, eighty-eight years of age, was shot as he came out of his door. The soldiers rolled him up in a cloth and set fire to it. I saw a German break into the stable of Elie Pierrot's house as the latter came running out of his burning home, carrying his stepmother of seventy-five. They tore the poor old woman out of his arms and shot him on the spot. He fell dead at the door of his house. We passed Henry Burniaux's house, it was on fire, and so was the tobacco factory and the offices. The house on the other side of the street was also on fire. Then we came to the postman, Léopold Burniaux's house. We heard the most heartrending screams—his wife, Eléonore, was imploring that her sons might be spared her. Her husband had been shot before her eyes; her son Armand, who had been ordained a priest the year before and was home on holiday, had been taken by the soldiers and killed without pity. They also killed her son Albert, who had broken his leg the day before, and therefore could not escape. The poor woman still kept her last son, Gaston. He was a teacher at the college of Malonne. He clung to his mother and was allowed to join our procession. As our procession of suffering went forward we passed the smoking ruins of their house where those terrible scenes had been enacted. A little further on I saw in a garden by the road the body of a woman whom I did not know, and two small children weeping by her side. We were driven on to the road to Romedenne. To right and left the houses were already all burnt down, amongst these the house of the Communal Secretary, Monsieur Pichon, that of the tax-gatherer, Monsieur Georges and those of Monsieur Stanilas Burniaux and the Mayor Monsieur Delcourt. All the workmen's cottages were also burnt. The school, the town-hall, and the church still stood.

"Thus we came to the place which is called 'Les Fosses.' Here in the ditches lay the bodies of French soldiers and dead horses. To the right and to the left were numbers of German soldiers with *mitrailleuses;* they shook their fists at us and pointed their revolvers at us. Shortly afterwards they drove us off the road over plowed fields, from which could be seen Romedenne and other more distant villages. We were about fifty or sixty persons in all, men and women.

It was about seven in the morning. The men were now made to stand on one side and the women on the other. An officer came forward and said in French with a strong German accent: 'You deserve to be shot—the whole lot of you. A young girl of fifteen has shot at one of our Generals. But the Council of War has decided that only the men are to be shot. The women are to go to prison.'

"What now took place it is impossible to describe. There were eighteen men. Beside the parish priests from Anthée and Onhaye and Pastor Gaspiard stood our parish priest and his brother-in-law, Dr. Jacques and his son Henri, a boy of barely sixteen. Then Gaston Burniaux, Leonard Soumoy, his son-in-law Durdu and Camille Soumoy. A little further on was Balbeur and Billy, the latter with his seventeen-year-old son, and lastly a man from Onhaye and another from Dinant who had come to take refuge at Surice, and two others whom I did not know. They nearly put with the others Dr. Schmidt's son of fourteen years, but the soldiers pushed and cuffed him to one side. At this point I saw a young German soldier so moved that great tears fell upon his uniform. He did not dry his eyes, but turned away so that the officer should not see him.

"Some minutes went by. Before our horrified eyes, whilst the women shrieked: 'Kill me too! Kill me too!' and the children wept, they stood the men up against a wall leading down from the high road to the lower part of the village. The men waved us good-by, some waved their hands, others their heads, or their hats. Young Henri Jacques supported himself against one of the priests as if to seek help and refuge from him, and shrieked: 'I am too young! I haven't the courage to die!' I could not bear to look any more. I turned aside and hid my face in my hands. The soldiers fired and the men fell. Some one said to me: 'You can look up—they have fallen!' Some were not killed at once; we saw them move a little still; the soldiers finished them off, striking them with the butt end of their rifles on the head. Amongst them M. le Curé of Surice was found afterwards with his head horribly battered. After this massacre the Germans plundered the bodies. They took watches, rings, purses and pocketbooks. Schmidt had about three thousand francs on him, his wife told me.

"At this moment a German came forward with a certain Victor Cavillot, and before he reached the spot where the others were shot they shot him. I saw him turn round and fall backwards.

"A deep anguish consumed us. The mother of our parish priest was so overcome at having seen her son killed— such a good, noble priest!—that she could not weep, but kept saying to herself: 'What a misfortune! What a misfortune!' Thérèse Poskin was white as a corpse and went backwards and forwards from her sister to her mother. Madame Schmidt wept. She could speak a little German and, holding her little child by the hand, she had in vain begged for mercy for her husband, declaring, which was true, that he did not belong to those parts and only happened to be there by chance. The poor little girl called at the last moment to her father: 'Forgive me, Papa, if I have ever given you pain!' It was agonizing. Madame Burniaux had for the third time seen one of her sons killed before her eyes. She walked about like a mad woman with staring eyes, repeating: 'Let us come away. Let us come away!' But they made us stay. All this time I had watched our house catch fire in its turn and also the church and the school. It was not till midday that these buildings fell in. When I saw the home of my father burning and so many cherished memories disappear my heart was torn with the thought of all the things I loved so much and shall never see again. Finally, they gave us a pass, or, more correctly, they gave it to a man who came from Romedenne with an order to conduct us, and we had the choice of going either to Romedenne or to Rosée. We were expressly forbidden to go anywhere else. Before we could start we had to wait until the troops which had begun to defile had passed by. There were infantry, cavalry, and a number of automobiles. There passed, too, a number of officers on horseback. It was said that one of the Kaiser's sons was with them, and that he was on his way to Rocroi. I forgot to say that before our wretched fellow-citizens were shot the Germans drove up a

mitrailleuse before us as though we were to be murdered
altogether. But shortly afterwards they took it in the opposite direction to join some others with which the Germans
had begun the destruction of the first house in Romedenne.
Since then I have heard that the church and a hundred and
twenty houses were reduced to ruins in Romedenne.

"We crossed the road by a roundabout way and reached
Omézée. The whole way along houses were burning and
the soldiers plundering, stealing even pots of jam.

"We reached the wood, and here I met my brother and
described to him the horrors I had just witnessed. When I
named Durdu, he reminded me that it was Durdu who, in
his capacity of Alderman, did all in his power to prevent
civilians from making any attack on the enemy. At the beginning of the war he had read aloud to the villagers at the
church door, as they came out from Benediction, a proclamation that had been sent to all the villages in the province, in
which calmness and strict obedience to the authorities was
enjoined, and also ordered that all arms should be deposited
in the Communal School; it had been so well obeyed that
even the old useless shotguns were collected and put under
lock and key. We were, therefore, unable to believe that a
young girl had shot a German officer and killed him. If he
was killed, it must have been, the neighbors say, by the
French soldiers who were lying in ambush behind the hedges
at the entrance to the village. Afterwards we heard that
both in Morville and Anthée they had given the same excuse for shooting people and plundering and burning the
houses. . . .

"I have described the things I saw. When we met my
brother and several other persons from Surice in the wood
of Omézée, they told us that Marron was shot in his house,
sitting in his chair—likewise Elisée Pierrard. Others were
killed here and there, but I do not know their names or the
circumstances of their death. I only know that old Adèle
Soumoy was burnt in her bed. My sister returned to Surice
on the 2nd or 3rd of September. Of the hundred and
thirty-one houses in the village only eight were not burnt.
The village was as though dead.

"All I have said is the most careful and complete truth. I declare it on my soul and conscience (*en mon âme et conscience*), and I am ready to take my oath to it."

Several times whilst I have been translating this most simple, unexcited, almost lugubrious narrative, I have had to get up and walk about the room, I was so overcome by it. In the whole of this long report there is not a phrase, scarcely an expression of feeling. It is all so minute, the witness even describes the view she saw of Romedenne from the field of death. And who can ever forget the seventeen-year-old boy who, before the relentless guns of the Boches, cried in uncontrollable anguish: "No, no, I cannot die—I am too young!" Or the little girl who begged her father's forgiveness . . . ?

It is all minute and most honest. Mdlle. Diericx does not call the German soldiers "jackals." She saw the tears of sympathy in the young German's eyes and does not forget them.

What happened at Surice we know was not a singular case. On the contrary it was only one case among hundreds of others. The path of the Germans through Belgium was marked the whole of its length with corpses and burnt-down homes.

The manner of proceeding was always the same.

First the cry: "Some one has fired upon us!" "Civilians have fired upon us!" And once that cry had gone forth *everything was permitted.* Murder, burning, ruthless execution, every sort of cruelty, plunder, violence, every sort of orgy. What proportion is there in reality between this one act of the killing of a German officer by a young girl (*tiré sur,* says the officer—but let us allow that she killed him), allowing that it happened, what connection is there between this one act of unlawful warfare and the whole sequel of cruel treatment with which the Germans punished it? Even if a new Charlotte Corday had killed one of the enemies of her country, does that justify the refined cruelty of the Germans in allowing a flock of defenseless and innocent women to witness the murder of their husbands, fathers, brothers and sons, while all around their homes are in flames?

Do the Germans think that by such methods they can prevent further attacks? In that case they can be very sure that their method has failed. For if one can believe their own statements, they had hardly come to the next village before the cry went forth again: *"Man hat geschossen!"* ("Somebody has fired") and once more began to murder, to burn and plunder.

In *Belgian Luxemburg* alone the list of the German punishments runs thus :—

NEUFCHÂTEAU, 21 houses burnt, 18 civilians shot.
ETALLE, 30 houses burnt, 30 civilians shot.
HOUDEMONT, 64 houses burnt, 11 civilians shot.
RULLES, half the village burnt.
ANSART, the whole village burnt.
TINTIGNY, only 8 houses remain, 157 civilians shot.
JAMOIGNE, half the village burnt.
LES BULLES, the same.
MOYEN, 42 houses destroyed.
ROSSIGNOL, the whole village destroyed.
MUSSY-LA-VILLE, 20 houses burnt.
BERTRIX, 15 houses burnt, 2 civilians shot.
BLEID, many houses destroyed.
SIGNEUX, the same.
ETHE, five-sixths of the village burnt, 300 civilians shot.
BELLE-FONTAINE, 6 houses destroyed.
LATOUR, only 17 males alive.
SAINT-LÉGER, 6 houses burnt, 11 civilians shot.
SEMEL, entirely burnt down.
MAISSIN, of 100 houses 64 burnt; 10 men. 1 woman, and 1 young girl shot.
VILLANCE, 9 houses burnt, 2 men shot.
AULOY, 26 houses burnt, 52 men and women shot.
CLAIREUSE, 2 men shot and 2 hanged.

List for the province of *Luxemburg:*—
Three villages completely destroyed.
One village five-sixths destroyed.
Three villages half destroyed.
In the other villages: 303 houses burnt down, in all 511 civilians dispatched to the other world.

And that is only one of the provinces of Belgium. The world knows that the others fared no better—that the German name has ended in being feared as was the name of the Huns.

But the ninety-three men of culture stood forth on October 23rd—after Surice and Andenne, after Dinant and Tamines and Termonde and Louvain—and gave their word and honor that "not a single Belgian citizen's life or property had been touched except under the greatest provocation."

What are that word and honor worth now?

BY MAJOR-GENERAL DISFORTH OF GERMANY

No object whatever is served by taking any notice of the accusations of barbarity leveled against Germany by our foreign critics. Frankly, we are and must be barbarians, if by this we understand those who wage war relentlessly and to the uttermost degree. There is nothing for us to justify and nothing to explain away. Every act of whatever nature committed by our troops for the purpose of discouraging, defeating and destroying our enemies is a brave act and a good deed, and is fully justified. . . . Germany stands as the supreme arbiter of her own methods, which in the time of war must be dictated to the world.

It is of no consequence whatever if all the monuments ever created, all the pictures ever painted, and all the buildings ever erected by the great architects of the world be destroyed, if by their destruction we promote Germany's victory over her enemies. The commonest, ugliest stone placed to mark the burial place of a German grenadier is a more glorious and venerable monument than all the cathedrals of Europe put together.

They call us barbarians. What of it? We scorn them and their abuse. For my part, I hope that in this war we have merited the title of barbarians. Let neutral people and our enemies cease their empty chatter, which may well be compared to the twitter of birds. Let them cease their talk of the cathedral at Rheims and of all the churches and all the castles in France which have shared its fate. These

things do not interest us.   Our troops must achieve victory.
What else matters?

BY A GERMAN DESERTER

[The writer of the following account tells how he, as
a Socialist, was unwilling to enter the War, was later
roused to enthusiasm for it as a patriotic necessity, and
finally became so disgusted with its horrors and so convinced of its autocratic purposes of conquest and massacre
that he fled from Germany.   We take up his narrative on his
first day with the army in Belgium.   He meets the first
homeless victims of the warfare.]

In a perambulator or a push-cart those unfortunate beings carried away all that the brutal force of war had left
them.   In marked contrast to the fugitives we had hitherto
met, these people were filled with the utmost fear, shivering
with fright, terror-stricken in face of the hostile world.
As soon as they beheld one of us soldiers they were seized
with such a fear that they seemed to crumple up.

How different they were from the inhabitants of the village in which we were, who showed themselves kind,
friendly, and even obliging towards us.   We tried to find
out the cause of that fear, and heard that those fugitives
had witnessed bitter street fighting in their village.   They
had experienced war, had seen their houses burnt, their simple belongings perish, and had not yet been able to forget
their streets filled with dead and wounded soldiers.   It became clear to us that it was not fear alone that made these
people look like the hunted quarry; it was hatred, hatred
against us, the invaders, who, as they had to suppose, had
fallen upon them unawares, had driven them from their
homes.

We marched away that very evening and tried to reach
our section.   When darkness fell the Belgians had concentrated still farther to the rear; they were already quite near
the fortress of Liege.   Many of the villages we passed were
in flames; the inhabitants who had been driven away
passed us in crowds; there were women whose husbands

were perhaps also defending their "Fatherland," children, old men who were pushed hither and thither, and seemed to be always in the way. Without any aim, any plan, any place in which they could rest, those processions of misery and unhappiness crept past us—the best illustration of man-murdering, nation-destroying war! Again we reached a village which to all appearances had once been inhabited by a well-to-do people, by a contented little humanity. There were nothing but ruins now, burnt, destroyed houses and farm buildings, dead soldiers, German and Belgian, and among them several civilians who had been shot by sentence of the court-martial.

Towards midnight we reached the German line which was trying to get possession of a village which was already within the fortifications of Liege, and was obstinately defended by the Belgians. Here we had to employ all our forces to wrench from our opponent house after house, street after street. It was not yet completely dark, so that we had to go through that terrible struggle which developed with all our senses awake and receptive. It was a hand-to-hand fight; every kind of weapon had to be employed; the opponent was attacked with the butt-end of the rifle, the knife, the fist, and the teeth. One of my best friends fought with a gigantic Belgian; both had lost their rifles. They were pummeling each other with their fists. I had just finished with a Belgian who was about twenty-two years of age, and was going to assist my friend, as the Herculean Belgian was so much stronger than he. Suddenly my friend succeeded with a lightning motion in biting the Belgian in the chin. He bit so deeply that he tore away a piece of flesh with his teeth. The pain the Belgian felt must have been immense, for he let go his hold and ran off screaming with terrible pain.

All that happened in seconds. The blood of the Belgian ran out of my friend's mouth; he was seized by a horrible nausea, an indescribable terror, the taste of the warm blood nearly drove him insane. That young, gay, lively fellow of twenty-four had been cheated out of his youth in that night. He used to be the jolliest among us; after that we could never induce him even to smile.

Whilst fighting during the night I came for the first time in touch with the butt-end of a Belgian rifle. I had a hand-to-hand fight with a Belgian when another one from behind hit me with his rifle on the head with such force that it drove my head into the helmet up to my ears. I experienced a terrific pain all over my head, doubled up, and lost consciousness. When I revived I found myself with a bandaged head in a barn among other wounded.

I had not been severely wounded, but I felt as if my head was double its normal size, and there was a noise in my ears as of the wheels of an express engine.

The other wounded and the soldiers of the ambulance corps said that the Belgians had been pushed back to the fortress; we heard, however, that severe fighting was still going on. Wounded soldiers were being brought in continuously, and they told us that the Germans had already taken in the first assault several fortifications like outer forts, but that they had not been able to maintain themselves because they had not been sufficiently provided with artillery. The defended places and works inside the forts were still practically completely intact, and so were their garrisons. The forts were not yet ripe for assault, so that the Germans had to retreat with downright enormous losses. The various reports were contradictory, and it was impossible to get a clear idea of what was happening. [His wound proving but slight, he rejoins the advance in a few days.]

The spirit of our soldiers, in spite of the hardships they had undergone, became better and gayer. They joked and sang, forgot the corpses which were still filling the roads and paths, and felt quite at ease. They had already accustomed themselves to the horrible to such a degree that they stepped over the corpses with unconcern, without even making the smallest detour. The experience of those first few weeks of the war had already brutalized us completely. What was to happen to us if this should continue for months?

At eleven o'clock all further philosophizing was put a

stop to; we were ordered to halt, and we were to receive our food from the field-kitchen.

We were quite hungry and ate the tinned soup with the heartiest of appetites. Many of our soldiers were sitting with their dinner-pails on the dead horses that were lying about, and were eating with as much pleasure and heartiness as if they were home at mother's. Nor did some corpses in the neighborhood of our improvised camp disturb us. There was only a lack of water, and after having eaten thirst began to torment us.

Soon afterwards we continued our march in the scorching midday sun; dust was covering our uniforms and skin to the depth of almost an inch. We tried in vain to be jolly, but thirst tormented us more and more, and we became weaker and weaker from one quarter of an hour to another. Many in our ranks fell down exhausted, and were simply unable to move. So the commander of our section had no other choice but to let us halt again if he did not want every one of us to drop out. Thus it happened that we stayed behind a considerable distance, and were not amongst the first that were pursuing the French.

Finally, towards four o'clock, we saw a village in front of us; we began at once to march at a much brisker pace. Among other things we saw a farm-cart on which were several civilian prisoners, apparently snipers. There was also a Catholic priest among them who had, like the others, his hands tied behind his back with a rope. Curiosity prompted us to inquire what he had been up to, and we heard that he had incited the farmers of the village to poison the water.

We soon reached the village and the first well, at which we hoped to quench our thirst thoroughly. But that was no easy matter, for a military guard had been placed before it, who scared us off with the warning, "Poisoned!" Disappointed and terribly embittered, the soldiers, half dead with thirst, gnashed their teeth; they hurried to the next well, but everywhere the same devilish thing occurred—the guard prevented them from drinking. In a square, in the middle of the village, there was a large village well which sent, through two tubes, water as clear as crystal into a large trough. Five soldiers were guarding it and had to watch that nobody drank of the poisoned water. I was just going to march past it with my pal when suddenly the second, larger portion of our company rushed like madmen to the well. The guards were carried away by the rush, and every one now began to drink the water with the avidity of an animal. All quenched their thirst, and not one of us became ill or died. We heard later on that the priest had to pay for it with his death, as the military authorities "knew" that the water in all the wells of that village was poisoned and that the soldiers had only been saved by a lucky accident! Faithfully the God of the Germans had watched over us; the captured Belgians did not seem to be under His protection. They had to die.

In most places we passed at that time we were warned against drinking the water. The natural consequence was that the soldiers began to hate the population, which they now had to consider to be their bitterest enemies. That again aroused the worst instincts in some soldiers. In every army one finds men with the disposition of barbarians. The many millions of inhabitants in Germany or France are not all civilized people, much as we like to convince ourselves of the contrary. Compulsory military service in those countries forces all without distinction into the army, men and monsters. I have often bitterly resented the wrong one did to our army in calling us all barbarians, only because among us—as naturally also among the French and English— there were to be found elements that really ought to be in the penitentiary. I will only cite one example of how we soldiers ourselves punished a wretch whom we caught committing a crime.

One evening—it was already dark—we reached a small village to the east of the town of Bertrix, and there, too, found "poisoned" water. We halted in the middle of the village. I was standing before a house with a low window, through which one could see the interior. In the miserable poverty-stricken working-man's dwelling we observed a woman who clung to her children as if afraid they would be torn from her. Though we felt very bitter on account of the want of water, every one of us would have liked to help the poor woman. Some of us were just going to sacrifice our little store of victuals and to say a few comforting words to the woman, when all at once a stone as big as a fist was thrown through the window-pane into the room and hurt a little girl in the right hand. There were sincere cries of indignation, but at the same moment twenty hands at least laid hold of the wretch, a reservist of our company, and gave him such a hiding as to make him almost unconscious. If officers and other men had not interfered the fellow would have been lynched there and then. He was to be placed before a court-martial later on, but it never came to that. He was drowned in the river at the battle of the Meuse. Many soldiers believed he drowned himself, because he was not only shunned by his fellow-soldiers, but was also openly despised by them.

We were quartered on that village and had to live in a barn. I went with some pals into the village to buy something to eat. At a farmer's house we got ham, bread, and wine, but not for money. The people positively refused to take our money as they regarded us as their guests, so they said; only we were not to harm them. Nevertheless we left them an adequate payment in German money. Later on we found the same situation in many other places. Everywhere people were terribly frightened of us; they began to tremble almost when a German soldier entered their house.

Four of us had formed a close alliance; we had promised each other to stick together and assist each other in every danger. We often also visited the citizens in their houses, and tried to the best of our ability to comfort the sorely tried people and talk them out of their fear of us. Without exception we found them to be lovable, kindly, and good people who soon became confidential and free of speech when they noticed that we were really their friends. But when, at leaving, we wrote with chalk on the door of their houses, *"Bitte schonen, hier wohnen brave, gute Leute!"* [Please spare, here live good and decent people] their joy and thankfulness knew no bounds. If so much bad blood was created, if so many incidents happened that led to the shooting by court-martial of innumerable Belgians, the difference of language and the mistakes arising therefrom were surely not the least important causes; of that I and many others of my comrades became convinced during that time in Belgium. But at first the systematically nourished suspicion against the "enemy," too, was partly responsible for it.

In the night we continued our march, after having been attached to the 21-centimeter mortar battery of the 9th Regiment of Foot Artillery which had just arrived; we were not only to serve as covering troops for that battery, but were also to help it place those giants in position when called upon. The gun is transported apart from the carriage on a special wagon. Gun-carriage and gun are drawn each by six horses. Those horses, which are only used by the foot artillery, are the best and strongest of the German army. And yet even these animals are often unable to do the work required of them, so that all available men, seventy or eighty at times, have to help transport the gun with ropes specially carried for that purpose. That help is chiefly resorted to when the guns leave the road to be placed in firing position. In order to prevent the wheels from sinking into the soil, other wheels, half a yard wide, are attached round them.

These guns are high-angle guns, i.e., their shot rises into the air for several thousand yards, all according to the distance of the spot to be hit, and then drops at a great angle. That is the reason why neither hill nor mountain can protect an enemy battery placed behind those elevations. At first the French had almost no transportable heavy artillery, so that it was quite impossible for them to fight successfully against our guns of large caliber. Under those conditions the German gunners, of course, felt themselves to be top-dog, and decorated their 21-centimeter guns with inscriptions like the following, "Here declarations of war are still being accepted."

We felt quite at ease with the artillery, and were still passably fresh when we halted at six o'clock in the morning, though we had been marching since two o'clock. Near our halting-place we found a broken German howitzer, and next to it two dead soldiers. When firing, a shell had burst

in the gun, destroying it entirely. Two men of the crew
had been killed instantly and some had been seriously
wounded by the flying pieces. We utilized the pause to bury
the two dead men, put both of them in one grave, placed
both their helmets on the grave, and wrote on a board: "Here
rest two German Artillerymen."

We had to proceed, and soon reached the town of Bertrix. Some few houses to the left and right of the road
were burning fiercely; we soon got to know that they had
been set alight because soldiers marching past were said to
have been shot at from those houses. Before one of these
houses a man and his wife and their son, a boy of fifteen
or sixteen, lay half burnt to cinders; all had been covered
with straw. Three more civilians lay dead in the same
street.

We had marched past some more houses when all at
once shots rang out; they had been shooting from some
house, and four of our soldiers had been wounded. For a
short while there was confusion. The house from which
the shots must have come was soon surrounded, and hand-
grenades were thrown through all the windows into the interior. In an instant all the rooms were in flames. The
exploding hand-grenades caused such an enormous air-pres-
sure that all the doors were blown from their hinges and
the inner walls torn to shreds. Almost at the same time,
five men in civilian clothes rushed into the street and asked
for quarter with uplifted hands. They were seized immediately and taken to the officers, who formed themselves into
a tribunal within a few minutes. Ten minutes later sentence
had already been executed: five strong men lay on the
ground, blindfolded, their bodies riddled by bullets.

Six of us had in each of the five cases to execute the
sentence, and unfortunately I, too, belonged to those thirty
men. The condemned man whom my party of six had to
shoot was a tall, lean man, about forty years of age. He
did not wince for a moment when they blindfolded him. In
a garden of a house nearby he was placed with his back
against the house, and after our captain had told us that it
was our duty to aim well so as to end the tragedy quickly,

we took up our position six paces from the condemned one. The sergeant commanding us had told us before to shoot the condemned man through the chest. We then formed two lines, one behind the other. The command was given to load and secure, and we pushed five cartridges into the rifle. Then the command rang out, "Get ready!" The first line knelt, the second stood up. We held our rifles in such a position that the barrel pointed in front of us whilst the butt-end rested somewhere near the hip. At the command, "Aim!" we slowly brought our rifles into shooting position, grasped them firmly, pressed the plate of the butt-end against the shoulder and, with our cheek on the butt-end, we clung convulsively to the neck of the rifle. Our right forefinger was on the trigger, the sergeant gave us about half a minute for aiming before commanding, "Fire!"

Even to-day I cannot say whether our victim fell dead on the spot or how many of the six bullets hit him. I ran about all day long like a drunken man, and reproached myself most bitterly with having played the executioner. For a long time I avoided speaking about it with fellow-soldiers, for I felt guilty. And yet—what else could we soldiers do but obey the order?

During the preceding night there had been encounters at Bertrix between the German military and the population. Houses were burning in every part of the town. In the market-place there was a great heap of guns and revolvers of all makes. At the clergyman's house they had found a French machine gun and ammunition, whereupon the clergyman and his female cook had been arrested and, I suppose, placed immediately before a court-martial.

Under those conditions we were very glad to get out of Bertrix again. We marched on in the afternoon. After a march of some three miles we halted, and received food from the field-kitchen. But this time we felt no appetite. The recollection of the incidents of the morning made all of us feel so depressed that the meal turned out a real funeral repast. Silently we set in motion again, and camped in the open in the evening, as we were too tired to erect tents.

It was there that all discipline went to pieces for the first

time. The officers' orders to put up tents were not heeded
in the slightest degree. The men were dog-tired, and suffered the officers to command and chatter as much as they
liked. Every one wrapped himself up in his cloak, lay down
where he was, and as soon as one had lain down one was
asleep. The officers ran about like mad shouting with redoubled energy their commands at the exhausted soldiers; in
vain. The officers, of course, had gone through the whole
performance on horseback and, apparently, did not feel sufficiently tired to go to sleep. When their calling and shouting
had no effect they had recourse to personal physical exertion and began to shake us up. But as soon as one of us
was awake the one before had gone to sleep again. At last
they ceased their efforts in despair.

TURKEY LENDS SUPPORT TO GERMANY

SHE SHELTERS THE FLEEING GERMAN WARSHIPS

HENRY MORGENTHAU   BARON GUILLAUME

When the Great War began, Turkey and the other states of the
Balkan peninsula were only just recovering from two successive and
exhaustive wars among themselves. They had known peace for only
a single year. In the first of these internecine wars Turkey had
been defeated by the united forces of Serbia, Bulgaria and Greece.
In the second, all the others had opposed Bulgaria, crushed her ambition to rule the peninsula, and deprived her of territory. Even
Turkey had ventured to snatch from the Bulgarians a portion of
her former losses. This she had done in defiance of Europe's command that she should remain passive during the second war.

Turkey had thus lost her fear of the united action of the European
Powers. She had also lost her faith in them and in herself. With
her Government torn to pieces by repeated revolutions, she was
ruled by "opportunists," adventurers raised by chance into unac-
customed power. Her Sultan was the merest figurehead. Control
lay with whichever leaders were most vigorous and most reckless.
These chanced at the moment to be two, Talaat Pasha, a statesman
of real ability though brutal, who had risen from the lowest rank to
become the leader of the "Young Turk" party, and Enver Pasha, a
young officer of thirty-two. He had led the Turkish army in revolution in 1908; and in 1914, after assassinating his predecessor in
office, he had been made "Minister of War." He thus controlled the
army, the only real power in Turkey.

Enver was an admirer of Germany. He had brought German
officers to train his troops and had finally placed these under command of a German general, Von Sanders. This general and Wangenheim, the German ambassador in Constantinople, were the youthful
leader's chief advisers. Through Enver in war and Talaat in diplomacy, the Germans held control of Turkey.

It was manifest, even to the ignorant Turks, that their country
was so exhausted by the preceding wars that another contest, immediately following, must mean utter ruin to her people. But Turkish
Governments have as a rule been wholly indifferent to the miseries
of their subject peoples. War means prosperity for Turkish officials,
and plunder for Turkish soldiers; the suffering falls upon the merchant class and on the poor. The moment the Great War began,
Enver Pasha called a general mobilization of the army, explaining that
this was a necessary step in order to preserve Turkish neutrality. In

93

reality, the mobilization made his own power secure, except against assassination, and rejoiced his soldiers by enabling them to "conscript" provisions and supplies at will.

The diplomats of Europe, outside of Germany, seem to have retained hope of Turkey's genuine neutrality, despite the Germanizing of her army and the mobilization of her forces. The United States Ambassador on the spot, Mr. Morgenthau, describes vividly the decisive incident which bound Turkey to follow the fortunes of Germany. The Belgian minister to Turkey at the time was Baron Guillaume, who here describes the general situation.

C. F. H.

BY HENRY MORGENTHAU [1]

On August 10th, I went out on a little launch to meet the *Sicilia,* a small Italian ship which had just arrived from Venice. I was especially interested in this vessel because she was bringing to Constantinople my son-in-law and daughter and their three little daughters. The greeting proved even more interesting than I had expected. I found the passengers considerably excited, for they had witnessed, the day before, a naval engagement in the Ionian Sea.

"We were lunching yesterday on deck," my daughter told me, "when I saw two strange-looking vessels just above the horizon. I ran for the glasses and made out two large battleships, the first one with two queer, exotic-looking towers and the other one quite an ordinary-looking battleship. We watched and saw another ship coming up behind them and going very fast. She came nearer and nearer and then we heard guns booming. Pillars of water sprang up in the air and there were many little puffs of white smoke. It took me some time to realize what it was all about, and then it burst upon me that we were actually witnessing an engagement. The ships continually shifted their position but went on and on. The two big ones turned and rushed furiously for the little one, and then apparently they changed their minds and turned back. Then the little one turned around and calmly steamed in our direction. At first I was somewhat alarmed at this, but nothing happened. She circled around us with her tars excited and grinning and somewhat grimy. They signaled to our captain many questions, and

[1] Reprinted by permission from "Ambassador Morgenthau's Story."

then turned and finally disappeared. The captain told us that the two big ships were Germans which had been caught in the Mediterranean and which were trying to escape from the British fleet. He said that the British ships are chasing them all over the Mediterranean, and that the German ships are trying to get into Constantinople. Have you seen anything of them? Where do you suppose the British fleet is?"

A few hours afterward I happened to meet Wangenheim.[2] When I told him what my daughter had seen, he displayed an agitated interest. Immediately after lunch he called at the American Embassy with Pallavicini, the Austrian Ambassador, and asked for an interview with my daughter. The two ambassadors solemnly planted themselves in chairs before her and subjected her to a most minute, though very polite, cross examination. "I never felt so important in my life," she afterward told me. They would not permit her to leave out a single detail; they wished to know how many shots had been fired, what direction the German ships had taken, what everybody on board had said, and so on. The visit seemed to give these allied ambassadors immense relief and satisfaction, for they left the house in an almost jubilant mood, behaving as though a great weight had been taken off their minds. And certainly they had good reason for their elation. My daughter had been the means of giving them the news which they had desired to hear above everything else—that the *Goeben* and the *Breslau* had escaped the British fleet and were then steaming rapidly in the direction of the Dardanelles.

For it was those famous German ships, the *Goeben* and the *Breslau,* which my daughter had seen engaged in battle with a British scout ship!

The next day official business called me to the German Embassy. But Wangenheim's animated manner soon disclosed that he had no interest in routine matters. Never had I seen him so nervous and so excited. He could not rest in his chair more than a few minutes at a time; he was constantly jumping up, rushing to the window and look-

[2] The German Ambassador.

ing anxiously out toward the Bosphorus, where his private wireless station, the *Corcovado,* lay about three-quarters of a mile away.   Wangenheim's face was flushed and his eyes were shining; he would stride up and down the room, speaking now of a recent German victory, now giving me a little forecast of Germany's plans—and then he would stalk to the window again for another look at the *Corcovado.*

"Something is seriously distracting you," I said, rising. "I will go and come again some other time."

"No, no!" the Ambassador almost shouted.   "I want you to stay right where you are.   This will be a great day for Germany!   If you will only remain for a few minutes you will hear a great piece of news—something that has the utmost bearing upon Turkey's relation to the war."

Then he rushed out on the portico and leaned over the balustrade.   At the same moment I saw a little launch put out from the *Corcovado* toward the Ambassador's dock. Wangenheim hurried down, seized an envelope from one of the sailors, and a moment afterward burst into the room again.

"We've got them!" he shouted to me.

"Got what?" I asked.

"The *Goeben* and the *Breslau* have passed through the Dardanelles!"

He was waving the wireless message with all the enthusiasm of a college boy whose football team has won a victory.

Then, momentarily checking his enthusiasm, he came up to me solemnly, humorously shook his forefinger, lifted his eyebrows, and said, "Of course, you understand that we have sold those ships to Turkey!

"And Admiral Souchon," he added with another wink, "will enter the Sultan's service!"

Wangenheim had more than patriotic reasons for this exultation; the arrival of these ships was the greatest day in his diplomatic career.   It was really the first diplomatic victory which Germany had won.   For years the chancellorship of the empire had been Wangenheim's laudable ambition, and he behaved now like a man who saw his prize within his grasp. The voyage of the *Goeben* and the *Breslau* was his personal triumph; he had arranged with the Turkish Cabinet for their passage through the Dardanelles, and he had directed their movements by wireless in the Mediterranean. By safely getting the *Goeben* and the *Breslau* into Constantinople, Wangenheim had definitely clinched Turkey as Germany's ally. All his intrigues and plottings for three years had now finally succeeded.

I doubt if any two ships have exercised a greater influence upon history than these two German cruisers. Few of us at that time realized their great importance, but subsequent developments have fully justified Wangenheim's exuberant satisfaction. The *Goeben* was a powerful battle cruiser of recent construction; the *Breslau* was not so large a ship, but she, like the *Goeben,* had the excessive speed that made her extremely serviceable in those waters. These ships had spent the few months preceding the war cruising in the Mediterranean, and when the declaration finally came they were taking on supplies at Messina.

I have always regarded it as more than a coincidence that these two vessels, both of them having a greater speed than any French or English ships in the Mediterranean, should have been lying not far from Turkey when war broke out. The selection of the *Goeben* was particularly fortunate, as she had twice before visited Constantinople and her officers and men knew the Dardanelles perfectly. The behavior of these crews, when the news of war was received, indicated the spirit with which the German navy began hostilities; the men broke into singing and shouting, lifted their Admiral upon their shoulders, and held a real German jollification. It is said that Admiral Souchon preserved, as a touching souvenir of this occasion, his white uniform bearing the finger prints of his grimy sailors!

For all their joy at the prospect of battle, the situation of these ships was still a precarious one. They formed no match for the large British and French naval forces which were roaming through the Mediterranean. The *Goeben* and the *Breslau* were far from their native bases; with the coaling problem such an acute one, and with England in possession of all important stations, where could they flee for safety? Several Italian destroyers were circling around the German ships at Messina, enforcing neutrality and occasionally reminding them that they could remain in port only twenty-four hours. England had ships stationed at the Gulf of Otranto, the head of the Adriatic, to cut them off in case they sought to escape into the Austrian port of Pola. The British navy also stood guard at Gibraltar and Suez, the only other exits that apparently offered the possibility of escape. There was only one other place in which the *Goeben* and the *Breslau* might find a safe and friendly reception. That was Constantinople. Apparently the British navy dismissed this as an impossibility. At that time, early in August, international law had not entirely disappeared as the guiding conduct of nations.

Turkey was then a neutral country, and, despite the many evidences of German domination, she seemed likely to maintain her neutrality. The Treaty of Paris, which was signed in 1856, as well as the Treaty of London, signed in 1871, provided that war-ships should not use the Dardanelles except by the special permission of the Sultan, which could be granted only in times of peace. In practice the government had seldom given this permission except for ceremonial occasions. Under the existing conditions it would have amounted virtually to an unfriendly act for the Sultan to have removed the ban against war vessels in the Dardanelles, and to permit the *Goeben* and the *Breslau* to remain in Turkish waters for more than twenty-four hours would have been nothing less than a declaration of war. It is perhaps not surprising that the British, in the early days of August, 1914, when Germany had not completely made clear her official opinion that "international law had ceased to exist," regarded these treaty stipulations as barring the German ships from the Dardanelles and Constantinople. Relying upon the sanctity of these international regulations, the British navy had shut off every point through which these German ships could have escaped to safety—except the entrance to the Dardanelles. Had England, immediately on the declaration of war, rushed a powerful squadron to this vital spot, how different the history of the last three years might have been!

"His Majesty expects the *Goeben* and the *Breslau* to succeed in breaking through!" Such was the wireless that reached these vessels at Messina at five o'clock on the evening of August 4th. The twenty-four hours' stay permitted by the Italian Government had nearly expired. Outside, in the Strait of Otranto, lay the force of British battle cruisers, sending false radio messages to the Germans, instructing them to rush for Pola. With bands playing and flags flying, the officers and crews having had their spirits fired by oratory and drink, the two vessels started at full speed toward the awaiting British fleet. The little *Gloucester,* a scout boat, kept in touch, wiring constantly the German movements to the main squadron. Suddenly, when off Cape Spartivento, the *Goeben* and the *Breslau* let off into the atmosphere all the discordant vibrations which their wireless could command, jamming the air with such a hullabaloo that the *Gloucester* was unable to send any intelligible messages. Then the German cruisers turned southward and made for the Ægean Sea. The plucky little *Gloucester* kept close on their heels, and, as my daughter had related, once had even audaciously offered battle. A few hours behind the British squadron pursued, but uselessly, for the German ships, though far less powerful in battle, were much speedier. Even then the British admiral probably thought that he had spoiled the German plans. The German ships might get first to the Dardanelles, but at that point stood international law across the path, barring the entrance.

Meanwhile Wangenheim had accomplished his great diplomatic success. From the *Corcovado* wireless station in the Bosphorus he was sending the most agreeable news to Admiral Souchon. He was telling him to hoist the Turkish flag when he reached the Strait, for Admiral Souchon's cruisers had suddenly become parts of the Turkish navy, and, therefore, the usual international prohibitions did not apply. These cruisers were no longer the *Goeben* and the *Breslau,* for, like an oriental magician, Wangenheim had suddenly changed them into the *Sultan Selim* and the *Medilli.* The fact was that the German Ambassador had cleverly taken advantage of the existing situation to manufacture a "sale." Turkey had two dreadnoughts under construction in England when the war broke out. These ships were not exclusively governmental enterprises; their purchase represented what, on the surface, appeared to be a popular enthusiasm of the Turkish people. They were to be the agencies through which Turkey was to attack Greece and win back the islands of the Ægean, and the Turkish people had raised the money to build them by a so-called popular subscription. Agents had gone from house to house, painfully collecting these small sums of money; there had been entertainments and fairs, and, in their eagerness for the cause, Turkish women had sold their hair for the benefit of the common fund. These two vessels thus represented a spectacular outburst of patriotism that was unusual in Turkey, so unusual, indeed, that many detected signs that the Government had stimulated it.   At the very moment when the war began, Turkey had made her last payment to the English shipyards and the Turkish crews had arrived in England prepared to take the finished vessels home. Then, a few days before the time set to deliver them, the British Government stepped in and commandeered these dreadnoughts for the British navy.

There is not the slightest question that England had not only a legal but a moral right to do this; there is also no question that her action was a proper one, and that, had she been dealing with almost any other nation, such a proceeding would not have aroused any resentment. But the Turkish people cared nothing for distinctions of this sort; all they saw was that they had two ships in England, which they had greatly strained their resources to purchase, and that England had now stepped in and taken them. Even without external pressure they would have resented the act, but external pressure was exerted in plenty. The transaction gave Wangenheim the greatest opportunity of his life. Violent attacks upon England, all emanating from the German Embassy, began to fill the Turkish press. Wangenheim was constantly discoursing to the Turkish leaders on English perfidy and he now suggested that Germany, Turkey's good friend, was prepared to make compensation for England's "unlawful" seizure. He suggested that Turkey go through the form of "purchasing" the *Goeben* and the *Breslau*, which were then wandering around the Mediterranean, perhaps in anticipation of this very contingency, and incorporate them in the Turkish navy in place of the appropriated ships in England. The very day that these vessels passed through the Dardanelles, the *Ikdam,* a Turkish newspaper published in Constantinople, had a triumphant account of this "sale," with big headlines calling it a "great success for the Imperial Government."

Thus Wangenheim's maneuver accomplished two purposes: it placed Germany before the populace as Turkey's friend, and it also provided a subterfuge for getting the ships through the Dardanelles, and enabling them to remain in Turkish waters. All this beguiled the more ignorant of the Turkish people, and gave the Cabinet a plausible ground for meeting the objection of Entente diplomats, but it did not deceive any intelligent person. The *Goeben* and *Breslau* might change their names, and the German sailors might adorn themselves with Turkish fezzes, but we all knew from the beginning that this sale was a sham. Those who understood the financial condition of Turkey could only be amused at the idea that she could purchase these modern vessels. Moreover, the ships were never incorporated in the Turkish navy; on the contrary, what really happened was that the Turkish navy was annexed to these German ships. A handful of Turkish sailors were placed on board at one time for appearance sake, but their German officers and German crews still retained active charge. Wangenheim, in his talks with me, never made any secret of the fact that the ships still remained German property. "I never expected to have such big checks to sign," he remarked one day, referring to his expenditures on the *Goeben* and the *Breslau.* He always called them "our" ships. Even Talaat told me in so many words that the cruisers did not belong to Turkey.

"The Germans say they belong to the Turks," he remarked, with his characteristic laugh. "At any rate, it's very comforting for us to have them here. After the war, if the Germans win, they will forget all about it and leave the ships to us. If the Germans lose, they won't be able to take them away from us!"

The German Government made no real pretension that the sale had been *bona fide;* at least when the Greek Minister at Berlin protested against the transaction as unfriendly to Greece—naïvely forgetting the American ships which Greece had recently purchased—the German officials soothed him by admitting, *sotto voce,* that the ownership still remained with Germany. Yet when the Entente ambassadors constantly protested against the presence of the German vessels, the Turkish officials blandly kept up the pretense that they were integral parts of the Turkish navy!

The German officers and crews greatly enjoyed this farcical pretense that the *Goeben* and the *Breslau* were Turkish ships. They took delight in putting on Turkish fezzes, thereby presenting to the world conclusive evidence that these loyal sailors of the Kaiser were now parts of the Sultan's navy. One day the *Goeben* sailed up the Bosphorus, halted in front of the Russian Embassy, and dropped anchor. Then the officers and men lined the deck in full view of the enemy embassy. All solemnly removed their Turkish fezzes and put on German caps. The band played *"Deutschland über Alles,"* the "Watch on the Rhine," and other German songs, the German sailors singing loudly to the accompaniment. When they had spent an hour or more serenading the Russian Ambassador, the officers and crews removed their German caps and again put on their Turkish fezzes. The *Goeben* then picked up her anchor and started southward for her station, leaving in the ears of the Russian diplomat the gradually dying strains of German war songs as the cruiser disappeared down stream.

I have often speculated on what would have happened if the English battle cruisers, which pursued the *Breslau* and the *Goeben* up to the mouth of the Dardanelles, had not been too gentlemanly to violate international law. Suppose that they had entered the Strait, attacked the German cruisers in the Marmora, and sunk them. They could have done this, and, knowing all that we know now, such an action would have been justified. Not improbably the destruction would have kept Turkey out of the war. For the arrival of these cruisers made it inevitable that Turkey, when the proper moment came, should join her forces with Germany. With them the Turkish navy became stronger than the Russian Black Sea Fleet and thus made it certain that Russia could make no attack on Constantinople. The *Goeben* and the *Breslau,* therefore, practically gave the Ottoman and German naval forces control of the Black Sea. Moreover, these two ships could easily dominate Constantinople, and thus they furnished the means by which the German navy, if the occasion should arise, could terrorize the Turks.

I am convinced that, when the judicious historian reviews this war and its consequences, he will say that the passage of the Strait by these German ships made it inevitable that Turkey should join Germany at the moment that Germany desired her assistance, and that it likewise sealed the doom of the Turkish Empire. There were men in the Turkish Cabinet who perceived this, even then. The story was told in Constantinople—though I do not vouch for it as authentic history—that the cabinet meeting at which this momentous decision had been made had not been altogether harmonious. The Grand Vizier and Djemal, it was said, objected to the fictitious "sale," and demanded that it should not be completed. When the discussion had reached its height Enver, who was playing Germany's game, announced that he had already practically completed the transaction. In the silence that followed his statement this young Napoleon pulled out his pistol and laid it on the table.

"If any one here wishes to question this purchase," he said quietly and icily, "I am ready to meet him."

A few weeks after the *Goeben* and the *Breslau* had taken up permanent headquarters in the Bosphorus, Djavid Bey, Minister of Finance, happened to meet a distinguished Belgian jurist, then in Constantinople.

"I have terrible news for you," said the sympathetic Turkish statesman. "The Germans have captured Brussels."

The Belgian, a huge figure, more than six feet high, put his arm soothingly upon the shoulder of the diminutive Turk.

"I have even more terrible news for you," he said, pointing out to the stream where the *Goeben* and the *Breslau* lay anchored. "The Germans have captured Turkey."

BY BARON GUILLAUME

Official Report to the Belgian Government by the Belgian Minister of Turkey

Constantinople, September 7, 1914.

Since I had the honor of announcing to you my return to Constantinople on August 16th, I have addressed to you no political dispatch, finding myself without any means of transmitting one to you.

I entrust the present letter to a special messenger of the French Embassy, in the hope that it will reach you.

On my return here, I found the situation very strained. The incident of the *Goeben* had just taken place.

The German Ambassador, all-powerful here, to the extent that the Ottoman ministers fairly frequently hold their Council meetings at his house, used all his efforts to push the Turks into an imprudent step, which might provoke war with the powers of the Triple Entente.

At this moment, Talaat Bey and Halil Bey, President of the Chamber, had just left for Sofia and Bucharest with the object, they said, of settling the question of the islands with Greece. But the real aim of their journey was to feel the ground with a view to constituting a compact group, which might engage in war against Russia.

They were soon able to assure themselves that this attempt had no chance of success, and it was at that moment that I had the honor of telegraphing to you that the Ambassadors of the Triple Entente were beginning to hope that the complication of a war with Turkey would not supervene.

Since then the situation has gone through different phases and more than once has looked dangerous.

Baron de Wangenheim, and especially General Liman von Sanders, are doing all they can to incite the Turks to war, and they have succeeded in creating here an absolutely German atmosphere in Ottoman circles.

A week ago a rupture appeared probable. The Government not only did not send back the German crews of the *Goeben* and the *Breslau,* but hundreds of sailors and artillerymen were seen arriving from Germany, to serve both in the naval forces and in the batteries guarding the Straits.

The moment therefore appeared near, when the sense of national dignity would oblige the three Allied Powers to put a limit to the provocations of Turkey. Their Ambassadors then began to prepare for departure and I had the honor of informing you of this by telegraph, adding that in the event of my receiving my passports myself, I proposed to entrust the protection of the Belgians residing in Turkey to the Ambassador of the United States.

But in consequence of energetic representations made on August 30th to the Grand Vizier, the situation has seemed to clear up somewhat. His Highness is personally in favor of peace. The same may be said of several members of the Cabinet, amongst others Djavid Bey, who sees the abyss into which the finances of the State will be hurled.

Unhappily the power of Enver Pasha is still very great and he would like to launch the country into the maddest adventures at any cost.

The mobilization which has taken place under his orders far surpassed in rigor that which took place during the Balkan War. This time, nobody is excepted between the ages of 20 and 45. Requisitions have assumed a character of a veritable spoliation. The military authorities not only require the provisions to be delivered to them which are found in the shops of private owners or at the Customs House, but also goods of every kind, from motor-cars to ladies' toilet articles.

Numerous boats coming from the Black Sea and going past on their way to the Mediterranean, have been stopped at the passage and unloaded by force.

These proceedings, which the Minister of a foreign Power has not hesitated to term piracy, in a note which he addressed to the Porte, have, as their result, made trading ships desert the Bosphorus.

I learn that the receipts of the customs at Constantinople have diminished by more than 75 per cent. As to tithes, they will amount to practically nothing, according to what I was told by a member of the Council of Debt. On the one hand, the harvest has been gathered in under adverse conditions, in consequence of lack of labor; on the other hand, the military authorities have seized a mass of agricultural produce, before there was opportunity for the tithe to be levied.

It will be possible for the September coupons of the Public Unified Debt to be paid, but that will probably not be the case with the following coupon, and, for the first time since the Decree of Muharram, a suspension of the service of the Public Debt will be seen, whilst the deficit, according to the British Delegate on the Council of the Debt, will reach the figure of £16,500,000.

It is not surprising that under these conditions Djavid Bey, as Minister of Finance, is exerting himself to stop the Government on the fatal incline, down which German influence and the chauvinism of Enver Pasha wish to drag them.

For the moment, it is especially war against Greece which is contemplated. As I was told yesterday by an Ambassador, the Hellenic Government are well aware that they can no longer hold without question all that was assigned to them by the Treaty of London. The European situation has changed and they will have to make some concessions. Athens would be willing to make concessions with regard to the government in Chios and Mytilene; for instance, it would be prepared to recognize the suzerainty of the Sultan over these islands. But the Turks, in accordance with their system of bargaining, are now formulating on this head such demands that it seems difficult for an understanding to be reached.

There are, nevertheless, various reasons which lead one to believe at present that Turkey will not decide to open hostilities against Greece.

Turkey could not attack Greece by sea, since England has given it to be understood that if the *Goeben* or the *Breslau* comes out of the Dardanelles, the British squadron has orders to sink them.

As to a campaign on land, that would need the consent of Bulgaria, and certain signs seem to indicate that there is little disposition at Sofia to yield an assistance which might involve the country in grave complications.

All the Ambassadors at Constantinople are, in fact, convinced that a rupture between Turkey and Greece will inevitably lead to a war with the three great allied Powers.

To sum up, the danger has diminished, but it is far from having disappeared. The Powers of the Triple Entente are doing their best to remove it, but German influence may bring things to such a pass that the dignity of the three allied countries will be compromised.

Finally, if war breaks out, this will mean political, as well as economic, ruin for Turkey, since the persons most competent to speak are of the opinion that the Turkish army is incapable of taking the field.

THE FRENCH INVADE ALSACE

GERMANY WINS THE BATTLE OF LORRAINE

AUGUST 7TH-20TH

GEORGE H. PERRIS   FREIHERR VON STEINACKER

The previous sections of our volume have shown the opening attacks of Germany and Austria in the Great War. We turn now to the response of France. As Britain alone had been prepared to meet the onslaught on the ocean, so was France alone in readiness on land. To the German attack she responded quickly by a counter-attack in Alsace. This is fully described by Mr. Perris, a British scholar and diplomat who was at the time in France, and who had previously been a sympathetic friend to Germany. Hence his narrative is without any coloring of partiality to France. He gives facts and shrewdly estimates their value. For the German account we follow the narrative of General von Steinacker, authorized by the German Government and issued as semi-official toward the close of the war. This battle of Lorraine, or of Morhange as the French call it, was the first large and equal battle on the western front.

BY GEORGE H. PERRIS

WE may now turn to the military plans of the western Allies and their chief enemy, taking France first, as the Power longest acquainted with the threat of a new invasion. The German Empire is bordered on the west, to the extent of nearly two-thirds of its extent, by Holland and Belgium, and to the extent of little more than one-third by France. During the armed rivalry that followed the war of 1870, this short Franco-German frontier—only 170 miles in length, counting all its indentations, from Longwy to Belfort—had been so effectively blocked by systems of fortification, centering in Diedenhofen (Thionville), Metz, Strassburg, and Neu-Breisach on the one side, Verdun, Toul, Epinal, and Belfort on the other, that any rapid invasion in either direction was generally considered impossible. It was, indeed, the prospect of over-pressure of millions of men in the gaps between these great fortresses that German military writers cited as justifying their assumption of a violation of Belgian, and perhaps also of Dutch and Swiss, neutrality. If these neutral States were barred, the defensive position of the German Empire on the west was very strong —the Italian Alliance apart—the possibility of any serious attack being limited to the gaps between the fortresses on the north of the Vosges and the gap of Belfort leading into the plain of southern Alsace. We have seen that the German Imperial Government was in no merely defensive mood, but had immediately struck out through neutral Luxemburg and the Liege gap. What was France doing, meanwhile?

She was playing the game on orthodox lines, all warnings notwithstanding. The mobilization progressing smoothly, the chief armies were hurried to the eastern frontier. A minor force was sent north to guard the gates of the Sambre and Meuse Rivers, and, generally, the neutral frontier from Maubeuge to Longwy. The western half of the northern frontier was left practically uncovered. An offensive was at once taken from Belfort into southern Alsace, supported by an advance along the crests of the Vosges, under the direction of General Dubail. Evidently, the plain round Mulhouse was only lightly held. Perhaps this French advance was deliberately permitted; certainly it absorbed in Paris and the country at large a great deal of attention which should have been directed elsewhere.

On Friday, August 7th, a French brigade, with cavalry and artillery, occupied the town of Altkirch, and on the following morning advanced along the railway across the low country, and, after another stiff fight with the retiring German troops, entered Mulhouse at 5 p. m. This was, politically speaking, a great event. At last, after forty-four years, French soldiers again trod the bank of the "German" Rhine. Much was made of the victorious march of twenty-five miles into Alsace; and General Joffre issued a proclamation in which he called his soldiers, "the first laborers in the great work of *la revanche.*" [1]

[1] The proclamation ran as follows:
CHILDREN OF ALSACE!
After forty-four years of sorrowful waiting, French soldiers once more tread the soil of your noble country. They are the pioneers in

Correspondingly acute was the disappointment of the following retreat.   On August 9th, the Austrian Government was reported to be sending troops through southern Germany to Alsace; and it was only then that the French Government broke off relations with the Dual Monarchy.   On the same day, Mulhouse was retaken by the German 14th Army Corps and a portion of the 15th, the direct attack being supported by a flank movement against Cernay (Sennheim).   The sequel is thus described in the French official statement.

"Our troops were enthusiastically received in Mulhouse by the Alsatians.   Some hours were spent in joyous excitement, and for a moment, perhaps too readily, the men forgot that they were in the enemy's country.   Beside the Alsatians fêting our arrival, there were a number of German immigrants who immediately informed the retreating Germans of our exact position and strength.   Mulhouse, difficult to defend against an attack from the north and east, was comparatively easy to recover if vigorously attacked.   That is what the Germans did during the night, advancing on the one side from the Forest of Hard and on the other from the direction of Neu-Breisach and Colmar, and marching toward Cernay in order to cut our retreat. If we had remained at Mulhouse with insufficient forces, we would have been in danger of losing our line of retreat toward the Upper Vosges and Belfort.   Orders were, therefore, given to retire.   Another plan might, indeed, have been conceived and carried out.   The troops we had left at Altkirch had not been attacked.   It would thus have been possible to counter-attack the enemy marching on Cernay by utilizing our reserves.   This plan was not carried out.   Our left was attacked near Cernay by greatly superior forces;

the great work of revenge.   For them what emotions it calls forth, and what pride!

To complete the work they have made the sacrifice of their lives. The French nation unanimously urges them on, and in the folds of their flag are inscribed the magic words, "Right and Liberty."   Long live Alsace.   Long live France.

General-in-Chief of the French Armies,
                                                JOFFRE.

our center was attacked at Mulhouse; and our right was inactive. The battle was badly begun, and the wisest solution was, therefore, to retreat. In order to carry out our initial plan, it was necessary to recommence the operations on a new basis, and under a new commander. The command was given to General Pau."

When the new start was made in the plain, the chief crests and passes of the Vosges had been captured after hard fighting, and were firmly held. The retirement five miles from the frontier on the eve of the war here involved a peculiarly hard penalty upon the mountain troops. The pass known as the Ballon d'Alsace (Welsche Belchen —4,085 feet), a famous viewpoint overlooking Thann, was the first to be secured. It is very steep on the Alsatian side, but less so on the French, where, moreover, the summit was commanded by the fort of Servance. From here, the Col du Busang was easily taken. Next, the Schlucht, the picturesque pass between Gerardmer and Münster, and the Hohneck (4,465 feet) were gained, under like advantageous conditions. More to the north, the central Vosges offered much greater difficulties, the French sides being the steeper, so that it was difficult to bring up artillery; while the Germans had been able to strengthen their positions on the narrow, thickly wooded summits by cutting down trees, putting up wire entanglements, and digging trenches. The Col du Bonhomme (3,120 feet) and the lower Col Ste. Marie, captured after a five-days' struggle before the middle of August, gave protection to the French right in its progress toward Saales, at the head of the valley leading to Schlestadt; but the direct way to Colmar was blocked by German field-works and by heavy artillery on the lower slopes. A further northward advance was, therefore, made along the mountain crests, and artillery was brought down from the head of the Bruche Valley upon the German flank. This operation, in which material losses were sustained, opened the way for the occupation of Mount Donon (3,300 feet), the most northerly of the Vosges summits, on August 14th. This quasi-Alpine campaign had been skillfully directed, and met with a deserved success. The numbers of men engaged were not large, varying at first from a battalion of Chasseurs to a regiment of infantry, and being gradually increased. The most considerable French loss officially named was 600 killed and wounded in the Bonhomme and Ste. Marie passes. Apart from cannon and material, the German losses were larger.

The little manufacturing town of Thann had now been reoccupied; and at St. Blaise, a village near Ste. Marie-aux-Mines, in a sharp combat, General von Deimling, commanding the 15th German Army Corps, was wounded, and the French took their first standard, to the great joy of Paris sightseers a few days later. On August 18th, General Joffre issued from eastern headquarters the first dispatch bearing his own signature. It reported steady advance along the Alsatian valleys, and declared that "the enemy retreated in disorder, everywhere abandoning his wounded and material." General Pau had received strong reënforcements with a view to a "decisive" action. Advancing simultaneously from Belfort and the Vosges, but on a narrower front than previously, with their right supported on the Rhone-Rhine Canal, they had stormed Thann and Dannemarie, and, bringing the left round toward Colmar, while the center attacked Mulhouse, threatened the German forces with a serious breach of their communications. After severe street fighting, in which twenty-four guns were taken, Mulhouse was again in French possession on August 20th.

The whole of the ground thus gained was abandoned a few days later. This was a grave blow to French pride, and brought a severe punishment upon the Francophile Alsatians. Naturally, the whole southern campaign aroused severe criticism. Several high officers were retired for mistakes in the first advance, which was afterwards officially described as "a mere reconnoissance." If any less eminent soldiers than General Joffre and General Pau had been responsible, there might have been more trouble. But Joffre "the taciturn," the cool-headed engineer whose powers had been tested in many a colonial field, and confirmed in long labors of fortification and organization, and the veteran

Pau, who had been second in consideration for the post of Generalissimo, could not be regarded as reckless adventurers, aiming at a political advantage they could not hold.

The Germans directed their advance—apart from the three first German armies and General von Emmich's Army of the Meuse, operating through Belgium—across the Belgian Ardennes and Luxemburg respectively, against the gap behind Longwy, while the Verdun army watched that of Metz, and the Nancy army watched that of Strassburg. Longwy, although without serious modern fortification, and having but a small garrison, refused to surrender on August 3rd, and, after being invested and losing half its effectives by repeated bombardments, capitulated only on the 27th. The gallant Governor, Lieutenant-Colonel Darche, was named officer of the Legion of Honor for this heroic defense.

The feat indicates, however, that the German effort in this direction was of a secondary character; and, in fact, it was checked at Mangiennes and Pillon on August 10th-12th, with a loss of several guns and a thousand prisoners. On this side Verdun was not to be approached.

After repelling attacks, and routing a Bavarian corps established on the hills above Blamont and Cirey, east of Nancy and Lunéville, General de Castelnau's army of five corps and reserve divisions now made a bold entry into the Lorraine lowlands. All the signs seemed favorable. The Minister of War boasted (on August 15th) that the expected German attack on Nancy had "scarcely been attempted," that the invasion of Belgium had been "foiled," that the movements of the Allied armies had been "perfectly coördinated," and that their supremacy at sea had secured the free passage of the Algerian troops and future foreign supplies. The British Expeditionary Force was known to have crossed the Channel. Mulhouse was lost, but the Vosges passes were won. The Generalissimo was sure as to the next move; the soldiers had already gained confidence in themselves, their bayonets, and their field-guns, especially their "75's."

On Sunday, the 16th, the French troops had a firm hold

on Avricourt, the frontier station on the main line from
Paris to Strassburg.   Saarburg was menaced from the
north, south and west.   A sleepy town, but an important
railway junction, the authorities of the Reichsland kept
here a considerable garrison, and the neighboring hills
were defaced with huge barracks.   To the south of the
town a strong artillery position had been established.   This
was taken by assault; and, on August 18th, the French entered Saarburg, thus effectually breaking the main railway
communications between Metz and Strassburg.   Zabern,
where Lieutenant von Forstner had so recently executed
Prussian military vengeance upon a lame cobbler, which
Herr von Jagow had described as "almost an enemy's
country," where the Prussian Minister of War had feared
"to see life for a German become less safe than life in the
Congo"—Zabern, the very name of which cried aloud of
the uniformed bully, was only a day's march further east,
and Strassburg itself only as much more.

Hope flashed over France like a sudden conflagration.
Count Albert de Mun published in Paris the narrative of a
refugee priest who declared that Metz was hungry and
terror-stricken.   General Bonnal, in the *Gaulois,* quoted a
prisoner as saying: "It is an officers', not a people's war,"
and from this concluded that there had been "a complete
reversal of rôles" since 1870.   The Abbé Wetterlé, a nota-
ble Alsatian member of the Reichstag, reached Paris on
August 19th, by way of Basel and Pontarlier, having narrowly escaped arrest and trial for high treason.   M. Blu-
menthal, another deputy, and ex-mayor of Colmar, had also
had an exciting journey from that town to the Swiss frontier.   Their adventures accentuated the general anticipation
that the lost provinces were about to be liberated.

The French positions were quickly extended to the
northwest of Saarburg, through Dieuze and Morhange to
Château-Salins and Delme, decayed country towns on a
strategic railway running to Metz, only twenty miles away.
Whether they had deliberately tempted Castelnau into this
dangerous salient, or had retired only to give time for the
bringing up of heavy reënforcements, the Crown Prince of

Bavaria and General von Heeringen were now able, with the aid of the Metz garrison, to fall upon the French from three sides at once.

The blow was sudden and decisive. The French 15th Corps, taken by surprise, gave way—some, at least, of these Southern troops fled, but they afterwards bravely retrieved their character—and the whole line had to be withdrawn. The Germans claimed to have captured 10,000 prisoners and 50 guns. The French questioned these figures, but could not deny a severe reverse. This was on August 20th, while the German cavalry was entering Brussels, the French were recovering Mulhouse, and the authorities in Paris were congratulating themselves that, except a corner of land at Audun-le-Roman, the frontier station between Longuyon and Thionville, every part of the national territory was free of the invader.

The retreat from Lorraine was arrested for a moment on the line of the Seille and the Marne-Rhine Canal. On August 22nd, it had reached the Moselle and the advanced works of Nancy on the left, Badonviller and the Donon on the right. On the 23rd, Lunéville was lost; the French retired to, and at some points beyond, the Murthe, the center of the defense being the ring of hills known as the Grand Couronné of Nancy. On the 25th, Mulhouse was evacuated, and all but the southern passes of the Vosges were abandoned. There was now something more important than Alsace for General Pau to look after. The danger in the north was unmistakable.

BY GENERAL FREIHERR VON STEINACKER

The powerful attack which the French undertook in the region between Epinal and Toul-Nancy in the direction of Saarburg, led to the battle of Lorraine.

The battle was preceded by small vanguard encounters on the borders of Lorraine. On the 11th of August, a mixed French brigade attacked a small Bavarian frontier-guard detachment near Lagarde. As the French left this place in order to reconnoitre the Seille district, they were halted by the Bavarians and thrown back into the forest of Parroy, situated northeast of Lunéville on the Marne-Rhine canal.   Thereby the Germans captured the first French flag, two batteries, four machine-guns and 700 prisoners.

By the 10th of August the German advance troops had already crossed the boundary in the Meurthe district and fought victoriously near Baronweiler.   These advance troops, however, were taken back as soon as the strength of the advancing enemy forces had been determined; for it did not appear expedient to offer the French battle within the artillery range of their great forts, Toul and Nancy. The French went forward to battle here with no fewer than 8 army corps of the first and second Armies, numbering about 300,000 men.   It was hard for the so recently victorious German troops of the Sixth Army to obey the order to fall back.   When, however, during the next few days they were incorporated into the main German position, extending through Morville and Pfalzburg, they realized their mission as frontier-guard was ended and that powerful forces were being placed here for a decisive battle.

During the period August 12-19, the main German position here was extended and strengthened in expectation of the French attack.   The town of Saarburg had to be abandoned for a few days, a favorable position for the heavy artillery being found to the north of it.   On August 19th, the French armies, under Dubail and Castelnau, had begun their advance, the German Sixth Army had been assembled in a fortified position on the line Mörchingen-Saarburg, while the Seventh German Army stood ready for attack between Saarburg and Strassburg.

On the morning of August 19th, French cavalry and guns appeared on the height before the German position. They were surprised, however, by German bombs which fell among them, and compelled them to seek cover.   The French infantry managed to approach within a few hundred meters of the German line of fire; but the attack, momentarily expected, did not materialize.

On the 20th, both German armies proceeded to the attack.   Although this was entirely unexpected by the enemy, the latter endeavored to stand his ground; and severe fighting took place near Dieuze and in several places to the north of it, as well as in the region of the Saar. Over vineyards and through fields where the oats grew high, the German attack went forward, and even the murderous artillery fire directed from the enemy's main position was powerless against it. The French infantry, which stood ready in dense masses in the forests near Saarburg and Saaraltdorf, suffered heavily under the fire of the German batteries. The right wing of the enemy was beaten by a brilliant bayonet charge. Thus, along the whole line of the Sixth Army, a great victory had been won on the evening of the 20th of August. Thousands of prisoners had been taken and a large number of guns had been captured.

A few attempts to recover lost ground proved unavailing. The defeated "Second Army" of the French flowed back and was forced back ever farther by the energetic pursuit which set in during the following days, being finally compelled in consequence of the defeat in the region of Beaumont, August 22nd, to retreat behind the Meurthe. Lunéville was also captured on that day.

The battle, so far as the Seventh Army was concerned, which developed along the line Saarburg-Lützelhausen, on the 20th, owing to the nature of the ground, resolved itself into a series of single engagements which led to bitter hand-to-hand combats. On the 22nd, the First French Army was beaten and commenced its retreat toward the Meurthe and the Mortagne, the Seventh Army following to the line Baccarat-Saint Dié. Here the German attack came to a standstill.

During this first great and successful encounter with the French right wing, the Fifth Army, under the command of the German Crown-Prince, advanced through Luxemburg along both banks of the Chiers. The French fortress Longwy, situated on this river near the boundary, could not arrest the advance of the Crown-Prince: it was surrounded, and the advance continued. On August 28th, Longwy fell into the hands of the Germans, being the first important French fortress to be captured.

THE "BATTLE OF THE FRONTIERS"

AND THE RETREAT TO THE MARNE

AUGUST 20TH-SEPTEMBER 5TH

MARSHAL JOFFRE   SIR JOHN FRENCH
HEINRICH HUEBNER   GENERAL VON STEINACKER

We come now to the beginning of the vast, coördinated main battle, the trial of military skill and strength between France and Germany, which began along the borders on August 20th and reached its culmination in the Battle of the Marne.

So complex and far-spread was this campaign, so brilliant in its strategy, like some mighty chess game between the chosen masters of the military art, that it can only be understood when looked at in detail. We present first, therefore, the first series of engagements, which history has named "the Battle of the Frontiers"; and we present it in the official narrative of Marshal Joffre, the ultimate victor in the game. The help that he received from his British allies is then fully emphasized by the equally official narrative of the British chief commander. The German commanders issued no such formal report, but the authoritative narrative of General von Steinacker groups this battle with the preceding one in Lorraine and covers both. A German "army order" issued by the Kaiser himself is also given as having an emphasis of its own in expressing the spirit of the German Headquarters. This is followed by the personal narrative of an enthusiastic and patriotic German officer, a former college professor, who was in the thick of the frontier battle and the eager advance upon Paris which followed the preliminary German success.

We must recognize that this first huge clash of the armies was decisively a German success. Since General Joffre himself asserts this, it is useless for the Allies' partisans to deny it and seek to explain the defeat away. In a great campaign at the opening of war, the opposing leaders are both venturing into the unknown. Despite all preliminary spy work in peace, they are sure neither of the opponent's weapons nor of his tactics. Even their own new inventions have yet to prove of actual value in war. Joffre had expected the attack from the east, as his report explains. When it came from the north through Belgium he was not taken by surprise or wholly unprepared; but he had much shifting of armies to accomplish. His own invasion along the eastern frontiers seems to have revealed to him the main German plan; but his adversaries had gained the quicker start. He would have fought them in Germany if he could. As it was, he had lost Belgium before he was ready to begin. The unexpected power of the new Teutonic artillery had swept aside the first Belgian fortress, Liege, with terrifying speed. It now proved equally effective in capturing Namur. After that, the French did not trust to fortresses. They saw that these were only death-traps. They retreated, while with this new knowledge, Joffre evolved new plans.

The strategy of his frontier battle broke down chiefly because the French army under Gen. Lanrezac allowed itself to be driven back from the easily defensible river banks east of Namur. This left the newly arrived British army exposed to an overwhelming attack, and the whole Allied line fell back, fighting as it went. We might talk of separate battles in this celebrated retreat, battles fought by the British at Mons, Landrecies and Le Cateau, by the French at Charleroi, St. Quentin, Guise, Marfée, Jaulnay and a dozen other danger spots. In reality, however, these were all but one vast struggle to protect the "retreat to the Marne."

BY MARSHAL JOSEPH JOFFRE
Official French Review of the Campaign in France

THE first month of the campaign began with successes and finished with defeats for the French troops. Under what circumstances did these come about?

Our plan of concentration had foreseen the possibility of two principal actions, one on the right between the Vosges and the Moselle, the other on the left to the north of Verdun-Toul line, this double possibility involving the eventual variation of our transport. On August 2nd, owing to the Germans passing through Belgium, our concentration was substantially modified by Marshal Joffre in order that our principal effort might be directed to the north.

From the first week in August it was apparent that the length of time required for the British Army to begin to move would delay our action in connection with it. This delay is one of the reasons which explain our failures at the end of August.

Awaiting the moment when the operations in the north could begin, and to prepare for it by retaining in Alsace the greatest possible number of German forces, the General in Chief ordered our troops to occupy Mulhouse, to cut the bridges of the Rhine at Huningue and below, and then to flank the attack of our troops, operating in Lorraine.

The purpose of the operations in Alsace was to retain a large part of the enemy's forces far from the northern theater of operations. Our offensive in Lorraine was to pursue the same purpose still more directly by holding before it the German army corps operating to the south of Metz.

This offensive began brilliantly on August 14th. On the 19th we had reached the region of Saarburg and that of the Etangs (lakes), and we held Dieuze, Morhange, Delme, and Château Salins.

On the 20th our success was stopped. The cause is to be found in the strong organization of the region, in the power of the enemy's artillery, operating over ground which had been minutely surveyed, and, finally, in the default of certain units.

On the 22nd, in spite of the splendid behavior of several of our army corps, notably that of Nancy, our troops were brought back on the Grand Couronné, while on the 23rd and 24th the Germans concentrated reënforcements— three army corps, at least—in the region of Lunéville and forced us to retire to the south.

This retreat, however, was only momentary. On the 25th, after two vigorous counter-attacks, one from south to north and the other from west to east, the enemy had to fall back. From that time a sort of balance was established on this terrain between the Germans and ourselves. Maintained for fifteen days, it was afterward, as will be seen, modified to our advantage.

There remained the principal business, the battle of the north—postponed owing to the necessity of waiting for the British Army. On August 20th the concentration of our lines was finished and the General in Chief gave orders for our center and our left to take the offensive. Our center comprised two armies. Our left consisted of a third army, reënforced to the extent of two army corps, a corps of cavalry, the reserve divisions, the British Army, and the Belgian Army, which had already been engaged for the previous three weeks at Liege, Namur, and Louvain.

The German plan on that date was as follows: From seven to eight army corps and four cavalry divisions were endeavoring to pass between Givet and Brussels, and even to prolong their movements more to the west. Our object was, therefore, in the first place, to hold and dispose of the enemy's center and afterward to throw ourselves with all available forces on the left flank of the German grouping of troops in the north.

On August 21st our offensive in the center began with ten army corps. On August 22nd it failed, and this reverse appeared serious.

The reasons for it are complex. There were in this affair individual and collective failures, imprudences committed under the fire of the enemy, divisions ill-engaged, rash deployments, precipitate retreats, a premature waste of men, and, finally, the inadequacy of certain of our troops and their leaders, both as regards the use of infantry and artillery.

In consequences of these lapses the enemy, turning to account the difficult terrain, was able to secure the maximum of profit from the advantages which the superiority of his subaltern complements gave him.

In spite of this defeat our maneuver had still a chance of success, if our left and the British Army obtained a decisive result. This was unfortunately not the case. On August 22nd, at the cost of great losses, the enemy succeeded in crossing the Sambre and our left army fell back on the 24th upon Beaumont-Givet, being perturbed by the belief that the enemy was threatening its right.

On the same day (the 24th), the British Army fell back after a German attack upon the Maubeuge-Valenciennes line. On the 25th and 26th its retreat became more hurried. After Landrecies and Le Cateau it fell back southward by forced marches. It could not from this time keep its hold until after crossing the Marne.

The rapid retreat of the English, coinciding with the defeat sustained in Belgian Luxemburg [at the Sambre], allowed the enemy to cross the Meuse and to accelerate, by fortifying it, the action of his right.

The situation at this moment may be thus summed up: Either our frontier had to be defended on the spot under conditions which the British retreat rendered extremely perilous, or we had to execute a strategic retirement which, while delivering up to the enemy a part of the national soil, would permit us, on the other hand, to resume the offensive at our own time with a favorable disposition of troops, still intact, which we had at our command. The General in Chief determined on the second alternative.

Henceforward the French command devoted its efforts to preparing the offensive. To this end three conditions had to be fulfilled:

1.   The retreat had to be carried out in order under a succession of counter-attacks which would keep the enemy busy.

2.   The extreme point of this retreat must be fixed in such a way that the different armies should reach it simultaneously, ready at the moment of occupying it to resume the offensive all together.

3.   Every circumstance permitting of a resumption of the offensive before this point should be reached must be utilized by the whole of our forces and the British forces.

The counter-attacks, executed during the retreat, were brilliant and often fruitful. On August 26th we successfully attacked St. Quentin to disengage the British Army. Two other corps and a reserve division engaged the Prussian Guard and the Tenth German Army Corps, which was debouching from Guise. By the end of the day, after various fluctuations, the enemy was thrown back on the Oise and the British front was freed.

On August 27th we also succeeded in throwing back upon the Meuse the enemy, who was endeavoring to gain a foothold on the left bank. Our successes continued on the 28th in the woods of Marfée and of Jaulnay. Thanks to them we were able, in accordance with the orders of the General in Chief, to fall back on the Buzancy-Le Chesne-Bouvellemont line.

Further to the right another army took part in the same movement and carried out successful attacks on August 25th on the Othain and in the region of Spincourt.

On the 26th these different units recrossed the Meuse without being disturbed and were able to join in the action of our center. Our armies were, therefore, again intact and available for the offensive.

On August 26th a new army composed of two army corps, five reserve divisions, and a Moorish brigade was constituted.   This army was to assemble in the region of Amiens between August 27th and September 1st and take the offensive against the German right, uniting its action with that of the British Army, operating on the line of Ham-Bray-sur-Somme.

The hope of resuming the offensive was at this moment rendered vain by the rapidity of the march of the German right wing.   This rapidity had two consequences, which we had to parry before thinking of advancing.   On the one hand, our new army had not time to complete its detraining, and, on the other hand, the British Army, forced back further by the enemy, uncovered on August 31st our left flank. Our line, thus modified, contained waves which had to be redressed before we could pass to the offensive.

To understand this it is sufficient to consider the situation created by the quick advance of the enemy on the evening of September 2nd.

A corps of cavalry had crossed the Oise and advanced as far as Château Thierry.   The First Army (General von Kluck), comprising four active army corps and a reserve corps, had passed Compiègne.

The Second Army (General von Bülow), with three active army corps and two reserve corps, was reaching the Laon region.

The Third Army (General von Hausen), with two active army corps and a reserve corps, had crossed the Aisne between the Château Porcien and Attigny.

More to the east the Fourth, Fifth, Sixth, and Seventh Armies, namely, twelve army corps, four reserve corps, and numerous Ersatz formations, were in contact with our troops, the Fourth and Fifth Armies between Vouziers and Verdun and the others in the positions which have been indicated above, from Verdun to the Vosges.

It will, therefore, be seen that our left, if we accepted battle, might be in great peril through the British forces and the new French Army, operating more to the westward, having given way.

A defeat in these conditions would have cut off our armies from Paris and from the British forces and at the same time from the new army which had been constituted to the left of the English. We should thus be running the risk of losing by a single stroke the advantage of the assistance which Russia later on was to furnish.

General Joffre chose resolutely for the solution which disposed of these risks, that is to say, for postponing the offensive and the continuance of the retreat. In this way he remained on ground which he had chosen. He waited only until he could engage in better conditions.

In consequence, on September 1st, he fixed as an extreme limit for the movement of retreat, which was still going on, the line of Bray-sur-Seine, Nogent-sur-Seine, Arcis-sur-Aube, Vitry-le-François, and the region to the north of Bar-le-Duc. This line might be reached if the troops were compelled to go back so far. They would attack before reaching it, as soon as there was a possibility of bringing about an offensive disposition, permitting the coöperation of the whole of our forces.

On September 5th it appeared that this desired situation existed.

The First German Army, carrying audacity to temerity, had continued its endeavor to envelop our left, had crossed the Grand Morin, and reached the region of Chauffry, to the south of Rebaix and of Esternay. It aimed then at cutting our armies off from Paris, in order to begin the investment of the capital.

The Second Army had its head on the line Champaubert, Etoges, Bergeres, and Vertus.

The Third and Fourth Armies reached to Chalons-sur-Marne and Bussy-le-Repos. The Fifth Army was advancing on one side and the other from the Argonne as far as Triacourt-les-Islettes and Juivecourt. The Sixth and Seventh Armies were attacking more to the east.

But—and here is a capital difference between the situation of September 5th and that of September 2nd—the envelopment of our left was no longer possible.

In the first place, our left army had been able to occupy

the line of Sézanne, Villers-St. Georges and Courchamps. Furthermore, the British forces, gathered between the Seine and the Marne, flanked on their left by the newly created army, were closely connected with the rest of our forces.

This was precisely the disposition which the General in Chief had wished to see achieved. On the 4th he decided to take advantage of it, and ordered all the armies to hold themselves ready. He had taken from his right two new army corps, two divisions of infantry, and two divisions of cavalry, which were distributed between his left and his center.

On the evening of the 5th he addressed to all the commanders of armies a message ordering them to attack.

"The hour has come," he wrote, "to advance at all costs, and to die where you stand rather than give way."

BY SIR JOHN FRENCH

Official Report of the British Commander Delivered to Lord Kitchener, Secretary of War

September 7th, 1914.

My Lord: I have the honor to report the proceedings of the field force under my command up to the time of rendering this dispatch.

1. The transport of the troops from England both by sea and by rail was effected in the best order and without a check. Each unit arrived at its destination in this country well within the scheduled time.

The concentration was practically complete on the evening of Friday, the 21st ultimo, and I was able to make dispositions to move the force during Saturday, the 22nd, to positions I considered most favorable from which to commence operations which the French Commander in Chief, Gen. Joffre, requested me to undertake in pursuance of his plans in prosecution of the campaign.

The line taken up extended along the line of the canal from Condé on the west, through Mons and Binche on the east. This line was taken up as follows:

From Condé to Mons inclusive was assigned to the Second Corps, and to the right of the Second Corps from Mons the First Corps was posted. The Fifth Cavalry Brigade was placed at Binche.

In the absence of my Third Army Corps I desired to keep the cavalry division as much as possible as a reserve to act on my outer flank, or move in support of any threatened part of the line. The forward reconnoissance was intrusted to Brig. Gen. Sir Philip Chetwode with the Fifth Cavalry Brigade, but I directed Gen. Allenby to send forward a few squadrons to assist in this work.

During the 22nd and 23rd these advanced squadrons did some excellent work, some of them penetrating as far as Soignies, and several encounters took place in which our troops showed to great advantage.

2. At 6 a. m. on August 23rd, I assembled the commanders of the First and Second Corps and cavalry division at a point close to the position and explained the general situation of the Allies, and what I understood to be Gen. Joffre's plan. I discussed with them at some length the immediate situation in front of us.

From information I received from French Headquarters I understood that little more than one, or at most two, of the enemy's army corps, with perhaps one cavalry division, were in front of my position; and I was aware of no attempted outflanking movement by the enemy. I was confirmed in this opinion by the fact that my patrols encountered no undue opposition in their reconnoitering operations. The observations of my aëroplanes seemed also to bear out this estimate.

About 3 p. m. on Sunday, the 23rd, reports began coming in to the effect that the enemy was commencing an attack on the Mons line, apparently in some strength, but that the right of the position from Mons and Bray was being particularly threatened. The commander of the First Corps had pushed his flank back to some high ground south of Bray, and the Fifth Cavalry Brigade evacuated Binche, moving slightly south; the enemy thereupon occupied Binche.

The right of the Third Division, under Gen. Hamilton, was at Mons, which formed a somewhat dangerous salient;

and I directed the commander of the Second Corps to be careful not to keep the troops on this salient too long, but, if threatened seriously, to draw back the center behind Mons. This was done before dark.

In the meantime, about 5 p. m., I received a most unexpected message from Gen. Joffre by telegraph, telling me that at least three German corps, viz., a reserve corps, the Fourth Corps and the Ninth Corps, were moving on my position in front, and that the Second Corps was engaged in a turning movement from the direction of Tournay. He also informed me that the two reserve French divisions and the Fifth French Army on my right were retiring, the Germans having on the previous day gained possession of the passages of the Sambre between Charleroi and Namur.

3. In view of the possibility of my being driven from the Mons position, I had previously ordered a position in rear to be reconnoitered. This position rested on the fortress of Maubeuge on the right and extended west to Jenlain, southeast of Valenciennes, on the left. The position was reported difficult to hold, because standing crops and buildings made the siting of trenches very difficult and limited the field of fire in many important localities. It nevertheless afforded a few good artillery positions.

When the news of the retirement of the French and the heavy German threatening on my front reached me, I endeavored to confirm it by aëroplane reconnoissance; and as a result of this I determined to effect a retirement to the Maubeuge position at daybreak on the 24th.

A certain amount of fighting continued along the whole line throughout the night and at daybreak on the 24th the Second Division from the neighborhood of Harmignies made a powerful demonstration as if to retake Binche. This was supported by the artillery of both the First and Second Divisions, while the First Division took up a supporting position in the neighborhood of Peissant. Under cover of this demonstration the Second Corps retired on the line Dour-Quarouble-Frameries. The Third Division on the right of the corps suffered considerable loss in this operation from the enemy, who had retaken Mons.

The Second Corps halted on this line, where they partially intrenched themselves, enabling Sir Douglas Haig with the First Corps gradually to withdraw to the new position; and he effected this without much further loss, reaching the line Bavai-Maubeuge about 7 p. m. Toward midday the enemy appeared to be directing his principal effort against our left.

I had previously ordered Gen. Allenby with the cavalry to act vigorously in advance of my left front and endeavor to take the pressure off.

About 7.30 a. m. Gen. Allenby received a message from Sir Charles Fergusson, commanding the Fifth Division, saying that he was very hard pressed and in urgent need of support. On receipt of this message Gen. Allenby drew in the cavalry and endeavored to bring direct support to the Fifth Division.

During the course of this operation Gen. De Lisle, of the Second Cavalry Brigade, thought he saw a good opportunity to paralyze the further advance of the enemy's infantry by making a mounted attack on his flank. He formed up and advanced for this purpose, but was held up by wire about 500 yards from his objective, and the Ninth Lancers and the Eighteenth Hussars suffered severely in the retirement of the brigade.

The Nineteenth Infantry Brigade, which had been guarding the line of communications, was brought up by rail to Valenciennes on the 22nd and 23rd. On the morning of the 24th they were moved out to a position south of Quarouble to support the left flank of the Second Corps.

With the assistance of the cavalry Sir Horace Smith-Dorrien was enabled to effect his retreat to a new position; although, having two corps of the enemy on his front and one threatening his flank, he suffered great losses in doing so.

At nightfall the position was occupied by the Second Corps to the west of Bavai, the First Corps to the right. The right was protected by the fortress of Maubeuge, the left by the Nineteenth Brigade in position between Jenlain and Bry, and the cavalry on the outer flank.

4. The French were still retiring, and I had no support except such as was afforded by the fortress of Maubeuge; and the determined attempts of the enemy to get round my left flank assured me that it was his intention to hem me against that place and surround me. I felt that not a moment must be lost in retiring to another position.

I had every reason to believe that the enemy's forces were somewhat exhausted and I knew that they had suffered heavy losses. I hoped, therefore, that his pursuit would not be too vigorous to prevent me effecting my object.

The operation, however, was full of danger and difficulty, not only owing to the very superior force in my front, but also to the exhaustion of the troops.

The retirement was recommenced in the early morning of the 25th to a position in the neighborhood of Le Cateau, and rearguards were ordered to be clear of the Maubeuge-Bavai-Eth Road by 5.30 a. m.

Two cavalry brigades, with the divisional cavalry of the Second Corps, covered the movement of the Second Corps. The remainder of the cavalry division, with the Nineteenth Brigade, the whole under the command of Gen. Allenby, covered the west flank.

The Fourth Division commenced its detrainment at Le Cateau on Sunday, the 23rd, and by the morning of the 25th eleven battalions and a brigade of artillery with divisional staff were available for service.

I ordered Gen. Snow to move out to take up a position with his right south of Solesmes, his left resting on the Cambrai-Le Cateau Road south of La Chaprie. In this position the division rendered great help to the effective retirement of the Second and First Corps to the new position.

Although the troops had been ordered to occupy the Cambrai-Le Cateau-Landrecies position, and the ground had, during the 25th, been partially prepared and intrenched, I had grave doubts—owing to the information I had received as to the accumulating strength of the enemy against me—as to the wisdom of standing there to fight.

Having regard to the continued retirement of the French on my right, my exposed left flank, the tendency of the enemy's western corps to envelop me, and, more than all, the exhausted condition of the troops, I determined to make a great effort to continue the retreat till I could put some substantial obstacle, such as the Somme or the Oise, between my troops and the enemy, and afford the former some opportunity of rest and reorganization. Orders were, therefore, sent to the corps commanders to continue their retreat as soon as they possibly could toward the general line Vermand-St. Quentin-Ribemont.

The cavalry, under Gen. Allenby, were ordered to cover the retirement.

Throughout the 25th and far into the evening, the First Corps continued its march on Landrecies, following the road along the eastern border of the Forêt de Mormal, and arrived at Landrecies about 10 o'clock. I had intended that the corps should come further west so as to fill up the gap between Le Cateau and Landrecies, but the men were exhausted and could not get further in without rest.

The enemy, however, would not allow them this rest, and about 9.30 p. m. a report was received that the Fourth Guards Brigade in Landrecies was heavily attacked by troops of the Ninth German Army Corps, who were coming through the forest on the north of the town. This brigade fought most gallantly, and caused the enemy to suffer tremendous loss in issuing from the forest into the narrow streets of the town. This loss has been estimated from reliable sources at from 700 to 1,000. At the same time information reached me from Sir Douglas Haig that his First Division was also heavily engaged south and east of Maroilles. I sent urgent messages to the commander of the two French reserve divisions on my right to come up to the assistance of the First Corps, which they eventually did. Partly owing to this assistance, but mainly to the skillful manner in which Sir Douglas Haig extricated his corps from an exceptionally difficult position in the darkness of the night, they were able at dawn to resume their march south toward Wassigny on Guise.

By about 6 p. m. the Second Corps had got into position with their right on Le Cateau, their left in the neighborhood of Caudry, and the line of defense was continued thence by the Fourth Division toward Seranvillers, the left being thrown back.

During the fighting on the 24th and 25th the cavalry became a good deal scattered, but by the early morning of the 26th Gen. Allenby had succeeded in concentrating two brigades to the south of Cambrai.

The Fourth Division was placed under the orders of the general officer commanding the Second Army Corps.

On the 24th the French cavalry corps, consisting of three divisions under Gen. Sordêt, had been in billets north of Avesnes. On my way back from Bavai, which was my "Poste de Commandement" during the fighting of the 23rd and 24th, I visited Gen. Sordêt, and earnestly requested his coöperation and support. He promised to obtain sanction from his army commander to act on my left flank, but said that his horses were too tired to move before the next day. Although he rendered me valuable assistance later on in the course of the retirement, he was unable for the reasons given to afford me any support on the most critical day of all, viz., the 26th.

At daybreak it became apparent that the enemy was throwing the bulk of his strength against the left of the position occupied by the Second Corps and the Fourth Division.

At this time the guns of four German army corps were in position against them, and Sir Horace Smith-Dorrien reported to me that he judged it impossible to continue his retirement at daybreak (as ordered) in face of such an attack.

I sent him orders to use his utmost endeavors to break off the action and retire at the earliest possible moment, as it was impossible for me to send him any support, the First Corps being at the moment incapable of movement.

The French cavalry corps, under Gen. Sordêt, was coming up on our left rear early in the morning, and I sent an urgent message to him to do his utmost to come up and support the retirement of my left flank; but owing to the fatigue of his horses he found himself unable to intervene in any way.

There had been no time to intrench the position properly, but the troops showed a magnificent front to the terrible fire which confronted them.

The artillery, although outmatched by at least four to one, made a splendid fight, and inflicted heavy losses on their opponents.

At length it became apparent that, if complete annihilation was to be avoided, a retirement must be attempted; and the order was given to commence it about 3.30 p. m. The movement was covered with the most devoted intrepidity and determination by the artillery, which had itself suffered heavily, and the fine work done by the cavalry in the further retreat from the position assisted materially in the final completion of this most difficult and dangerous operation.

Fortunately the enemy had himself suffered too heavily to engage in an energetic pursuit.

I cannot close the brief account of this glorious stand of the British troops without putting on record my deep appreciation of the valuable services rendered by Gen. Sir Horace Smith-Dorrien.

I say without hesitation that the saving of the left wing of the army under my command on the morning of August 26th could never have been accomplished unless a commander of rare and unusual coolness, intrepidity, and determination had been present to personally conduct the operation.

The retreat was continued far into the night of the 26th and through the 27th and 28th, on which date the troops halted on the line Noyon-Chauny-La Fère, having then thrown off the weight of the enemy's pursuit.

On the 27th and 28th I was much indebted to Gen. Sordêt and the French cavalry division which he commands for materially assisting my retirement and successfully driving back some of the enemy on Cambrai.

Gen. D'Amade also, with the Sixty-first and Sixty-second French Reserve Divisions, moved down from the neighborhood of Arras on the enemy's right flank and took much pressure off the rear of the British forces.

This closes the period covering the heavy fighting which

commenced at Mons on Sunday afternoon, August 23rd, and which really constituted a four days' battle.

At this point, therefore, I propose to close the present dispatch.

I deeply deplore the very serious losses which the British forces have suffered in this great battle; but they were inevitable in view of the fact that the British Army—only two days after a concentration by rail—was called upon to withstand a vigorous attack of five German army corps.

It is impossible for me to speak too highly of the skill evinced by the two general officers commanding army corps; the self-sacrificing and devoted exertions of their staffs; the direction of the troops by divisional, brigade, and regimental leaders; the command of the smaller units by their officers; and the magnificent fighting spirit displayed by non-commissioned officers and men.

I wish particularly to bring to your Lordship's notice the admirable work done by the Royal Flying Corps under Sir David Henderson. Their skill, energy, and perseverance have been beyond all praise. They have furnished me with the most complete and accurate information, which has been of incalculable value in the conduct of the operations. Fired at constantly both by friend and foe, and not hesitating to fly in every kind of weather, they have remained undaunted throughout. Further, by actually fighting in the air, they have succeeded in destroying five of the enemy's machines.

I wish to acknowledge with deep gratitude the incalculable assistance I received from the General and Personal Staffs at Headquarters during this trying period.

September 17, 1914.

My Lord: In continuation of my dispatch of September 7th, I have the honor to report the further progress of the operations of the forces under my command from August 28th.

On that evening the retirement of the force was followed closely by two of the enemy's cavalry columns, moving southeast from St. Quentin.

The retreat in this part of the field was being covered
by the Third and Fifth Cavalry Brigades. South of the
Somme Gen. Gough, with the Third Cavalry Brigade, threw
back the Uhlans of the Guard with considerable loss.

Gen. Chetwode, with the Fifth Cavalry Brigade, encountered the eastern column near Cerizy, moving south.
The brigade attacked and routed the column, the leading
German regiment suffering very severe casualties and being
almost broken up.

The Seventh French Army Corps was now in course of
being railed up from the south to the east of Amiens. On
the 29th it nearly completed its detrainment, and the French
Sixth Army got into position on my left, its right resting
on Roye.

The Fifth French Army was behind the line of the Oise,
between La Fère and Guise.

The pursuit of the enemy was very vigorous; some five
or six German corps were on the Somme, facing the Fifth
Army on the Oise. At least two corps were advancing
toward my front, and were crossing the Somme east and
west of Ham. Three or four more German corps were opposing the Sixth French Army on my left.

This was the situation at 1 o'clock on the 29th, when I
received a visit from Gen. Joffre at my headquarters.

I strongly represented my position to the French Commander in Chief, who was most kind, cordial, and sympathetic, as he has always been. He told me that he had directed the Fifth French Army on the Oise to move forward
and attack the Germans on the Somme, with a view to
checking pursuit. He also told me of the formation of the
Sixth French Army on my left flank, composed of the Seventh Army Corps, four reserve divisions, and Sordêt's corps
of cavalry.

I finally arranged with Gen. Joffre to effect a further
short retirement toward the line of Compiègne-Soissons,
promising him, however, to do my utmost to keep always
within a day's march of him.

In pursuance of this arrangement the British forces retired to a position a few miles north of the line Compiègne-Soissons on the 29th.

The right flank of the German Army was now reaching a point which appeared seriously to endanger my line of communications with Havre. I had already evacuated Amiens, into which place a German reserve division was reported to have moved.

Orders were given to change the base to St. Nazaire, and establish an advance base at Le Mans. This operation was well carried out by the Inspector General of Communications.

In spite of a severe defeat inflicted upon the Guard Tenth and Guard Reserve Corps of the German Army by the First and Third French Corps on the right of the Fifth Army, it was not part of Gen. Joffre's plan to pursue this advantage; and a general retirement to the line of the Marne was ordered, to which the French forces in the more eastern theater were directed to conform.

A new Army (the Ninth) had been formed from three corps in the south by Gen. Joffre, and moved into the space between the right of the Fifth and left of the Fourth Armies.

While closely adhering to his strategic conception to draw the enemy on at all points until a favorable situation was created from which to assume the offensive, Gen. Joffre found it necessary to modify from day to day the methods by which he sought to attain this object, owing to the development of the enemy's plans and changes in the general situation.

In conformity with the movements of the French forces, my retirement continued practically from day to day. Although we were not severely pressed by the enemy, rearguard actions took place continually.

On September 1st, when retiring from the thickly wooded country to the south of Compiègne, the First Cavalry Brigade was overtaken by some German cavalry. They momentarily lost a horse artillery battery, and several officers and men were killed and wounded. With the help, however, of some detachments from the Third Corps operating on their left, they not only recovered their own guns, but succeeded in capturing twelve of the enemy's.

Similarly, to the eastward, the First Corps, retiring south, also got into some very difficult forest country, and a somewhat severe rearguard action ensued at Villers-Cotterets, in which the Fourth Guards Brigade suffered considerably.

On September 3rd the British forces were in position south of the Marne between Lagny and Signy-Signets. Up to this time I had been requested by Gen. Joffre to defend the passages of the river as long as possible, and to blow up the bridges in my front. After I had made the necessary dispositions, and the destruction of the bridges had been effected, I was asked by the French Commander in Chief to continue my retirement to a point some twelve miles in rear of the position I then occupied, with a view to taking up a second position behind the Seine. This retirement was duly carried out. In the meantime the enemy had thrown bridges and crossed the Marne in considerable force, and was threatening the Allies all along the line of the British forces and the Fifth and Ninth French Armies. Consequently several small outpost actions took place.

On Saturday, September 5th, I met the French Commander in Chief at his request, and he informed me of his intention to take the offensive forthwith, as he considered conditions very favorable to success.

ARMY ORDER ISSUED BY EMPEROR WILLIAM II. ON AUGUST 19TH

It is my Royal and Imperial command that you concentrate your energies, for the immediate present, upon one single purpose, and that is that you address all your skill and all the valor of my soldiers to exterminate first the treacherous English and walk over General French's contemptible little army.[1]

Headquarters, Aix-la-Chapelle.

[1] It was from this order that the British seized the phrase "contemptible little army" and used it as a badge of honor. Doubts have been raised as to the genuineness of the order. The British Government has vouched for its reality.

BY CAPTAIN HENRY HUEBNER

[Captain Huebner's narrative begins with his enthusiastic and patriotic departure for the front, hints at rapine and drunkenness in Belgium, and continues as follows:]

Before reaching Louvain we bivouacked near a large well-built village, and here we had the wettest and merriest evening in the whole campaign. Some of our battalion water-carriers discovered a wine-cellar in the village. On going into a cellar they noticed a stack of fagots, and guessed that they were put there with a purpose. The fagots were quickly cleared away, and behind them appeared a door. It led to a cellar filled with thousands of bottles of wine. They loaded themselves inside and out with the precious liquid, so that it is no wonder they walked into camp with unsteady gait.

Louvain, which afterwards attained so sad a fame, received us in quite a friendly manner. The inhabitants put vessels of drinking water in the streets. During a long halt in one of the suburbs they willingly brought us food, drinks, and cigars.

Towards evening we marched past a splendid red sandstone building, the Congo Museum. It is surrounded by a beautiful park, through the trees of which we caught glimpses of the royal palace, Tervueren. Soon afterwards we entered the southern suburbs of the Belgian capital. The streets reëchoed the tramp of thousands of feet and the marching-songs of the troops. Thousands of the inhabitants lined the street, watching the endless columns with curiosity and dismay. . . .

August 23rd brought us into touch with the hated English.

A report came that about 30,000 English were in position on the other side of the canal, and our two divisions had to attack them. Our regiment was in reserve in a forest intersected by a railway. As we marched to our position in the forest we could hear the rattle of rifle-fire and the thunder of artillery in the distance. But we were soon ordered forward.

We marched over a railway crossing, and at the quick step along the wide, dusty street of a large village with a burning August sun overhead, while the kindly villagers handed our men supplies of water and fruit.

A short halt was called under the high wall of a park, and there we learned to our great joy that the artillery had successfully bombarded the station at J——, near Mons, thus preventing the detrainment of English troops. In advancing we passed the munition wagons of our heavy artillery, then, taking a path to the left, crossed meadows straight for the village. A part of it was already in flames, and the rifles were cracking in the park of a large château on the right.

Large numbers of wounded were carried past us; they were from the gallant X—— regiment, which had stormed forward on its own, and, after heavy street fighting, had captured the station and some factories. We lay down for a short time while our artillery continued to pour shells into the village. Cries of jubilation greeted a well-aimed shot which took away the top of the church-tower with the Belgian flag fluttering on top and set the tower on fire.

It was nearly seven o'clock before the English, who had obstinately defended the place, evacuated it and retreated at top speed. They had had their first taste of the *furor teutonicus*. Our regiment did not come under fire again that day, but now we rushed forward and crossed the canal by an excellent bridge which our pioneers had erected. On the other side were the ruins of the railway station; a little further on we saw the first English prisoners—a corporal and eight men—sitting with their backs against a wall. Our men were standing round gazing at the helpless Britons. I must admit that they made an exceedingly good impression—strongly-built, sun-burnt, well-equipped soldiers. I was sorry that I could not speak English, but a one-year volunteer [2] noticed my embarrassment and offered to interpret.

---

[2] All young Germans who pass a certain examination at the end of the sixth class in a State Secondary School get the privilege of serving only one year in the German Army. They have to bear the entire expenses of the year's training, and are called *Einjährige-Freiwillige*.

This young soldier then narrated this extraordinary story: "I know the second prisoner from the left quite well; he is an old school friend of mine. My parents lived in England for twenty years, and we sat on the same school-bench together. We have met again here, but, it is true, under very different circumstances." The world is indeed small!

The farther we penetrated into the village the traces of the fight became more evident. Large buildings had been literally riddled by the German shells; the rifle bullets had split the red bricks in the houses, and as we turned a street corner there lay before us the first dead Englishman. In a signalman's cottage we found quite a number of the enemy's dead, for it is said that the British—if it is at all possible—carry the dead as well as the wounded into cover.

It was an industrial village, but the streets were quite deserted. Beyond it the country sloped upwards to various single hills, on the highest of which we could plainly see a huge stone obelisk, topped by a gilded object. We recognized the gigantic granite monument erected by the French in memory of their victory over the Austrians at the battle of Jemappes, 1792.

Our battalion encamped at the foot of the obelisk. But while the shadows of evening fell upon the landscape our artillery advanced to pursue the retreating English with their fire. On the left the neighboring division was still hotly engaged with them. They were only able to force a passage over the canal, which the English had defended with obstinate bravery, and were now endeavoring to drive the enemy out of the factories, woods, colliery-buildings, and villages, in order to come into line with our division. Across there the fire swelled to one long tremendous roar, then weakened, and after sunset ceased entirely. I shall never forget the scene, nor our own feelings, as we sat around on the monument steps. We felt a kind of mad joy that at the first set-to the hated English had got some good German blows and been hurled back.

But we were compelled to admit that these English mercenaries—whom many of us before the war had looked down upon with disparagement and contempt—had in every case fought valiantly and tenaciously. This was sufficiently obvious from the heavy losses which our German troops had suffered here.

After a hurried meal from the field-kitchen, we marched on a good distance in the waning light, in spite of the day's exertions. The English, however, had vanished; so the regiment assembled in the long, desolate street of a neighboring village for a halt. We all sank absolutely exhausted on the cobble-stones, and very soon loud snoring sounded between the long rows of houses.

It was by no means inspiring when an order was brought for us to return and act as a cover for the heavy guns. It seemed as if our superiors were determined that we should be quite pumped out, for the march back through blazing Jemappes to the village of G—— was an endless, racking strain. Our feet and legs almost refused to fulfill their functions; no word was spoken, and we rejoiced when, after two hours, a halt was called.

Towards midnight we arrived at G——, where the heavy artillery had marched up; guards and double sentries were detailed, and we looked for quarters. After a long search and much hammering of doors I found excellent quarters for four of us in the house of a frightened but very obliging schoolmaster. After I had got to bed the good man brought me a bottle of red wine and some roast beef which his wife had just prepared. During the whole campaign I have seldom slept so well and comfortably as in the house of these good people.

The first day of the great battle with the English, of which our fight was only a part, was a Sunday. With us Sunday came to be synonymous with *Schlachttag* (battle-day), for nearly every important engagement fell on that day. On the first day our regiment had not actually gone into action, but what we had missed was more than made good on Monday, August 24th.

First of all we had to cover again the long march of the night before, and while on the road we could hear the roar of battle ahead. Our regiment was allotted the task of driving the English out of the village F——, in which they had

employed all sorts of devices to defend the houses.   The
village stood on a moderate height before us; on the left it
turned back almost at right angles, while on the right a number of factories and collieries stretched down the slope.
Open, stubble land rose gently between these two wings to
the village.

While our battalion halted behind a huge slag heap, the
other two battalions of our regiment were heavily engaged
with the enemy.   From our covered position we could see
the English projectiles exploding with great exactness above
our comrades, but they were already pushing forward, and
finally our turn came too.   We had hardly swerved into
the open when English bullets began to whistle round our
heads.   We at once advanced in open formation, while a
battery came up on the right and, after a short duel, silenced
the enemy's guns, but his rifle-fire increased in violence, and
we had to cross 1,200 yards of open field.

Here and there one or other of our men sank with a
short scream or dragged themselves groaning to the rear.
Finally we rushed to a railway bank, across the top of which
the enemy's bullets fled through the air like swarms of bees.
But we could not lie there forever; the two first battalions
were heavily engaged about 300 yards in advance of the railway, and badly in need of our support.   So I yelled the
order: *Sprung auf, marsch! marsch!*   (Up and forwards!)

A veritable hail of bullets greeted us as we rushed over
the bank.   Then we advanced by short rushes; throwing
ourselves flat after each short rush we worked our way into
the first line.   While our artillery was hurling shells into the
village and into the factories on the right we climbed the
height and entered the village from behind.   Just as on the
previous day, however, the English had completely vanished.
They must have run at an extraordinary speed.   We got
into the houses through the back gardens and by breaking
open doors and windows, for everything was locked and
bolted; the English had even put sand-bags against the cellar
windows.   In order to get into the street we had to break
open the front doors, and I was nearly shot by my own men

in the process, for they mistook me for an Englishman trying to escape.

Three of the enemy's wounded were discovered, two of
whom were able to walk, but the third had had his shin-bone
shattered by a bullet and lay in great pain behind a house.
As we put a first dressing on the wound he screamed in
agony under our clumsy, inexperienced fingers, but nevertheless he managed to stammer his "thank you."

Thus ended our second day in the great battle of Maubeuge,[3] and again we had driven the English out of their
fortified positions, although we had to attack across the
open.   It is true our losses had been heavy, but so had
theirs.   We had discovered that the British are brave and
doughty opponents, but our Army had inspired in them a
tremendous respect for the force of a German attack.   Captured English officers said that they had not believed it possible for us to storm across such open country.

Several of our companies had suffered very severe losses
through the enemy's artillery fire and the machine guns
which the English had very cleverly placed so as to catch
our troops in the flank.   There was desperate street and
house-to-house fighting, but the same regiment which had
met the English the day before succeeded in driving them
out at the left side of the village and in making many prisoners.

An incident which I witnessed characterizes the feeling
of our soldiers towards the English people.   A number of
prisoners were being escorted past us when our men shook
their clenched fists and rained down curses of the foulest
kind on Tommy Atkins, who marched past erect, with his
head up and a smile on his face.   When, later, French prisoners were brought in, I never observed any similar out-
bursts of a national hate which is only too well founded.

After the English had been thrown back along the whole
line we bivouacked in an open place in the village of F——.
The straw was already spread out, but nothing came of it.
We had only a two hours' rest, then started again; after a

---

[3] The German designation of what we call the battle of Mons.

long march we reached the village of W——, where we found passable sleeping quarters but nothing to eat.

On August 25th a period of tremendous forced marches began, which brought us in a few days across the Marne to the southeast of Paris. Our armies were close on the heels of the retreating enemy, the purpose of the General Staff being to push him away from Paris and hurl his armies back on to the line of fortresses (Belfort, Verdun, etc.) in the west. Unfortunately the scheme failed, for various reasons which I cannot and may not discuss in this place.

Nevertheless, that hurried rush through Northern France—a rush which called for the most tremendous exertions of both man and horse—will remain forever in my memory. In those breathless forced marches I did succeed, however, in keeping at least a list of the towns and villages which we passed through.

On August 25th our battalion was detailed to cover the light munitions column of the X Field Artillery Regiment, and on the same day we crossed the French frontier at 3.15 p. m. Only a small ditch marked the dividing line between the two countries, and our two companies crossed the little wooden bridge with loud hurrahs.

On the 26th, after a long march, we reached B——, and found decent quarters. The news that two English divisions had been annihilated aroused great enthusiasm; but the fact that I had received no news from my family for twenty-six days considerably damped my share of joy.[4] Furthermore, in those days of forced marches the food supply was exceedingly irregular. There was no bread to be had, although the field-kitchens worked fairly well. But it was quite impossible for the provision-columns to keep pace with us. I was exceedingly glad to find a large boiled ham in the village shop, and promptly requisitioned it.

On the following day we continued the pursuit of the English. In order to stop our advance they made another

[4] During the first weeks of the war the German authorities "held up" all correspondence between the German Armies and the folk at home in order to veil the mobilization and concentration of their Armies.

stand at Le Cateau, but, in spite of a most gallant defense, received a crushing defeat. Our regiment did not participate in this fight, but as we marched near to the battlefield, on our way southwards, we found numerous traces of the English retreat. The enemy artillery had left great heaps of their ammunition on both sides of the road, in order to save at least the guns. For quite an hour we were marching between these remarkable monuments of German victories and English defeats, and never have we enjoyed a higher degree of malicious joy [5] than during that day's march.

The countryside teemed with small parties of English troops who had got cut off from the main body. As it was easy for them to hide in the woods, and as one was never sure of their strength, a lot of valuable time was lost in rounding them up.

One of our cavalry patrols discovered a party of them near the village W——, and our battalion, with my company in front, was detached to clear them out. Very soon we got glimpses of the well-known English caps, and here it must be admitted that in making use of cover and in offering a stubborn defense the English performed wonders.

When we advanced against their first position we were received with rifle-fire, then they vanished, only to pop up in a second position. They were dismounted cavalrymen whose horses were hidden farther back, and, after decoying us to their third line, they mounted and fled. Between two of their trenches we found the dead horses of a patrol of Uhlans which they had apparently ambushed.

After a very fatiguing march we reached the townlet of B—— about 7 p. m., and were lucky to find some excellent beer in an inn by the market-place. Of course the place was packed with thirsty soldiers; the hostess and her daughter did splendid business that evening.

August 28th was another day of tremendous exertion. Our course led at some distance past St. Quentin, and this day brought our first fight with the French.

During the ensuing march to find our regiment again,

[5] *Schadenfreude ist die reinste Freude* (Malicious joy is the purest joy) is a well-known German saying.

we were amazed on entering a village to see the inhabitants welcoming us with shouts and other signs of jubilation. They had mistaken us for English, and it was exceedingly funny to see the transformation in their faces, and how quickly they disappeared into the houses, when they discovered their mistake.

I have forgotten where we slept after the terrible fighting and marching exertions of that day; but in my diary is the short notice: "Disgusting quarters." Next morning, by 7.30, we had reached the Somme. Our men were gradually getting accustomed to this race across France. The number of those who dropped out decreased from day to day; the feet got hardened, but our bodies, it is true, got thinner.

It is noteworthy that on these tremendous marches one suffered comparatively little from hunger. A swede or turnip from the next field, some chocolate, a cigarette, or a cigar, was often sufficient for a whole day. Further, the exultation of having defeated the enemy helped us to endure anything. . . .

September 1st, the anniversary of Sedan, was just as beautiful a day as forty-four years before. We crossed the Aisne in the early morning by Vic, and crossed a wide stretch of open country to a plateau in the hilly forest district of Villers Cotterets.

At the edge of this plateau we could hear our guns in front bombarding the village V——, and soon afterwards we heard heavy infantry fire—a sure sign that we were close to the enemy. As a matter of fact, our brigade-regiment was heavily engaged with the English rear guard. Unfortunately, we only came up in time to congratulate our comrades on their splendid success.

A forest fight is always a difficult affair, but the woods in France claim particularly heavy sacrifices, because the French allow the undergrowth to grow very thick. This forms a great obstacle to an advance, and at the same time affords the defender great advantages. The English had chosen a height commanding a turning in the road which led through this huge forest, and spent several days in strengthening the position. Yet our gallant brigade-regiment, in a fight of a few hours, had hurled them back and inflicted heavy losses on them.

When the last shots had echoed through the magnificent forest, several companies of our regiment were ordered to accompany the Field Artillery through the forest. At intervals of ten steps we marched by the side of the guns in case of a surprise attack. As we passed the scene of the fight which was just ended we met numbers of our stretcher-bearers and small groups of captured British. At the top of the height in the forest we saw a large number of the enemy's killed and seriously wounded.

Apparently the fight had raged hottest at the turn in the road, for just there the dead and wounded lay thick around, some 900 in all, in comparison to which our losses had been relatively light. . . .

The strain and exertion which we endured on September 3rd were almost beyond human capacity. From 6 a. m. till 10 p. m. we tramped along the dusty roads under a hot September sun, with only a couple of hours' rest at noon, till we reached the neighborhood of the Marne. Towards evening several hostile airmen circled above us at a great height.

At S——, in the Marne valley, we found passable quarters, and, after the terrific efforts of the day, sank exhausted into a deep sleep. Still these terrible marches did not bring us to the desired goal; we could not overtake the retreating enemy, and it was said that the French and English were marching to the southeast, towards Italy.

On Friday, September 4th, we crossed the Marne at 7.30 a. m. in beautiful autumn weather. But this delightful day was to be impressed on our memories by another tremendous march. We passed through the district where Blücher had been well thrashed by Napoleon a hundred years ago, and crossed the Morin (a tributary of the Marne) in the vicinity of Montmirail, reaching our quarters in the village, M——, just as darkness fell. Several officers, including myself, were in a miller's house at the exit of the village. A strong barricade of plows, wagons, etc., was erected, and a strong guard placed about 100 yards down the road.

We had not slept long when we were roused by heavy rifle fire. The guards had seen a troop of soldiers marching towards them in the moonlight and opened fire. Our companies were alarmed and awaited an attack which never came. The sentries asserted that they had shot a number of the enemy, and, as a matter of fact, we found several dead and wounded by the roadside, among them a French colonel.

The other companies in the village had also made some captures, among them being Turcos and some Zouaves, with their unpractical, theatrical uniforms. From the prisoners we learned that the English and French Armies, defeated at St. Quentin and Maubeuge, had fallen into great confusion. Portions of these armies had completely lost themselves and were wandering about aimlessly between the German columns advancing to the south. Again and again they collided with German troops on the right or left, till at last they did not know which way to turn.

The enemy, therefore, was more exhausted and suffering more than we were; added to this we were the victors, a fact which enabled us to endure all the demands put upon our energies. It is true that we suffered greatly in those days from want of food. In my diary is the remark: "Nothing to eat for three days; abjectly wretched."

BY GENERAL FREIHERR VON STEINACKER.

The Second German Army, under General von Bülow, advanced from Liége along the Meuse in the direction of Namur. His scouting cavalry detachments, on August 19th, encountered at Perwez, 18 k.m. north of the fortress, the 5th French cavalry division, and defeated it. Then the German artillerists, screened by their cavalry, succeeded unobserved in bringing their heavy guns up into position against Namur.

Austrian 30.5 cm. mortars joined the German 42cm. howitzers in opening fire on the fortress of Namur on the evening of August 20th. Just as General von Emmich had previously done at Liége, General von Gallwitz—who was entrusted with the siege of Namur, dispensed with a complete investment and formal attack, directing his guns against the nearest fort within range, Fort Maizeret, situated on the eastern side; against the northeastern forts, Marchevolette and Cognelée; and against the southeastern forts. Dug in, behind the batteries, lay the German infantry, ready to go forward. But only when the fire of the forts had noticeably slackened on the 22nd, and when, during the following night, the searchlights suspended their activity, was it possible for the infantry to work its way up closer to the fortress. On the 23rd, the cannons were also directed against the intermediate fortified places, and the garrison driven out; and when, at dawn of the 23rd, the artillery-fire once more set in with vigor, Fort Maizeret was evacuated, while the fire of Marchevolette and Cognelée subsided.

Through the breach thus made, the neighboring works could now also be attacked from the rear, the attacking infantry, however, being compelled to engage in a fierce struggle with the garrison. Nevertheless the forts were taken and the enemy thrown back into the city. The antiquated citadel was then bombarded from noon until half past three o'clock. Meanwhile the Belgian general staff had already vacated the fortress at 5 o'clock a. m., to be followed at noon by the garrison, consisting of Belgians and French, these effecting their retreat under the shelter of the western forts which continued fighting. On the 25th, these forts also surrendered, and Namur was in the possession of the Germans.

While the advance now proceeded in a southerly direction, measures for the prevention of attacks on the part of the enemy lying at Antwerp became necessary, in order that the rear communications might not be imperilled. On August 24th and 25th, King Albert, with five divisions, undertook an attack from the fortress in the direction of Mechelin-Villevorde in order to relieve the meanwhile hard-pressed French troops in the Sambre. A counter-attack on the part of the Germans resulted in a complete failure of the enterprise. Probably it was in order to support the above undertaking that the population of Louvain, on August 25th, organized a surprise attack, in all probability carefully planned with the coöperation of disguised Belgian soldiers. In cunning and cruelty it surpassed every known incident of this kind. It resulted in street-fighting which lasted 24 hours and ended with a partial destruction of the city.[1]

On the 22nd the armies along the entire front, Longwy-Mons, clashed. The Fifth French army, reinforced by Belgians who had not been able to reach Antwerp, advanced in the space between the Meuse and the Sambre and came upon the armies of Von Bülow and Von Hausen. In combats lasting several days, Mons and Charleroi being the scene of the hottest contention, the Allies were here forced back on French territory. The Germans followed them on August 27th, proceeding east of Maubeuge, the investment of that fortress being inaugurated by parts of Von Bülow's army.

In those same August days General Von Kluck began the battle with the left wing of the enemy forces, signalized by the first encounters with larger British bodies. On August 22nd the English occupied a position to the east and northeast of Maubeuge. On the evening of the 23rd, General French retired to a position between Valenciennes and Maubeuge, where, on the 24th, he became involved in vanguard conflicts with the advancing Germans. On the 25th the latter succeeded in forcing back the English troops to the line Cambrai-Landrecies-Le Cateau. Although General French could have occupied positions prepared there, he retreated precipitately to the line Vermand-St. Quentin-Ribemont, taking with him as reinforcement three French divisions. But the German cavalry was quicker. It succeeded in arresting the flood of the English retreat until the pursuing army corps could come up and gain the great victory of St. Quentin on the 27th.

[1] This is an impressive example of the official German insistance on the assertion that a considerable armed force attacked them in Louvain. The absurdity of this charge has been proven and reproven; but no wonder the German people still believe it.

THE DESTRUCTION OF LOUVAIN

THE CULMINATION OF GERMAN MILITARISM

AUGUST 25TH-27TH

LEON VAN DER ESSEN   GOTTLIEB VON JAGOW
MANUEL GAMARRA

We have already seen by what grim means the German High Command sought to stamp out the national spirit of the Belgians, by what devices the German soldiery were roused to the necessary pitch of rage to make them fit distributers of "frightfulness." We turn now to the particular resulting deed which most of all aroused the world to horror. In the black calendar of German repressive measures against Belgium, the single incident that will be most long remembered is the sacking of Louvain.

Louvain was a university city of about forty thousand inhabitants, a celebrated center of learning, noted for its Roman Catholic college, its seminary for priests, and above all for its ancient and much treasured library of over a quarter million of volumes. It would be impossible to conceive a less warlike town, or one more intelligently awake to the necessity of obedience to its captors, and to the suicidal uselessness of resistance. Moreover, Louvain had been for a week in possession of the Germans, and had suffered their insolence in quiet dignity. Then the Germans threw themselves suddenly on the helpless populace, slaughtering them by hundreds and burning the center of the city with most of its treasured ancient edifices and its unreplaceable library.

Probably we shall never know whether this destruction was deliberately planned by the German leaders so as to reduce the surviving Belgians to a more abject submission, or whether it was but an accidental consequence of their general policy of urging their soldiers to savagery. The weight of opinion leans rather to the first alternative, though Professor Van der Essen in his judicial summing up of the case, here given, inclines to the theory of a chance destruction. He as a noted leader of learning in Louvain itself is by far the best authority for picturing the catastrophe as a whole. His description is here supplemented by the official statement by Germany's Minister of State, explaining the matter as Germany declares she understood it. Then follows a brief statement by a neutral eye-witness and sufferer, a priest from Paraguay in South America, who was studying in Louvain at the time. See also the statement by General Steinacker in the preceding section.

C. F. H.

150

BY LEON VAN DER ESSEN

APART from requisitions and constant vexations, the Germans had committed no excesses in Louvain after their entry on August 19th. They continued to make hostages, who took it in turn to live at the town-hall and were responsible for the behavior of their fellow-citizens. Every day, in all the churches of the place, an urgent warning was given at the instance of the German authorities, telling the inhabitants to remain calm and promising them, in that case, not to take any more hostages.

The troops which reached the town the following week, however, seemed to be animated by a violently anti-clerical spirit. They followed the priests who showed themselves in public with buffoonery, insults, and even threats. They were also very excitable. One day, when a municipal official was taken through the town, preceded by soldiers with drums, and forced to read a proclamation, the Germans hurried up at once from all sides in the hopes of seeing a civilian executed.

The attack by the Belgian 2nd and cavalry divisions on the German positions between Malines and Louvain on the day of August 25th produced considerable excitement in the town. The gun-firing was distinctly heard, and became more violent in the course of the afternoon. It drew closer.

On this day Louvain was crammed with troops. Some 10,000 men had just arrived from Liege and were beginning to take up quarters in the town. A few hundred hussars were coming along the Malines road, covered with dust and leading their horses by the bridles. It was plain that the struggle was not going well for the Germans and that re-enforcements were necessary. At the town-hall dispatch-bearers followed one another quickly, bringing messages which made the members of the *Kommandantur* anxious. At 5 p. m. firing was heard of particular violence, and seemed to be extremely close to the town. At this moment some horsemen galloped through the streets, giving the alarm. At once officers and soldiers ran together and formed up in a disordered column. Motor-cars were coming and going every way, and ranging themselves up confusedly on the borders of the boulevards. Artillery and commissariat wagons were mixed up with them. Along the roads the horses, lashed till they bled, stiffened themselves and rattled along in a mad dash the guns which were going to reenforce the German troops on the Malines road. As if to raise the confusion to its height, carts were coming back full-tilt and in the greatest disorder from the field of battle, their drivers all excitement, with revolvers in their hands. After the departure of the hastily formed battalions a great silence fell upon the town. In view of the gravity of affairs, everybody had gone home, and soon nothing more was heard except the ever closer and more distinct sound of guns.

Suddenly, at 8 p. m., when twilight had already fallen and every one, in obedience to the rules of the occupying army, had to be already at home, a shot rang out, followed rapidly by two more, and then by a terrible fusillade. This was heard simultaneously at several points of the town, in the Boulevard de Tirlemont, at the Tirlemont Gate, in the Rue de Tirlemont, at the Brussels Gate, in the Rue and Place de la Station, in the Rues Léopold, Marie-Thérèse, and des Joyeuses-Entrées. With the cracking of rifles was mingled the sinister "tac-tac" of machine guns. The windows of the houses splintered under a hail of bullets, the doors and walls were riddled by the machine guns. In their cellars and other places where they had taken shelter on the first shots the inhabitants heard, through the din, the quick and crowding steps of the soldiers, the noise of whistles followed at once by volleys, and at times the heavy sound of a body falling to the ground. Those who had ventured to go up to their upper stories or attics soon saw the heavens reddened with a dreadful light. The Germans had set fire to several quarters of the town—the Chaussée and Boulevard de Tirlemont, the Place and Rue de la Station, and the Place du Peuple Soon, too, the Palais de Justice, the University with the celebrated Library, and the Church of St.Pierre were ablaze, systematically set on fire with fagots and chemicals. Through the streets the German soldiers were running like madmen, firing in every direction. Under the orders of their officers, they smashed in the doors of the houses, dragged the inmates from their hiding-places, with cries of *"Man hat geschossen! Die Zivilisten haben geschossen!"* (There has been firing! Civilians have fired!), and hurled hand-grenades and incendiary pastilles into the rooms. Several of the inmates were haled out and instantly shot. Those who tried to escape from their burning houses were thrust back into the flames or butchered like dogs by the soldiers, who were watching along the pavements, with their fingers on the triggers of their rifles. From several of the houses the officers had the objects of value taken out before giving the order to burn them. Every one who showed himself in the street was shot down. In the Rue de la Station an officer on horseback, bursting with rage, was directing the incendiaries.

In the morning certain of the inhabitants, who had passed the night in their cellars or their gardens, ventured to go out. They then learnt that the Germans pretended that a plot had been hatched amongst them, that there had been firing on the troops, and that the whole responsibility for what had happened was thrown on the civilians. From dawn squadrons of soldiers entered the houses, searched them from top to bottom, and turned out the inhabitants, forcing them towards the station. The poor wretches were compelled to run with their hands uplifted. They were given blows with the fists and with rifle-butts. Soon a large number of townspeople were collected in the Place de la Station, where dead bodies of civilians were lying on the ground. During the night a certain number of people had been shot, without serious inquiry. While they were being hustled along, the townspeople were searched by officers and soldiers, and their money was taken from them (some officers gave a receipt in return), as well as any objects of value. Those who did not understand an order, who did not raise their arms quick enough, or who were found carrying knives larger than a penknife, were at once shot. While these horrible scenes were enacted, the guns were constantly booming in the Malines direction, but the noise gradually grew more distant. In the streets numerous civilian corpses lay, and in some places corpses of German soldiers, who had been killed by one another in the night. Victims of panic and obsessed by the thought of francs-tireurs, they had fired on every group which they met in the darkness. Fights of this kind had taken place in the Rue de Bruxelles, near the station, in the Rue de Paris et Vieux-Marché, the Rue des Joyeuses-Entrées, near the canal, and in the Rue de Namur. On all sides lay dead horses. The Germans had unharnessed them from their wagons, driven them into the streets and killed them, to lend belief to an attack by civilians.

As the houses burned and the soldiers continued to loot and to drive the inhabitants down the streets, the townspeople who had been carried off to the station were brutally separated into two groups. The women and children were shut up in the station and the tram-shed, the men ranged up in the Place de la Station. The Germans selected by haphazard from among them the victims destined to be executed. Some of them had to lie on their stomachs, and were butchered by shots in the head, neck, or back. Others were collected in groups, surrounded by soldiers with fixed bayonets, and carried off to the outskirts of the town, to the accompaniment of curses, threats, and blows. They were forced to march and countermarch through Herent, Thildonck, Rotselaer, Campenhout, etc. Wherever they went the prisoners saw houses in flames and corpses of civilians stretched on the road or charred by fire. In the country district of Louvain the Germans had committed the same excesses as in the town itself. In order to terrorize them, these groups of prisoners were hunted along the roads, without any precise object except to drive them mad. Sometimes they were made to stop, and a mock shooting took place. They were forced to run, to lift up their arms, etc. Those who fell through fatigue or attempted to escape were slaughtered. When the mournful procession passed through a village they found their ranks swollen by numbers of inhabitants of these places, who had already spent the night in the church. At last, after having thus wandered over the country for hours, several of these groups were taken

back to Louvain and put on board cattle-trucks.   Piled on
to these like cattle, old men, women, children, and able-
bodied men were dispatched to Germany.   We cannot stop
to describe the tortures which the deported had to endure on
the journey and the cruelties inflicted on them by the fanatical inhabitants of the towns through which they passed.
Some were taken to Cologne and exhibited to the crowd;
others were sent as far as Münster, where they were interned.

During these explosions of violence on the part of the
troops there was no respect of persons.   Dutch, Spaniards,
South Americans pleaded their neutral status in vain; they
were jeered at and subjected to the same outrages as the
Belgians.   The flags of foreign nations floating over certain
houses were no protection to them.   The Spanish *pédagogie*
in the Rue de la Station was burnt, and in the house of Professor Noyons, of Dutch nationality, a pile of fagots was
lighted.

Meanwhile those of the inhabitants who had not fled
towards the station, or who had not been driven in that direction, were running madly about the streets.   A large
number took refuge in the Hospital of Saint-Thomas, in the
neighborhood of the Institut Supérieur de Philosophie.
About 9 a. m. on Wednesday, August 26th, the shooting
ceased and quiet temporarily returned.   A picket of soldiers
traversed the streets, taking an unarmed policeman with
them to announce that able-bodied men must come together
in certain places to help to put out the flames.   The civil
guards were specially invited to repair, in civilian clothes, to
the St.-Martin barracks.   All who obeyed the summons
were made prisoners and taken, some to the station, bound
for Germany, others to the neighboring villages, where they
swelled the troops of prisoners already there.   Several
groups were taken to Campenhout in particular.   After
spending the night there, insulted and threatened with death
all the time, they were ordered the next day or the day after
to Louvain and shut up in the Riding School.   There atrocious scenes were witnessed.   Women went mad and children died.

On this Wednesday the soldiers started again to fire at intervals, to plunder, and to burn. They could be seen strolling about the town, drunk, laden with bottles of wine, boxes of cigars, and objects of value. The officers let them do it, roared with laughter, or set the example themselves. The Vice-Rector of the University and the Prior of the Dominicans were led through the town, escorted by soldiers, and forced to stop at certain spots to read a German proclamation warning the people "not to fire again upon the soldiers." A gloomy comedy, indeed! In several places soldiers were seen entering the houses and the gardens, firing shots, so as to prolong the mystification and the looting. Some walked along firing phlegmatically into the air. If a house was of fairly good appearance, a group of soldiers would assail it with shouts of "There was firing from here," and at once began to loot.

On the third day, Thursday, August 27th, some soldiers went through the town in the morning, announcing to the terrified population that Louvain was to be bombarded at noon and that every one must leave at once. Often they added special instructions to go to the station. Those who obeyed these orders were put on to cattle-trucks and sent to join their hapless fellow-citizens in Germany. Others, better advised, took refuge at Heverlé, the property of the Duke of Aremberg, a member of the Prussian House of Lords, who was serving in the German army, and there they were not molested.

Along the Tirlemont and Tervueren roads rolled the wretched flood of fugitives, old men, women, children, invalids, nuns, priests, in a rout which cannot be described. German soldiers followed, compelling the unfortunates to raise their arms, striking them and insulting them. The fury of the Germans raged particularly against the priests. On the Tirlemont road several of them were arrested, taken to a piggery, and stripped of everything. They were accused of having incited the people to revolt, and there was talk of shooting them. One officer, more humane than the rest, had them released. The scenes were the same on the Tervueren road. There the Rector of the University, several ecclesiastical professors, the President of the American Seminary, and a number of Jesuits were treated in a disgraceful fashion and penned in a field. A young Jesuit, Father Dupierreux, on whom was found a diary with notes on the war, some of them very unflattering to the invaders, was shot before the eyes of his colleagues. Certain of these priests were taken to Brussels, where they were at last released. The Rector of the University, some professors and monks were set free through the intervention of a Dutchman, M. Grondys, who was present at the sack of Louvain.

At 11 o'clock on this Thursday, August 27th, the town was as dead. Nothing could be heard to break the profound silence except the sinister crackle of houses on fire. Then, the inhabitants having disappeared, the regular sack began. There was no more talk of bombardment. The sack was organized methodically like the burning, which also continued at the same time. The doors of wardrobes and drawers of desks were smashed with rifle-butts. Safes were broken open with burglars' tools. Every soldier took his pick amid the heap of furniture spread over the floor. Silver-plate, linen, works of art, children's toys, mechanical instruments, pictures—everything was taken. Whatever could not be carried off was broken. The cellars were emptied. Then the looters finished up by depositing their filth in all the corners.

This lasted eight days. Every time fresh troops reached Louvain, they rushed on their prey. Recalling his entry and his stay at Louvain on August 29th, a Landsturm soldier from Halle wrote in his diary: "The battalion . . . arrive dragging along with it all sorts of things, particularly bottles of wine, and many of the men were drunk. . . . The battalion set off in close order for the town, to break into the first houses they met, to plunder—I beg pardon, I mean to requisition—wine and other things too. Like a pack let loose, each one went where he pleased. The officers led the way and set a good example."

And Gaston Klein, the soldier in question, concludes: "This day has inspired me with a contempt I could not describe."

The burning continued, simultaneously with the sack, down to September 2nd. On that day the last houses were set on fire in the Rue Marie-Thérèse. In the evening drunken German soldiers were still dragging to the station heavy bags full of things stolen in the Rue Léopold.

On the afternoon of Friday, August 28th, the Germans committed a particularly odious crime. From August 20th the little town of Aerschot had been abandoned to the mercy of all the troops passing through. The parish priest of Gelrode had been put to death there in barbarous circumstances, and the burning of houses and terrorization of the remaining inhabitants had gone on. On the morning of August 28th a large group of people from Aerschot was carried off in the direction of Louvain. When they reached the Place de la Station they were made to wait, being told that they were to be put on a train and deported to Germany. While the human herd stood there, suddenly, without motive, some enraged soldiers began to fire into the mass. Some were killed and wounded, including women and children. Certain German soldiers, who took two of the wounded to the Hospital of St.-Thomas, could not themselves conceal the disgust inspired in them by this barbarous act.

Meanwhile some energetic citizens, among whom was M. Nerinckx, professor of the University, had somehow managed to form a new municipal council, with the help of some members of the old council who had escaped the massacre or had returned after the early days of terror. By their firm attitude they were at last able to obtain from the commandant of the town the cessation of all acts of disorder on the part of the troops.

Such is the story of the sack of Louvain. What was the motive of it? We shall not stop to consider the odious and lying accusation made against the inhabitants by the military authorities and adopted by the Emperor himself in his famous telegram to the President of the United States. It has been reduced to nothing by the evidence of disinterested neutrals and by the inquiries of an Austrian priest, made on the spot.

In Louvain itself the following explanation is given. On the night of August 25th, at the moment when soldiers and vehicles were coming back in disorder from Malines, some shots rang out. The German soldiers in the town imagined, some that the enemy was coming, others that the civilians were beginning an attack. The former fired on their own comrades, taking them for Belgian or French soldiers; the latter riddled the fronts of the houses with bullets. The supposition is that there was a mistake, and then a panic.

It must be the truth with regard to a great number of German soldiers. We have already said that the soldiers quartered in Louvain seemed very nervous, that the troops who flocked back into the town during the battle were very excited; and, on the other hand, it is established that during the night several groups of Germans fired on one another in the streets. In such a state of mind, constantly haunted by visions of francs-tireurs, the German soldiers were very liable to sudden panic. A single shot was sufficient to produce it. We have the histories of Aerschot, Liege, Namur, and above all Andenne, to guide us on the subject.

Now, the evidence of witnesses establishes that a few moments before the fusillade began a shot was heard, followed immediately by two others. By whom was this shot fired? That will probably never be known. Was it fired by an unnerved sentry, by a drunken soldier, by a civilian? Considering the numerous warnings given to the townspeople, the threats of the Germans themselves, the excited state of the troops returning to the town, and the numbers of the soldiers in the garrison, it is very unlikely that a civilian would have been guilty of this act of folly, knowing that thereby he was exposing the whole population to nameless horrors. The fate of Aerschot was in every one's memory. Those events were recent.

If the first shot was fired by a German soldier, did that soldier act with the intention of starting a catastrophe? Was he obeying superior orders, and was he giving the signal for the carrying out of a German military "plot"?

Some have replied to the German accusation with a

charge of premeditation on the part of the invaders. Louvain must have been condemned in advance, they say, and the attack of the Belgian troops on August 25th can only have hastened the execution of the plan.

History, while rejecting the German accusation, will demand serious proofs before accepting the victims' counteraccusation of German premeditation. Doubtless the German methods of terrorization do not entirely exclude the possibility of systematic and premeditated destruction of a town. But did this premeditation exist positively in this one particular case of Louvain? That is the whole question.

After carefully examining the mass of documents within our reach, we believe we may say that, in the present state of the evidence, it is impossible to consider proved the charge of premeditation with regard to Louvain—premeditation signifying to us the plan conceived long beforehand of giving Louvain up to the flames.

No doubt there are singular facts which, at first sight, seem to justify the defenders in their hypothesis of German premeditation. The fusillade breaking out almost simultaneously at several points some distance apart, the several centers of incendiarism started at the same time, the presence of a company of incendiaries armed with up-to-date appliances, the luminous signals said to have been sent up a few moments before the fusillade began, certain remarks let drop by soldiers or officers, the removal of the German wounded on the eve of the disaster, the warnings given long in advance to the inhabitants living in places 20 to 30 kilometers away from Louvain by soldiers or officers—the whole setting of the drama, taken in its entirety, cannot fail to be suspicious.

Still, when one examines the weight of these facts, one by one, many of them lose their conclusive force. The data are not precise enough or are insufficiently established; the facts and the words themselves seem capable of different interpretations.

On the other side, certain facts seem to negative premeditation, in the sense which we attach to the word. It is established that many soldiers, and even officers, believed for a moment that "the French were there." On the hypothesis of a preconceived plan, would they not have understood that the first shots were the signal for the massacre? At the start, and in the night, the Germans fired upon one another; there can be no doubt of that. This can be easily understood on the hypothesis of a panic, less easily on that of a German plot.

We therefore exclude, provisionally, the supposition of a German plot, conceived long before its execution. It does not seem to us proved by the documents published so far.

What we do not exclude is the hypothesis of premeditation on the part of the soldiers. In the state of excitement in which they were, particularly those coming back in disorder from Malines, they may have fired a shot, knowing that "the rest" would follow.[1] This story was repeated so often in other places that we have the right to apply it hypothetically in the case of Louvain.

There is more. On the night of the 25th and the following days, certain soldiers and non-commissioned officers fired shots,[2] so as to have a pretext for continuing the pillage. Many of the soldiers and officers may have believed, at the beginning, for a few moments, that they were being attacked by the enemy entering the town or that a civilian attack was taking place. But this mistake cannot have lasted long. It remains established that, in cold blood and without any idea of a serious inquiry, the military authorities persisted in the error and subjected Louvain to eight days' martyrdom, without raising a finger to stop the orgy. Whether the responsibility falls upon Major Von Manteuffel or must be referred back to the highest personalities in the Empire does not matter. It is the prolonged sack of the town, without previous inquiry, which makes what has been called "the crime of Louvain" so enormous.

[1] There were at Louvain soldiers of the 165th Infantry Regiment, which committed the worst excesses in the villages around Liege.
[2] At Professor Verhelst's house; before the houses of Professors Dupriez and Noel; before the Hospital of St. Thomas.—Declaration of the Rector of the University in regard to the Rue de Namur.

Such an inquiry was possible. The example of Huy proves that. On August 25th Major Von Bassewitz, commandant of that place, published the following order of the day :—

August 25, 1914.

Last night shooting took place. It has not been proved that the inhabitants of the town were still in possession of arms. Nor has it been proved that the civil population took part in the shooting; on the contrary, it would seem that the soldiers were under the influence of alcohol and opened fire under an incomprehensible fear of an enemy attack.

The conduct of the soldiers during the night produces a shameful impression, with a few exceptions.

When officers or non-commissioned officers set fire to houses, without permission or order from the commandant, or in the present case from the senior officer, and when they encourage the troops by their attitude to burn and loot, it is an act of the most regrettable kind.

I expect severe instructions to be given generally as to the attitude towards the life and property of the civil population. I forbid firing in the town without officers' orders.

The bad conduct of the troops has had as its result the serious wounding of a non-commissioned officer and a soldier by German shots.

VON BASSEWITZ, Major,
Commandant.

If this had been the state of mind of the military authorities in Louvain, it is certain that there would not have been the horrors which we have described above. We cannot help thinking that the military authorities, when once the machine was accidentally thrown out of gear, were not at all annoyed. They took care not to give the necessary sign to avert the consequences.

How many victims were there at Louvain? We do not know. The Capuchin Father Valère Claes himself discovered 108, of whom 96 had been shot, the others having perished in the ruins of the houses. In his Pastoral Letter,

Cardinal Mercier speaks of 176 persons shot or burnt in the whole neighborhood of Louvain and the adjoining communes. With regard to material destruction, 1,120 houses were burnt in the area of the commune of Louvain, 461 in the adjacent commune of Kessel-Loo, and 95 in that of Héverlé, these three parts making up the urban district of Louvain. In Louvain itself, apart from private houses, fire destroyed the Church of St.-Pierre, the central University buildings, the Palais de Justice, the Académie des Beaux-Arts, the theater, and the School of Commercial and Consular Science belonging to the University.

The Church of St.-Pierre was methodically set on fire, as was the University Library. A Josephite Father called the attention of the officer in command of the incendiaries to the fact that the building which he was about to set on fire was the Library. The officer replied, *"Es ist Befehl"* (It is ordered). It was then about 11 p. m. on Tuesday, August 25th.

This was not the end, however, of the excesses committed by the Germans during the first sortie of the Belgian troops from Antwerp. The region round Louvain and the villages situated between this town and Malines were engulfed in the "punishment." Bueken, Gelrode, Herent, Wespelaer, Rymenam, Wygmael, Tremeloo, Werchter, Wesemael, Wackerzeel, Blauwput, Thildonck, Rillaer, Wilsele, Linden, Betecom, Haecht were partly burnt and plundered, a number of the inhabitants being shot. Others were dragged along for many hours, loaded with insults, used as shields against the enemy's troops during the battle, and finally chased in the direction of the Belgian lines. Some were thrown into wells after being horribly illtreated. Here, too, the German soldiers were bitter against the priests. The Rev. Father Van Holm, a Capuchin, and Father Vincent, a Conventual; Lombaerts, parish priest of Boven-Loo; de Clerck, parish priest of Bueken, and Van Bladel, parish priest of Herent, were killed, as also were a Josephite Father and a Brother of Mercy. The parish priests of Wygmael and Wesemael were shamefully treated. Finally, in this neighborhood the Germans committed the same outrages against women and young girls as in the neighborhood of Hofstade, Sempst, etc. Crimes of a Sadic character were also found. Neither old men, women, nor children were respected.

BY GOTTLIEB VON JAGOW

Official Statement by the German Minister of State, Addressed to the United States Government

Long ago the Belgian Government had organized an insurrection of the people against the invasion of the enemy. Some stores of arms had been established, and upon each gun was the name of the citizen who was to use it.[3] Since the Hague Conference it has been recognized, at the request of the little powers, that an insurrection of the people is in conformity with international law, if weapons are carried openly and the laws of war respected. Such an insurrection, however, could be organized only to combat an enemy who invaded the country. At Louvain, on the other hand, the city had already surrendered and the population had then abandoned all resistance. The city was occupied by German troops.

Nevertheless the population attacked from all sides the German garrison and the troops who were in the act of entering the city, by opening upon them a murderous fire. Because the attitude of the population was obviously pacific these troops arrived at Louvain by railroad and autos. In the present case, then, there is no question of a measure of defense in conformity with international law, nor an admissible ruse of war; but it was a traitorous attack on the part of the civilian population. This attack is the more unjustifiable because it has been proved that it had been planned long before and was to have taken place at the same time as the sortie from Antwerp. The weapons were not carried openly. Some women and young girls took part in the combat, and gouged out the eyes of the wounded.

[3] Belgian authorities claim in refutation of this charge that these arms had been handed in by the civil population in response to disarmament proclamations, and that the names were those of the owners who had surrendered the guns.

The barbarous acts of the Belgian people in almost all the territories occupied by the German troops have not only justified the most severe reprisals on the part of the German military authorities but have even compelled the latter to order them for safeguarding the troops. The intensity of the resistance of the population is proved by the fact that it took our troops twenty-four hours to overcome the attacks by the inhabitants of Louvain.

In the course of these combats the city of Louvain has been destroyed in large part by a conflagration which broke out after the explosion of a convoy of benzine, and this explosion was occasioned by shots fired during the battle. The Imperial Government is the first to deplore this unfortunate result, which was in no way intentional. Nevertheless, because of the acts of the francs-tireurs, it was impossible to avoid such an outcome. Moreover, any one who knows the conciliatory character of the German soldier could not seriously assert that he has been led to act in such a manner without serious provocation. Under these circumstances the Belgian people, who respect neither right nor law, bear all the responsibility, in conjunction with the Belgian Government, which, with a criminal nonchalance, has given to the people orders contrary to international law by inciting them to resistance, and which, in spite of reiterated warnings by the German authorities, did nothing, after the capture of Liege, to induce the people to take a pacific attitude.[4]

[4] As to the general charges here iterated without detail, they are fully refuted in the preceding article on "Belgium's Agony." The specific "francs-tireurs" [free shooters, civilians] charge is perhaps best answered in the protest to the German authorities, issued by the Bishop of Namur. It says, in part:

"We assert, with all the inhabitants of our villages, without exception, and with the whole Belgian population, that the *story of the Belgian francs-tireurs is a legend, an invention, a calumny.*

"It is evident that the German army trod the Belgian soil and carried out the invasion with the preconceived idea that it would meet with bands of this sort, a reminiscence of the war of 1870. But German imagination will not suffice to create that which does not exist.

"*There never existed a single body of francs-tireurs in Belgium.*

"This is so certain that we have no hesitation in solemnly challenging the German authorities to prove the existence of a single band

BY MANUEL GAMARRA

Testimony of a Neutral Eye-witness, a Paraguayan Priest Studying
at Louvain

The vanguard of the Army of Von Kluck occupied Louvain, without striking a blow, on the 18th of August at noon. The first error to rectify is the following: Louvain was not

of francs-tireurs formed either before or after the invasion of the territory.

"*No 'isolated instance' even is known of civilians having fired upon the troops,* although there would have been no occasion for surprise if any individual person had committed an excess. In several of our villages the population was exterminated because, as the military authorities alleged, a major had been killed or a young girl had attempted to kill an officer, and so forth. . . .

"Let us however accept for one moment, not by way of admission, but of supposition, this hypothesis of a legitimate repression of *francs-tireurs.* We assert that it will be made clear, by the examination of each particular instance of the destruction of a village and the extermination of the civilians, that the punishment is so greatly out of proportion to the alleged crime that it could not be justified by any kind of argument. Such are the events that happened at Andenne, Tamines, Dinant, Leffe, Neffe, Spontin, Surice, Ethe, Tintigny, Houdemont, and many other places, *events so abominable that they will one day rouse the conscience of the whole world,* and that one day a sense of justice in Germany itself will stigmatize them in scathing terms when she has a true knowledge of the facts, and has recovered her equanimity.

"Further, still on the supposition that what took place, in certain parts at least, was merely the repression of *francs-tireurs,* what civilized mind would dare to justify, on behalf of soldiers, the following acts: *the infliction in some cases of blows and wounds, atrocities of all kinds, barbarities and sanguinary methods, cruel and infamous treatment, on mere hostages or prisoners; the dispatch of the wounded, the shooting of peaceful and unarmed civilians, pillage by armed men to an extent almost incredible, the employment of priests, young people, old men, women and children as a shield against the bullets and shells of the enemy; the imputation to the civil population of acts of war for which Belgian or French soldiers were legitimately responsible, and the severe punishment inflicted on the population in consequence thereof; summary executions by shooting, without any form of inquiry or regular sentence, extermination of entire families and even villages; incendiarism in more than 200 villages of the two provinces, independently of the destruction caused by the fighting; moral torture inflicted on persons of weak constitution and sometimes upon whole populations. Outrage and murders of women, young girls, and children at the breast. . . .*

"Now these crimes are so numerous that one or another of them

bombarded. There was no fighting, except in the direction of Tirlemont and Dieste to the north and south of Louvain. The destruction of this town was carried out deliberately by a company of incendiarists seven days after its occupation. The commander of the place who gave the orders was named Manteuffel, and it was the 52nd Regiment of Infantry which was established there during these early days.

The burning began at half-past seven in the evening of August 25th. Whilst the town was burning on all sides the Germans shot the unfortunate people as they fled from their burning houses. It was a night of unimaginable horror. Most of the inhabitants, however, succeeded in escaping by the courtyards and gardens. I myself succeeded in doing so when, about midnight, the houses adjoining the one which I occupied in Juste Lipse Street began to blaze.

The following morning I was taken prisoner and conducted to the station at about 10 o'clock.

With me was a Spaniard, Father Catala, Spanish Vice-Consul, who had been for some little time principal of a college in Station Street, which had been burnt down, in spite of the Spanish flag flying over its door. The first group of prisoners, from 70 to 80 in number, included some distinguished persons, advocates, medical men, etc. Five of us

and often all of them at once, have been committed in hundreds of our villages.

"An impression of dismay and horror provoked by these barbarities remains with those of our population who have lived through these terrible events and have suffered on account of them in a way which it is impossible to describe. It is, they say, a *monstrous war,* carried on, not against soldiers, but against *unarmed civilians.* They have one and all forgotten the events, horrible as they are in themselves, of the war properly so called, and remember only the sufferings during less than a week by an entire population unarmed, terror-stricken, and given up to the mercy of ferocious soldiers. It has been said (but can it be true?) that the number of civilians killed is not far behind that of soldiers who have fallen in battle. It is astonishing indeed that there have not been still more victims, and we cannot but admire the ingenuity with which the inhabitants of such localities as Dinant, Tamines, Spontin, Houdemont and numerous villages lying between the Sambre and the Meuse escaped to the full extent of the destruction to which they had been doomed.

"Millions of eye-witnesses are ready to affirm these facts upon oath as soon as the regular committee of inquiry shall have been appointed."

were foreigners, Father Catala, three young Spaniards, and myself. We were placed in files of four, surrounded by soldiers, who insulted us and treated us in a brutal manner. At the beginning of the Station Street there was a corpse partially carbonized. In the corridors of the station were lying fifteen or twenty bodies of civilians who had been shot. The town, especially in this quarter, was enveloped in smoke and flames. These were days of indescribable terror.

I had in my hand my passport proving my foreign nationality. I was looking for a means of saving myself from the death that I felt was threatening, for the German soldiers, as well as officers were, at that moment, no longer men but ferocious beasts. God alone could, by a miracle, save us. They did not wish to hear anything about my passport. Every time that I tried to prove my innocence and my American nationality the officers threatened and struck me. When I saw that all was useless I resigned myself and prepared for death. My companions did the same. . . .

Towards eleven o'clock they began to conduct us towards Malines, in the environs of which fighting was going on between Belgians and Germans. To the right and left of the road everything was in flames. At Héront, five kilometers from Louvain, I saw in a corner of the wall the body of a little girl of 12 or 13 years of age burned alive. We were terribly ill-treated during the whole of the journey whether we were made to run or to stop, or to walk slowly, it was all by blows with a saber, the butt end of a rifle or a lance. We were kicked and spat upon, and, O my God! to what insolence we were subjected! I supported a sick old man who dragged himself along with the help of my arm in order to escape death, for if he had stopped he would have been pierced by a bayonet or shot by a bullet. We glanced towards one another from time to time in a state of stupefaction at such barbarity. At length we arrived in a field nine or ten kilometers from Louvain. There a halt was made and an officer told us that we were about to be shot. When I repeated to him that I was a South American, as was proved by my passport, he cried out, with fire flashing from his eyes, that it was I who would be shot the first "because I had kept concealed in my church mitrailleuses and other arms." He ordered me to hold my tongue. They then tied our hands behind our backs with our own handkerchiefs. The soldiers drew themselves up in line and every preparation was made for our execution, and we were left there for a quarter of an hour.

Presently we were divided again into groups, with our hands still bound, with the soldiers drawn up in front of us as shooting parties, and we were then made to proceed through the fields from village to village towards the Belgian lines.

At nightfall we arrived at Campenhout, where we passed the night imprisoned in the church where fighting was going on all around. The following day Father Catala, the three young Spaniards and myself were set at liberty.

The remaining inhabitants of Louvain were no better treated. Many were conducted as prisoners into the interior of Germany (Munsterlagen). Several thousands were dragged as far as Tirelmont. Thousands of others passed a whole week in the woods, living only on potatoes which they gathered in the fields. During August 27th, 28th and 29th Louvain remained denuded of its inhabitants and the Germans seized the occasion to pillage systematically house after house, everything in fact which had not been burned, so that the families which subsequently returned, if their dwellings were still standing, found nothing but the walls.

What the Germans have done at Louvain, and in the whole of Belgium, is indescribable. A narrative of these events would fill volumes. As for myself, since God has saved my life, I am pleased to have been able to be in a position to see and verify all those iniquitous doings which cover with opprobrium German militarism, of which many other foreigners have been witnesses, if indeed they have not been the victims, and amongst them South Americans, Uruguayans, Brazilians, Colombians, etc., who are able to testify, like myself, to the truth.

TANNENBERG: RUSSIA'S FIRST DISASTER

THE INVASION OF EAST PRUSSIA AND ITS BRILLIANT REPULSE BY HINDENBURG

AUGUST 26TH-SEPTEMBER 1ST

GABRIEL HANOTAUX   GENERAL VON HINDENBURG
GENERAL BASIL GOURKO

The suddenness and completeness of the Russian defeat at Tannenberg gave to that battle a widespread fame, causing it to stand out more prominently than many another of greater size and more important result. The unexpected swiftness of the Russian invasion of East Prussia at the opening of the War caused something very like a panic in the streets of Berlin, and a corresponding rejoical in the Allies' lands. The Russians, however, had never intended this advance to progress very far into Germany. In fact, it was undertaken with troops singularly unprepared. Only the complete unexpectedness of the move gave it an even temporary success.

To check it without disarranging their French campaign the German Staff dispatched into East Prussia Von Hindenburg, a general who had been previously retired from service, partly because of age, partly because of disfavor at Court. The story is told that during one of the "practice campaigns" with which German generals drilled in time of peace, Hindenburg, a native of East Prussia, had been placed in command of one army there, and pitted against another under command of the Kaiser himself. Hindenburg had been so uncourtly as to take full advantage of his intimate knowledge of the region, and to defeat his august opponent with staggering completeness. That had caused his retirement then, and his recall now in the hour of East Prussia's need.

He defeated his Russian opponents with apparent ease, though it should be noted that Von Ludendorff, his chief lieutenant, has described this first Hindenburg success as a gamble. He declares that the German leaders took a desperate chance; they left one Russian army, under General Rennenkampf, wholly unopposed, and hurled all their forces at General Samsonof's army. Had Rennenkampf advanced, he would have destroyed the Germans. His delay was at one time attributed to treason; but the charge remains unproven.

Nevertheless, Hindenburg's every step against the Russians impresses us as the move of a master playing a game against the merest beginners—and a merciless master. He spares the beginners not at all; he exacts from them the utmost penalties of defeat. At Tannenberg the Russians were driven into the vast and often bottomless swamps of the region, where they floundered helplessly or sank to suffocation beneath the surface. Their cries of surrender were un-heeded. The German troops were ordered to continue firing upon them, and they were massacred by thousands. We have included in our account an apparently authentic letter published in Germany, in which a German participant in the slaughter cries out against the horror of it.

Despite the quick repulse of this invasion of East Prussia, it caused the most extensive ravaging which any German territory received during the entire War. When the world exclaimed in protest against the "frightfulness" deliberately employed in Belgium and Serbia, German apologists spoke of equal horrors as having been perpetrated by the Russians in East Prussia. Convincing proof of such charges will probably never be forthcoming. We may fairly conclude that there were individual cases of brutality and even murder; yet upon the whole the Russians during the first years of the War proved themselves a kindly foe, quick to fraternize with a defeated enemy. And even if we accept the tales of Russian barbarity at their worst, it was never an official barbarity, like that of Germany, originating at headquarters. The Russian officers did their best to restrain their ignorant troops not to delude them into greater excesses. It is a vivid commentary upon the German state of mind, that the Germans should feel their own excesses justified by the excuse that the less civilized Russians had thus imitated the German savagery and had proved equally murderous.

Hindenburg's own account of the battle is here given as told in his autobiography. The story is also quoted from Gabriel Hanotaux, the most renowned of contemporary French historians. The Russian viewpoint is then given by the Russian general best fitted to attempt it, General Gourko. He was chief of staff and afterward commander-in-chief upon the Russian western front.

C. F. H.

BY GABRIEL HANOTAUX

THE German military chiefs applied the doctrines of encirclement in the east also; but there they won success with them. The campaign in East Prussia presents a positive proof that fully confirms the negative proof of the battle on the French frontier.

Two Russian armies had invaded East Prussia; one, commanded by Rennenkampf, followed the great railway that binds Petrograd to Berlin by way of Gumbinnen, Insterburg, Allenstein, Eylau, on toward Thorn on the Vistula. While besieging or masking Königsberg, Elbing, Dantsic, it counted upon occupying East Prussia and there awaiting the success of the general maneuver aimed against Austria by the Grand Duke Nicholas.

The other Russian army came from Warsaw and the

banks of the Narew.   It advanced from south to north in
order to march, like the other, upon the Vistula in the direction of Dantsic, there to join Rennenkampf's army and
clear the way to Berlin.

The preliminary mission intrusted to the two armies of
the north was singularly facilitated by the fact that Germany, not foreseeing so rapid a mobilization of the first
Russian armies, had left on that frontier only three active
army corps and some reserve formations.   The two Russian
armies—separately weaker than the German army—would
be much stronger than it when once united.   Unfortunately, they were not in close communication with each
other, being separated by the almost impenetrable region of
the Masurian Lakes.

The first commander of the German army, von Prittwitz, advanced on the frontier before Rennenkampf; he
was beaten at Gumbinnen on August 20th.   Rennenkampf
advanced as far as Insterburg on the railway north of the
Masurian Lakes; he installed his army in East Prussia and
threatened Königsberg.   Meanwhile Samsonof, coming
from the Narew, was debouching to the southwest of the
lakes and skirting them with the object of joining Rennenkampf near Osterode-Eylau.

The German army, which was still facing Rennenkampf
near Gumbinnen, saw its communications menaced by this
advance of Samsonof.   It beat a precipitate retreat, and
von Prittwitz believed he had no choice but to retire behind
the Vistula.   The population was fleeing as far as Berlin.

There was a great sensation in the headquarters of the
German General Staff, which had staked everything on the
western front, and which at that moment (August 20th-
22nd) still had some painful fighting to do at Charleroi, in
the Ardennes, and on the Lorraine frontier, so that it did
not feel any too sure of victory.

It was in this hour of peril that a dispatch, dated at
Namur, went to seek at Hanover in a tavern where he was
smoking his pipe and drinking his habitual bock an old,
retired General, Hindenburg, and named him at one stroke
the commander of the army on the eastern front.   For his

second in command they gave him Ludendorff, who, leaving Namur with all necessary instructions, came to seek him at Hanover. The two men took the train together in the night of August 22nd, studying their maps on the journey, formulating their plan, and writing their orders.

Far from thinking of retiring behind the Vistula, Hindenburg and Ludendorff decided to resume the offensive against the Russian armies, attacking them separately while they were still divided by the Masurian Lakes. Hindenburg first turned his attention to Samsonof's army, which had come from Warsaw and the Narew, and which most directly menaced his communications. Samsonof was an impetuous man; having excellent troops, he was full of confidence, and was marching straight ahead; he was just the man to fall headforemost into the trap that his enemy was setting for him.

This was the trap. Hindenburg arranged his troops in a vast semicircle formed by the lines of hills on each side of Allenstein, the one toward Usdau on the west and the other toward Willenberg on the east. The Twenty-second German Army Corps, at the entrance of the semicircle, at Soldau, on the railway from Warsaw, received an order to engage Samsonof's army, and to retreat while fighting, thus luring it as far as possible into the curve of the German lines. At the proper moment the two sectors of the semicircle were to close in upon Samsonof, envelop and crush him; it was Schlieffen's maneuver, the extension of the front and the action of both wings.

Samsonof entered the semicircle in pursuit of the Twenty-second German Corps, the Twenty-second fell back, Samsonof followed, forcing it westward, and finally establishing his headquarters at Allenstein. He believed he had won a victory. His right, finding no enemy forces before it, extended itself northward and reached the Petrograd-Berlin railway near Rastenburg.

The position of Samsonof may be compared to that of the classic runner, with his right hand stretched high in the air toward Rennenkampf, the body in full career, but the left foot delaying in the rear toward Usdau. It was exactly at this moment when Samsonof was hurling himself forward, that Hindenburg, beginning the real maneuver, seized him by that left foot. A German force, coming partly from Thorn, and reënforced by all the units available, appeared at Usdau and threw itself against the communicating lines of Samsonof in the direction of Soldau.

Samsonof failed to grasp the meaning of this movement, and went on pursuing his idea of breaking the German front at the middle. He hurled himself against the Hohenstein-Tannenberg lines, which Hindenburg had garnished with his heavy guns and his best troops. The latter withstood the shock of Samsonof's desperate assaults, which were renewed for three days—August 26th-29th.

Meanwhile Hindenburg's extreme right wing continued its turning movement, gained the first advantage at Usdau, and marched next upon Soldau with the object of closing the door on Samsonof at that point. In the other direction Mackensen, who held the eastern sector of the semicircle, turned Samsonof's flank on the east, defeated his right wing, and pushed on toward Willenberg, the other door. Without pausing in the pursuit he turned toward Samsonof's main force, which was still fighting desperately in the direction of Hohenstein-Tannenberg, and fell upon its rear. It was the same as if von Hausen had succeeded in his Meuse maneuver on the western front and had fallen upon the rear of Lanrezac at Charleroi.

Apparently at that moment Samsonof realized what was happening. He tried to snatch himself out of the trap; he evacuated Allenstein in haste and rushed toward Soldau to open a way toward the Narew and Warsaw. It was too late. Hindenburg's right wing had entered Soldau. The doors of escape were closed one after the other. In the swamps and network of little lakes Samsonof's army was surrounded. It fought heroically, a hopeless fight. Even surrender, if it had been desired, was impossible. After the incredible efforts of five whole days of battle there remained only the shattered fragments of a great army, strewn about in the trackless maze of swamp lands; troops wandering through the woods, units mixed in a hopeless mob, cannon mired in the stagnant water, regiments formed from soldiers of all arms, the most vigorous débris gathered up by the most energetic officers in order to break through the circle by charging at random!

Some divisions got through. Others clung in rags to the thickets of thorn trees, or wandered in circles, completely lost. Samsonof did not wish to survive the disaster; he placed himself in the first ranks and was killed by a shell, which also struck his Chief of Staff. Thus ended what the German historians call emphatically "the greatest battle of destruction in history." They all give the credit to the strategic teachings of Schlieffen. I have before me a German brochure explaining the battle of Tannenberg with diagrams; its title is "From Hannibal to Hindenburg," and it contains this sentence: "It was Schlieffen who before his death dictated the whole plan of the great war against France and Russia."

BY GENERAL VON HINDENBURG

In the pocket-book of a dead Russian officer a note had been found which revealed the intention of the enemy Command. It told us that Rennenkampf's Army was to pass the Masurian Lakes on the north and advance against the Insterburg-Angerburg line. It was to attack the German forces presumed to be behind the Angerapp while the Narew Army was to cross the Lötzen-Ortelsburg line to take the Germans in flank.

The Russians were thus planning a concentric attack against the Eighth Army, but Samsonof's Army now already extended farther west than was originally intended.

What, indeed, could we do to meet this dangerous enemy scheme? It was dangerous less on account of the audacity of the conception than by reason of the strength in which it was to be carried out—at any rate, strength from the point of view of numbers. We could hope that it would be otherwise as regards strength of will. During the months of August and September Russia brought up no fewer than 800,000 men and 1,700 guns against

East Prussia, for the defence of which we had only 210,000 German soldiers and 600 guns at our disposal.

Our counter-measures were simple. I will attempt to make the broad outlines of our plan clear to the reader even if he is not an expert.

In the first place we opposed a thin center to Samsonof's solid mass. I say thin, not weak. For it was composed of men with hearts and wills of steel. Behind them were their homes, wives and children, parents and relatives and everything they had. It was the 20th Corps, brave East and West Prussians. This thin center might bend under the enemy's pressure, but it would not break. While this center was engaged two important groups on its wings were to carry out the decisive attack.

The troops of the 1st Corps, reënforced by Landwehr —likewise sons of the threatened region—were brought for the battle from the right, the northwest, the troops of the 17th Corps and the 1st Reserve Corps, with a Landwehr brigade, from the left, the north and northeast. These men of the 17th Corps and 1st Reserve Corps as well as the Landwehr and Landsturm also had behind them everything which made life worth living.

We had not merely to win a victory over Samsonof. We had to annihilate him. Only thus could we get a free hand to deal with the second enemy, Rennenkampf, who was even then plundering and burning East Prussia. Only thus could we really and completely free our old Prussian land and be in a position to do something else which was expected of us—intervene in the mighty battle for a decision which was raging between Russia and our Austro-Hungarian Ally in Galicia and Poland. If this first blow were not final the danger for our Homeland would become like a lingering disease, the burnings and murders in East Prussia would remain unavenged, and our Allies in the south would wait for us in vain.

It was thus a case for complete measures. Everything must be thrown in which could prove of the slightest use in manœuvre warfare and could at all be spared. The fortresses of Graudenz and Thorn disgorged yet more

Landwehr fit for the field. Moreover, our Landwehr came from the trenches between the Masurian Lakes, which were covering our new operations in the east, and handed over the defence there to a smaller and diminishing number of Landsturm. Once we had won the battle in the field we should no longer need the fortresses of Thorn and Graudenz, and should be freed from anxieties as regards the defiles between the lakes.

Our cavalry division and the Königsberg garrison with two Landwehr brigades were to remain facing Rennenkampf, who might fall upon us like an avalanche from the north-east at any time. But at the moment we could not yet say whether these forces would really be sufficient. They formed but a light veil which would easily be torn if Rennenkampf's main columns moved or his innumerable cavalry squadrons advanced, as we had to fear. But perhaps they would not move. In that case the veil would be enough to cover our weakness. We had to take risks on our flanks and rear if we were to be strong at the decisive point. We hoped we might succeed in deceiving Rennenkampf. Perhaps he would deceive himself. The strong fortress of Königsberg with its garrison and our cavalry might assume the proportions of a mighty force in the imagination of the enemy.

But even supposing Rennenkampf cradled himself in illusions to our advantage, would not his High Command urge him forward in forced marches to the south-west—in our rear? Would not Samsonof's cry for help bring him in hot haste to the battlefield? And even if the sound of human voices echoed in vain, would not the warning thunder of the battle reach the Russian lines north of the Lakes, nay, to the enemy's Headquarters itself?

Caution with regard to Rennenkampf was therefore necessary, though we could not carry it to the extent of leaving strong forces behind, or we should find ourselves weaker on the battlefield than we ought to be.

When we considered the numbers on both sides a comparison with the probable Russian forces showed a great disparity against us, even if we counted in on our side the two Landwehr brigades which were then coming from Schleswig-Holstein, where they had been employed in coast protection (and assuming that they would arrive in time for the battle), and even if Rennenkampf did not move and indeed played no part. Moreover, it must be remembered that large bodies of Landwehr and Landsturm had to fight in the first line. Older classes against the pick of Russia's youth! We had the further disadvantage that most of our troops and, as the situation decreed, all those which had to deliver the *coup de grâce*, had just been engaged in heavy and expensive fighting. Had they not just been compelled to leave the battlefield of Gumbinnen to the Russians? The troops were not therefore marching with the proud feeling of being victors. Yet they pressed forward to the battle with stout hearts and unshaken confidence. We were told that their *moral* was good, and it therefore justified bold decisions. Where it was somewhat shaken such decisions could not fail to restore it. It had been thus before; could it be otherwise now? I had no misgivings on the score of our numerical inferiority.

He who reckons solely by the visible in war is reckoning falsely. The inherent worth of the soldier is everything. It was on that that I based my confidence. What I thought to myself was this:

The Russian may invade our Fatherland, and contact with the soil of Germany may lift up his heart, but that does not make him a German soldier, and those who lead him are not German officers. The Russian soldier had fought with the greatest obedience on the battlefields of Manchuria although he had no sympathy with the political ambitions of his rulers in the Pacific. It did not seem unlikely that in a war against the Central Powers the Russian Army would have greater enthusiasm for the war aims of the Tsar's Empire. On the other hand, I considered that, taking it all round, the Russian soldier and officer would not display higher military qualities in the European theatre than they had in the Asiatic, and believed that I was entitled to credit our side with a plus on the ground of intrinsic value instead of a minus for our numerical inferiority.

Such was our plan and such our line of reasoning before and for the battle. We compressed these ideas and intentions into a short report which we sent from Marienburg to Main Headquarters on August 23:

"Concentration of the army for an enveloping attack in the region of the 20th Corps planned for August 26."

On the evening of the 23rd I took a short walk on the western bank of the Nogat. From there the red walls of the proud castle of the Teutonic Knights, the greatest brick monument of Baltic Gothic, made a truly wonderful picture in the evening light. Thoughts of a noble chivalry of the past mingled involuntarily with conjecture as to the veiled future. The sight of the refugees flying past me from my home province deepened the sense of responsibility that possessed me. It was a melancholy reminder that war not only affects the fighting man, but proves a thousandfold scourge to humanity by the destruction of the very essentials of existence.

On August 24 I motored with my small Staff to the Headquarters of the 20th Corps, and thus entered the village which was to give its name to the battle so soon to blaze up.

Tannenberg! A word pregnant with painful recollections for German chivalry, a Slav cry of triumph, a name that is fresh in our memories after more than five hundred years of history. Before this day I had never seen the battlefield which proved so fateful to German culture in the East. A simple monument there bore silent witness to the deeds and deaths of heroes. On one of the following days we stood near this monument while Samsonof's Russian Army was going to its doom of sheer annihilation.

On our way from Marienburg to Tannenberg the impression of the miseries into which war had plunged the unhappy inhabitants were intensified. Masses of helpless refugees, carrying their belongings, pressed past me on the road and to a certain extent hindered the movements of our troops which were hastening to meet the foe.

Among the Staff at the Corps Headquarters I found the confidence and resolution which were essential for the success of our plan. Moreover, they had a favorable opinion of the *moral* of the troops at this spot, which was at first the crucial point for us.

The day brought us no decisive information either about Rennenkampf's operations or Samsonof's movements. Apparently it only confirmed the fact that Rennenkampf was moving forward very slowly. We could not see the reason for this. Of the Narew Army, we knew that its main columns were pressing forward against the 20th Corps. Under its pressure this corps refused its left wing. There was nothing doubtful about this measure. Quite the contrary. The enemy, following up, would all the more effectively expose his right flank to our left enveloping column which was marching on Bischofsburg. On the other hand the hostile movement which was apparently in progress against our western wing and Lautenburg attracted our attention, as it caused us some anxiety. We had the impression that the Russians were thinking of enveloping us in turn at this point and coming in on our flank.

August 25 gave us a rather clearer picture of Rennenkampf's movements. His columns were marching from the Angerapp, and therefore on Königsberg. Had the original Russian plan been abandoned? Or had the Russian leaders been deceived by our movements and suspected that our main force was in and around the fortress? In any case we must now have not the slightest hesitation in leaving but a thin screen against Rennenkampf's mighty force. On this day Samsonof, obviously feeling his way, was directing his main columns towards our 20th Corps. The corps on the Russian right wing was undoubtedly marching on Bischofsburg, and therefore towards our 17th Corps and 1st Reserve Corps, which had reached the district north of this village on this day. Apparently further large Russian forces were concentrating at Mlawa.

This day marked the conclusion of the stage of expectation and preparation. We brought our 1st Corps round to the right wing of the 20th Corps. The general attack could begin.

August 26th was the first day of the murderous combat

which raged from Lautenburg to north of Bischofsburg. The drama on which the curtain was rising, and whose stage stretched for more than sixty miles, began not with a continuous battle line but in detached groups; not in one self-contained act, but in a series of scenes.

General von François was leading his brave East Prussians on the right swing. They pushed forward against Usdau with a view to storming the key to this part of the southern battle front next day. General von Scholtz's magnificent corps gradually shook off the chains of defence and addressed themselves to the business of attack. Fierce was the fighting round Bischofsburg that this day witnessed. By the evening magnificent work had been done on our side at this point. In a series of powerful blows the wing corps of Samsonof's right had been defeated and forced to retreat on Ortelsburg by the troops of Mackensen and Below (10th Corps and 1st Reserve Corps), as well as Landwehr. But we could not yet realize how far-reaching our victory had been. The Staff expected to have to meet a renewed and stout resistance south of this day's battlefield on the following day. Yet was their confidence high.

It was now apparent that danger was threatening from the side of Rennenkampf. It was reported that one of his corps was on the march through Angerburg. Would it not find its way to the rear of our left enveloping force? Moreover, disquieting news came to us from the flank and rear of our western wing. Strong forces of Russian cavalry were in movement away there in the south. We could not find out whether they were being followed up by infantry. The crisis of the battle now approached. One question forced itself upon us. How would the situation develop if these mighty movements and the enemy's superiority in numbers delayed the decision for days? Is it surprising that misgivings filled many a heart, that firm resolution began to yield to vacillation, and that doubts crept in where a clear vision had hitherto prevailed? Would it not be wiser to strengthen our line facing Rennenkampf again and be content with half-measures against Samsonof? Was it not better to abandon the idea of destroying the Narew Army in order to ensure ourselves against destruction?

We overcame the inward crisis, adhered to our original intention, and turned in full strength to effect its realization by attack. So the order was issued for our right wing to advance straight on Neidenburg, and the left enveloping wing "to take up its position at 4. A. M. and intervene with the greatest energy."

August 27 showed that the victory of the 1st Reserve Corps and 17th Corps at Bischofsburg on the previous day had had far-reaching results. The enemy had not only retired, but was actually fleeing from the battlefield. Moreover, we learned that it was only in the imagination of an airman that Rennenkampf was marching in our rear. The cold truth was that he was slowly pressing on to Königsberg. Did he, or would he, not see that Samsonof's right flank was already threatened with utter ruin and that the danger to his left wing also was increasing from hour to hour? For it was on this day that François and Scholtz stormed the enemy's lines at and north of Usdau and defeated our southern opponent. Now, when the enemy's centre pushed forward farther towards Allenstein—Hohenstein, it was no longer victory but destruction that lured it on. For us the situation was clear. On the evening of this day we gave orders for the complete encirclement of the enemy's central mass, his 13th and 15th Corps.

The bloody struggle continued to rage on August 28.

On the 29th a large part of the Russian Army saw itself faced with total annihilation at Hohenstein. Ortelsburg was reached from the north, Willenberg, through Neidenburg, from the west. The ring round thousands and thousands of Russians began to close. Even in this desperate situation there was plenty of Russian heroism in the cause of the Tsar, heroism which saved the honor of arms but could not longer save the battle.

Meanwhile Rennenkampf was continuing to march quietly on Königsberg. Samsonof was lost at the very moment when his comrade was to give proof of other and better military qualities. For we were already in a position to draw troops from the battle front to cover the work of destruction in which we were engaged in the great cauldron, Neidenburg—Willenberg—Passenheim, and in which Samsonof sought for death in his despair. Swelling columns of prisoners poured out of this cauldron. These were the growing proofs of the greatness of our victory. By a freak of fortune it was in Osterode, one of the villages which we made our Headquarters during the battle, that I received one of the two captured Russian Corps Commanders, in the same inn at which I had been quartered during a General Staff ride in 1881 when I was a young Staff officer. The other reported to me next day at a school which we had converted into an office.

As the battle proceeded we were able to observe what splendid raw material, generally speaking, the Tsar had at his disposal. I had the impression that it doubtless contained many qualities worth training. As in 1866 and 1870, I noticed on this occasion how quickly the German officer and soldier, with their fine feeling and professional tact, forgot the former foe in the helpless captive. The lust of battle in our men quickly ebbed away and changed to deep sympathy and human feeling. It was only against the Cossacks that our men could not contain their rage. They were considered the authors of all the bestial brutalities under which the people and country of East Prussia had suffered so cruelly. The Cossack apparently suffered from a bad conscience, for whenever he saw himself likely to be taken prisoner he did his best to remove the broad stripe on his trousers which distinguished his branch of the service.

On August 30th the enemy concentrated fresh troops in the south and east and attempted to break our encircling ring from without. From Myszaniec—that is, from the direction of Ostrolenka—he brought up new and strong columns to Neidenburg and Ortelsburg against our troops, which had already completely enveloped the Russian centre and were therefore presenting their rear to the new foe. There was danger ahead; all the more so because airmen reported that enemy columns twenty-three miles long—

therefore very strong—were pressing forward from Mlawa. Yet we refused to let go of our quarry. Samsonof's main force had to be surrounded and annihilated; François and Mackensen sent their reserves—weak reserves, it is true— to meet the new enemy. Against their resistance the attempt to mitigate the catastrophe to Samsonof came to naught. While despair seized on those within the deadly ring, faint-heartedness paralyzed the energies of those who might have brought their release. In this respect, too, the course of events at the Battle of Tannenberg confirmed the human and military experience of yore.

Our ring of fire round the Russian masses, crowded closely together and swaying this way and that, became closer and narrower with every hour that passed.

Rennenkampf appears to have intended to attack the line of the Deime, east of Königsberg and between Labiau and Tapiau, this day. From the region of Landsberg and Bartenstein his masses of cavalry were approaching the battlefield of Tannenberg. However, we had already concentrated strong forces, weary but flushed with victory, for defence in the neighborhood of Allenstein.

August 31 was the day of harvesting for such of our troops as were still engaged, a day of deliberation about the further course of operations for our leaders, and for Rennenkampf the day of the retreat to the Deime—Allenburg—Angerburg line.

As early as the 29th the course of events had enabled me to report the complete collapse of the Russian Narew Army to my All-Highest War Lord. The very same day the thanks of His Majesty, in the name of the Fatherland, had reached me on the battlefield. I transferred these thanks, in my heart as with my lips, to my Chief of Staff and our splendid troops.

On August 31st I was able to send the following report to my Emperor and King:

"I beg most humbly to report to Your Majesty that the ring round the larger part of the Russian Army was closed yesterday. The 13th, 15th and 18th Army Corps have been destroyed. We have already taken more than 60,000 prisoners, among them the Corps Commanders of the 13th and 15th Corps. The guns are still in the forests and are now being brought in. The booty is immense though it cannot yet be assessed in detail. The Corps outside our ring, the 1st and 6th, have also suffered severely and are now retreating in hot haste through Mlawa and Myszaniec."

The troops and their leaders had accomplished extraordinary feats. The divisions were now in bivouacs and the hymn of thanks of the Battle of Leuthen rose from them.

In our new Headquarters at Allenstein I entered the church, close by the old castle of the Teutonic Knights, while divine service was being held. As the clergyman uttered his closing words all those present, young soldiers as well as elderly Landsturm, sank to their knees under the overwhelming impression of their experiences. It was a worthy curtain to their heroic achievements.

BY A GERMAN SOLDIER

[This letter, descriptive of the massacre of the entrapped Russians at Tannenberg, appeared in a German socialistic paper, and purports to have been written by a participant:]

It was frightful, heartrending, as these masses of human beings were driven to destruction. Above the terrible thunder of the cannon could be heard the heartrending cries of the Russians: "O Prussians! O Prussians!"—but there was no mercy. Our Captain had ordered: "The whole lot must die; so rapid fire." As I have heard, five men and one officer on our side went mad from those heartrending cries. But most of my comrades and the officers joked as the unarmed and helpless Russians shrieked for mercy while they were being suffocated in the swamps and shot down. The order was: "Close up and at it harder!" For days afterwards those heartrending yells followed me and I dare not think of them or I shall go mad. There is no God, there is no morality and no ethics any more. There are no human beings any more, but only beasts. Down with militarism.

This was the experience of a Prussian soldier. At present wounded; Berlin, October 22, 1914.

If you are a truth-loving man, please receive these lines from a common Prussian soldier.

BY GENERAL BASIL GOURKO [1]

Tannenberg took its name from a large wood behind the battlefield into which the two central corps were driven and surrounded by the Germans, the entire forces, with all their remaining officers, being captured. The plans which had been made, owing to tactical errors on the part of the corps commanders on the flanks, were never carried out, and the two corps in the center, left entirely without support and surrounded by the living wall of the enemy, had no option but to lay down their arms after a heavy fight.

Fighting began on the morning of September 28th, and from the beginning the corps on the flanks met with some resistance, the Germans threatening an attack on their exterior, which was but poorly protected with cavalry. Probably this resistance was unexpected, for both corps, without half their troops having come into action, began to retire at the moment the two central corps were heavily engaged. On the front the battle had been going well for the Russian troops; a few thousand prisoners had been taken, and there was every possibility of a great victory. Things moved normally for some time afterwards and heavy losses had been incurred by both sides, when suddenly fresh German columns made their appearance, marching to strike a blow at both flanks of the Russian troops attacking in the northerly direction. It was reported at the same time that these enemy columns could turn both flanks of our forces, which, of course, would mean that both army corps would be encircled.

Headquarters of the central corps were entirely without information as to what had happened to the corps on the flanks. They were supposed to be holding in check any turning movement attempted by the Germans. In reality they were retreating and had altogether lost touch with the enemy. Probably it is quite natural to ask why General

[1] Reprinted from Gourko's "Russia, 1914-1917," by permission of the publishers, the Macmillan Co.

Samsonof did not give orders to compel the flanking corps to stop their retreat, to reattack and by a single frontal blow strike hard at the flank and rear of the German columns which were then beginning to surround the two corps in the center. Failing this in any case he could have given orders in due time to withdraw from a fight that was fast threatening to become unequal.

General Samsonof and his Staff were at an observation post in company with General Martson, the commander of the 15th Corps, watching, within the limits of their visibility, the attack which was successfully developing before them. It was subsequently reported by eye-witnesses that during the battle Samsonof several times inquired from General Martson if any information had been received from the corps on the flanks. Each time the answer was in the negative. The absence of news was due to the difficulty of maintaining connection in such open fighting and also to the fact that both the flanking corps were moving, and had the utmost difficulty in maintaining any kind of communication with the other commanders. Destitute of any information concerning the other troops under his control, Samsonof lost all power of directing operations and thus infringed one of the elementary rules of military strategy, that which provides that the commander of an army shall choose as his headquarters some spot where information can readily be brought to him and whence he can communicate with all the forces under his command.

The worse the organization of communication, the more an army commander is disinclined to come close to the actual scene of the fighting and by personal supervision counterbalance the failure to maintain communication between himself and the unit under his command. Again the tendency to generalize, which nearly every man possesses, will inevitably lead an army commander to imagine that an operation happening before his eyes must be similar to that of the other areas where fighting is taking place, which he cannot see. The defeat or success of a unit under the immediate observation of the army commander may result in such orders being given to the whole army as would certainly meet the situation immediately within vision but might prove disastrous taking the battle altogether.

In the Battle of Tannenberg the preliminary success enjoyed by the troops under General Samsonof's immediate observation was such an encouraging picture that final victory appeared a matter of certainty. Unfortunately, just at this time the retreat of the two flanking corps, of which Samsonof was totally unaware, was leading from hour to hour towards the catastrophe which was ultimately to overtake the corps in the center. Every hour that passed brought confirmation of the fact that the 13th and 15th Corps were being more and more completely surrounded by the Germans. General Martson set out for the scene of the frontal attack to issue orders for a gradual retirement, for the divisions to withdraw one by one. Simultaneously, Samsonof set off in a different direction, presumably to get in touch with the other army corps of his army. But these measures were taken too late.

Disaster had already overtaken the 13th and 15th Corps; German turning columns had already penetrated their flanks and rear so deeply that only a portion of the transport and a comparatively insignificant number of infantrymen managed to escape from the ring of German masses which every minute became more contracted. The two army corps fell back slowly into the shades of Tannenberg Wood, absolutely helpless and unable to use their artillery. The result of this disaster was that the Germans captured, almost in full strength, two army corps with all their officers, and recovered possession of their own troops who had been captured earlier during the battle. Caught in the ring, although the Germans did not know it, was General Samsonof and his personal staff.

Night fell. Samsonof, accompanied by five other staff officers, was guiding himself through the thick forest towards the Russian frontier. Their motor-cars had been abandoned, for it was too risky to use the roads. The little party mounted on horseback, passing out of the forest, despite the darkness were seen by a party of German infantry armed with machine guns. Amidst a hail of bullets the party dismounted and continued their way on foot, into another belt of forest. Utter darkness surrounded them. The sounds of fighting died away, and all that could be heard was the trampling of the undergrowth and an occasional voice as members of the little party called out to each other in order to keep together. From time to time a halt was called and all drew closer to make sure that nobody was missing.

General Samsonof, who suffered from heart trouble, and found his breathing more and more difficult, lagged behind. There came a time when everybody had been called and all had answered but Samsonof. General Postovski, the Chief of his Staff, immediately called a halt and in the thick darkness led a search for the missing general. It was fruitless.

RUSSIA CRUSHES THE AUSTRIANS

THE LEMBERG DEFEAT REDUCES AUSTRIA TO GERMAN VASSALAGE

AUGUST 26TH-SEPTEMBER 2ND

ERNEST VIZETELLY   PRINCESS RADZIWILL

The chief Russian forces in the opening phases of the War were concentrated, not upon the German frontier where Tannenberg was fought, but against the Austrians. Here a brief and brilliant Russian campaign directed by Gen. Russky culminated in a crushing defeat of the main Austrian armies at Lemberg, the chief city of the frontier Austrian province of Galicia. The Austrians, retreating in confusion, left all Galicia in Russian hands, except for the strong fortress city of Przemysl.

Great as was this victory, in the number of men engaged, in the losses and in the resulting booty, nevertheless it was not of decisive military importance; for the Russians did not succeed in advancing beyond Galicia into the heart of the Austrian domains. The importance of the battle of Lemberg lies in another direction. In a way, the Russians had aided Germany's game, for they had so completely broken the Austrian spirit and self-confidence, that thereafter the Austrian military authorities did what the Germans bade them. Thus Lemberg ultimately, by placing the Austrian soldiers under the iron German system, made them much more formidable than at first.

Such results, however, were of later development. For the moment Russia rejoiced whole-heartedly over her great triumph. This spirit is well shown in the account of the victory by the Russian princess, Catharine Radziwill. The Russians regarded the campaign of Lemberg as equaling that of the Marne in importance, and excelling it in fullness of success. A more impartial view is here presented by the British authority on Austrian affairs, Mr. E. Vizetelly.

BY ERNEST A. VIZETELLY

RUSSIA did not wait for the complete mobilization of her troops. On August 2nd—the very day when a *Te Deum* for victory was chanted outside the Winter Palace at St. Petersburg (whose name was soon to be changed to Petrograd), and when, in the presence of statesmen, courtiers, soldiers, and seamen, the Emperor Nicholas took a solemn pledge that he would not conclude peace so long as a single enemy remained on Russian soil—a first army crossed the East Prussian frontier under the orders of General Rennenkampf, an officer of German extraction, who had previously commanded at Vilna. The post of generalissimo of the Russian forces had been conferred on the Grand Duke Nicholas Nicholaïevitch, one of the Czar's uncles, and the control of the principal army intended for the operations against Austria was allotted to General Russky, until then commander at Kiev.

Some German detachments had already penetrated to various Polish frontier villages and towns, but they refrained from going farther in that direction when Rennenkampf's troops made their appearance in East Prussia, where several minor engagements took place during the ensuing week. More important operations were imminent when on August 14th the Grand Duke Nicholas issued a momentous proclamation to the whole Polish people. Poland, it will be recollected, was dismembered twice during the eighteenth century, one part (Posen and Danzig) going to Prussia, another (Galicia) to Austria, and the remainder (the Warsaw territory) to Russia. For several years prior to the Great World War, Prussia, as is well known, had grossly ill-treated her Polish subjects, whom she vainly strove to "Germanize." In Galicia Austria had exercised a milder sway, while Russia, anxious to obliterate the unhappy memories of the past, had recently promised a number of reforms in the administration of her Polish territory. At the moment of the declaration of war, the Austrian Poles or Galicians gave numerous signs of loyalty. In response to the appeals of the Emperor Francis Joseph they flocked to the Austrian colors, and tendered large war offerings of money, Cracow alone contributing over £40,000. Prussia, on her side, suddenly strove to conciliate the more or less disaffected inhabitants of Posen by dint of blandishment and cajolery; and, carrying her intrigues as well as some of her forces across the frontier, she endeavored to stir up revolt among the Russian Poles.

Russia retorted in a very remarkable manner, for the Grand Duke Nicholas's manifesto to the Poles promised the reunion of all the severed regions of Poland under the Russian scepter, with freedom in faith, language, and self-government.   In a striking passage of his proclamation the Grand Duke said: "A century and a half ago the living flesh of Poland was torn asunder, but her soul did not die." —words which recalled the legendary retort of the heroic Polish patriot, Kosciusko, who, on being finally overcome in 1794, was said to have exclaimed: *"Finis Poloniæ!"* "I said no such thing," he afterwards declared indignantly; "it would have been blasphemy.   Poland will live!"

Galicia being now seriously threatened by the army of General Russky and another under General Brusiloff, the Austrians endeavored to check their advance by a bold counter-stroke, which consisted in invading Poland with strong composite forces of Austro-Germans, Poles, and Hungarians.   These troops advanced from Cracow into the Kielce, Radom, and Lublin districts of Russian Poland, where they made considerable progress, thereby creating a hope that they might be able to turn the right of the Russian troops who were operating against Galicia from the east. Russia, however, disposed of ample forces to defeat this design, and her plans with respect to Galicia remained unchanged.

These were carried out in the careful methodical manner which was to be expected of such a commander as General Russky—an officer of the scientific type, sixty years of age, spectacled, and slightly bent, even as Moltke became bent, patient also like Moltke with respect to the accomplishment of his designs, but quick in his decisions.   His fellow commander, General Brusiloff, was an officer of a more dashing stamp, but also one of high attainments.   In opposition to these leaders Austria put forth Field-Marshal von Ost-Auffenberg, Field-Marshal von Hoetzendorff, General Dankl, the Archduke Frederick—a brother of the Queen-mother of Spain, and reputed to be the best military man of the Austrian imperial family—and also the young Archduke Joseph, heir to the empire since the assassination of his uncle, Francis Ferdinand, at Serajevo.

On August 25th there began a great battle for the possession of Lemberg, the seat of the Austrian Government in Galicia, though Cracow, at the other extremity of the province, was the capital of all Poland in the days of the country's independence. The contest for Lemberg raged during seven days, and extended over a distance of 200 miles from the Lublin district in Russian Poland to Halicz, south-southwest of the threatened city. By September 2nd the Austrians were completely defeated. There were thousands of killed and wounded, and the Russians claimed to have taken no fewer than 70,000 prisoners, in addition to 200 guns and several standards. Many of the Austrian losses were incurred on the Halicz front, where they desperately attempted a flanking movement but were decisively routed by General Brusiloff. At this point alone the Russians buried 5,000 of the enemy's dead. Lemberg, several of whose fortified positions had previously been taken, now surrendered to General Russky.

Meanwhile Russky and his colleagues were dealing further severe blows at the Austrian forces. On September 5th the latter were attacked in the vicinity of Tomaszow, near the frontier, and retreated in disorder towards Rawaruska, northwest of Lemberg, where, after four days' fighting, they were again severely defeated. The result of these engagements was that the Russians were able to cross the lower part of the River San—driving the Austrians before them into a marshy triangle between that stream and the Vistula—and to lay siege to the great fortress of Przemysl, which offered, however, so determined a resistance that the invaders ultimately contented themselves with isolating it, relying on time to contribute to its reduction.

Meantime Russky, Brusiloff, and Dimitrieff were inflicting further defeats on the Austrians under Auffenberg and his colleagues, Dankl and Boverig. On September 17th these commanders were routed in Galicia with terrible losses, the estimates supplied by the Russians being so huge as to appear almost incredible. On the 21st the important fortified town of Jaroslav, commanding the railway line between Lemberg and Cracow, was stormed by the Russians, and although Przemysl still stanchly resisted bombardment, the end of the month found the Austrian armies in a most woeful plight, and the Russians steadily prosecuting their advance towards Cracow.

In these circumstances several Austrian commanders were superseded, and the victor of Tannenburg, the much-belauded German General von Hindenburg, became, in connection with the campaign against Russia, generalissimo of the forces of the Dual Monarchy. It was asserted at the time that his appointment had been imposed on Austria by the German Kaiser, but there is evidence that the aged Emperor Francis Joseph was profoundly dissatisfied with the conduct of his own generals. They had failed on all sides. In vain, too, had every available man of the eleven nationalities of the empire been called to the colors. Nothing seemed to stem the tide of disaster. Cossacks had driven back the Austrian forces in the Carpathians and descended into the Hungarian plain, where their presence seemed to threaten a speedy advance on Budapest. Vienna, crowded with an ever-increasing number of refugees, was reported to be almost in a state of panic.

BY PRINCESS RADZIWILL

The whole attention of the public became concentrated upon Galicia, where the Grand Duke had thrown the whole weight of our armies. He guessed, quite rightly, that the vulnerable point of our enemies lay in the weakness of the Austrian troops. The Austrians had at first occupied certain portions of the so-called Kingdom of Poland—the province of Lublin—and we had considerable trouble to dislodge them; but once on their own ground, they had broken down in what seemed an almost incredible manner. Events proved, later on, that the cause of this sudden collapse had been the utter incapacity of the officers, who, owing to the happy-go-lucky way in which they considered everything, had failed to grasp the determination with which Russia invaded Austrian territory. Besides this, the German Staff still believed that it could allow the Austrians to act independently, and could trust them to bring into execution the plan which had been settled by mutual agreement. The

Austrians, however, showed themselves miserable tacticians, and defeat upon defeat followed, until Berlin, exasperated by the succession of reverses which gave up the whole of Galicia into Russian hands, insisted upon the Austrian troops being led by Prussian officers. After this, things most unfortunately changed for us; we were obliged to evacuate Galicia, and thus were stultified our enormous sacrifices to conquer the region.

Hostilities against Austria were conceived upon a considerable scale, and were executed with great talent and knowledge by General Russky, the commander of the troops forming part of the Kiev army, who showed singular perspicacity and great decision in all the operations which he executed. The Austrians thought that by attacking us with all their forces they would be able to prevent our mobilization being accomplished in time, and thus, from the outset, secure a very real advantage. They began by attacking and taking Lublin and Chelm, with the evident intention to force our lines from the West to cross the Bug, and thus attack from the rear the army which we were concentrating around Warsaw, and in flank the troops which we had sent into Eastern Prussia. To be able to execute this movement, the Austrians developed their forces on a front of more than 150 versts,[1] occupying and leaning on the following points, which they had strongly fortified: Zavilost, Janov, Bilgoraj, Tomaszov, and Belcez.

To accomplish this very important operation it was indispensable, however, to protect the right wing of the Austrian Army from the possibility of an attack by the Russian troops occupying the Kiev military district. In order to do this, the intention of the Austrian commanders had been to bring forward the second Austro-Hungarian Army, composed of the third, eleventh and twelfth corps, and five cavalry divisions. According to the reckonings of the Austrian Staff, the mobilization of the Austro-Hungarian Army, as well as its concentration in South Galicia, ought to have been accomplished on the fourteenth day after the order for the general mobilization had been issued; but two weeks after

[1] A verst is 1,161 3/5 yards.

war had begun the Austrians had not succeeded in gathering all their forces. This delay placed our enemies in a worse strategical position than they had imagined possible, and they found themselves compelled to reënforce the troops which they had in South Galicia by bringing up part of their seventh, thirteenth and fourteenth corps, amounting to twelve divisions of infantry, and a few brigades of Landsturm and some cavalry and artillery—approximately 220,-000 to 230,000 men,—who were instructed to cover the operations that had been intrusted to the main body occupying Southern Galicia. In the meanwhile the Russian mobilization had been effected far more quickly than our adversaries had anticipated, and already, on the 16th of August, a bare fortnight following the declaration of war by Austria upon Russia, the army forming part of the Kiev military district had developed itself around Lutzk, Dubno and Proskurov—that is, on a front extending to something like 175 versts—and began steadily marching toward the enemy's territory.

During seventeen days these troops, which formed the left wing of our main army, covered a space of 220 versts, or something like thirteen versts per day, fighting nearly the whole of the time. If one takes into account that troops on the march in peaceful times are not supposed to cover more than fifteen versts in twenty-four hours, whilst we managed to do thirteen, fighting and forcing all kinds of obstacles, Russia may justly feel proud of the endurance shown by our soldiers upon this occasion, where everything depended on the promptitude of our movements.

The main forces of our enemy in South Galicia were gathered together in a very strongly fortified position at Kamenka and Kalisz, and extended upon a front of more than 110 versts. We attacked this position, and after a most desperate struggle, which lasted several days, the Austrians were completely routed on September 1st. They lost something like a hundred and thirty thousand men killed and wounded, whilst, in addition, two hundred guns and vast quantities of ammunition were left in our hands.

After this defeat, due to the clever strategy of General

Russky, who was most ably seconded by General Brusiloff, the commander of the Second Army engaged in Galicia, the principal Austrian forces reassembled opposite Opol and Belcez, but they did not succeed in establishing themselves on a wide front. We had crossed the frontier on the 19th of August, and fought all the time from that day to the moment when at last we entered Lemberg. Our march forward was very difficult, owing to the many small rivers, affluents of the Dniester, which had to be crossed, as well as to the various fortified points that we had to take by storm; but already, on the 20th of August (September 2nd), our army found itself in sight of Lemberg, the forts of which showed no resistance whatever, and on August 21st (September 3rd), at eleven o'clock in the morning, the town itself was taken by our troops after a short engagement. The greatest success of the campaign had been achieved with relatively very little loss, and the name of General Russky became famous all over Russia.

The Grand Duke Nicholas immediately telegraphed the good news of Lemberg to the Emperor, asking the Czar to award the Cross of St. George, of the third class, a most rare distinction, to General Russky. All over Russia solemn thanksgiving services were celebrated, and great manifestations of joy as well as popular demonstrations took place in Petrograd and in Moscow. People began speaking of the invincible Russian armies and expected to hear every day that we were on the road to Vienna, if not in actual possession of that capital. In the general joy it was entirely forgotten that Germany existed, and through the glasses of a rose-colored optimism she was seen already conquered just as completely as her Austrian ally. As for our reverses in Eastern Prussia, they had already sunk into insignificance, the more so that, as a revenge for all the horrors of Tannenburg, the Emperor had seen fit to change the name of Petersburg into the truly Russian "Petrograd," and the government had forbidden German to be spoken in the streets or to be taught in schools. Surely this was enough to satisfy the most fervent patriot!

THE ABANDONMENT OF PARIS

WITHDRAWAL OF THE FRENCH GOVERNMENT TO BORDEAUX

SEPTEMBER 3RD

GENERAL GALLIÉNI   GEORGE PERRIS

We turn again to France, the main theater of the Great War. As the victorious Germans swept on from the frontier and over northeastern France, there seemed no stopping them. Battles were reported every day; and still the British and the French fell back. To all except Joffre, the master strategist, this seemed to imply disaster falling thick upon disaster. The public could not realize how the Germans were being worn to exhaustion, their lines of communication stretched to the uttermost, their munitions squandered. Then came the moment when Joffre warned the Paris government that he would not even guarantee the safety of the capital. That too might become the spoil of war; the government must withdraw.

Heroically President Poincaré and all his ministers accepted the situation. France must fight to her utmost, must sacrifice everything else, even Paris, if her military chances were thereby improved. Indeed, there is no single element of the War more impressive than the splendid firmness wherewith Frenchmen met every call upon their courage and resources, even to the end. Mr. Perris, who here describes the Paris of those dark September days, was himself an eyewitness, an English one not over-sympathetic with the French. Their own feeling in the matter is best expressed by the Government Proclamation of withdrawal, and by the brief, decisive words in which General Galliéni announced that, with the government officials gone, he was in command of the capital, and would defend it to the end. Both then and later Galliéni well won his fame as one of the foremost French heroes of the War.

BY GENERAL GALLIÉNI

ARMY OF PARIS, INHABITANTS OF PARIS,

THE members of the Government of the Republic have left Paris to give a fresh impulse to national defense.

I have been intrusted with the task of defending Paris against the invader.

That task I will fulfill to the end.

GALLIÉNI,
Commandant of the Army of Paris.

[Here follows the Government Proclamation signed by all the civil and military authorities, including Galliéni.] PEOPLE OF FRANCE!

For several weeks relentless battles have engaged our heroic troops and the army of the enemy. The valor of our soldiers has won for them, at several points, marked advantages; but in the north the pressure of the German forces has compelled us to fall back.

This situation has compelled the President of the Republic and the Government to take a painful decision.

In order to watch over the national welfare, it is the duty of the public powers to remove themselves temporarily from the city of Paris.

Under the command of an eminent Chief, a French Army, full of courage and zeal, will defend the capital and its patriotic population against the invader.

But the war must be carried on at the same time on the rest of its territory.

Without peace or truce, without cessation or faltering, the struggle for the honor of the nation and the reparation of violated rights must continue.

None of our armies is impaired. If some of them have sustained very considerable losses, the gaps have immediately been filled up from the reserves, and the appeal for recruits assures us of new reserves in men and energy tomorrow.

Endure and fight! Such must be the motto of the Allied British, Russian, Belgian, and French armies.

Endure and fight, while at sea the British aid us, cutting the communication of our enemy with the world.

Endure and fight, while the Russians continue to advance to strike the decisive blow at the heart of the German Empire.

It is the duty of the Government of the Republic to direct this stubborn resistance.

Everywhere Frenchmen will rise for their independence; but, to insure the utmost spirit and efficacy in the formidable fight, it is indispensable that the Government shall remain free to act.

At the request of the military authorities, the Government is therefore temporarily transferring its headquarters to a place where it can remain in constant touch with the whole of the country.

It requests members of Parliament not to remain away from it, in order that they may form, with their colleagues, a bond of national unity.

The Government leaves Paris only after having assured the defense of the city and of the entrenched camp by every means in its power.

It knows that it does not need to recommend to the admirable population of Paris that calm, resolution, and coolness which it is showing every day, and which is on a level with its highest traditions.

People of France, let us all be worthy of these tragic circumstances. We shall gain the final victory; we shall gain it by unflagging will, endurance, and tenacity.

A nation which refuses to perish, and which, in order to live, does not flinch either from suffering or sacrifice, is sure of victory.

BY GEORGE PERRIS

On the night of Monday, August 31st, I received privately the alarming news that the Government of France was abandoning its capital, the first city of Continental Europe. At four o'clock on that afternoon, 1,200 of the 1,500 employees of the Ministry of War, of all grades, had received notice, first to send their families into the country immediately, then to go themselves to Tours, taking with them what they could of the material for which they were responsible. The loading of automobiles with office documents, typewriters, and other effects was then proceeding at full pressure. Many of the men had already left. At other Ministries, there was the same scene of hurried packing in corridors full of boxes, and a rapid succession of motor-cars carried away the official property as soon as it was ready. Some was taken to the Quai d'Orsay and Austerlitz stations; other motor-cars had gone southward by road. The decision to abandon Paris and to shift the seat of Government to Bordeaux was come to on the Monday afternoon at a Cabinet Council, of which a usually trustworthy official gave me a grievous account. This climax had been reached so rapidly, and it is so easy for the stolid Englishman to misunderstand the French temperament—in which wild gesticulations are perfectly consistent with an heroic courage—that I will not repeat my informant's words, lest it should be supposed that there was a flagrant hour of sheer panic. Suffice it that the Ministers were not agreed whether to go or stay, but that it was ultimately decided to go.

It is difficult now to recall the sense of impending calamity that then seemed so real, and lay hourly more heavily upon us. At the Central Telegraph Office that Monday evening, I was told that, since the early morning, there had been no communication with London. Letters were three days late. We were, or appeared to be, nearly isolated. There might have been a great defeat. We did not know. When I went to the War Office at eleven o'clock that night to receive the usual late communiqué, I already knew the facts cited above, and had, beside, a bundle of rumors hot enough then to set the Seine on fire; but not now. The officer in charge of the Press service did not usually come in person, but sent an orderly with a parcel of typewritten sheets which were distributed without comment. There had been an unusually long communiqué at 5 p. m.—a réchauffé of the former news which did not indicate any new defeat or cause for anxiety. At 11 p. m. Commandant Thomasson came to us himself, and, after announcing that no official bulletin would be issued, made a short statement, in course of which he admitted that a second aëroplane had appeared over Paris that day and left the usual missiles. Not a word as to what many of the responsible French journalists present must, like myself, have been thinking about. And therefore no guidance in the next morning's papers for the hundreds of thousands of anxious hearts in a city that had been at full stretch of its nervous powers for a month.

Or, rather, there were two notes, faintly struck, in either of which some comfort might be found, but that neither had any apparent authority, and they were quite **irreconcilable**. Paris is all right, said the one voice; she can stand a long siege, and by that time the Russians will be in Berlin. Paris may be invested, said the other voice, and it is evidently inadvisable for the Ministry to be locked up or captured by the enemy. Naturally, it will retire, as the Belgians retired from Brussels to Antwerp. Putting aside for a moment the question of the power of the city to resist assault and to bear a siege, it will be seen that the analogies were unsound. It was supposed that, if the Russians reached Berlin, everything would be over but the shouting, while, when the Germans reached Brussels and Paris, the Governments would move away and the resistance be maintained as if nothing had happened. An impartial observer would say that, if the Russians continued their successful march, the Prussian Government would leave Berlin—and the German people would not lose much by that. The Belgian Government was in being; but there was this great difference between Brussels and Paris—Brussels was an open town, and could not be defended. Paris had a double ring of fortifications, and we had been told, with every kind and degree of positiveness, that it would resist capture to the last. Evidently, the Government, or the main body of it, should be moved whenever there was any danger of its being captured; but a premature movement of the kind could not but be a severe shock to the Parisian public, and it was a matter of no little local importance that shocks should be avoided if possible, apart from any general effect upon the feeling of the nation.

No news more alarming than statements that the defenses were being put in readiness, and that it was advisable for people having relations in the country to send their women and children thither, had been allowed to appear in the Paris Press for a week past. Yet an exodus, now much accentuated, had begun on Saturday, August 29th; throughout that and the following days, lines of cabs, many of them filled with household goods, were racing through the boulevards to the southern and western railway stations; and a very large part of the population of the city was en-

gaged in discussing whether, and if so how, it should remove itself. A lady who had arranged some time before to
leave Paris on the Saturday night for Biarritz had to be
content at the last moment with a seat on a rough bench in
a cattle truck, into which thirty passengers or more were
crowded, without a glimmer of light. The train carried
nothing but third-class and trucks, and, stopping at most
stations, it took about thirty hours to reach its destination.
I went down to the St. Lazare Station on the Sunday morning
to see how it was with the British and American passengers
leaving at 9.30 by the Havre route. A quite orderly, but
tired, anxious, and uncomfortable crowd of about a thousand persons surrounded the entry to the platform, and
more were constantly arriving. At noon there were 10,000
persons in and around the Mont Parnasse Station, trying to
get train for Rennes, St. Malo, and Brest; and at the In-
valides Station, which had been more carefully reserved for
military use, the officials said that enough passengers had
been booked in advance for Brittany to fill all the trains for
a week.

The odd thing was that there was an inflow as well as an
outflow, though not on so large a scale. First, there was an
uninterrupted stream of refugees from the immediate scene
of fighting—the region of Mons, and then the region around
Laon. More than 30,000 of these poor people were landed
at the Nord Station on the 29th. Many of them were carrying oddments of property with them, and some of the children had been allowed to bring a favorite dog or canary.
All of this vast social disturbance was not directed upon
Paris. A lady who had a summer cottage near Pontoise described vividly the abandonment of many of the villages on
this northwestern road by their inhabitants, who had not yet
seen the Germans, and were resolved not to see them. Add
to the influx of refugees that of wounded soldiers—all the
hospitals of the city were not full, but even when expecting a siege, Paris is a great distributing center—and a
smaller number of German prisoners; then offset against
these the flight of Parisian families and foreigners, and
there is given a problem of social migration that would be

very grave even if there were no urgency about getting troops mobilized and to the front. So far, the railways had worked marvelously; and it was not till Sunday, the 30th, that some little effervescence was perceptible among the people of Paris. The cool courage with which the agonies of the past month had been borne deserved every word that the best living French prose writers (there was here no tendency to cheap versification) said in its praise. But this patient loyalty could not safely be abused; and the migration problem could not safely be allowed to be aggravated by an open alarm.

There were various and potent warnings of the gravity of the situation other than the statements of refugees and wounded soldiers. On the evening of August 30th, the president of the City Council, M. Mithouard, made a statement advising residents having friends in the country to send their women and children thither, as a siege would mean privation, whatever efforts were made to assure the food supply. On the same day, the papers were forbidden to issue more than one daily edition; and news became scantier than ever. Englishmen, getting through with difficulty by Dieppe and Beauvais, and arriving many hours late, reported that the enemy was at Compiègne, and rumor added falsely that this town, only 45 miles away, was in flames. The War Office admitted that the French army was continually retreating, but gave no details. It was safe to conclude that the enemy was within two days' march. All round the northern suburbs and outlying districts of Paris, the inhabitants were ordered to get away immediately; and many of these were pouring into the city by the Maillot, St. Ouen, and Clignancourt gates, while others more sensibly took suburban roads to the south. The telegraphs were working subject to many hours' delay, and to England only two wires, via Havre, were open on September 3rd. Orders had been given for all the wounded to be removed outside the "intrenched camp of Paris." Those in hospital at Versailles, sufficiently recovered to be moved, were taken by train to such distant points as Rennes and Nantes.

Secrets, like bombs, are a worrying cargo; and it was
with a sigh of relief that I read over my coffee and crust
(no fancy rolls in these days!), on the morning of September 3rd, the proclamation announcing the shifting of the
Government to Bordeaux.

Not a hint of this grave step had appeared in the Paris
Press till now, although thousands of officials knew of it,
and a number of journalists had scented sensation afar off.
I had learned that an announcement would be issued before
midnight on Thursday, September 3rd; and this was my excuse for troubling the British Embassy with a call.   The
great door in the Rue du Faubourg St. Honoré, surmounted
with the royal arms, was closed, and the porter had received
orders, on this sad and busy day, not to admit any visitors.
The reason was soon apparent; indeed, two furniture vans
and many half-packed cases in a corner of the courtyard,
the unusual bustle on the stairs and in the upper rooms, and
large labels showing that many boxes of papers and other
property would be left in charge of the American Ambassador, told the whole story so eloquently that there was no
need for me to do more than wish the courteous Secretary
bon voyage.   All the same, there was something very grievous about this retreat—something, for a civilian, like what
the soldier feels when he witnesses a forced retirement on
the battlefield.

On Wednesday evening, September 2nd, their various
Excellencies left the Quai d'Orsay Station; and none who
saw it is ever likely to forget the scene.   Groping my way
in the deep, narrow streets about the War Office, on the
south side of the river, during the past few nights, I had
conceived a perfectly practical affection for the much-slan-
dered moon.   You see, they were saving coal and electric-
ity; moreover, it is advisable to give no guidance to hostile
airships.   So, off the boulevards, the streets were hardly lit
at all.   We may see again a mild alarm such as had carried
scores of thousands of Parisians southward in these critical
days; but we are never likely again to see the abandonment
of the first city of Europe at dead of night by a cosmopoli-
tan crowd of diplomatists.   There was Sir Francis Bertie,

in black suit and bowler hat, and Mr. Graham, very tall and fair, talking to the Marquis Visconti-Venosta—the Italian Ambassador himself, Signor Tittoni, being another distinguishable figure, in gray and a soft felt hat.   Mr. Myron T. Herrick, the United States Ambassador, had come down with his wife to say good-by to his confrères, and M. Isvolsky, the Czar's envoy, was chatting with the Spanish Minister, who, like Mr. Herrick, was remaining in Paris to perform the duties of courtesy that fall upon neutrals at such a time.   The windows of each carriage of the special train were labeled with the names of the countries whose representatives it was carrying off—there was even an inscription for the more or less imaginary Republic of San Marino; but no one appeared to answer to this honorific name. There was the Persian Minister, and M. Romanos, the black-bearded Greek, and a Russian military attaché in uniform, and some Belgians, and all sorts of servants, including a Chinese nurse feeding a yellow baby, with coal-black eyes.   And, at last, a soft horn was blown, and the train rolled away.   Whatever might be said about the adventurous Herr Taube, and the possibly approaching legions of his still more reckless Kaiser, it was no pleasant thing to see the world's delegates pack up their traps, and leave the splendid city of Paris to its fate.

President Poincaré, accompanied by all the members of the Ministry, left for Bordeaux at 5 a. m. on Thursday, and they were followed in two special trains by the Presidents and members of the Senate and Chamber of Deputies, with other official persons.   The main body of the staff and the reserves of the Banque de France had already been removed.   Of the major Embassies, only those of Spain and the United States remained, and the neutrality of the American Republic was oddly marked by the fact that Mr. Herrick had taken charge of the records of the British, the German, and the Austrian Ambassadors.   A like transfer of the higher legal machinery of France had been made by sending to Bordeaux fifteen magistrates selected from among the three sections of the Cour de Cassation.   During the day, the Presidents of the City Council and the Council of the Seine Department formed a committee, under the authority of the Military Governor, the Prefect of Paris, and the Prefect of Police, for the government of the capital. A new Prefect of Police, M. Laurent, was appointed in place of M. Hennion, a change warmly welcomed, and connected by rumor with official discussions as to whether, if a breach were made in the line of forts, the city should be surrendered. Thousands of people continued to crowd into the southern railway stations, but there was still no panic. The quietude of the population was a worthy reflection of the courage of the children of the Republic under arms. As one writer said, "It was a moment for those who act, not those who talk"; and General Galliéni enjoyed unbounded confidence, both as organizer and as soldier.

Thus was Paris derobed of her accustomed majesty. Long afterwards, we learned that many of the treasures of the Louvre and other museums and public galleries had been secretly removed. Other monuments, and those the most characteristic, if not the most precious, remained only because they could not be shifted. The perspective of the Champs-Elysées was no less glorious because the Presidential palace was closed. We could walk among the flower-beds, the splashing fountains, and the statuary, of the Tuileries gardens, and reflect upon the hollowness of worldly hopes, or discover with a more genuine surprise that nothing avails to extinguish love's young dream. A column of Chasseurs click-clacked along the Rue de Rivoli: what were they thinking of it all? Perhaps only that the thin moonshine was worth a hundred searchlights to General Galliéni, now master of our immediate destinies. To me, the vague mist of light made all that had seemed so terribly real a few hours before most unreal; and I saw only the ghosts of the soldiers of olden times, called from forgotten graves by the sound of cannon and the cry of the blood-lust, the ghosts of the conquering fighters who built these palaces and arches—and, far behind, under one blue star, the pale ghost of a man who was crucified.

The Chasseurs passed, and then a regiment of infantry; a little donkey-cart piled with the poor property of a workman's home passed; and a procession of such refugees urged onward to the south through the dead city. With the early daylight, some of the shutters fell, the doors opened, and through these miles of streets, men and women awoke to ask what news there was from Compiègne.

Did I say Paris had lost something of her majesty? But she had gained a majesty higher than the glitter of any official uniforms can give. Let me confess it. I had feared, half expected, trouble in this still crowded population. *Rien du tout!* Where had the volatile, explosive, rather vicious Parisian of forty-four years ago gone? There was no sign of him to-day. I have no belief in easy generalizations— you do not know much of the mind of two millions of people by observing the faces of two thousand, or by a closer knowledge of two hundred. But, without overestimating the worth of such evidence as one man can gather, it must yet be said that the quietude of the city, the appearance of a grave confidence and resolution, the perfect order in public places, were things to impress the most skeptical. So far, I do not believe that any human society in time of peril could display in a higher degree than Paris was doing the virtues of calmness, courage, loyalty, and endurance. Used to enjoy her powers and amenities in perfect security, she had suddenly become a frontier town, imminently threatened with a blow hardly less grave in its effect on the national spirit than in its material injuries. Pride and calculation, it is true, combined to throw a ray of light upon this prospect. Many of these Parisians, elders who had given their last and dearest for the national defense, recalled 1870, and could see that it was not now as it was then with France, that the daily work of industrialism and of political democracy, the progress of education and humane influences, have created a new Republic, more sober, stable, and strong. As for the Government, they were not indifferent to its departure, and they did not hurl after it the open scorn reserved for more wealthy and less responsible fugitives. They watched stoically, sure of the future. Many old Parisian traditions are dead; new and better have grown, and the city has no peer in the Latin world.

THE TURNING OF THE TIDE

THE ATTACK ON EASTERN FRANCE BROKEN AT THE GRAND COURONNÉ

MAURICE BARRÈS   COUNT DE SOUZA
COLONEL FROBENIUS   GOMEZ CARILLO

Those days of the opening of September in 1914 were to the Allied peoples the darkest of the War. The news of Lemberg was as yet uncertain; the disaster of Tannenberg was retold in exaggerated form; and in the west Paris was abandoned. Nothing seemed able to check the German onrush. Then suddenly, sharply, all along the French line from Paris to the Swiss frontier came the abrupt checking of the Germans. Nothing more dramatic has ever occurred in history. The French still call it "the miracle of the Marne."

The first step in this vast victory, however, came not in the Marne region but east of it on the Lorraine frontier, where the French had made their original invasion of Germany and been driven back in the battle of Lorraine. In this eastern region General Castelnau was in immediate command, General Joffre's first headquarters at Nancy having been quickly shifted to a more central spot to meet the main German attack. Castelnau, forced out of Germany by overwhelming defeat, prepared himself as best he could for a defensive battle, holding to the east of Nancy the long range of hills whose principal summit is known as the Great Crowned Mountain or the *Grand Couronné*.

It must be remembered that every leader was still unsure of what new tactics must be used to meet new weapons. Fortresses were obviously useless against the huge Teutonic howitzers; mass attacks were hopeless against modern machine guns. Hence arose the technic of movable defense. Guns were protected from the huge howitzers by being hidden in pits and moved when discovered; and against these was developed the huge, blind artillery bombardment, covering every suspected hiding-place with a rain of shells and then launching an infantry assault before the stunned and battered line of gunnery could be reformed. The second battle of Nancy saw these new tactics in their infancy. Castelnau concealed his guns along the wooded hill crests, and there was an artillery battle of a week's duration before the Germans ventured to launch their massed infantry attack. Even then their bombardment had been insufficient. Those remarkable French cannon, the 75's, were still in good condition after a week of constant usage; and they mowed down the foe by thousands. Thus Castelnau was able to hold his ground against far larger forces.

To the general German plan it was absolutely necessary that this French line should be broken. Thus the armies of Joffre were to be caught in the rear. That was the essential point of the whole German campaign. And it must be accomplished at once! That is why the Germans repeated their costly mass attacks day after day, why the Kaiser himself came upon the scene to inspire his heroes in the main assault. But even the Kaiser's presence could not enable his men to achieve the impossible. So long as those 75's continued to rage with their steady accuracy, every advance meant death. The Germans learned that lesson at awful cost. The assaults dwindled away in exhaustion. The thin French line, almost equally exhausted both in men and munitions, held firm until the end; and Joffre's armies were saved. They could fight along the Marne on equal terms with their opponents, instead of being smothered in an encircling net. That was the first German breakdown.

The event is here described first by a celebrated French lyric writer, Barrès. He rejoices with fervid patriotism over the opening of the struggle. The account is then taken up by a cool-headed strategist, the great French military authority, De Souza. Next comes the brief semi-official account by the German military authority, Colonel Frobenius, of the High Staff. And then, since German narratives of the disaster are all too vague and scant to be of value, we conclude with the summing up by a neutral, the noted Spanish writer, Carillo, who visited the scene.   C. F. H.

BY MAURICE BARRÈS

IN August, 1914, our enemies could well believe themselves masters of the world. With what proud confidence they advanced after the battles of Saarburg, and Morhange, and Charleroi! Yet they were stopped so sharply and so definitely that they never tried to capture Paris, and Nancy, and the passage of the Moselle. Let us recall those days of our extreme peril, let us understand by what virtues of our soldiers and commanders, by what complete unity of the French people, we obtained that miracle of victory.

Visiting Lorraine to help my fellow-countrymen celebrate at Rozelieures, at Gerbéviller, at Mesnil-sur-Belvitte, the great deeds done by the armies of Castelnau and Dubail, I traversed daily the scenes of the "battle of Charmes," which others call the battle of Borville or the opening phase of the battle of Grand Couronné. The culminating point, decisive of a long battle which was itself the pivot of all the maneuvers of the Marne, was a day of immense importance. It assured the safety of Lorraine and of France.

The gratitude of Lorraine and of France ought to be inscribed upon the school of Pont Saint Vincent, where

General Castelnau—working amid the absolute confidence of his army and of the people, because of his knowledge of Lorraine and his admirable character, seconded and supported by a General Staff whose chief was General Anthoine—directed the battles of Charmes and of the Grand Couronné. It was on August 22nd, one hour after noon, that Castelnau came to establish his headquarters in that modest structure, now venerable. Whence did he come?

On August 19th, 20th, and 21st the armies of Dubail and Castelnau had fought at Saarburg and Morhange—fought without success. Nevertheless, the Germans, who had suffered heavy losses in those battles, made no attempt to cut off our line of retreat. They had lost contact. Our two armies fought during their retreat by a combined movement in which the two commanders helped each other. I hope some day to tell the story of General Dubail as he stood in the City Hall of Rambervillers and directed the victorious resistance of his troops and of the Twenty-first Corps.

From the Blandan Barracks at Nancy on August 20th General Castelnau had, under pressure of necessity, taken all precautions to assure the defense of Nancy and to permit his main forces to establish themselves behind the Meurthe and the fortified front of the Grand Couronné. His wish was not to give battle until after all the army corps were completely remade. The country people described the scene to me along the routes of march—the columns finding their way, the isolated men regrouping themselves, the trains, the parks of artillery, the convoys winding along the left bank of the Meurthe. Recovery of contact with the Germans took place on the 22nd; they had received re-enforcements, and our rear guards and cavalry sought to check them and understand their direction.

Would there be time to finish the preparations on the heights of the Grand Couronné? Could the armies stop up the hole just in front of the forest opening at Charmes, that is to say, at one of the decisive points between Castelnau's right and Dubail's army? Would there be troops enough to guard that thirty-seven-mile front from Sainte Geneviève to Dorville? Those expected from the Alps—released by Italy's assurances—could they arrive for the decisive hour?

All those problems were thought out and controlled by Castelnau in the little schoolhouse of Pont Saint Vincent, where, hour by hour, depending upon his air scouts and cavalry, he knew or divined what the enemy was doing or intended to do, leaving his maps only to walk back and forth with hands behind him, or to throw himself for a few hours fully dressed upon a couch in a corner of the room, surrounded by his staff.

On the evening of the 23rd, and still more in the night of the 24th, he emerged from his keenest anguish, being convinced that he could stop the retreat, that his troops were in condition to fight. All his positions were ready and solidly held. To guard against every contingency, the destruction of the bridges over the Moselle and lower Meurthe was arranged for—even down in the forest opening of Neufchâteau—and the fort of Bourlemont was armed and reoccupied. In the region of Lenoncourt he got together a strong group which he held ready with all the available forces of the Twentieth Corps to execute a powerful counterattack.

Where will the shock come? The first part of the morning of August 24th passes in the expectation of an assault by the Germans on the Rembêtant, that is to say upon Nancy, but behold! at 8 o'clock from all directions comes the information to Pont Saint Vincent that two German army corps are marching southward in all haste toward Charmes.

In place of attacking Castelnau on the heights, the Germans evidently have taken for their objective the possession of the bridgeheads on the Moselle. They are going to be able, in the neighboring woods of Charmes, to approach the river without being seen or touched. Even before reaching it they will seize, on the right bank, the line Vesoul-Epinal-Nancy, which at this moment has become one of the great arteries in which flow the life and hope of France. Ten miles further on, at Tantonville, on the left bank, is another artery no less active, the line of Chalindrey-Mirecourt-Nancy, which brings to the Grand Couronné night and day the means for its resistance.   Beyond lie Neufchâteau, Chaumont, the death of all our hopes.

In his haste Prince Rupprecht of Bavaria refuses to believe that Castelnau and Dubail have been able to reëstablish themselves; he executes before them "the maneuver of scorn," as von Kluck was to do a little later before Galliéni and Maunoury; he does not try to join battle with them, but to outstrip them on their lines of communication.   He rushes forward, he pushes his columns along, thus laying his flank open to the blows of the Grand Couronné.

Instantly Castelnau profits by this imprudence of pride. He orders an offensive upon the flank and rear of the enemy columns, yet a limited offensive, without engaging his principal force, without relinquishing the support of his positions, which he continues to reënforce for the reception of any attack.   And at the same time (about 10 o'clock in the morning) his cavalry corps, which is commanded by General Conneau, and which includes the famous regiments from Lunéville, pushed by the Germans in the direction of Charmes, makes a stubborn stand on the crest of Morviller, inflicts serious losses with its artillery, and, finally, in the evening, falls back in good order upon Dorville, thus assuring the union of Castelnau and Dubail and stopping up the neck of the bottle in the direction of the Moselle.

BY COUNT DE SOUZA

The eyes of the world were fixed on Paris and the western extremity of the battlefield in France, not only because the British were there; not only because the situation of the apparently threatened capital seemed desperate; but because representatives of the world-wide Press—who were allowed to follow the operations from a safe distance—found it easier, and no doubt more interesting, to confine their attention to that sector of the line.   This favorite way of talking or writing about the war has almost condemned to oblivion what can well be considered, without exaggeration, as the finest achievement of the campaign.

This is the defense of Nancy, an action which if the field of operations had been reversed, if it had been fought out in Belgium or near Paris, would have immediately received from the world the amount of attention that it deserved. For, on the defense of Nancy, or rather of the positions surrounding it and the approaches to the fortress of Toul, depended entirely the course of events in the west, and therefore the success of the retreat to, and of the battles on, the Marne. Furthermore, it was the longest and most bitterly contested action of the first phase of the campaign; and the material results achieved, apart from the strategic, were of paramount importance to the successful prosecution of the war by the Allies; for, at little cost to the French, it swept off the surface of the earth a number of first-rate German units. In other words, the Germans at Nancy more than anywhere else (until the battles of Flanders in the second phase of the war) squandered their strength in the most ineffective and useless fashion, not to mention the moral effect of the failure, which was immense, for it was the first time that German soldiers were defeated in the presence and under the very eyes of their Emperor.

Apart from all this the battle of Nancy would still take precedence over those on the Marne if for the only reason that it started a whole week previously, and reached its climax before the other efforts of the Germans elsewhere reached theirs. To realize this one must keep in account that the German attack on the "Grand Couronné" began at the moment that Joffre abandoned the line of the Somme in order to carry out the Great Retreat, and that when he resumed the offensive east and south of Paris, the German efforts at Nancy were practically spent. Beyond the taking of Nancy and the investment of Toul, the Germans had what constituted a more important object at this stage of developments: the weakening of Joffre's left and center armies, and the "pinning down" in Lorraine of a considerable portion of the French forces. This end, the last strategic hope of the Germans during their first offensive, was not attained.

Thus can the battle of Nancy alone be appraised at its

true worth, and its decisive character impressed on the minds of men.

The German attack on the Grand Couronné was a direct answer to Joffre's refusal to accept battle on the line of the Somme. Up to August 30th the Germans, having failed to gain control of the gap of Mirecourt, meant to attack or isolate Verdun and pierce the French line north of Toul, at St. Mihiel. Suddenly, as it became known that the Allies were falling back from the Somme, the Germans wheeled sharply round to the south, towards Pont à Mousson, and the position of St. Geneviève, which is the northern extremity of the Grand Couronné. Concurrently the garrisons of Metz and Strassburg were drawn upon in material and men to reënforce the army of Bavaria, whose losses along the banks of the Moselle and the Meurthe had been fearful. What happened further south, from Gerberviller to St. Dié, after Castelnau's successful counter-attacks from the 26th to the 30th of August, was only a parallel action along the line of the Meurthe, in which the Germans, now on the defensive in that region, endeavored to protect their flank and the communications of the Bavarian army, whilst this army transferred its activities to the north, aiming first at Verdun, then, in obedience to the change of plan, at Nancy.

The terrific artillery actions that took place east of Nancy on the 27th and 28th were the outcome of the German flank march past positions, where they thought the French might attack in great strength, as they had done two days earlier to check the German effort against the gap of Mirecourt. This is rendered more illuminative by the fact that it was not there, but on the *northern* sector of the "Grand Couronné" that the Bavarians began their infantry assaults, when they would have saved time and the fatigues of a march by beginning with the southern sector.

Thus the importance of Joffre's retreat is more and more emphasized, for by so doing he not only saved his left wing, which was in jeopardy on the Somme, but he also saved Verdun. Verdun had no Grand Couronné to protect it, and even without taking it the Germans could isolate the fortress and surround from the south the army of Sarrail, which at the time (August 30th-31st) was still disputing with the Crown Prince the passage of the Meuse north of Verdun.

Instead the Germans turned their attention to Nancy and concentrated their efforts against the Grand Couronné, a course of action which allowed Sarrail to keep a tight hold on Verdun and play his part in the Great Retreat.

The attacks on the Grand Couronné were preceded by the most terrific bombardment, no less than 400 heavy guns, brought from the arsenal of Metz, being massed against it. The French, who had already had a taste of the German heavy gun fire at Saarburg, were fully prepared for it, and not being able to reply to this weight of metal, they had taken all the precautions necessary to reduce to a minimum the effects of the German siege ordnance. The troops had dug themselves in and improvised all sorts of ingenious shelters against shell fire, and the field guns (*Rimailho's* and "75's"), to be used only at short range against infantry attacks (since these weapons were outranged by the howitzers and siege guns of the enemy), were cleverly concealed in the folds of the ground.

Thus the effective defense of the positions was made possible by an extreme minimum of men. The position of St. Geneviève, for instance (which to many was the key of the Grand Couronné) was only held by a regiment of reserve (Territorials). But the ground in front of it, especially in the valley of the Moselle, was elaborately prepared; it was covered with wire entanglements and other obstacles of a more or less deadly kind. To the west of the Moselle there was a division based on Toul; the plateau of Amance, northeast of Nancy, was occupied by the 20th army corps. Further south a thin line of troops—perhaps two divisions—extended as far as the Rhine-Marne Canal, where they were in connection with Dubail's army based on Epinal, Dubail having in front of him, from that point to the Vosges, the main body of von Heeringen's army.

The positions around Nancy, from Pont à Mousson to Dombasle, near Lunéville, were attacked by no less than eight army corps, or their equivalent in number of men (about 350,000).

The infantry assaults began, as we have said, in the north, on August 31st, and gradually extended south, the Germans employing everywhere the same tactics; issuing in dense masses from the thick woods, they rushed on the positions with the greatest bravery and determination. Invariably they were shot down at short range by the thousand, and were finished off with the bayonet. Thus they were able to realize the small impression that their big guns had made on the French. Again and again Bavarians, Prussians and Saxons returned to the attack. The result was the same; they never permanently conquered an inch of ground, and their slain kept accumulating in heaps on the slopes and at the foot of the Grand Couronné. At one single spot near St. Geneviève, in the valley, the French found 4,000 German dead. The Germans christened the locality "The Hole of Death."

The only momentary progress was made by von Stranz, who took Pont à Mousson, and carried the tall hill of the same name, whence he raked with artillery fire the flank of the St. Geneviève position. But a counter-attack by the French division based on Toul made the Germans lose these gun positions.

The forlorn attacks of the Germans on the Grand Couronné culminated on September 6th in a grand and general assault on the plateau of Amance. This assault, or series of assaults, was delivered by masses of 50,000 men at a time, under the eyes of the German Emperor, who had hurried from his headquarters at Metz with the intention, it is said, of entering the capital of Lorraine on that day or the next, at the head of his white cuirassiers who formed his escort. From a hill in the rear of his troops he anxiously watched the action. He knew from his staff, as well as from the early developments of the campaign, that things had not been going too well; that the enemy was wily, resourceful and intelligent, and that up to now the German arms had scored no decisive success. The attack on Nancy, if it succeeded, would put everything right. It would, at any rate, help the sweeping moves near Paris.

So the Kaiser hoped, and he came to put some heart into

his soldiery, to give more impetus to their attacks. From afar his lonely figure could be seen on the top of a sunny hill on that fatal day, peering through his glasses. He was pointed out as a great favor to some French soldiers who had been captured near St. Geneviève. The French soldiers were not in the least awed. One of them, a reservist, having escaped, wrote home to say that he had at last seen "the scoundrel who had plunged Europe into this calamitous war!"

At the sight of their Kaiser the German troops were truly inspirited. They dashed from the woods in serried ranks, with flags unfurled and bands playing. Three times on that day they ascended the deadly slopes of the Grand Couronné, already strewn with slain; and three times, under the terrific fire of the "75's" and the bayonet charges of the 20th French corps, they reeled back in confusion. In the evening the Kaiser returned to Metz, where he received ominous tidings of the developments of affairs near Paris. He had lost all hope.

Not so his commanders, who, on the 7th and the 8th, renewed their attacks in less theatrical fashion. But the troops were exhausted, disheartened, and terribly diminished in numbers. To have an idea of their losses it is only necessary to know that in front of the positions of the Grand Couronné alone the French picked up afterwards more than 40,000 identification discs of German dead. The other casualties have not been estimated, and probably never will be. Whole brigades, entire regiments had vanished; divisions and army corps were sorely depleted, whilst the losses of the French in comparison were insignificant.

On the 9th, when the battles of the Marne were nearing their climax, the German efforts against the Grand Couronné had already slackened. It was on the evening of that day that, more out of spite than any effective design, the Germans pushed up, under cover of darkness, an advanced battery, which dropped some seventy shells in the suburbs of Nancy. On the next day the battery was destroyed by the French guns. On the 11th a German division issuing from Einville made a dash against Dombasle, with the apparent design of cutting into the French line there. But this division was trapped by the French artillery in and around the woods of Crevic and practically annihilated. The French counted there more than 3,000 German bodies. Einville marks the end of all German offensive action in Lorraine. It was the last kick of a baffled foe, of an army in distress. By this time the issue on the Marne had been decided.

BY COLONEL FROBENIUS

At the time the five armies of the right wing were performing their great marches and rapid evolutions alternating between attack and defense, the two armies on the left wing had to contend in French Lorraine with the First and Second French Armies, which had been thrown back on Epinal and Nancy. With the intention of surrounding these points of support (Nancy also had been fortified) the troops, on occupying Lunéville on the 23rd, had crossed the Meurthe at this place and to the south of it. Here, however, the French had converted the only 40 kilometres broad space between St. Nicolas and the Vosges Mountains into an exceedingly strong defensive position.

Nevertheless the Bavarians advanced so far in the vicinity of Nancy that they came within range of the batteries of the fortress, a circumstance which made it imperative for the Germans also to bring up heavy guns with which the city could be bombarded. The approach to the fortress, however, had been provided with so many difficult impediments, that the advance could not be effected.

As an attempt to break through between Toul and Epinal also failed, the Germans, when Saint Dié also had fallen on August 27th, confined themselves to holding the enemy fast. On September 10th the two German armies, in consequence of the withdrawal of the right wing to the Aisne, were ordered to fall back to the boundary; a large part of the Seventh Army was transferred to the Aisne, whither also the Sixth Army soon followed.

BY GOMEZ CARILLO

For the last three days we have been studying the battle-fields in which the crosses on the graves mark out the fighting points like the little flags upon a map. We have seen Sainte-Geneviève, Amance, the wood of Champenoux, and all the heights of Grand Couronné. We have traversed a front of over fifty kilometers, on which hundreds of thousands of men have been engaged. We have been down into the holes where innumerable batteries established their line of fire, and finally, we visited a great many villages converted into heaps of ruins. A staff captain explained the principal military operations at the beginning of September to us, and declared that they constitute one of the most formidable and glorious episodes in the history of France.

"Over there, on the right," said our learned guide to us to-day, "is the army that is defending Pont-à-Mousson. To the left, another army is holding back the advance of the enemy on the banks of the river. Look for yourself."

In vain did I try to verify all this; I could see nothing but the peaceful Lorraine landscape, undulating in the tranquil tide of its hills, stretching away and away to infinity. The huge graveyard is the only thing that marks the limits of the picture. But because, alas! it is so huge, the picture disconcerts us and prevents us from forming a concrete image of the drama.

Placing himself opposite the wood of Champenoux, the black branches of which stood out like a mourning veil on the winding-sheet of snow, our captain described the furious attack of September 7th.

"Towards morning," he said, "the Prussian troops, who were ordered to take Nancy that the Emperor might make his solemn entry into the capital of Lorraine, and establish himself in Duke René's palace, marched down the slopes of the Seille, and crossed the river by the bridges of Chambley, Moncel, Brin, and Bioncourt. After a general attack they placed their siege-guns on the crests of Doncourt, Bourthecourt, and Rozebois. The shells poured upon Amance and its environs, at once set fire to the villages of

Bouxières-aux-Chênes, Fleur-Fontaine, and Laître. The church towers collapsed like houses of cards. The woods crackled and flamed in the hurricane of fire and steel. Protected by this infernal artillery, the battalions advanced in perfect order, and as our field guns decimated them, tearing convulsive breaches in the grandiose human wall, other troops hurried forward to fill the gaps, passing over the corpses of their comrades. The solemn clamor of *'Deutschland über Alles,'* intoned by thousands of voices, rose in the air mingling dirge-like with the roar of the guns. It was like an avalanche advancing, an avalanche so mighty, so compact, and so methodical that no dyke seemed capable of resisting it. Amance was given up for lost. And if once Amance were in the power of the enemy, the high road, open and defenseless, would be but a broad avenue for a triumphal march, the goal of which would necessarily have been Nancy.

"The information received at Headquarters stated that William II., with 10,000 cavalry of the Guard, was in the wood of Morel, ready for the great advance which was to bring him with banners flying and fifes sounding, to the Place Stanislas. It would be an exaggeration to say that our chiefs, with their relatively small numbers, hoped to offer a successful resistance to the onslaught of our enemies. All they were bent on for the moment was to gain a few hours. 'If we can hold our own all day,' said a general, 'we shall have performed a miracle.' And this miracle actually came to pass. When night began to fall the avalanche had not yet overwhelmed us; our 75's kept them at bay; our fire broke the mass at several points. Night came at last, lighted by incendiary fires, and with the night a ray of hope dawned in the French soul.

"But on the following day the turmoil became more violent, the attack more intense, the enemy stronger. Velaine soon succumbed, and the defile between the two hills of Amance was filled with Uhlans. 'We are lost,' thought the most valiant of our chiefs. At this moment our reënforcements, which had just come up, advanced from all our positions, not in close formation, but in slender lines of marksmen. The guns of Amance suddenly came into action again, mowing down the fields of pointed helmets like ripe corn. The trumpets sounded in our ranks; something like a fever ran through every soul; the very woods seemed to quiver joyously. The Emperor, whose white silhouette dominated the tumult, ordered up his reserves, and a whole army corps from the rear advanced towards the bridges which the first columns had crossed the day before without difficulty. But we had now got the range so perfectly that not a single enemy succeeded in passing the river. No matter! The white horseman shook his golden eagle, crying: 'Forward, forward! *Deutschland über Alles!'*

"For a few hours the shock was so terrific that the air vibrated, shaken by the fire of the guns. A kind of frenzy ran through the lines on both sides. The Emperor, livid, continued to cry: 'Forward.' But suddenly, as if moved by an irresistible impulse, the avalanche fell back, sweeping with it in its retreat the 10,000 horsemen of the Imperial Guard, who galloped towards Metz in disorder. What was a victory the day before had become a rout.

"On the following day, when our general was preparing for a fresh struggle, a messenger with a flag of truce arrived, asking for an armistice of twenty-four hours to bury the dead. 'In the name of His Majesty,' he said. The French commander bowed and replied: 'In twenty-four hours, when the Emperor has buried his thousands of corpses, we will expect him again.' But His Majesty has not been seen here since."

The captain made a sweeping gesture with his arms as if to embrace the whole scene of the struggle. Instinctively I looked into the distance for some point that might suggest a battlefield. The hills cut across the landscape, and through the defiles, all that can be seen beyond are other white hills, crowned by black pine-woods. In spite of all my efforts I can form no idea of a modern battle, fought with guns that have a range of six kilometers. I have to recall all the terrible details, to think of the thousands of German dead, to imagine the distant masses of the human avalanche, in order to grasp the grandeur of the struggle.

"The battle you have just described to us," said I to our cicerone, "must have been one of the most terrible in the present war."

An enigmatic and contemptuous smile rises to the officer's lips.

"The action I have been talking about," he said, "was merely an episode in the Battle of Nancy, and the Battle of Nancy was only an episode in the great Battle of the Marne."

One cannot but feel utterly disconcerted at the proportions of these military operations of the twentieth century. An extent of ground which the eye cannot even take in, is not the picture, but a little corner of the picture. And this little corner would have sufficed for all the campaigns described by Froissart, which have thrilled us throughout the ages.

"The Battle of Nancy," said our guide, turning to the left, "took place on a line of over fifty kilometers and lasted more than a fortnight. Ever since August 20th, one of our divisions had been in the valley of the Moselle, ready to defend the road leading to the capital of Lorraine. At Morhange we suffered a cruel defeat, which enabled the Germans to take possession first of Nomeny, and then, in the early days of September, of Pont-à-Mousson. On September 4th, when the enemy's forces began to descend the heights of Château-Salines to attack our center, they succeeded after a fierce struggle in bombarding our positions at Sainte-Geneviève.

"On the 6th the Germans, finding the ground poorly defended, turned, confident of success, to Loisy, where they were well aware that we had only a single company. What is a company nowadays? Nothing at all. Nevertheless, the company at Loisy, by entrenching themselves in the cemetery, and taking advantage of the hollows in the ground, succeeded not only in making a good defense all the evening of the 6th, but forced those who were attacking them to abandon their frontal advance and make for the road to Sainte-Geneviève by a flanking movement. Do you know what troops were engaged against the company at Loisy?

A whole regiment. This regiment was almost completely annihilated in the marshy ground, without achieving the slightest result. But the Germans don't spare their men. On the following day a formidable column rushed the heights of Cuittes, where they placed batteries which commanded our center. Major M., who was in command at Sainte-Geneviève, saw his soldiers falling under a hail of shell. No matter. 'We won't give way an inch,' he cried. And the general had to send him a written order to induce him to retire towards the rearguard lines, here on the northern hills. It was then that the Emperor, seeing the way clear before his troops, gave the famous order of the day on the morning of the 7th, which ended thus: 'To-morrow, on to Nancy.' But to realize this dream it was necessary to dislodge our troops at Amance."

The captain, understanding that it was impossible for us to follow the movements of the army on the actual territory, unfolded his map, and pointed out the vast outlines of the battle. For three weeks several hundred thousands of men were maneuvering in this space, which stretches from the gates of Saint-Nicholas to the woods of Lunéville. Following on the paper the red lines that pass by Dommartin, Laneuvelotte, Champenoux, Réméréville, Drouville, Sommerviller, and Héréménil, we grasped the immensity of the battle as a whole. Every position, with its height indicated by figures, is the key to a road; every road is the bulwark of a valley; every stream serves as a trench to defend a pass. For all its epic grandeur the conflict was made up of minute episodes. The company which by holding out for a whole day in a cemetery against several battalions enabled the reserves to come up in time, was a decisive and symbolic pawn on the general chess-board. But all this, which became clear upon a map, with the officer's commentary, was an impenetrable mystery when we attempted to picture it upon the actual landscape.

"It was down there the avalanche came," we heard.

But we could see only the closed horizon. And this was hardly surprising, when we consider that looking out over the plain itself, and knowing that it was occupied at that very moment by a large number of batteries and many regiments, we could distinguish nothing but the undulating landscape, silent and deserted. In this strange modern warfare, so different from that of old, what one sees least is war itself. The guns are buried. The men are buried. The words of command, passing over telephone wires also buried, call forth from the bowels of the earth torrents of fire which are like the eruption of a volcano. And the warriors who fight and die, unseeing and unseen, know nothing of their valor, their triumphs and their reverses, until a *communiqué* from the staff brings the final echoes of battle to them in their holes.

The learned officer who is our guide, talks with the enthusiasm of an expert of the methodical and occult character of the campaign.

"It is scientific war," he exclaims, and his short-sighted blue eyes sparkle behind his spectacles.

But far from sharing his joy, I feel sorrowful when I evoke, as I do on every contemporary battlefield I visit— great battlefields, no doubt, and steeped, no doubt, in valiant blood—other fields less immense, in which History conjures up a vision of brilliant banners spread, and of the armies of the knights of old, who fell in the full light of day, and in the full flush of joy and pride.

THE BATTLE OF THE OURCQ

"THE TAXICAB ARMY THAT SAVED PARIS"

SEPTEMBER 5TH-8TH

GENERAL CLERGERIE   LOUIS MADELIN
GENERAL VON MOLTKE   GENERAL VON KLUCK

If Castelnau's victory on the Grand Couronné was the first step in
Germany's defeat, Maunoury's victory before Paris was the second.
The contest is now usually called, from the stream along which it was
chiefly fought, the Battle of the Ourcq. It was in its day the most
talked of event of the War, and probably the least understood, the
most confusing. Its most picturesque incident was the sudden launching into the fray of several thousand Paris troops by employing all
the taxicabs of the metropolis to rush them to the front. This has
naturally been magnified in importance, until it has become fixed in
a phrase as "the taxicab army that saved Paris." Hence the incident is here given in the authoritative words of General Clergerie, one
of the men who devised it. He was the chief-of-staff of General Galliéni, commander of Paris.

Far more important, and at the time bewildering, was the question
of General Von Kluck's sudden change in the direction of his advance.
By this he abandoned his threatened attack on Paris, and sapped the
high hopes of his soldiers. These had been chanting "On to Paris"
for a week, as they struggled mightily onward against every obstacle
of battle, of scorching heat and of physical exhaustion. We know now
that the change was part of the German general plan to encircle the
French armies and destroy them. Where Von Kluck erred was only
in assuming that the move could be made in safety, that the French
forces left around Paris were too feeble, and the Britons retreating
across the Marne were too crushed, to assail his flank as he marched
past them. Had his assumption been correct, had a small covering
force been sufficient to hold back the Paris attack, then Von Kluck
would have performed from the west that encirclement of the French
which Castelnau was so magnificently preventing in the east.

The next disputed problem of the battle is the part played in it by
the British army. Britons have been inclined to assume that Sir John
French by a final well-timed attack won the battle and so saved
France. They include this struggle as part of the main battle of the
Marne; and our volume in its account of that battle presents Sir
John's own report, so the reader may judge from that the weight of
the British claim. Here we have given instead a moderate French
account by the historian Madelin. There can be no question that the
main fighting of the battle was done by the French 6th Army under

General Maunoury, and that his chief help came from Paris. There have even been French critics to point out that the Britons, who were expected to attack with Maunoury, left him unsupported for two whole days, that they did not, in fact, turn upon Von Kluck until the brunt of the battle was over, and that when they did advance it was only against an already retreating remnant of Von Kluck's defeated troops. Of the splendid fighting of the Britons during their long and most disheartening retreat from Belgium, there exists no question whatsoever. But as to the degree of promptitude with which their commander renewed the needed aggressive movement in harmony with Maunoury, there ensued much criticism even in British circles.

Our German accounts of the battle include the brief official report of the Headquarters chief strategist, Gen. Von Moltke, and then the fuller narrative of General Von Kluck himself. He wrote a book on this battle to explain and defend his course, a defense necessitated because some of the German leaders sought to cast upon him the blame of having been needlessly defeated here and of having thereby lost the entire battle of the Marne. He was removed from command of his army somewhat abruptly by General Von Moltke and never again held a high position in the field. Military opinion in other lands has regarded him as the "scapegoat" of Germany's High Staff who had to blame someone for the obvious breakdown of their vaunted plan of crushing France.

BY GENERAL CLERGERIE

FROM August 26, 1914, the German armies had been descending upon Paris by forced marches. On September 1st they were only three days' march from the advanced line of the intrenched camp, which the garrison were laboring desperately to put into condition for defense. It was necessary to cover with trenches a circuit of 110 miles, install siege guns, assure the coming of supplies for them over narrow-gauge railways, assemble the food and provisions of all kinds necessary for a city of 4,000,000 inhabitants.

But on September 3rd the intelligence service, which was working perfectly, stated, about the middle of the day, that the German columns, after heading straight for Paris, were swerving toward the southeast and seemed to wish to avoid the fortified camp.

General Galliéni and I then had one of those long conferences which denoted grave events: they usually lasted from two to five minutes at most. The fact is that the military Government of Paris did little talking—it acted. The conference reached this conclusion: "If they do not come to us, we will go to them with all the force we can muster."

Nothing remained but to make the necessary preparations. The first thing to do was not to give the alarm to the enemy. General Maunoury's army immediately received orders to lie low and avoid any engagement that was not absolutely necessary.

In the night of September 3rd, knowing that the enemy would have to leave only a rear guard on one bank of the Ourcq, General Galliéni decided to march against that rear guard, to drive it back with all the weight of the Maunoury army, to cut the enemy's communications, and take full advantage of his hazardous situation. Immediately the following order was addressed to General Maunoury:

"Because of the movement of the German armies, which seem to be slipping in before our front to the southeast, I intend to send your army to attack them in the flank, that is to say, in an easterly direction. I will indicate your line of march as soon as I learn that of the British Army. But make your arrangements now so that your troops shall be ready to march this afternoon and to begin a general movement east of the intrenched camp to-morrow."

General Joffre gave permission to attack and announced that he would himself take the offensive on the 6th. On the 5th, at noon, the army from Paris fired the first shot; the battle of the Ourcq, a preface to the Marne, had begun.

General von der Marwitz, cavalry commander of the German First Army, made intemperate use of the wireless telegraph and did not even take the trouble to put into cipher his dispatches, of which the Eiffel Tower made a careful collection. In the evening of September 9th, an officer of the intelligence corps brought me a dispatch from this same Marwitz couched in something like these terms: "Tell me exactly where you are and what you are doing. Hurry up, because XXX."

The officer was greatly embarrassed to interpret those three Xs. Adopting the language of the poilu, I said to him: "Translate it, 'I am going to bolt.'" True enough, next day we found on the site of the German batteries, which had been precipitately evacuated, stacks of munitions; while by the roadside we came upon motors abandoned for the slightest breakdown, and near Betz almost the entire outfit of a field bakery, with a great store of flour and dough half-kneaded. Paris and France were saved. Von Kluck could not get over his astonishment. He has tried to explain it by saying he was unlucky, for out of a hundred Governors not one would have acted as Galliéni did, throwing his whole available force nearly forty miles from his stronghold. It was downright imprudence. Of course, it was Galliéni who was in the wrong!

BY LOUIS MADELIN

On August 30th Von Kluck was nearing Paris, he was at Chantilly, only twenty-two and a half miles distant. The great town, encouraged and comforted by Galliéni's words, which will become historic,[1] but abandoned by the Government, awaited the barbarous hordes with outward calm,— just as in former days, Geneviève de Nanterre had calmed the people of Lutetia menaced by Attila's Huns.

But already on September 3rd it seemed as if Von Kluck, heading towards Meaux and Coulommiers, was turning away from Paris—for the time being. It is said that he was applying Moltke's doctrine: "Defeat and throw back the French beyond the Marne, the Yonne and the Loire, and only then march upon Paris." Was this posthumous order necessary? Had Von Kluck attempted to enter the capital without fighting, it would have been a great risk—Maunoury would have barred the way and Galliéni was there behind Maunoury, what magnificent strength wasted just when it was going to be proved that the entire German Army massed together could not withstand the French Army! Of what worth would Von Kluck's troops have been, hampered as they were by conquest, and drunk with something that did not resemble pride, before our armies so easily victorious?

Nevertheless, Von Kluck pushed on towards the Marne, possessed with the idea that he would attack our left, the British Army and d'Espérey's, and enveloping it, turn the entire French Army. The maneuver was an obvious one

[1] See article on "The Abandonment of Paris."

and imposed itself on strategy, it would have succeeded had not Maunoury been on Von Kluck's right flank. But, curiously enough, and most inexplicable, the German general who prided himself on his knowledge of everything seems to have ignored the existence of a French Army on his right, or if he knew of it, he underestimated its strength and continued marching south, while Maunoury let him get encircled and spread out his own forces fan-wise from north to south, facing east.

The mistake was all the graver since Von Kluck, and the other German generals, were going to encounter an army no longer in retreat, but an army which by order of its chief was ready to hold and determined to attack.

The mistake rested mainly with Von Kluck and was due in a measure to his misconception of the opponent and to his unbounded audacity. Galliéni had warned Joffre on the 4th of Von Kluck's daring advance, and everything since had confirmed the news received from Paris. In agreement with the Governor of the city, our Generalissimo clearly saw what steps the event immediately necessitated. He wants the battle fought on our left. Kluck hopes to envelop Sir John French and d'Espérey, but it is Maunoury, disregarded by Kluck, who will attempt to envelop Von Kluck with the help of Sir John French and d'Espérey.

The mission of the armies on the left is thus already defined by General Joffre's order of the 4th:

"1st. It is expedient to take advantage of the *foolhardy position of the 1st German Army* and hurl against it the strength of our left flank. All steps will be taken on the 5th for an attack on the 6th."

The first days are more especially Maunoury's. The latter has scarcely moved, threatening to envelop and crush the 40,000 men of Schwerin's corps, when the Prussian general, alarmed, calls for help. Von Kluck, at the very moment when he engages the four-fifths of his army against Sir John French and d'Espérey, learns that a recently formed army is menacing his left flank. With a promptitude that enhances his reputation as a strategist, he does not hesitate to abandon his plan in order to break the attack prepared against him. He turns round and faces Maunoury, certain that after having crushed him, he can turn again south and finish off Sir John French and d'Espérey.

Everything will therefore depend on Maunoury's resistance. If he is able to hold, Sir John French and d'Espérey can repulse the troops left against them and in their turn menace Von Kluck, not on his right, but on his left flank. And menaced he was on the third day, obliged to admit he is vanquished and beat a retreat for fear of being caught between Maunoury, French and d'Espérey.

This battle is the battle of the Ourcq. By losing it and retreating prudently, Von Kluck laid Von Bülow's front bare and weakened the entire German front, which could not be strengthened owing to Foch's violent attacks elsewhere. That is why the battle of the Ourcq has been termed the decisive factor in the victory of the Marne.

The first encounter between Maunoury and Schwerin's corps took place in Monthyon at 2 p. m. on the 5th. Meanwhile, the light cavalry, charging on Penchard, spread death there, and the soldiers of the 56th reserve division carried Marcilly and Chambry, while those of the 55th took Barcy, thanks to the deadly fire of our artillery. Already in one little corner of the battlefield, infantry, cavalry, zouaves, at the cost of cruel losses, display a courage which, read of later on, moves one to enthusiasm. It has been said that "Barcy and Chambry became the tombs of our reserve divisions," but tombs that already predicted the salvation of France!

We continue to advance on the 6th; the entire 4th reserve corps is thrown eastwards and seems in a bad way when the first reënforcements reach it from the south. Von Kluck has begun to realize the impossibility of his position. Through lack of precise information, he had run a great risk. He immediately recalls the 2nd and 4th corps, thus uncovering part of the front facing the British army and d'Espérey, in order to meet a more pressing danger, and he places his heavy artillery between Varreddes and May-en-Multien.

The Germans cannot, however, regain their positions and

by the end of the afternoon the 4th reserve corps, badly shattered, falls back towards the woods of Meaux. Maunoury on the 7th, reënforced by the 61st division sent from Paris, is advancing steadily and beginning his enveloping movement. The 4th reserve corps is giving way. At this juncture, Von Kluck crosses the Marne again and intervenes with the bulk of his army. General Vauthier (7th corps) is engaged in a desperate struggle at Etavigny with the 2nd corps, and thrown back on Acy-en-Multien. The fighting everywhere is very fierce. The German artillery from Trocy shells our positions in vain, our men take and retake them time after time. Thus the farm at Nogeon where we captured a flag, was lost and recovered three times.

Von Kluck, however, seems to be averting his peril; he decides to take the offensive on the 8th, calling on his reserves left in the south. But our troops are determined no further ground shall be lost and the fighting on the 8th becomes more and more desperate. We advance till midday, but the 45th division, attacking in the Varreddes direction, is repulsed by curtain fire, and the 7th corps falls back from Betz and Thury-en-Valois. Maunoury immediately sends a reënforcement of three regiments from the 61st reserve division, and elsewhere the advance continues towards Trilport and Changis. Von Kluck, now fully aware of his danger and extremely anxious, is repeatedly calling up reënforcements from the south. Maunoury is also greatly reenforced by the entire 4th army corps (General Boëlle) taken from Sarrail's army and transferred rapidly to the other end of the battlefield. The action on the Ourcq turns into a huge battle. Von Kluck means it to be so, and realizing now the strength of his adversary, seems to have given up all idea of an offensive beyond the Marne, for he orders all the bridges to be destroyed; this, he thinks, will insure the safety of his left flank. Almost the entire bulk of his army is now massed against Maunoury.

Will the latter, in this torrid heat, be able to hold on with men who have been fighting for three days?

It is at this critical moment that Galliéni, warned of the situation by the 6th army commander, intervenes once again.

From the beginning of operations, the Military Governor of Paris has followed step by step the preparations for the battle now about to rage on the east of the great capital. His warnings and advice had been often listened to and he proved a valuable lieutenant, cool-headed, never ceasing to provide Maunoury's army with all the reënforcements at his disposal. On the 9th, acting upon his own initiative, he sent him the most precious of all in the shape of the 62nd division freshly disembarked in Paris. And so that it might from the first take part in the battle, he mobilized in a few hours the Paris taxicabs. These modern vehicles thus had their small share in the "miracle" and the troops transported in this manner to the Ourcq were thoroughly amused by the Governor's act.[2] Such troops would at any time have been most valuable. At the same moment, Von Kluck receives a message from General Von Marwitz, left in the south against the British, that does not tend to reassure him.

The British had been severely attacked on the morning of the 6th by the 2nd corps on the Vaudoy-Hautefeuille line, whilst the 4th corps pressed forward on the left. Sir John French was preparing to counter-attack when, to his surprise, the fighting calmed down and suddenly ceased. It was at this moment that Von Kluck, realizing the danger of his position in the north, sent for reënforcements. The British could make nothing of it. In classical fashion, Von Kluck then covers the sudden retreat of his 80,000 men by the incessant noise of artillery and a great display of cavalry. The British hesitate about moving northwards; they allow the 4th corps to cross the Petit-Morin and only decide towards evening to push their advance guard in the direction of Villiers-sur-Morin-Choisy. Sir John French's infantry becomes bolder and bolder, advancing rapidly it dislodges the enemy and holds the heights occupied that very morning by the German artillery. Marwitz's cavalry continues to

---

[2] The number of these valiant little cabs has been strangely exaggerated, 9,000 have been mentioned, but in reality only one thousand were used. As was explained to me by some one who organized the affair, both chauffeurs and *taxis* yielded such a return that it explains the temptation to increase them tenfold.—MADELIN.

cover the retreating German corps so that they are able to recross the Marne on the 7th. The British, however, move beyond Coulommiers and on the 8th, having received intelligence from their airmen concerning Von Kluck's right wing, which had recrossed the Marne and was blocking the way, they destroy the bridges, notably at la Ferté-sous-Jouarre, while the infantry of the 3rd corps quickens its march. The British infantry now succeeds in dislodging the enemy between St. Cyr and La Trétoire after stubborn resistance. The whole of Sir John French's army has forced the Petit-Morin and is pressing hard on the 2nd cavalry division which, unable to halt as it had hoped, is continuing its retreat. Encouraged by this, the British advance faster and faster, they cross the Marne between Luzancy and Nogent-l'Artaud; there where the bridges had been blown up by the enemy their engineers throw over pontoon bridges, they only succeed in securing the passage of the river at Varreddes under enemy fire after having thrown across, with true British tenacity, 17 bridges, unfortunately part of the army was delayed in crossing. Marwitz now completely realizes that the danger is deepening on Von Kluck's left. A detachment of English soldiers is hurled against two German squadrons, "piercing through," in Sir John French's words: "with the ease of a penknife through packing paper." The German cavalry are now in full retreat; d'Espérey, on Sir John French's right, is advancing quicker and quicker, thus adding to the enveloping movement which is growing more and more dangerous for Von Kluck.

D'Espérey advancing from Montmirail routs the enemy as he goes and comes into touch with Sir John French's army also in pursuit of the enemy—thus both armies reach and cross the Marne. Von Kluck is now directly menaced on his flank, while Maunoury, who has received reënforcements, continues to oppose him. It can be easily understood that the 1st German Army Commander, spurred on by the anger surging against him at Imperial Headquarters, made fierce efforts to reduce his adversary. The issue of the battle perhaps depended on this moment.

Von Kluck at the same time tries to outflank Maunoury in the north at Nanteuil and to throw him back south towards Etrépilly.

The 4th corps is hurled from Betz to Nanteuil and encounters our 4th corps, which had arrived on the battlefield on the preceding evening. The struggle is fierce, bloody and desperate. Nanteuil is evacuated, General Boëlle orders the defending troops to fall back while the enemy occupies Droiselles and menaces Silly-le-Long from Montigny-Sainte-Félicité. Boëlle's corps is in danger of being turned. It is a dramatic moment—everywhere else the German effort is broken, Etrépilly, heavily bombarded, still holds, but the danger for us lies at Nanteuil and it would seem that Von Kluck has discovered the weak spot in our armor. Are we in our *extremis* going to be turned? Maunoury sends word to Boëlle that he is not to move a step backwards but on the contrary to advance, *and if necessary be slain where he stands;* the latter had not waited for this order to reform his corps and face the enemy, already the 1st battalion of the 103rd supported by two batteries, holds the enemy behind Nanteuil in a kind of fierce rage. General Boëlle advances, certain of being cut to pieces and finds himself before a faltering enemy. Von Kluck was beating a retreat.

For Marwitz's warnings had become pressing. "He could no longer withstand the combined Franco-British attacks," Sir John French and d'Espérey would in a few hours thrust him on Von Kluck, for whom the position had become so dangerous that no further hesitation was possible. The German High Command, we have proof of it to-day, already knew then that the game was up. The Emperor, abandoning France, had gone to Luxemburg; on every hand Von Kluck's mistake aroused the fiercest anger.

"With a heavy heart," says a German account, "he gave the order for a general retreat northwards." He and his many thousand soldiers were vanquished and so as to avoid imminent and terrible disaster, this general, who had the greatest reputation for strategy in the German army, fell back defeated to the north. From every side, mournfully, German columns are pouring forth; some in bad array having suffered heavily and all now experiencing a fatigue not felt the day before when they hoped to carry all before them. No more cries of *"Nach Paris,"* but everywhere stupefying silence. They were unable to pick up their wounded or bury their dead, for they had to give way as they went. The earth was strewn with dead. To quote one instance: The Magdeburg regiment was torn almost to shreds in a desperate struggle near d'Acy-en-Multien.

Maunoury helps to clear up the field; he sends from right to left wing the necessary reënforcements to dislodge the German detachments from Nanteuil. He presses closely on the rear of the retiring columns, following both banks of the Ourcq, whilst the Germans retreat hastily towards the forest of Villers-Cotterets, whence they are obliged to push on towards Soissons the next day.

The 6th army, having forced Von Kluck to abandon abruptly his offensive against the British and the 5th army, had in this way attracted the attention of the greater bulk of the powerful German army and for four days had offered a firm front to a formidable attack. Finally, helped by the menacing advance of the Armies of the Marne, it forced the "incomparable" army and its eminent chief to beat a hasty retreat in order to avoid utter ruin.

GENERAL JOFFRE'S PROCLAMATION TO MAUNOURY'S ARMY

The 6th army has just sustained, during five entire days, without interruption or rest, an engagement against a numerous enemy whose previous successes had raised their *morale* to a high pitch. The struggle has been a severe one, and the losses from fire, as well as from fatigue due to want of sleep, and occasionally of provisions, have surpassed any that have been hitherto imagined; you have supported all this with a valor, a firmness, and an endurance to which no words can possibly give adequate expression.

Comrades! Your General asked you, for the sake of your country, to do more than your plain duty; your answer has exceeded his most sanguine expectations. Thanks to you, victory has crowned our colors. Now that you have realized the glorious satisfaction of victory, you will in future never let it fall from your grasp.

As for myself, if I have been able to help I have been fully compensated by the greatest honor of my long career, namely, to have commanded troops such as you are. For all you have done I thank you with sincerest emotion, because to you I owe that to which all my efforts and energy for the last forty-four years have been directed—Revenge for 1870! My thanks to you; honor to all the combatants of the 6th army!

JOFFRE.

BY GENERAL VON MOLTKE

Announcement from German Military Headquarters

[This statement from the German strategist at the head of the High Staff is the only official German recognition of Von Kluck's defeat. He was, however, promptly removed from command.]

Berlin, September 10, 1914.

East of Paris [German] detachments which had advanced to the Marne and across it have been attacked by superior enemy forces coming from Paris, and between Meaux and Montmirail. These detachments held the enemy, and after hard fighting, which lasted two days, they have gained ground. News having been received as to the approach of new and strong enemy columns, the [right] wing of these detachments has fallen back without being anywhere pursued.

BY GENERAL VON KLUCK

A chance of dealing a decisive blow against the British Army was now no longer to be hoped for, and it was therefore decided to move the two corps on the left wing, the III., and IX., in the general direction of Château Thierry against the flank of the French retreating from Braisne-Fismes on Château Thierry-Dormans in front of the Second Army.

In coöperation with the Second Army it might be

possible to damage the French western flank very considerably. The First Army by its deep formation was in a position both to cover the flank and rear of such an attack and also to hold in check the garrison of Paris and the British.

During the night of the 2nd-3rd September a wireless message arrived from the Supreme Command: "The intention is to drive the French in a south-easterly direction from Paris. The First Army will follow in echelon behind the Second Army and will be responsible for the flank protection of the Armies." The general directions of August 28th, which had ordered the First Army to move west of the Oise towards the lower Seine, had therefore been abandoned, and the wheel inwards of the First Army towards the Oise and its passage of the river about Compiègne and Noyon on the 31st August in order to exploit the success of the Second Army had evidently been approved by the Supreme Command. On the evening of the 2nd September, when that day's movements had been completed, the four corps of the First Army and the Cavalry Corps were still in the region of Creil-La Ferté Milon, north-east of Paris, ready for any operation west of the capital, against it, or east of it, whilst the IX. Corps, like an arm of the Army reaching out to the left, was making the most creditable efforts to fulfil its mission and hold up the western flank of the retreating French Army by Château Thierry.

The First Army Commander considered that to force the enemy away from Paris in a south-easterly direction (which would involve the passage of the Marne and the Seine) would be a difficult and risky undertaking. There would probably be initial successes, but it would be scarcely possible in the circumstances to continue the offensive until the enemy was decisively defeated or partially annihilated. Another group of four or five divisions was needed by the Armies on the German right wing, in order effectively to guard the right flank against Paris and protect the long communications of the First and Second Armies, if the advance was to be continued into the centre of France. The Supreme Command, however, seemed to be firmly convinced that the garrison of Paris need not be taken into account for any operations outside the line of forts of the capital.[1] It is true that all the reports up to date seemed to confirm this point of view, but the situation of the flank armies might and would be most dangerous as soon as the French Higher Command was in a position to move a mass of troops from a part of the front where they could be spared through Paris, and thence begin a big offensive, making use of the great facilities for deployment from behind its extensive line of forts. The Supreme Command, however, had no anxieties with regard to the risks here suggested, and evidently placed complete confidence in the accuracy of its intelligence service on that point. At First Army Headquarters this view of the general situation also found many adherents. All the more urgently, therefore, did the First Army Commander renew his request for the long-delayed transfer to the front of the Brigade of the IV. Reserve Corp retained by the Governor-General of Brussels, and for the relief by *Landsturm* and *Landwehr* troops of all the active units on the line of communications, so that they also might be brought up to the front. A further appreciation of the tasks of the First Army in these critical days was finally concentrated into a memorandum sent by the First Army Commander to the Supreme Command.

"The First Army Commander had up till then—at La Ferté Milon—imagined that the German plan of campaign had so far been carried out as arranged, that all the armies were advancing from victory to victory, and that the enemy was being decisively beaten along the whole front. That such was not the case—particularly that the German left wing to the south-west had withdrawn from the front of the French line of fortresses—was not realized at First Army Headquarters, owing to the scanty information which was given to it on the general situation of all the armies.

[1] The Supreme Command orders of the 2nd/3rd September quoted above ordered the First Army "to follow in echelon behind the Second Army and to be responsible for the flank protection of the Armies." These provided against attack from Paris direction. Von Kluck did not carry out these orders. His explanation for his disobedience follows below.

The rapidity of the advance frequently made it difficult to maintain the telephonic cables leading to the rear, which were often destroyed by the inhabitants or by fire, sometimes accidentally by our own troops, and in other ways. Communication with the Supreme Command had therefore to be carried on mainly by wireless stations, which again were overworked in keeping touch with the Cavalry Corps and the neighboring armies, a fact which the Army Commander was frequently made aware of by personal experience. There was consequently no means for the personal exchange of views so urgently needed between Army Headquarters and the General Staff of the Supreme Command. Nevertheless, no doubt existed at First Army Headquarters that the protection of the flank of the armies was increasing in importance as they advanced, and that the troops at the disposal of the First Army, which, under force of circumstances, had to be used for purposes of attack and flank protection simultaneously, would not suffice in the end for this. The reinforcement of the right wing by a group of about two corps appeared, therefore, to be absolutely indispensable."

These reflections found expression in a wireless message sent to the Supreme Command on the morning of the 4th September, which ran as follows: "The First Army requests to be informed of the situation of the other Armies, whose reports of decisive victories have so far been frequently followed by appeals for support. The First Army, which has been fighting and marching incessantly, has reached the limits of its endurance. It is through its efforts alone that the crossings of the Marne have been opened for the other Armies, and that the enemy has been compelled to continue his retreat. The IX. Corps has won the greatest merit by its bold action in this respect. It is now hoped that every advantage will be taken of this success.

"The message of the Supreme Command No. 2220, in accordance with which the First Army was to follow in echelon behind the Second, could not be carried out under the circumstances. The intention to force the enemy away from Paris in a south-easterly direction was only practicable by advancing the First Army. The necessary flank protection weakens the offensive strength of the Army, and immediate reinforcements are therefore urgently needed. Owing to the ever-changing situation, it will not be possible for the commander of the First Army to make any further important decisions unless he is kept continuously informed of the situation of the other armies who are apparently not so far advanced. Communication with the Second Army is constantly maintained."

On the evening of the 5th September detailed instructions arrived from the Supreme Command, and from them it appeared that the enemy was transporting troops from the front Belfort-Toul westwards, and was also withdrawing troops from the front of our Third, Fourth, and Fifth Armies. The Supreme Command, therefore, calculated that very strong enemy forces were being concentrated near Paris to protect the capital and threaten the German right flank. The bearer of these instructions from the Supreme Command, Lieut.-Colonel Hentsch, gave a verbal account of the general situation, and, to the amazement of First Army Headquarters, who believed all the Armies to be advancing victoriously, it appeared that the left wing of the German Armies—namely, the Fifth, Sixth, and Seventh Armies—was held up in front of the French eastern fortresses, so much so that it could scarcely pin the enemy in front of it to his ground. There was consequently a possibility that the enemy would move troops by rail from his eastern wing towards Paris.

A very different aspect was thus given to the situation confronting the First Army. It was intensified by a report which arrived late in the evening of the presence of strong enemy forces about Dammartin, to the north-east of Paris.

During the night of the 5th September it became obvious that further and more drastic changes in the movements of the First Army were essential, if the danger of an envelopment was to be effectively countered in time. Owing to the reports of the IV. Reserve Corps in its fighting during the 5th, a special order was sent to the II. Corps to begin its march in the early hours of the 6th, so as to be ready to support the IV. Reserve Corps on the 6th if needed. Its commander, General von Linsingen, moved the 4th Infantry Division by Lizy towards Trocy and the 3rd by Vareddes, to the relief of the IV. Reserve Corps, which in the meantime had been attacked by about a corps of the enemy on the front Bregy-St. Soupplets-Penchard. The 3rd Infantry Division came up against strong British forces west and north of Vareddes.[1] The first strong reinforcement to deal with the new opponent had thus arrived on the scenes.

By an Order issued at 5.30 p. m. the IV. Corps was withdrawn across the Marne to the district north of La Ferté-sous-Jouarre, so that in case of necessity it could be put into the fight, the enemy having now brought superior forces into action. At 10.30 p. m. the IV. Corps was ordered to move again that same night, so that at dawn it would be in a position to attack across a line Rozoy-en-Multien-Trocy. Thus, on the morning of the 7th September, the II. Corps, the IV. Reserve Corps (still without its Brussels Brigade), and the IV. Corps stood between the Thérouane and the Gergogne (a tributary of the Ourcq), with their units rather intermingled, with the 4th Cavalry Division immediately to the north of them: they were to hold up the Army of Maunoury, of the strength and composition of which nothing was known at First Army Headquarters. The pressure of superior forces was perceptible from the very first.[2]

The Second Army, wheeling round, pivoted on its right flank at Montmirail, intended to continue the pursuit up to the Seine with its centre and left wing, the latter moving on Marigny-le-Grand. The III. and IX. Corps thus came in front of the right wing of the Second Army. By an Army Order issued at 10 p. m. that evening both these corps were therefore withdrawn to the line Sablonnières-Montmirail

[1] There were no English forces within ten miles of Vareddes, nor did any of them come in contact with the II. Corps on the 6th. The Moroccan Brigade is probably meant.

[2] Von Kluck's own account of Maunoury's Army, taken from Major Gedel's book, disproves that it was on the 6th/7th September superior in force to his troops.

on the northern bank of the Petit Morin. They gained touch again with the right flank of the Second Army at Montmirail, and, to ensure united action, were to conform to its instructions. Marwitz's Cavalry, which had advanced to Lumigny and Rozoy, covered the right flank of the III. Corps against the enemy forces.

During the morning of the 8th September it became evident that the British were advancing towards the Marne, while strong forces. An order was therefore sent to the IX. Corps at 11.20 a. m. to occupy the line of the Marne from La Ferté-sous-Jouarre to Nogent-l'Artaud, so as to guard it against this flanking movement of the British, but in the end only an infantry brigade and two field artillery regiments were sent, and the General Reserve at Montreuil-aux-Lions was handed over to the Corps Commander. The Marne bridges were to be prepared for destruction, and, if necessary, to be demolished; in the latter case, the fact was to be notified to headquarters.

Meanwhile, the French attempt to break through our front at Trocy on the morning of the 8th had been frustrated without the assistance of the 5th Infantry Division, which was ready at hand in support. Late in the evening, Army Headquarters went to La Ferté Milon in order to be close to the critical part of the battle. At dusk an audacious detachment of French cavalry[1] had attacked an aeroplane station south of La Ferté Milon, just as the line of cars of Army Headquarters was approaching the scene of action. All the members of the Staff seized rifles, carbines, and revolvers, so as to ward off a possible advance of the French cavalrymen, and extended out and lay down, forming a long firing-line. The dusky red and clouded evening sky shed a weird light on this quaint little fighting force. The thunder of the artillery of the IX. and IV. Corps boomed and roared defiantly, and the gigantic flashes of the heavy guns lit up the deep shadows of the approaching night. In the meantime, the French squadrons had been

[1] This was Gironde's squadron of the 22nd Dragoons in the raid of the 5th Cavalry Division led by General Cornulier-Lucinière. (See "Le Rôle de la Cavalerie Française à l'aile gauche de la première bataille de la Marne," by J. Héthay.)

apparently shot down, dispersed, or captured by troops of the IX. or another Corps.[1] These bold horsemen had missed a goodly prize!

The Army Operation Order for the 9th September issued from La Ferté Milon late in the evening of the 8th, stated that the First Army had maintained its position on the whole front from Cuvergnon, north of Betz-Antilly, to the Marne salient at Congis; also that enemy reserves were reported south and west of Crépy-en-Valois. A decision would be arrived at on the morrow by the enveloping attack of General von Quast with the IX. Corps and the 6th Infantry and 4th Cavalry Divisions from the wooded country north of Cuvergnon.

Shortly after 1 p. m. the following wireless message arrived from the Second Army: "Airmen report the advance of four long enemy columns towards the Marne; at 9 a. m. their advanced troops were on the line Nanteuil-Citry-Pavant-Nogent-l'Artaud. The Second Army is beginning to retreat; its right flank on Damery." This retreat widened the gap between the two Armies, which up till now had been screened, into a serious breach in the western wing of the German Armies, extending—with every possibility of a further increase—from Château Thierry to about Epernay—that is to say, on the breadth of front of an Army. Not till twenty hours later did the Second Army Headquarters correct their message by another to say their right flank was retiring not on Damery, but on Dormans.[2]

The attack of General von der Marwitz against the British ended successfully, and part of the enemy who had crossed the Marne was thrown back into the vicinity of Montbertoin by evening.

Towards midday the situation of the First Army was thoroughly favorable, even taking into consideration the withdrawal of the Second Army north-eastwards. For victory seemed assured on the decisive wing of attack, the left wing was standing firm, and the flank appeared to be

[1] There was only one squadron. It lost 2 officers and 25 men *vide* Héthay, quoted above.

[2] Damery is ten miles east of Dormans. The mistake made the gap forty miles instead of thirty.

sufficiently guarded by General von der Marwitz with two cavalry divisions, the 5th Infantry Division, and Kraewel's Brigade. At about this period Lieut.-Colonel Hentsch, on the Staff of the Supreme Command, arrived at Mareuil from Second Army Headquarters. His arrival was only made known to the Army Commander after he had already hastily departed—a regrettable circumstance, which would have been avoided had the Colonel personally reported himself to the Army Commander; the latter at the moment was close to the scene of the meeting.[1]

Colonel Hentsch made the following communication, which was taken down in the form of a minute in the still existing records of First Army Headquarters:

"The situation is not favorable. The Fifth Army is held up in front of Verdun and the Sixth and Seventh in front of Nancy-Epinal. The retreat of the Second Army behind the Marne is unalterable: its right wing, the VII. Corps, is being forced back and not voluntarily retiring. In consequence of these facts, all the Armies are to be moved back: the Third Army to north-east of Châlons, and the Fourth and Fifth Army, in conjunction, through the neighborhood of Clermont-en-Argonne towards Verdun. The First Army must therefore also retire in the direction Soissons-Fère-en-Tardenois, and in extreme circumstances perhaps farther, even to Laon-La Fère. (Lieut.-Colonel Hentsch drew the approximate line to be reached by the First Army with a bit of charcoal on the map of General-major von Kuhl, Chief of the Staff.) A new Army was being assembled near St. Quentin, so that a fresh operation might be begun. General von Kuhl remarked that the attack of the First Army was in full swing and that a retreat would be a very delicate operation, especially as the Army was in an extremely exhausted condition and its units intermingled. To this Lieut.-Colonel Hentsch replied that there was nothing else to be done; he admitted that, as the fight-

---

[1] It would appear to be the fault of Von Kluck's Chief of Staff that Colonel Hentsch did not see him. Hentsch, of course, as is the service custom, would report first to the General Staff. An unproven rumor represents Von Kluck as having been intoxicated on French wines.

ing stood at the moment, it would not be convenient to retire in the direction ordered and better to go straight back to behind the Aisne with the left flank at least on Soissons. He emphasized the fact that these directions were to remain valid regardless of any other communications that might arrive and that he had full powers."

It must be repeated that information of such a kind, throwing an entirely different light on the whole situation, should have been given by Lieut.-Colonel Hentsch direct to the Commander of the First Army.

From French sources now available, it is clear that General Maunoury had so early as the evening of the 8th considered the advisability of a retreat to a position of defence on the line Monthyon-St. Soupplets-Le Plessis Belleville. A tactical victory of the First Army over the Army of Maunoury on the extreme left wing of the French forces seemed indeed certain, and it was possible that by the continuation of the offensive on the 9th a far-reaching success might have been obtained. It is probable also that the British could not have come forward very rapidly at first after the fight at Montbertoin. Nevertheless, after the instructions from the Supreme Command, there could be no longer any doubt as to the necessity for the retreat ordered.

The full advantages of the success begun against Maunoury could be reaped with certainty within the next few days; but the breaking away from the enemy and the reorganization of units which would then be necessary, as well as the bringing up of fresh supplies of ammunition and food, moving forward the trains and making the communications secure—all being measures requiring time to carry out—would enable the British force only temporarily held up at Montbertoin and other British columns immediately east of it, as well as the left wing of the more mobile Army of General d'Esperey, to come up on the flank and in rear of the First Army, which had already reached the limits of its powers of endurance. Unless it is assumed that the enemy would make extraordinary mistakes, the First Army would then have to isolate itself from the other Armies by a withdrawal in a north-westerly direction towards Dieppe, or in more favorable circumstances towards Amiens—in any case, a long march, with a corresponding wastage of man-power.

In view of the completely altered situation, the Army Commander, fully conscious of the tremendous consequences of his decision, decided to begin the withdrawal immediately in a northerly direction towards the lower Aisne, between Soissons and Compiègne. Once the decision was made, the situation called for its execution without delay. Not a single hour was to be lost. Army Operation Orders were issued from Headquarters at Mareuil at 2 p. m. and at 8.15 p. m., as follows:

"The situation of the Second Army has necessitated its withdrawal behind the Marne on both sides of Epernay. By order of the Supreme Command, the First Army is to be withdrawn in the general direction of Soissons, to cover the flank of the Armies. A new German Army is being assembled at St. Quentin. The movement of the First Army will begin to-day. The left wing of the Army, under General von Linsingen, including the group under General von Lochow, will therefore be first withdrawn behind the line Montigny-Brumetz. The group under General Sixt von Armin will conform to this movement so far as the tactical situation will allow, and take up a new line from Antilly to Mareuil. The offensive of the group under General von Quast will not be proceeded with any further than is required for the purpose of breaking away from the enemy, so that it will be possible to conform to the movement of the other Armies.

"(*Signed*)   Von Kluck."

THE MARNE

THE BATTLE THAT SAVED FRANCE

SEPTEMBER 6TH-11TH

LOUIS MADELIN   JOSEPH REINACH
SIR JOHN FRENCH   MARSHAL JOFFRE
               PRESIDENT POINCARÉ

With the preliminaries of this World Battle made clear by the pictures of them drawn in the preceding sections of this volume, the main battle is easily understood. With his two flanks splendidly protected by Castelnau in the east and Maunoury in the west, General Joffre was now ready to concentrate his utmost power in beating back the German main attack. He meant to check that line, break it if he could, hurl it back in utter rout and capture if fortune turned so far in his favor.

The first step, the checking of the advance, he accomplished in terrific battle all along the line from September 6th-10th. The second step, the breaking of the line, was achieved at its very center on the evening of September 9th by the Ninth French Army under General Foch. By September 11th the necessary result, the retreat of the Germans to a new line of defense, was begun, reluctantly enough, all along the front. But the final hoped for step, the rout and ruin and capture—this was beyond the Allies' power.

Nevertheless, the first stage of the war was here ended. The intended German rush to immediate victory was foiled. A new war began, with new plans, new strategies. There have been military critics to assert that in none of the later campaigns was there any practical chance of Germany's victory, that only that first rush held for her any real probability of success, and that hence the Marne was really the one all-important contest of the War.

Following the careful general account of the battle by the French historian Madelin, we give here a summary of the various German accounts by Joseph Reinach, then the official narrative of the British commander, the terse concluding commentary of General Joffre, and the public announcement of triumph to the world by President Poincaré.

BY LOUIS MADELIN

FROM the 5th to the 10th September, the destiny of France and probably of the whole of western civilization was at stake on the plains of the Marne. On a battlefield nearly 200 miles in area, barring the way from Paris to Verdun against the most formidable invasion that has ever menaced France, the Nation in arms checked the invasion, and if, during that memorable week she did not completely shatter it, she at all events in some measure brought it to a standstill.

In those days, the French army, aided by a few British regiments, not only saved a country from ruin, but also rescued Europe from the formidable yoke that was threatening her. Between the river Seine and the Aisne, and between the banks of the Meuse and the suburbs of Paris, more than two million men, representing not only two nations, hereditary enemies, but two ideals, and if I may so term it two worlds, were face to face in battle array. It was not as at Jena or Sedan a matter of deciding a quarrel for which certain provinces were the prize. A question was put to France and perhaps to Germany on that memorable 4th September, 1914: *To be or not to be?* But in addition, the defeat of France meant the slavery of Europe, and her victory its deliverance.

The Battle of the Marne marks one of the most solemn hours that France has ever known, one of the five or six moments when from the brink of the abyss she staked all and won.

It was an onslaught! The invasion of the Huns in the 4th century, and that of the Allies in 1814, had been nothing compared with this formidable flood of men and artillery. The mass hurled against us consisted of about 1,500,000 men, more than a million of whom were rushing towards Paris from every side with 4,000 field guns, 450 batteries of heavy guns and 700 enormous trench mortars. The armies of von Kluck and Bülow (I and II) alone hurled 520,000 Germans through the gap at the Oise on l'Ile de France, the first army, following the right bank of the Aisne, seemed to be marching on Paris; the second, for a moment dislodged in Guise, rolled like a flood towards Laon on the Epernay road. Witnesses declare that the Germans moved forward like an enormous wave. Hausen, with the III Army (120,000 men), had penetrated into France by the right bank of the Meuse and was marching from Rethel on to Châlons; the Duke of Wurtemberg (IV Army), whose 200,000 men were being held in check with difficulty but successfully by General Langle de

Cary, was advancing from Sedan in the direction of Vitry, whilst the V Army, under the command of the Imperial Crown Prince himself, with a force of 200,000 men, after having skirted Verdun on the north, crossing the Meuse and part of Argonne, came down the valleys of Ornain and of Basse-Saulx.

They marched very rapidly imbued with the idea that it was vital for Germany to "crush France" by a swift blow before Russia could develop her full fighting strength and before England developed a taste for warfare. Soldiers' diaries bear witness to the fact that they had to march from 21 to 24 miles a day under the scorching sun of the last week in August. They reached the regions between the Aisne and the Maine, and Argonne and Ornain in a somewhat exhausted condition early in September. They amused themselves, by spreading grief and shame in the places they passed through, plundering, burning, violating, killing; the most human among them were content with the spoils of the cellar and the larder, carrying away in their knapsacks the most unlikely booty which, however, they were often obliged to leave on the roadside, and in Champagne especially they gave themselves up recklessly to that bacchanalian orgy which had colored their earliest dreams. At the rear or in the midst of this flood of men rolled the heavy artillery, the pride and hope of this modern horde, crushing under its heavy wheels meat that had rotted, broken treasures and empty bottles. The inhabitants of our northeastern provinces watched them pass, they seemed part of the machinery of an enormous destroying force, stiff, and automatic in the ranks, but like wild beasts let loose when at rest, trying to revenge themselves for the torment they endured on their victim, France, yelling *"nach Paris"* in a sort of frenzied lust. For they all thought, like the officer just now, that they would go straight to the "Moulin Rouge," whereas they were to encounter, strangely magnified, the Moulin de Valmy.

Our army continued to retreat, but not without difficulty at first, for crowds of terrified fugitives from the northern provinces mingling with our columns in their mournful exodus greatly encumbered them. And the grave defeat just

sustained weighed heavily upon us.   Order reigned once
again, but we marched along with no light step, for it was sad
to leave French soil to the invader, yet discipline was maintained, and if a few sighs were heard there were no murmurs.
"I had no skin left under my feet," said a soldier to me later
on, "but my heart alone ached at the idea we were going backwards."

Those who were directed to make counter-attacks and
local offensive movements, considered it a great privilege.
General Maleterre, a year later, described in striking terms
the wonderful spirit of the soldiers under his command. The
enemy was often checked and repulsed, got rid of for 48
hours, and ground was thus gained towards the goal, which,
according to the incidents of the retreat, followed by our
Commander-in-Chief with the utmost attention, he had determined in his mind. Thus Maunoury's troops having reached
the immediate vicinity of Paris, formed a rampart against
the town, while the other troops early in September crossed
the rivers Aisne and Marne and methodically destroyed the
bridges behind them.

On September 1st, Joffre, quartered with his General
Staff at Bar-sur-Aube, assigned the extreme limit of the retreating movement to the Seine, the Aube and the region
north of Bar-le-Duc. "That line will be reached only if we
are forced to move on. The attack will take place before
reaching it as soon as dispositions are completed that will
allow of the entire coöperation of all forces."[1]   And in the
orders addressed to the Commanding Officers, the General-in-
Chief on the same day instructs his lieutenants very clearly as
to the conditions necessary for achieving the pivoting movement on our right. The pivot was Verdun defended by Sarrail who with his back against the entrenched camp had orders
to retreat as little as possible: de Langle de Cary was on his

---

[1] The resuming of the offensive was from that date absolutely
decided on. All orders issued on September 2nd insist on the offensive
"which I shall command to be resumed in a few days," writes the
Generalissimo. He adds in order No. 2: "The effectives must be as
complete as possible, the units formed and the *morale* of the Army
at the height of the new tasks ahead *for the approaching renewal of
the offensive which will give us final success.*"

left, then Foch who had just moved into the line, then d'Espérey and finally Sir John French who all executed their
wheeling movements with greater amplitude as they approached the advancing wing. Meanwhile, contact had been
secured everywhere and the Army commanders are now in
closer and closer touch.

From start to finish the operations were carried out with
the utmost calm and method. I will mention two instances
out of twenty. On August 27th General Langle de Cary, who
was holding the enemy in check very successfully, asked if he
could remain on his positions. "I see nothing against your
remaining till to-morrow the 28th," the Generalissimo wisely
replied, "in order to consolidate your success and *show that
our withdrawal is purely strategic,* but on the 29th, every one
must be in retreat." At the other end of the retreating line we
have another proof of the same composure, this time on the
part of one of Joffre's lieutenants, and, curiously enough, by
one of the most impetuous. The Commander-in-Chief sent
him word that circumstances seemed favorable to giving battle on the 5th. After some consultation, General d'Espérey
replied that he did not consider the battle should take place
before the 6th. All this gives a decided impression of coolness
and perspicacity. It was in this spirit on the 4th that the
Commanding Officers of the principal units were warned that
the retreating movement towards the Seine would continue
only "in order to execute the operations which will lead to the
resuming of the offensive by the bulk of our armies." Thus
each one was able to take the necessary steps; an ideal disposition is attained; the armies are welded together and occupy
favorable positions, facing the German armies, who, in the
intoxication of what they consider as certain triumph, have
crossed the Marne and are convinced they will carry all before
them.

It is at this moment that the Generalissimo sends forth
to his lieutenants his now famous message: *"The hour has
come to hold at all costs and allow oneself to be slain rather
than give way."*

This battle in which the destiny of France is at stake is

about to be fought on soil essentially French, that of Ile-de-France, Valois, Brie, Champagne, and Barrois.

In its first phase the battle of the Ourcq, from east to west, is fought on the sunny land of Ile-de-France and historic Valois. Its boundaries are the Marne, to the confluent of the Ourcq and its many tributaries, the Ourcq de Lizy to the Ferté-Milon, and the southern edge of the forests of Villers-Cotterets and Chantilly whence rises the plateau of Multien, von Kluck's artillery base for his heavy guns during a short period. It is a land of forests with parks, still green, in spite of the heat of this torrid August. The town of Meaux lies at the extreme eastern limit.

To the east of the river Ourcq rises the vast triangular plateau of Brie, a country first rich, then poor, bounded by the valleys of the Marne, the Petit-Morin and the Seine; this is the region around Coulommiers, la Ferté-sous-Jouarre, Montmirail and Saint-Prix. Formerly it was one vast forest, the soil has remained wooded and hilly, hence the prefix *mont* so frequently met with. Coulommiers lies in the valley, but the vast plateau that rises above the town on the south is covered with a line of heights that have always passed for excellent strategic positions. These ridges have been fought for from the epoch when lords built their *fertés* on them to the time when Napoleon struggled hard to remove them. From these heights and from the plateau, Montmirail, Saint-Prix and Mondement rise above the clay pocket, ten miles long, called the Marshes of Saint-Gond bordered on the north by the forest of Epernay; a land famous in France's history and already reddened by French, and still more by German blood, when the Emperor rushing from the Seine to the Marne, won those memorable victories over his enemies marching upon Paris which a hundred years later the soldiers of d'Espérey and of Foch were going to commemorate.

The chalky Champagne country lies to the east on both banks of the Marne, whiter than ever under the pitiless sun of this late summer, the monotony of the plain is only broken by the pine and fir woods which under the blinding dust have assumed a grayish color; it is in this dust that Foch's right wing and Langle de Cary's army will give battle. At Vitry,

where the fighting will be very fierce, the river Saulx swelled
by the Ornain, flows into the Marne. The valleys of the
Saulx and Ornain are green though also somewhat dulled by
the terrible white dust of Champagne; pretty villages and
small towns make bright spots here and there, but to-morrow
a mass of ruins, and dead, will alone remain.—From Blesmes
to Revigny the valley reaches Barrois, which stretches from
Ligny to Saint-Mihiel; Sarrail has placed the bulk of his army
on the Barrois plateau, which separates the Ornain from the
Aire.

The Marne is the link between these different places : from
Ligny, where Sarrail has his headquarters, to the region of
the Ourcq, where Maunoury intends to deliver battle, flow the
waters gathered by the Marne until its juncture with the Seine
on the very threshold of Paris : the valley of the Marne,
French above all others, for it connects the great capital with
the eastern frontier towns, for it stretches from the capital to
Rheims where kings formerly were crowned, and leads to the
Argonne rampart called by the Convention "The Thermopy-
læ of France," to those plateaus where for three months
Napoleon struggled and delivered France from the spoil of
Europe.

It is there that Joffre led his armies, it is there he intended
they should fight. In contact with the soil where France took
her existence, Frenchmen will discover in themselves superhuman strength, like Antea, the giant in the fable, who became invincible every time Hercules allowed him to embrace
his Mother, the Earth. And, verily, I seem to see on September 5th, a giant suddenly returned firmly fixed with obstinate
front towards the attack and elbows resting securely on the
camps of Paris and Verdun.

The enormous front massed together on September 5th
stretches between those two cities. The 6th army under
Maunoury now lies from north to south between Dammar-
tin-en-Goele and the right bank of the Marne, and forms our
extreme left; it is composed of the 7th army corps, the 45th
division, the 55th and 56th reserves and three cavalry divisions. It forms an angle with the British army, three army
corps strong under the command of Sir John French, which

occupies the region southwest of Coulommiers, between
Hautefeuille and Vaudoy and is in touch on the right with
the 5th army under General Franchet d'Espérey. This army
extends from the north of Provins to Sézanne and is composed of the 18th, 3rd, 1st and 10th Army Corps, the 51st,
53rd and 69th reserve divisions, and a cavalry corps. The
three armies together form the left wing of our army.

General Foch at the head of the 9th army is in the center
with the 9th and 11th army corps, the 42nd division, the
Morocco division, the 52nd and 60th reserve divisions and
the 9th cavalry division. His front runs from Sézanne to
the Camp de Mailly.

This front (with a gap barely covered by a cavalry division) is prolonged by the 4th Army under the command of
General de Langle de Cary who, to the south of the Ornain
from Sompuis to Sermaize, offers resistance with the 17th
and 12th Army Corps, the colonial troops, and the 2nd Army
Corps.

The 3rd Army under Sarrail forms behind Revigny, an
angle to the right of the 4th Army, for from S. W. to N. E.
from Revigny to Souilly, on the evening of the 5th, the 15th,
5th, and 6th army corps (the 42nd division having been lent
to the 9th Army), and the reserve divisions under the command of General Paul Durand, are facing each other.

These six armies offer, from the forest of Chantilly to the
forest of Souilly, a front that may be termed harmonious, for
while the French-d'Espérey-Foch-de Cary line runs from
west to east, slightly bulging in the center, the two wings
from left to right form with this center two obtuse angles of
almost equal size; and while Maunoury has his back to Paris,
Sarrail has his back to Verdun. In fact Sarrail is not covered by Verdun alone. To the right of the great army which
stretches from the Ourcq to the Meuse, the 2nd Army under
General Castelnau holds the *Couronné* de Nancy and the 1st
Army under General Dubail is firmly in position on the
Vosges; they keep the German armies in check in the east,
thus allowing their brothers-in-arms in Champagne and in
Barrois to oppose the onslaught from the north. In this way

the two armies in Lorraine in the valleys of the Meurthe and Moselle contribute largely to the Victory of the Marne.

The German Army hurled itself without thought as to results against the enormous hemicycle which from Maunoury's left to Sarrail's right contained the French armies.

Von Kluck's Army, it will be remembered, held the right with the II, III, IV, IX Army Corps, the IV reserve corps and the Marwitz cavalry corps. Von Kluck crossed the Marne and occupied the Montherand-Esternay front on the 5th, leaving on the right bank the IV reserve corps under General von Schwerin—he deemed this support sufficient for his right flank. The Commander of the I army marches straight on Sir J. French and d'Espérey's armies, apparently neglecting Maunoury—he is thus caught between the two legs of a pair of compasses that may easily close on him unless he breaks the hinge or twists off one of the legs.

Von Bülow at the head of the II Army on Kluck's left makes Montmirail his headquarters. Facing d'Espérey's right and nearly all Foch's army, he occupies a front running west of Montmirail to Écury-le-Repos with the VII and X Army Corps, the X reserve corps and last but not least the Guards, for if Kluck's army possesses Kluck, a reputed strategist, von Bülow's army has the Guards whose prestige is as yet intact.[2]

Hausen, with the III Army, for the greater part composed of Saxons, held the front southeast of the marshes of Saint-Gond and west of Vitry-le-François with the XII and XIX Army Corps and the XII reserve corps. He faces Foch's right wing and de Cary's left.

The Duke Albrecht of Wurtemberg's army has its back towards Châlons, and it occupies a slightly oblique position with regard to Hausen, whose front runs north of Vitry and south of Sainte-Menehould with the VIII and XVIII Army Corps and the VIII and XVIII reserve corps.

Finally on the extreme left of the German line the Im-

---

[2] It is true that this crack Corps had been somewhat routed at Guise during the retreat and had previously been rather badly treated in Belgium. But it had been re-formed and its mishaps were as yet unknown. At St. Gond only, its prestige became seriously compromised.

perial Crown Prince, whose army has the important mission of breaking the French pivot, or at least of paralyzing it, lies between Bar and Verdun. Following the Meuse towards the river Ornain on both slopes of the Argonne, his VI corps reaches the region to the north of Revigny on the 5th, his VI reserve corps reaches Passavant and Charmontois, his XIII corps Triaucourt, and his XV corps Froidos. One corps remains near Montfaucon and a reserve corps near Consenvoye; both these corps keep in touch with the others by the Aire valley, while the Crown Prince is continuing to advance on the Ornain, for if he does not reach Bar-le-Duc he will occupy Revigny at Langle de Cary's and Sarrail's weak spots.

Thus the entire enormous German Army is engaged between the two wings opened out by us. On the evening of the 5th the great danger is not even suspected. Von Kluck will begin to realize it on the 6th.

On the 6th, however, the formidable strength of the German center is also being realized by General Foch in command of the 9th French army. His advance corps, severely attacked, is unable to maintain itself north of the marshes of St. Gond, and toward evening is obliged to retreat. The Tenth German corps takes Saint-Prix on Foch's left. The Prussian Guards drive the French from the marshes and fix their defenses there.

On the 7th the German attack became fiercer. General Foch remained calm. He continually repeated, "If they are trying to throw us back with such fury, that means things are going badly for them elsewhere and they are seeking compensation." He concluded that the best way was to hold on with the greatest possible energy.

On the 8th, the German attack grows fiercer than ever. The 42nd division supported by d'Espérey's right, manages to retake Saint-Prix, but the 9th corps can only just hold on and the 11th is struggling against the repeated assaults of the Guards and has to fall back. General Foch is forced to move his headquarters from Pleurs to Plancy further south.

On the next morning, September 9th, the situation is extremely critical. The enemy obviously aimed at taking the higher ground which, with the marshes, separates the Petit-

Morin valley from the plain of the Aube. Had our line been forced back on the Aube, the results would have been incalculable, probably obliging d'Espérey, who was advancing north, to fall back and exposing de Langle de Cary who continued to hold on desperately in the valley of the Saulx and Ornain. That is why the struggle for Saint-Prix was so fierce; during the first four days of the battle it was taken and retaken five times, so was the Castle of Mondement, which, according to a witness attached to General Humbert who commanded the Morocco division, was lost, retaken, lost and retaken again and again. The 10th corps of the 5th army came to the help of the 9th army on the morning of September 9th, but in vain; the Prussian Guards intending to keep up their reputation hurl themselves on Fère-Champenoise, our line gives way under the assault: Fère-Champenoise is lost. General Foch shows no discouragement, Fère is lost, but Fère will be recaptured. "The situation is excellent," he writes on the 9th. Excellent! what faith there is in such optimism! and he adds: "I command that the offensive be resumed."

In truth, such optimism was not only on the surface. With his quick eye the Commander of the 9th army had just perceived a break in the German line. Von Bülow, influenced by von Kluck, had to his great disappointment been forced to fall back in this maneuver, and, as happens sometimes in improvised retrograde movements, a gap occurred between Hausen and himself. Foch in his turn thought of driving a wedge into the weak spot.

The first thing was to reconstitute our line. The 42nd division attack and carry Fère-Champenoise. Then Mondement becomes the center of a deadly struggle. General Humbert has butted himself against it. This old castle, torn by our shells, and the enemy's, becomes for a moment the center of the battle. "Forward, boys," cries Colonel Lestoquoi, to his men who are storming for the third time; "and we shall succeed." And we did succeed. General Humbert once again took up his post of observation in the old tower, now a mass of ruins, while 3,000 German corpses strewed the avenue of the park.

"One last effort and we shall succeed!" General Foch might have used Colonel Lestoquoi's cheering words to his entire army. The high ground above the marshes is now ours, the enemy is giving way, the valley is open to us and we rush through it.

The marshes are not what legend (for there is already a legend of the Marne) has made of them. No one stuck in the quagmire, for during those months such a thing would be impossible. After a very hot summer and in spite of slight rains, they were like a dry river-bed in which, among the gray-cracked earth, grew reeds and grasses. But the Prussian Guard are forced to fight here exposed to our artillery and, though they do not actually *stick* there as romantic writers have described, they suffer heavily from our deadly fire. Eight thousand fall under the guns brought hastily into position on the higher ground wrested only the evening before from the Germans, while Foch pushes on his victorious divisions against these exposed German detachments.

By the evening of the 10th he held the marshes, and thanks to the energy with which he had transformed his difficult defensive movement into a victorious offensive, the troops advanced northwards and at a blow carried the line Vertus-Vatry. Foch took up his headquarters in La Fère-Champenoise, occupied a few hours previously by the Prussian Guard, who gorged themselves and drank to the certain destruction of the French army. "Let the troops eat the bread made for the enemy," wrote Napoleon to Murat; "that bread will taste better to them than cake." Our soldiers not only found bread baked by the enemy, but thousands of empty bottles, the sight of which made them smile and explained certain shortcomings. Many drunken soldiers belonging to the Guard and other corps, the victims of champagne, were taken prisoner that day.

However, d'Espérey's 10th corps, which so valiantly supported Foch, continues on the 9th its victorious forward march towards Vauchamps, Baye, and Champaubert. General d'Espérey congratulates his troops in an enthusiastic army order in which he evokes "the memorable fields which a century ago witnessed the victories of our ancestors over

Blücher's Prussians and where the soldiers of the third Republic forced the retreat of the most renowned army corps of old Prussia." From La Fère-Champenoise, facing the marshes, where fell a century ago to the cries of "Long live the Emperor" Pachtod's valiant soldiers, General Foch could have echoed that order which showed such legitimate pride. From the heights that Marmont had been unable to hold, he had just witnessed the foundering of the Imperial Prussian Guard and seen in this retreat of drunken soldiers, not only the loss of Germany's blood, but of her honor.

With the 4th army supporting his right, and the 5th army his left, Foch was able to face a situation which for a time was extremely critical.

While Maunoury on the Ourcq was making a "bulge" and the armies of Sir John French and d'Espérey threatening to envelop von Kluck, so contributed to his retreat, d'Espérey's right wing seconded the valiant 9th army which repulsed the great piercing movement attempted against our center. The two armies on the right meanwhile fulfilled their mission, which was to protect the "pivot" by hurling the enemy back from the triangle formed by the heights of Verdun, Bar and Vitry.

De Langle de Cary's and Sarrail's troops were prepared "morally" for victory inasmuch as frequent successes during their retreat had encouraged them. But these triumphant counter-attacks had been extremely fatiguing. A general is reported to have said: "We won the day with men dazed by fatigue." As an example of this: the 12th corps, with whom for a fortnight General Roques had gained repeated successes, is now composed of only six battalions fit to take part immediately in an offensive.

The 5th and 4th armies reach the line Humbeauville-Maurupt. Brienne is their headquarters. Sarrail is stationed at Ligny-en-Barrois, his left wing lies to the east of Revigny, his center covers Bar on the heights between the Ornain and the Aire, and his right wing covers Verdun on the plateau between the Aire and the Meuse. The two armies form an obtuse angle to the back of Revigny, and menace the front and the left flank of the two German armies coming down from the Ardennes and Argonne.

However, the Duke of Wurtemberg and the Imperial Crown Prince do not in the least mean to let themselves be menaced but rather intend to menace in their turn. If they manage to pierce through between Vitry and Bar, Saint-Dizier would be in danger, the French right wing turned, and Verdun, the pivot of our movement paralyzed, cut off and perhaps captured. Already on the 6th, the 2nd corps to the right of the 4th army and the connecting link between the two armies is violently attacked at Sermaize; the line holds however. But on the 7th, the enemy strikes again even more desperately, and still on the right of the 4th army, and this time succeeds. Sermaize is taken and Pargny-sur-Saulx stormed. The 2nd corps retreating calls for help. Sarrail immediately sends forward a brigade of the 15th corps, which menaces the advancing enemy on its flank while the bulk of the corps moves on towards Contrisson and the 5th corps gives battle beyond Laimont.

The left of the 4th army now seems in danger. The Saxons (XIX corps) compel our 17th corps to give way a little after fierce fighting, in which Colonel Breton's battalions cover themselves with glory. But our reinforcements are assured for the morrow, the 21st corps from the Vosges disembarks to the rear of de Langle de Cary's forces.

On the evening of the 8th the situation is extremely critical. But the enemy has to deal with the "tenacious 4th army" and no one will admit of being beaten. On the contrary it is intended that the ground lost shall be regained on the morrow. A tremendous effort is made, on both sides, and the J.-B. Dumas corps (17), supported by a division of the 21st holds the line on the 9th. The Saxons defend their position furiously at Sompuis, but finally falter before our attack and give way. Our artillery plays havoc among them, they retreat in great disorder, and whilst the center of the 4th army holds its positions, the 2nd corps on the right resumes the offensive pushing on towards Andernay and Sermaize still supported by Sarrail's two army corps pressing heavily on the German front near Contrisson-Mogneville.

The situation seems saved. At this hour, on the banks of the Ourcq, the lower Marne and Foch's front, in spite of fierce fighting, the battle is turning in our favor, but is still in full swing on the banks of the Saulx and the Ornain. De Langle de Cary, however, is beginning to feel the effects of the retreat of the German right wing. The Saxons who had fortified Vitry are obliged to abandon the place. Langle de Cary's soldiers press closely on their heels harassing the enemy who crosses to the other side of the Marne. Vitry is in our hands and already the 21st and 17th corps are pushing northeast and threatening to envelop the Duke of Wurtemberg's forces. The enemy, on the point of being turned, is obliged to retreat and is followed by the other troops stationed between Revigny and Triaucourt.

In accordance with their former exploits, they set fire to the villages and towns. A recent enquiry has enabled me to collect thoroughly reliable evidence of their crimes, I have handled the incendiary bombs that were picked up, seen the rags soaked in paraffin-oil which were thrown into the houses, and the carbonized ruins so unlike those caused by shells. Oh! ye ruins of Sermaize, of Saint-Lumier, Maurupt, Contrisson, Revigny, of ten other villages, what cries rise up from you against Germanic "culture!" But the honor of two defeated Princes had to be avenged. From the top of the southern hills "a very curtain of flames met our gaze," said an artilleryman to me, "during the night of the 9-10th we saw 17 villages burning."

For on the 10th, the Imperial Crown Prince was obliged to relinquish his great dream. Sarrail had shaken his army and was pushing it to the north of Verdun.

But with what confidence in his own powers had the Crown Prince attacked! Bearing down in the neighborhood of Revigny, he intended to seize the bridges of the Ornain as far as Bar and enter the little ducal town in a few hours. It is reported that on the 6th, an officer informed an inhabitant of Vaubecourt that "To-morrow we shall burn Poincaré's town." And in fact the XVI corps intended to occupy, if not destroy Bar, while the IV cavalry corps, no doubts being entertained as to victory, would move south, towards Saint-Dizier, Langres, and la Bourgogne.

A great danger had threatened Sarrail's flank; it caused the last incident in the huge battle. German forces were reported to be massing near Woevre and preparing to attack Saint-Mihiel. This is very serious news, for if the Germans should succeed in piercing through to Saint-Mihiel and cross the Meuse there, Verdun would be cut off from the 3rd army and the latter would be turned. Once again our pivot is threatened. The danger does not, however, divert the Commander of the 3rd army from his first duty; at daybreak on the 8th, he sends forward troops who dislodge the German corps from the valley of the Ornain and push them on to Vassincourt, Villers-aux-Vents, Triaucourt, while the 6th artillery corps crushes the XV corps at Aire. The menace is, however, increasing on the Heights of the Meuse, the enemy glides towards Saint-Mihiel; at 1 p. m. he has begun to bombard Fort Troyon. In the meantime, General Sarrail, in order to protect his right flank, gives the order to destroy the bridges at Saint-Mihiel. This, though it did not paralyze the attack of the 3rd army, made things harder. The repulse, on the 9th, of the enemy's advance on every side had to suffice for the time being. The situation becomes worse in the rear; after Troyon, Génicourt is bombarded, and the guns at Troyon now seem silent. General Coutanceau, who has just sent an urgent appeal to the 2nd army (under Castelnau), telegraphs to the Commander of the fort: "General situation of our armies excellent. It is of consequence that the fall of Troyon should not open a way to the Germans. *Hold indefinitely.*" [3] But the German columns continue to advance on Saint-Mihiel. On the 10th Sarrail's army holds the whole

[3] A special study might be made of the part played by Verdun in the Battle of the Marne. Verdun's garrison intervened actively on Sarrail's right, the 72nd Division under General Heymann harassed and held back the German columns while General de Morlaincourt, supporting General Coutanceau, attacked in the direction of Dombasle. During the bombardment of Fort Troyon, General Coutanceau sustained the defenders' courage with pressing messages and, as we shall see, called General Castelnau, Commander of the 2nd army, to the rescue.

day through, the battle rages and spreads destruction among the enemy (7,000 casualties) from Revigny to Vaubécourt. The situation is extremely critical, a defeat in the Saint-Mihiel direction may jeopardize everything at a moment when things are turning in our favor from the Ourcq to the Ornain.

No faltering, however, occurred. Troyon shelled, and half in ruins, repels the attack, the enemy is unable to cross the Meuse; General Castelnau sends the 73rd division and the 2nd cavalry division, detached from the 2nd army, to support the threatened forts which in their turn menace the assailant. On the 11th, the German cannon suddenly ceases firing. "The calm was impressive," said an officer. For the Crown Prince has just been informed that the German armies, defeated on the Ourcq and thrown back on the Marne, are beating a retreat. Even he wavers now. Sarrail pushes forward his offensive, the 5th corps captures Laimont and Villotte, while on his left, the 15th corps advances beyond the *Marne au Rhin* canal. The 6th corps and the reserve divisions on our right, try to take part in this forward movement in spite of the German howitzers covering the Prince's retreat. By the end of the day, the 15th corps has occupied Rancourt and Revigny, and has advanced to Brabant-le-Roi, making enormous captures of light and heavy artillery taken from the XVI corps in retreat. Our 6th corps meets with fierce opposition from the XVI corps southwest of Souilly. The Germans attempt one last bombardment of Troyon: the fort stands firm. All is over! Defeated all along the line, the enemy is unable to play his trump card at Saint-Mihiel. Our pivot has held and we are saved. The enemy owns himself vanquished on every side, for his retreat becomes more and more marked and so rapid that in certain places it looks very like flight. It is, at any rate, a formal admission of defeat.

BY JOSEPH REINACH

In the year 1916 a German book called "The Battles of the Marne" made a great stir in Germany. I hear that the volume has since been ordered withdrawn from circulation.

In any case, it is almost impossible to find a copy in neutral countries, though Germany has otherwise deluged them with a war literature as voluminous as misleading. The book is anonymous; but the author is manifestly an authority and an eye-witness. He claims to write simply a narrative; but in reality he aims to prove that the battle of the Marne "was interrupted for purely strategical motives"; consequently, that it was not "an immense victory" for the armies of France; that General von Moltke's plan was one of the greatest of all time, and that the commander of the First German Army is above all reproach. In all probability, he is an officer of the staff of von Moltke or of von Kluck. I am inclined to believe that he was attached to the latter, because of the very special attention which he pays to the actions of the First Army, and the eulogies which he lavishes on the commander who was beaten at the Ourcq. At times, one would say he writes at von Kluck's dictation. But he is equally attached to General von Moltke, who was at the head of the Grand General Staff from August, 1906, and who was to be forced into retirement before the end of the first year of the war. It is thus easy to understand how the book should be first authorized and then withdrawn.

He explains the plan of the German General Staff with great lucidity; a strict defensive from the Swiss frontier to the Donon; a defensive-offensive, according to Marshal von Moltke's formula, between the Donon and Verdun, where the chief mission of the Fifth Army will be to retain the enemy forces opposed to it; a vigorous offensive of the first four armies which, starting from the base Thionville-Aix-la-Chapelle, are to penetrate France through Luxemburg and Belgium "in order to endeavor later to extend the right wing more and more toward the sea."

This movement of conversion "full of genius" authorized the greatest hopes. "In the great curve which, through Brussels, Valenciennes, Compiègne, Meaux, passed to the east of Paris, we should throw the French armies back beyond the Aisne, the Marne, and, perhaps, beyond the Seine, in order eventually to outflank them to the south of Fontainebleau, and thus to roll up the whole French battle line.

So far as human foresight could tell, this plan could have been carried out at the end of September, 1914." Many army corps would have been liberated, and could have been hurled against Russia.

It will have been observed that our author indicates, as having formed a part of the German plan, the passage "to the east of Paris" after the first successes. So that the German Staff did not hesitate, we are told, on the morrow of the battles of Mons and Charleroi, between pushing straight on to Paris and seeking the French army on the Marne or on the Seine. . . . It can be seen at once what a brilliant exculpation of von Kluck and von Moltke is contained in this affirmation. All Germany was convinced, in August, and, with it, almost the whole world, that her victorious armies had Paris as their objective. *"Nach Paris!"* shouted all her soldiers, when entering Belgium, and, later, all along our roads, deafening and frightening all those who saw them rushing forward at the rate of forty kilometers a day. But the General Staff and the Emperor himself were already resolved not to attack Paris before having destroyed the French armies "to the south of Fontainebleau."

Is this the truth? I think so. Or is it an invention, after the disillusion, after the failure of the "plan of genius," and the defeat? Evidently, this will not be known for certain until the German archives disclose to us the original plan of the General Staff, as it was before the war or during its first days.

However great is the admiration of the German author for the German plan, he finds one fault with it: "The tasks imposed upon the armies of the center and, even more, those of the right wing were really excessive." In fact, "not only were they to break the resistance of the Belgians and their forts, but they were also, through the stifling heat of August, to execute an altogether extraordinary march, before they could come to grips with the French, who held good positions chosen by themselves, and who had to reckon with no supply problem." There are, as we know, other causes for the German defeat on the Marne—and our author himself will indicate them; but these causes are manifestly accurate. To march, in the hottest part of the summer, at the rate of forty kilometers a day, and even though inspired by victory and sure of an early triumphal entry into the enemy's capital, would have undermined the offensive vigor of armies of steel and iron and sapped their power of resistance. This was the case of the soldiers of von Kluck and von Bülow, when they arrived at the Ourcq and the Marne. They were weary. Without doubt, our troops and the English had also endured heavy fatigues; but they had not had to pass through all Belgium fighting. Thus the violation of Belgian neutrality, decided on for reasons of strategy, weighed heavily at this point also on the German armies. Finally, it cannot be denied that the German supply service became more difficult as the invading armies got further from their base. We, on the contrary, were fighting near ours. It was an appreciable advantage.

Must we add that the German armies drank more as they ate less? The German author is silent as to this, but there are certain and numerous evidences of it. These beer drinkers were not used to our wines. Weary and sweating, they rushed into our cellars. The wine of France had its part in our victory.

The confession of this is found in the notebook of an officer on von Kluck's staff, a prisoner to-day. On September 2nd he notes:

"Our soldiers are worn out. For four days they have been marching forty kilometers a day. The ground is difficult, the roads are torn up, trees felled, the fields pitted by shells like strainers. The soldiers stagger at every step, their faces are plastered with dust, their uniforms are in rags; one might call them living rag-bags. They march with closed eyes, and sing in chorus to keep from falling asleep as they march. The certainty of victory close at hand and of their triumphal entry into Paris sustains them and whips up their enthusiasm. Without this certainty of victory they would fall exhausted. They would lie down where they are, to sleep at last, no matter where, no matter how. Only the delirium of victory keeps our men going. And, to give their bodies a drunkenness like that of their souls, they drink enormously. But this drunkenness also helps to keep them up. To-day, after an inspection, the General was furiously angry. He wanted to put a stop to this collective debauch. We have just persuaded him not to give severe orders. It is better not to be too strict, otherwise the army could not go on at all. For this abnormal weariness abnormal stimulants are needed. In Paris we shall remedy all this. We shall forbid the drinking of alcohol there. When our troops are at last able to rest on their laurels, order will be restored."

"They drink enormously." It is a German officer who writes it, before the battle. They kept it up during the battle, on the evenings of the battle, in our villages of the Ile-de-France and Champagne, drinking enormously in our well-filled cellars. One of the cavalry officers who led the pursuit has told me that he found the main street of a village so strewn with wine bottles and broken glasses that he had to make his way through the fields.

Our author underlines the importance of the nomination of Galliéni (as Military Governor of Paris): "One of the best Generals of Republican France, who was absolutely the right man in the right place." But his admiration goes especially to Joffre, the reasoned admiration of a soldier who does not feel the need of diminishing his enemy, thus diminishing himself by a back stroke. It is natural that he calls the victories of the Sambre and the Meuse "prodigious." We do not deny that they were great, and that they filled the world with astonishment and anxiety. Let us quote textually:

"During the last third of August, 1914, the defeats of the French and English, especially on their left wing, had been so prodigious that only a general of very high gifts could have stopped the march of the Germans or obliged the adversary to evacuate a part of the territory occupied. The man who attempted this was General Joffre. Gathering all available reserves, a general with less decision would, perhaps, have tried to stop the enemy at several points. But a partial success gained in this way would have had no influence on the final result. Joffre immediately saw that it would not do to stop at half measures, and he found both the means and the efficient secondary commanders to carry out his ideas."

To begin with, Joffre did not allow himself to be disturbed "by the messages of misfortune which succeeded each other without interruption" during the closing days of August. He immediately recognized "at the first glance" that, on the one hand, "the strongly occupied line between Belfort and Verdun could hold at least for several days or weeks" and "contain the German attack"; and that, on the other hand, the danger to be guarded against was that of the immense enveloping movement—pursued "with a rapidity that had never been reached by armies of that size"—by the moving right wing of the enemy. Sure of his own right, Joffre therefore ordered the splendid strategic retreat—according to the expression of Marshal French—which was to end in the victory of the Marne.

An uneasiness begins to show through the following pages, in which the German Army is seen growing weaker as Joffre compels it to follow him still further. We may suppose that the understanding of the famous maneuver was reached by the German Staff only after their defeat, and that the homage rendered to Joffre is part of the special pleading for von Moltke and von Kluck. But this supposition is not essential, and we may well believe that such able soldiers perceived the growing peril which they could not avoid. In either case, we can indorse almost all the views of the German narrative.

"The further the Germans advanced, and the longer the French and English were able to escape without engaging in a decisive action, the more did the initial advantage of the Germans pass into the hands of their adversaries. The Germans got further and further from their base, and grew more and more exhausted by their forced marches. They were using up their munitions and their food supplies with alarming rapidity, and the least dislocation of the supply service might become fatal to armies so vast as those which the Germans launched, in the month of August, against Belgium and the north of France.

"But Joffre, who, it must not be forgotten, was fighting

on interior lines, was coming closer and closer to his supply bases. Every day new, fresh troops were arriving behind his lines of battle; day by day the first lines could be provided with food supplies and munitions, and, finally, the French Staff found itself in the agreeable situation of bringing into battle far fewer wornout troops than its adversary, who, for a month, had been marching almost day and night. In addition to this, it was a piece of good fortune for the French that their front, however thin it might be at certain points, had not yet been pierced.

"When Joffre had taken the resolution only to accept battle under particularly favorable circumstances, he gave the order to his subordinate commanders to withdraw before the enemy and to march further and further south. If his preparations had not been completed in time, he would eventually have accepted battle to the south of the Seine, and have abandoned Paris. He then took measures to reenforce his threatened left wing and center, and, before all, to prevent the army which was marching on the (German) extreme right wing from outflanking his battle line."

We are familiar with these measures; it is not doubtful that the German intelligence department was acquainted with them at the time when they were taken, or very soon afterward. They were "the creation of two new armies: the Sixth Army, which, under the command of General Maunoury," should have been formed, according to the initial plan, in the neighborhood of Amiens, and which "because of the rapid German advance, was actually formed to the northeast of Paris and in its vicinity"; the Ninth Army, "which was slipped in between the Fourth and Fifth Armies, and intrusted to General Foch, a very able commander."

These armies were made up of divisions, very accurately enumerated, some of them brought by rail from Alsace and Lorraine, "drawn from Castelnau's large Second Army," from the First Army, commanded by General Dubail, and from the Second Army, under General Sarrail; others were drawn from the Paris garrison and the Moroccan contingents. Another part of these measures was "the submission to Joffre's orders of the troops of the entrenched camp of

Paris which were commanded by General Galliéni," the Sixth Army being at the same time "put at the disposition of the Governor of Paris, that is, indirectly intrusted to the Commander-in-Chief," and this, "because, at all times, unity of command has been one of the principal factors of success." Finally, "in order that nothing might be neglected which could contribute to the success of the great plan, Joffre, who had already replaced Ruffey by Sarrail, put the Fifth Army under the orders of Franchet d'Espérey.

While Joffre's armies withdrew step by step on the Marne, where they were to halt on September 5th and be joined by the English army, "the German armies of the right wing were marching forward into France without a halt. It seemed as though a wall of iron were ceaselessly moving forward. A single thought animated this colossal gray mass: the annihilation of the French field army, in order to end at a stroke the war on the western front. It was everywhere believed that Paris was the goal of the German Generals, and every day the newspapers announced the diminution of the distance which separated the German advance guard from the French capital. And then suddenly—it was on September 4th—the German First Army, leaving Paris on its right, swerved toward the south!"

The exclamation mark stands in the German text, but, without doubt, only to mark the final point. "The point is all." The narrator has explained, as we have seen, at the beginning of his narrative, that "the passage to the east of Paris" had been written beforehand in the plan "full of genius" of Moltke, and not the march upon Paris. This affirmation must suffice as an answer to all the criticisms which have been raised in the sequel against the abandonment, assuredly only for a very brief period, in the thought of the German Staff, but which in fact became final, of the direct attack against the capital. *Magister dixit.* Thus the younger Moltke had decided. Thus the elder Moltke had prescribed in his famous note of 1859: "Even though the fate of Paris decides everything, as in 1814," it would be right to "turn away from Paris" in case a French army should be gathered in the neighborhood of Rheims. It would then be necessary to attack the French behind the Aisne, to throw them back across the Marne, the Seine, the Yonne, and, finally, the Loire. After that, we could march on Paris.

In contrast with this, here is what may be read in the notebook of the German officer already mentioned, under date of September 3rd. The bulk of the army had taken up its quarters in the forest of Ermenonwille. The columns were advancing toward Betz:

"We are leaving Paris on our right, and we shall concentrate toward the southeast, opposite the remnants of the Franco-English army, which is trying, it is true, to reassemble its broken fragments in the plain of the Marne. Our soldiers have no suspicion that we are temporarily leaving the road to Paris. They are counting so completely on finding themselves at the gates of Paris to-morrow, or the day after, that it would be cruel to tell them the truth. They would lose all their spring. Our soldiers believe that the epoch of battles is ended, that the decimated French Army is hiding, and that we are going to enter Paris singing and drinking."

Paris is not only the great triumph; it is rest and peace:

"One of our battalions was marching wearily forward. All at once, while passing a crossroad, they discovered a signpost, on which they read: Paris, thirty-seven kilometers (twenty-three miles). It was the first signpost that had not been erased. On seeing it, the battalion was as though shaken up by an electric current. The word Paris, which they have just read, drives them crazy. Some of them embrace the wretched signpost, others dance round it. Cries, yells of enthusiasm, accompany these mad actions. This signpost is their evidence that we are near Paris, that, without doubt, we shall soon be really there. This notice board has had a miraculous effect. Faces light up, weariness seems to disappear, the march is resumed, alert, cadenced, in spite of the abominable ground in this forest. Songs burst forth louder, and no longer the traditional songs, but Parisian ditties, stupid enough in all conscience."

Then on the next day (September 4th) General von Kluck himself comes to make a visit of inspection to Lizy-on-Ourcq. The officer of the notebook talks with a Major in his escort. Is von Kluck only the well-disciplined interpreter of the decisions of Moltke, the supreme chief? In any case, "he feels certain that the Germans will soon crush the crumbs of the French Army. The reports of spies who have watched the retreat of the enemy army are very encouraging. They are a dejected horde, discontented, without any spring. There is no chance of their regaining a biting edge. The General fears nothing from the direction of Paris. We shall come back to Paris, after having annihilated what is left of the Franco-British army. The Fourth Corps of reserves will be intrusted with the triumphal entry into the great capital."

On September 5th, the eve of the general attack, the officer of the notebook records that the high German command foresees a flank attack, "although our reconnoissances have not brought any certain information on this point." Orders are given to dig trenches, to hasten defensive works. "These orders are very badly executed." Von Kluck makes a tour of inspection; "he is evidently very displeased." The soldiers work badly or not at all. They are "worn out by forced marches, or drunk." But there is something more: "Persuaded that they have already attained complete success, they are full of disillusionment when they learn that they will have to dig defensive trenches. Our soldiers have been too much accustomed to singing hymns of victory and triumph."

This is very good military psychology. Here is a German who can read more than is in his books. Note the phrase that follows: "If the French were not so profoundly demoralized, they might become very dangerous, for our First Army is very far from possessing the energy and discipline which were its strength in Belgium and on the northern frontier of France." Also, on September 7th (battles of Marcilly, Barcy, and Chambry) and September 8th (capture of Chambry) what surprise: "The French troops appear to be full of ardor. Our men hold the heights, but the French have become demons, they charge in the face of machine-gun fire, joyfully let themselves get killed. The valor of the French is superhuman! Like spontaneous generation, troops appear from all sides."

On September 8th the officer of the notebook writes:

"Gen. von Kluck has inspected the posts. I saw him. His eyes, usually so brilliant, are dull. He, so energetic in his whole attitude, speaks in a faint voice. He is quite cast down. I question the Major who accompanies him. Our reconnoissances have just unmasked considerable French formations. To-day's battles have been terrible for us. And all our armies, from the Marne to Alsace, are bearing an unendurable burden. We must parry this danger at any cost, even by retreat."

It was, writes the German historian of the Marne, "to escape the danger of being outflanked that the French Commander-in-Chief had created a new army on the extreme French left. This new army, the Sixth, and the German Fifth Army, against which Joffre created it, were only fighting on the Ourcq, for four days now, in order to try to outflank each other. Neither succeeded. However, von Kluck was only able to stop Maunoury's turning movement by drawing strong reënforcements from Bülow, whose Second Army was thereby greatly weakened; the English, and the French Fifth Army, under Franchet d'Espérey, concentrated all their efforts on the point of least resistance in front of them; the English recrossed the Marne; the French Fifth Army pushed north; thus the German forces facing our Sixth Army on the Ourcq were taken in the flank. Here is the German account:

"September 9th was a very critical day for Maunoury. The Germans had been marching unceasingly for five weeks, they had fought numerous battles, and lacked munitions and even more, food. Yet, in irresistible assaults, they had the force to throw the French back at all points. Instead of yielding, they compelled the French to yield; instead of being outflanked, they outflanked the French, and even captured Nanteuil-le-Haudouin. But the finest energy must grow weak when it is not supported and refreshed. Reduced in power, weakened and melted away by fighting and fatigue, even these valiant warriors lost their power.

"The French, on the contrary, who were only a few kilometers from Paris, not only received continual reënforcements, but were further supplied with all kinds of munitions. General Galliéni ceaselessly watched with vigilant eye over the movements of the Sixth Army, and made every imaginable effort to furnish it, as rapidly as possible, with every kind of support. He requisitioned thousands of automobiles in Paris, and, during the night, sent them to Maunoury with reënforcements, which were brought to him by rail from the interior and other parts of the front. One of the most remarkable of these transports was that of the Sixty-second Division (Zouaves) toward Creil and Senlis, carried out in the night of September 8th-9th, with a view to hindering at all costs the outflanking of the French left wing.

"Finally, on the same day, Maunoury asked that the division which he had lent to the Marshal should be returned to him, because the danger of being beaten by the cavalry corps of General von Marwitz no longer existed for the three English corps. This Eighth Division was sent, by rail, from Paris toward Maunoury's extreme left wing.

"On the evening of September 9th, in spite of all the reenforcements they had received, the situation of the French Sixth Army was anything but brilliant. But it had to hold its ground at all costs, and could not withdraw even an inch further, no matter what it might cost.

"But on the German side the offensive power was equally paralyzed. After all their efforts, and all the prodigious battles of the last days, the iron legions of von Kluck's army had arrived at the extreme limit of what they could give. On September 9th, toward noon, General von Marwitz had to announce, with an unwilling heart, to his chief that it was no longer possible for him to resist the whole English Army and the French Eighteenth Corps. To spare the blood of the English, Marshal French had in fact asked his neighbor on the right, the commander of the Fifth Army, for a whole corps, the Eighteenth.

"In accord with the Chief of the General Staff, von Kluck was forced, unwillingly, to give the order to cease fighting, because the superiority of the enemy left wing grew continually. During the night of September 9th-10th the German armies withdrew toward the north in complete order. When, on the next morning, the French wished to continue the battle, von Kluck and his army had disappeared. Strong rearguards alone covered his retreat and for a long time occupied Nanteuil-le-Haudouin."

Thus reads this early German admission of military defeat at the Marne.

A retreat in good order! The officer of the notebook writes: "At Lizy the retreat is organized. If that helter-skelter can be called organization." The anonymous narrator, as was to be expected, remains faithful to his ill-starred chief: "The skill with which the Germans succeeded in withdrawing from their adversary is evidenced by the fact that von Kluck only abandoned a small number of guns and almost no prisoners." He also praises him for having retired toward Compiègne and Soissons, and not toward Rheims, for if he had bent toward the east, "the Germans, when Antwerp fell, would not have been in a position to extend and carry their front as far as the coast." This is accurate.

Necessarily, as von Kluck, with his army of the extreme right wing, "served in a certain way as guide for the other armies," his retreat compelled that of Bülow's army, which, in its turn, involved that of von Hausen's Saxon Army and of the Guard, in the center of the German front. Duke Albert of Wurtemberg and the Crown Prince, not wishing to lose contact, withdrew in their turn.

Of all the battles in progress, that of September 9th before General Foch's army was much the hardest and bloodiest. Von Hausen's furious offensive was the *ultima ratio* of Moltke, requiring of an action of the center a decision which he no longer hoped to be able to win on his wings. And Foch immediately proclaimed his faith in the famous Order of the Day, like a challenge, which destiny did not accept: "The situation is excellent; I order that the offensive shall be renewed. The key of the day will be to debouch by Fère-Champenoise." The very name of Fère, like that of Mondement and Marais, fails to appear in the narrative.

Our center might not have broken on September 10th; Dubois, Humbert, Grossetti, and all the others, firm in their reconquered positions, were masters of the hour.

The marshes of Saint-Gond in their turn witnessed a flanking maneuver which had a decisive share in the victory. The narrative admits, however, that Langle de Cary's attack, on Foch's right, against the Nineteenth German Corps—the retaking of Sermaize and of the crest west of Vassincourt—"had a certain influence on the course of the battle," and "to a certain degree hastened the retreat of the (German) center." He also admits that the energetic resistance offered by our Third Army "to the Crown Prince's violent and able attacks," stopped them on the heights of the Meuse and between Verdun and Saint-Mihiel. "The ring of iron around Verdun and the forts of the Meuse was also slackened—for a time."

Everything is linked together in the maneuver of battle, but on condition that no link bends or breaks. It would have availed Maunoury nothing to hold like a rock if Foch had yielded, nor Foch to have pierced the German center if Maunoury had been enveloped on his left. And everything would have smashed if Franchet d'Espérey and French had not pierced their hole between the First and Second German armies, or if Langle de Cary had been pushed back or Sarrail had been repulsed on the extreme right wing.

Finally, the German writer, while he still refuses to utter the word defeat, marks in clear enough lines the failure of Moltke's plan, which was "to smash the French Army at the first shock, to cut it into pieces and dislocate it." But, he says, "Joffre succeeded still less in turning the Germans, in rolling up their battle line and in throwing them out of France, across the Rhine."

In other words, we lost the battle of the frontiers; the Germans lost the battle of the Marne.

These are the facts as they appear to a German officer, who is not a Jomini, but who understands what he sees and whose mind is well balanced. The moral significance of the Marne escapes him. "Moltke withdrew the front of the German battle line about a day's march to the north." That is all he sees. It was "a battle interrupted for tactical reasons."

BY SIR JOHN FRENCH

Gen. Joffre on September 5th announced to me his intention of wheeling up the left flank of the Sixth Army, pivoting on the Marne and directing it to move on the Ourcq; cross and attack the flank of the First German Army, which was then moving in a southeasterly direction east of that river.

He requested me to effect a change of front to my right —my left resting on the Marne and my right on the Fifth Army—to fill the gap between that army and the Sixth. I was then to advance against the enemy in my front and join in the general offensive movement.

These combined movements practically commenced on Sunday, September 6th, at sunrise; and on that day it may be said that a great battle opened on a front extending from Ermenonville, which was just in front of the left flank of the Sixth French Army, through Lizy on the Marne, to Esternay and Charleville, the left of the Ninth Army under Gen. Foch, and so along the front of the Ninth, Fourth and Third French Armies to a point north of the fortress of Verdun.

This battle, in so far as the Sixth French Army, the British Army, the Fifth French Army, and the Ninth French Army were concerned, may be said to have concluded on the evening of September 10th, by which time the Germans had been driven back to the line Soissons-Rheims, with a loss of thousands of prisoners, many guns, and enormous masses of transport.

About September 3rd the enemy appears to have changed his plans and to have determined to stop his advance south direct upon Paris, for on September 4th air reconnoissances showed that his main columns were moving in a southeasterly direction generally east of a line drawn through Nanteuil and Lizy on the Ourcq.

On September 5th several of these columns were observed to have crossed the Marne, while German troops, which were observed moving southeast up the left flank of the Ourcq on the 4th, were now reported to be halted and facing that river. Heads of the enemy's columns were seen crossing at Changis, La Ferte, Nogent, Château Thierry, and Mezy.

Considerable German columns of all arms were seen to be converging on Montmirail, while before sunset large bivouacs of the enemy were located in the neighborhood of Coulommiers, south of Rebais, La Ferté-Gaucher, and Dagny.

I should conceive it to have been about noon on September 6th, after the British forces had changed their front to the right and occupied the line Jouy-Le Chatel-Faremoutiers-Villeneuve Le Comte, and the advance of the Sixth French Army north of the Marne toward the Ourcq became apparent, that the enemy realized the powerful threat that was being made against the flank of his columns moving southeast, and began the great retreat which opened the battle above referred to.

On September 7th both the Fifth and Sixth French Armies were heavily engaged on our flank. The Second and Fourth Reserve German Corps on the Ourcq vigorously opposed the advance of the French toward that river, but did not prevent the Sixth Army from gaining some headway, the Germans themselves suffering serious losses. The French Fifth Army threw the enemy back to the line of the Petit Morin River after inflicting severe losses upon them, especially about Montceaux, which was carried at the point of the bayonet.

The enemy retreated before our advance, covered by his Second and Ninth and Guard Cavalry Divisions, which suffered severely.

Our cavalry acted with great vigor, especially Gen. De Lisle's brigade, with the Ninth Lancers and Eighteenth Hussars.

On September 8th the enemy continued his retreat northward, and our army was successfully engaged during the day with strong rearguards of all arms on the Petit Morin River, thereby materially assisting the progress of the French armies on our right and left, against whom the enemy was making his greatest efforts. On both sides the enemy was thrown back with very heavy loss. The First Army Corps encountered stubborn resistance at La Trétoire (north of Rabais). The enemy occupied a strong position with infantry and guns on the northern bank of the Petit Morin River; they were dislodged with considerable loss. Several machine guns and many prisoners were captured, and upward of 200 German dead were left on the ground.

The forcing of the Petit Morin at this point was much assisted by the cavalry and the First Division, which crossed higher up the stream.

Later in the day a counter-attack by the enemy was well repulsed by the First Army Corps, a great many prisoners and some guns again falling into our hands.

On this day (September 8th) the Second Army Corps encountered considerable opposition, but drove back the enemy at all points with great loss, making considerable captures.

The Third Army Corps also drove back considerable bodies of the enemy's infantry and made some captures.

On September 9th the First and Second Army Corps forced the passage of the Marne and advanced some miles to the north of it. The Third Corps encountered considerable opposition, as the bridge at La Ferté was destroyed and the enemy held the town on the opposite bank in some strength, and thence persistently obstructed the construction of a bridge; so the passage was not effected until after nightfall.

During the day's pursuit the enemy suffered heavy loss in killed and wounded, some hundreds of prisoners fell into our hands and a battery of eight machine guns was captured by the Second Division.

The advance was resumed at daybreak on the 10th up to the line of the Ourcq, opposed by strong rearguards of all arms. The First and Second Corps, assisted by the cavalry divisions on the right, the Third and Fifth Cavalry Brigades on the left, drove the enemy northward. Thirteen guns, seven machine guns, about 2,000 prisoners, and quantities of transport fell into our hands. The enemy left many dead on the field. On this day the French Fifth and Sixth Armies had little opposition.

As the First and Second German Armies were now in full retreat, this evening marks the end of the battle which practically commenced on the morning of the 6th inst.

Although I deeply regret to have had to report heavy losses in killed and wounded throughout these operations, I do not think they have been excessive in view of the magnitude of the great fight, the outlines of which I have only been able very briefly to describe, and the demoralization and loss in killed and wounded which are known to have been caused to the enemy by the vigor and severity of the pursuit.

ORDER OF THE DAY BY GENERAL JOFFRE

September 11th.

The battle which we have been fighting for the last five days has ended in an undoubted victory. The retreat of the 1st, 2nd, and 3rd German Armies before our left and center becomes more and more marked. The enemy's 4th Army in its turn has begun to withdraw to the north of Vitry and Sermaise.

Everywhere the enemy has left on the field numerous wounded and a quantity of munitions. Everywhere we have made prisoners while gaining ground. Our troops bear witness to the intensity of the fight, and the means employed by the Germans in their endeavors to resist our *élan*. The vigorous resumption of the offensive has determined our success.

Officers, non-commissioned officers, and men! You have all responded to my appeal; you have all deserved well of your country.   JOFFRE.

REPORT FROM GENERAL JOFFRE TO THE MINISTER OF WAR

(Telegraphic.)   September 13th.

The completeness of our victory becomes more and more apparent. Everywhere the enemy is in retreat. The Germans are abandoning prisoners, wounded, and material in all directions. After the heroic efforts displayed by our troops during this formidable battle, which has lasted from the 5th to the 12th of September, all our armies, exhilarated by success, are carrying out a pursuit which is without parallel in its extension.

On our left we have crossed the Aisne below Soissons, thus gaining more than 100 kilometers in six days of battle. In the center our armies are already to the north of the Marne. Our armies of Lorraine and the Vosges are reaching the frontier. Our troops, as well as those of our Allies, are admirable in morale, endurance, and ardor. The pursuit will be continued with all our energy. The Government of the Republic may be proud of the army which it has prepared.

JOFFRE.

OFFICIAL LETTER FROM PRESIDENT POINCARÉ TO THE MINISTER OF WAR

BORDEAUX, September 11th.

MY DEAR MINISTER,

Our valiant armies have, during the last four days' fighting, again given striking proofs of their bravery and high spirit.

The strategic idea, conceived with so much clear-sightedness by the Commander-in-Chief and realized with so much coolness, method, and resolution, has been carried out in recent operations by faultless tactics.

Far from being fatigued by long weeks of marching and unceasing battle, our troops have shown more endurance and keenness than ever. With the vigorous assistance of our English Allies they have forced back the enemy to the east of Paris, and the brilliant successes they have gained and the magnificent qualities they have shown are sure guarantees of decisive victories.

I beg you, my dear Minister, to be good enough to transmit to the General Commanding-in-Chief, to the officers and the rank and file, the congratulations and good wishes of the Government of the Republic, and with them the personal expression of my own deep admiration.

RAYMOND POINCARÉ.

THE GERMAN RALLY ON THE AISNE

THE BEGINNING OF TRENCH WARFARE

SEPTEMBER 12-20

COLONEL E. D. SWINTON   COLONEL O. FROBENIUS
ANONYMOUS GERMAN LETTERS

Animated by hopes raised over-high by the victory of the Marne, the French rushed eagerly, perhaps recklessly, on the withdrawing Germans. The latter, steady and undismayed in their necessary retreat, fell back only until they could reform their lines. For this purpose they selected the strongest natural position they had passed, the line of hills north of the Aisne River, with the ancient road along their summit known as the *Chemin des Dames,* the "Ladies' Road."

Here in comparative security the Germans turned on their pursuers. The latter, especially the British, endeavored with desperate valor to cross the Aisne River and compel a continuance of the Germans' retreat. But the heavier Teutonic artillery had reached this new front and after a week of tragic losses, the assailants learned, as the Germans had learned before, the impossibility of advance against modern artillery.

So each side screened itself in trenches; and the art of "camouflage" began, both roads and guns being carefully hidden or disguised to protect them from the enemy's fire. Barbed wire also came into use; and soon the newly invented methods of defense so far outclassed the methods of attack, both old and new, that the war became a deadlock. Neither side could advance except by inches and at heavy cost. This fact, first proven along the Aisne, soon spread to the other fronts. By 1915 it had completely changed the character of the War.

The chief account of the Aisne battle, or rather of its frenzied opening week, since it became ultimately a perpetual trench battle, is here given by Colonel Swinton, a British participant. His day by day narrative of the doings of the British army was at first issued anonymously, under the pen-name of "Eye Witness." It was everywhere recognized as the clearest, most honest and most valuable of all the records which presented the story from the British view. It is here supplemented by the official German view of Colonel Frobenius, and by German soldiers who, like Colonel Swinton, were actually enduring the ordeal.

BY COL. E. D. SWINTON

General Headquarters,
September 18, 1914.

SEPTEMBER 14th, the Germans were making a determined resistance along the River Aisne. Opposition, which it was at first thought might possibly be of a rearguard nature, not entailing material delay to our progress, developed and proved to be more serious than was anticipated.

The action, now being fought by the Germans along their line, may, it is true, have been undertaken in order to gain time for some strategic operation or move, and may not be their main stand. But, if this is so, the fighting is naturally on a scale which as to extent of ground covered and duration of resistance, makes it undistinguishable in its progress from what is known as a "pitched battle," though the enemy certainly showed signs of considerable disorganization during the earlier days of their retirement phase.

Whether it was originally intended by them to defend the position they took up as strenuously as they have done, or whether the delay, gained for them during the 12th and 13th by their artillery, has enabled them to develop their resistance and force their line to an extent not originally contemplated cannot be said.

So far as we are concerned the action still being contested is the battle of the Aisne. The foe we are fighting is just across the river along the whole of our front to the east and west. The struggle is not confined to the valley of that river, though it will probably bear its name.

The progress of our operations and the French armies nearest us for the 14th, 15th, 16th, and 17th will now be described:

On Monday, the 14th, those of our troops which had on the previous day crossed the Aisne, after driving in the German rear guards on that evening, found portions of the enemy's forces in prepared defensive positions on the right bank and could do little more than secure a footing north of the river. This, however, they maintained in spite of two counter-attacks delivered at dusk and 10 p. m., in which the fighting was severe.

During the 14th, strong reënforcements of our troops were passed to the north bank, the troops crossing by ferry, by pontoon bridges, and by the remains of permanent bridges. Close coöperation with the French forces was maintained and the general progress made was good, although the opposition was vigorous and the state of the roads, after the heavy rains, made movements slow. One division alone failed to secure the ground it expected to.

The First Army Corps, after repulsing repeated attacks, captured 600 prisoners and twelve guns. The cavalry also took a number of prisoners. Many of the Germans taken belong to the reserve and Landwehr formations, which fact appears to indicate that the enemy is compelled to draw on other classes of soldiers to fill the gaps in his ranks.

There was a heavy rain throughout the night of September 14th-15th, and during the 15th. The situation of the British forces underwent no essential change. But it became more and more evident that the defensive preparations made by the enemy were more extensive than was at first apparent.

In order to counterbalance these, measures were taken by us to economize our troops and to secure protection from the hostile artillery fire, which was very fierce; and our men continued to improve their own intrenchments. The Germans bombarded our lines nearly all day, using heavy guns, brought, no doubt, from before Maubeuge, as well as those with the corps.

All their counter-attacks, however, failed, although in some places they were repeated six times. One made on the Fourth Guard Brigade was repulsed with heavy slaughter.

An attempt to advance slightly, made by part of our line, was unsuccessful as regards gain of ground, but led to the withdrawal of part of the enemy's infantry and artillery.

Further counter-attacks made during the night were beaten off. Rain came on toward evening and continued intermittently until 9 a. m. on the 16th. Besides adding to the discomfort of the soldiers holding the line, the wet weather to some extent hampered the motor transport service, which was also hindered by broken bridges.

On Wednesday, the 16th, there was little change in the situation opposite the British. The efforts made by the enemy were less active than on the previous day, although their bombardment continued throughout the morning and evening. Our artillery fire drove the defenders off one of the salients of their position, but they returned in the evening. Forty prisoners were taken by the Third Division.

On Thursday, the 17th, the situation still remained unchanged in its essentials. The German heavy artillery fire was more active than on the previous day. The only infantry attacks made by the enemy were on the extreme right of our position, and, as had happened before, were repulsed with heavy loss, chiefly, on this occasion, by our field artillery.

In order to convey some idea of the nature of the fighting it may be said that along the greater part of our front the Germans have been driven back from the forward slopes on the north of the river. Their infantry are holding strong lines of trenches among and along the edge of the numerous woods which crown the slopes. These trenches are elaborately constructed and cleverly concealed. In many places there are wire entanglements and lengths of rabbit fencing.

Both woods and open are carefully aligned, so that they can be swept by rifle fire and machine guns, which are invisible from our side of the valley. The ground in front of the infantry trenches is also, as a rule, under crossfire from the field artillery placed on neighboring features and under high-angle fire from pieces placed well back behind the woods on top of the plateau.

A feature of this action, as of the previous fighting, is the use by the enemy of their numerous heavy howitzers, with which they are able to direct long-range fire all over the valley and right across it. Upon these they evidently place great reliance.

Where our men are holding the forked edges of the high ground on the north side they are now strongly intrenched.

They are well fed, and in spite of the wet weather of the last week are cheerful and confident.

The bombardment by both sides has been very heavy, and on Sunday, Monday and Tuesday was practically continuous. Nevertheless, in spite of the general din caused by the reports of the immense number of heavy guns in action along our front on Wednesday, the arrival of the French force acting against the German right flank was at once announced on the east of our front, some miles away, by the continuous roar of their quick-firing artillery, with which their attack was opened.

So far as the British are concerned, the greater part of this week has been passed in bombardment, in gaining ground by degrees, and in beating back severe counter-attacks with heavy slaughter. Our casualties have been severe, but it is probable that those of the enemy are heavier.

The rain has caused a great drop in the temperature, and there is more than a distinct feeling of autumn in the air, especially in the early mornings.

On our right and left the French have been fighting fiercely and have also been gradually gaining ground. One village has already during this battle been captured and recaptured twice by each side, and at the time of writing remains in the hands of the Germans.

The fighting has been at close quarters and of the most desperate nature, and the streets of the village are filled with dead on both sides.

The Germans are a formidable enemy, well trained, long prepared, and brave. Their soldiers are carrying on the contest with skill and valor. Nevertheless they are fighting to win anyhow, regardless of all the rules of fair play, and there is evidence that they do not hesitate at anything in order to gain victory.

A large number of the tales of their misbehaviors are exaggeration and some of the stringent precautions they have taken to guard themselves against the inhabitants of the areas traversed are possibly justifiable measures of war. But, at the same time, it has been definitely established that they have committed atrocities on many occasions.

Among the minor happenings of interest is the following: During a counter-attack by the German Fifty-third Regiment on positions of the Northampton and Queen's Regiments on Thursday, the 17th, a force of some 400 of the enemy were allowed to approach right up to the trench occupied by a platoon of the former regiment, owing to the fact that they had held up their hands and made gestures that were interpreted as signs that they wished to surrender. When they were actually on the parapet of the trench held by the Northamptons they opened fire on our men at point-blank range.

Unluckily for the enemy, however, flanking them and only some 400 yards away, there happened to be a machine gun manned by a detachment of the Queen's. This at once opened fire, cutting a lane through their mass, and they fell back to their own trench with great loss. Shortly afterward they were driven further back, with additional loss, by a battalion of Guards which came up in support.

The following special order has been issued to the troops:

"September 17, 1914.

"Once more I have to express my deep appreciation of the splendid behavior of the officers, non-commissioned officers, and men of the army under my command throughout the great battle of the Aisne, which has been in progress since the evening of the 12th inst., and the battle of the Marne, which lasted from the morning of the 6th to the evening of the 10th, and finally ended in the precipitate flight of the enemy.

"When we were brought face to face with a position of extraordinary strength, carefully intrenched and prepared for defense by an army and staff which are thorough adepts in such work, throughout the 13th and 14th, that position was most gallantly attacked by the British forces and the passage of the Aisne effected. This is the third day the troops have been gallantly holding the position they have gained against most desperate counter-attacks and the hail of heavy artillery.

"I am unable to find adequate words in which to express the admiration I feel for their magnificent conduct.

"The French armies on our right and left are making good progress, and I feel sure that we have only to hold on with tenacity to the ground we have won for a very short time longer when the Allies will be again in full pursuit of a beaten enemy.

"The self-sacrificing devotion and splendid spirit of the British army in France will carry all before it.

"J. D. P. FRENCH, Field Marshal,
"Commander in Chief of the British Army in the Field."

The enemy is still maintaining himself along the whole front, and, in order to do so, is throwing into the fight detachments composed of units from different formations, the active army, reserve, and Landwehr, as is shown by the uniforms of the prisoners recently captured.

Our progress, although slow on account of the strength of the defensive positions against which we are pressing, has in certain directions been continuous; but the present battle may well last for some days more before a decision is reached, since it now approximates somewhat to siege warfare.

The Germans are making use of searchlights. This fact, coupled with their great strength in heavy artillery, leads to the supposition that they are employing material which may have been collected for the siege of Paris.

A buried store of the enemy's munitions of war was also found, not far from the Aisne, ten wagon loads of live shell and two wagon loads of cable being dug up. Traces were discovered of large quantities of stores having been burned—all tending to show that as far back as the Aisne the German retirement was hurried.

On Sunday, the 20th, nothing of importance occurred until the afternoon, when there was a break in the clouds and an interval of feeble sunshine, which was hardly powerful enough to warm the soaking troops. The Germans took advantage of this brief spell of fine weather to make several counter-attacks against different points. These were all repulsed with loss to the enemy, but the casualties incurred by us were by no means light.

The offensive against one or two points was renewed at dusk, with no greater success. The brunt of the resistance has naturally fallen upon the infantry. In spite of the fact that they have been drenched to the skin for some days and their trenches have been deep in mud and water, and in spite of the incessant night alarms and the almost continuous bombardment to which they have been subjected, they have on every occasion been ready for the enemy's infantry when the latter attempted to assault, and they have beaten them back with great loss.

BY COLONEL FROBENIUS

The retreat of the German army was effected, upon the whole, in an exemplary manner in spite of the tremendous overexertion imposed upon the troops and the difficulties of the situation. Criss-crossing on the lines of retreat on the part of several corps was unavoidable. Kluck's eccentric retreat toward the northeast will always be classed among the strategical masterpieces of the war.

On September 15th the new defensive battle on the Aisne was already in full swing. Kluck now fought against Manoury on the line Ribecourt—east of Soissons; Huringen's Seventh Army, composed of several constituents previously mentioned, fought along the Aisne from Vailly to Brimont, facing General French and the left wing of Franchet d'Esperey. Bülow, reënforced by the 18th Artillery Corps of the Fourth Army, attacked the eastern front of Rheims, defended by Franchet. Hausen attacked Foch's Ninth Army on the line Prosnes-Somme Py; Duke Albrecht found his old opponent Langle de Cary on the line Tahure-Varennes; and the German Crown Prince assembled his army again on the northern and eastern fronts of Verdun. At the same time the Sixth and Seventh Armies withdrew from the line of forts toward the border, only the Camp des Romains was won by us in September.

When, on September 18th, the Crown Prince of Bavaria advanced against this line, and, more particularly Fort Camp des Romains, his several corps had to surmount. First, the steep eastern edge of the Côte Lorraine, defended by the 8th French Corps, and this accomplished (September 21st amid great difficulties), had to encounter on the furrowed ground of the plateau the French infantry who, in carefully prepared positions, supported by batteries, were nevertheless put to flight.

In spite of their vigorous sorties even the garrisons of Toul and Verdun were powerless to stay the advance of the attacker. By the 23rd of September heavy artillery had been brought into action against the forts Troyon, Les Paroches, Camp des Romains and Liouville, which in a short time produced effective results. On the 24th of September Camp des Romains seemed ripe for attack. This was executed by Lieutenant-General von Höhn with the 6th Bavarian Infantry Division supported by detachments of Prussian foot artillery and sappers. Every foot of ground was hotly disputed during a hand-to-hand struggle lasting three hours. Under an uninterrupted heavy fire the sappers removed obstacles and smoked the enemy out of his holes. On the 25th the totally destroyed fort was forced to surrender. Thus was a powerful and conspicuous wedge driven into the French positions and the St. Mihiel salient established.

GERMAN LETTERS FROM THE AISNE

My Dear Wife: I have just been living through days that defy imagination. I should never have thought that men could stand it. Not a second has passed but my life has been in danger, and yet not a hair of my head has been hurt.

It was horrible! It was ghastly! But I have been saved for you and for our happiness, and I take heart again, although I am still terribly unnerved. God grant that I may see you again soon, and that this horror may soon be over.

None of us can do any more; human strength is at an end. I will try to tell you about it. On September 5th the enemy were reported to be taking up a position near St. Prix, southeast of Paris.

The Tenth Corps, which had made an astonishingly rapid advance, of course, was attacked on Sunday. Steep slopes led up to the heights, which were held in considerable force.

With our weak detachments of the Seventy-fourth and Ninety-first regiments we reached the crest and came under a terrible artillery fire that mowed us down. However, we entered St. Prix. Hardly had we done so than we were met with shell fire and a violent fusillade from the enemy's infantry.

Our Colonel was badly wounded—he is the third we have had. Fourteen men were killed around me. We got away in a lull without being hit.

The 7th, 8th, and 9th of September we were constantly under shell and shrapnel fire and suffered terrible losses. I was in a house which was hit several times. The fear of death, of agony, which is in every man's heart, and naturally so, is a terrible feeling.

How often I have thought of you, my darling, and what I suffered in that terrifying battle, which extended along a front of many miles near Montmirail, you cannot possibly imagine.

Our heavy artillery was being used for the siege of Maubeuge. We wanted it badly, as the enemy had theirs in force and kept up a furious bombardment. For four days I was under artillery fire. It was like hell, but a thousand times worse.

On the night of the 9th the order was given to retreat, as it would have been madness to attempt to hold our position with our few men, and we should have risked a terrible defeat the next day. The First and Third Armies had not been able to attack with us, as we had advanced too rapidly. Our morale was absolutely broken. In spite of unheard-of sacrifices we had achieved nothing.

I cannot understand how our army, after fighting three great battles and being terribly weakened, was sent against a position which the enemy had prepared for three weeks, but naturally I know nothing of the intentions of our Chiefs; they say nothing has been lost.

In a word, we retired toward Cormontreuil and Rheims by forced marches by day and night. We hear that three armies are going to get into line, intrench and rest, and

The Ill-fated Churchill Expedition
British Marines landing in
Belgium to aid the Antwerp
Defense

then start afresh our victorious march on Paris. It was not a defeat, only a strategic retreat. I have confidence in our Chiefs that everything will be successful.

Our First Battalion, which has fought with unparalleled bravery, is reduced from 1,200 to 194 men. These numbers speak for themselves.

Cerny, South of Laon, September 14, 1914.

My Dear Parents: Our corps has the task of holding the heights south of Cerny in all circumstances until the Fourteenth Corps on our left flank can grip the enemy's flank. On our right are other corps. We are fighting with the English Guards, Highlanders, and Zouaves. The losses on both sides have been enormous. For the most part this is due to the too brilliant French artillery.

The English are marvelously trained in making use of ground. One never sees them, and one is constantly under fire. The French airmen perform wonderful feats. We cannot get rid of them. As soon as an airman has flown over us, ten minutes later we get their shrapnel fire in our positions. We have little artillery in our corps; without it we cannot get forward.

Three days ago our division took possession of these heights and dug itself in. Two days ago, early in the morning, we were attacked by an immensely superior English force, one brigade and two battalions, and were turned out of our positions. The fellows took five guns from us. It was a tremendous hand-to-hand fight.

How I escaped myself I am not clear. I then had to bring up supports on foot. My horse was wounded, and the others were too far in the rear. Then came up the Guards Jager Battalion. Fourth Jager, Sixth Regiment, Reserve Regiment Thirteen, and Landwehr Regiments Thirteen and Sixteen, and with the help of the artillery we drove the fellows out of the position again. Our machine guns did excellent work; the English fell in heaps.

In our battalion three Iron Crosses have been given, one to C. O., one to Capt. ———, and one to Surgeon ———.

[Names probably deleted.]   Let us hope that we shall be the lucky ones next time.

During the first two days of the battle I had only one piece of bread and no water.   I spent the night in the rain without my overcoat.   The rest of my kit was on the horses which had been left behind with the baggage and which cannot come up into the battle because as soon as you put your nose up from behind cover the bullets whistle.

War is terrible.   We are all hoping that a decisive battle will end the war, as our troops already have got round Paris. If we beat the English the French resistance will soon be broken.   Russia will be very quickly dealt with; of this there is no doubt.

We received splendid help from the Austrian heavy artillery at Maubeuge.   They bombarded Fort Cerfontaine in such a way that there was not ten meters a parapet which did not show enormous craters made by the shells.   The armored turrets were found upside down.

Yesterday evening, about 6, in the valley in which our reserves stood there was such a terrible cannonade that we saw nothing of the sky but a cloud of smoke.   We had few casualties.

THE SUBMARINE'S FIRST TRIUMPH

THREE BRITISH WARSHIPS SUNK BY A SOLITARY U-BOAT

SEPTEMBER 22ND

LIEUT. OTTO WEDDIGEN
COMMANDER BERTRAM NICHOLSON

Before the War there had been much talk of the power of the newly invented "submarines" against the old style surface ships of war. Especially the discussion turned on the chances of the U-boats or Undersea-boats, as the Germans called their submarines, against the British battleships. For the first month the U-boats did nothing to justify their reputation. Then suddenly—and very startlingly for Britain's friends—came the impressive achievement of Lieutenant Weddigen.

In one attack he sank three British ships. They were not battleships, to be sure, but only "cruisers," that is faster but less powerful ships than those of the main battle fleet. Still they were splendid ships, each of some 12,000 tons, and each manned by about 800 sailors; and their combined loss constituted a menace for the future which was awesome beyond words. Fortunately, however, this case proved exceptional. Never again during the War did a submarine achieve anything even approaching such a wholesale success. In fact, the loss of these ships was soon learned to have been only another case of the need of new tactics to meet new weapons.

In the first place, the sea at the time was so rough as to hide the submarine's periscope, a condition thereafter recognized as "submarine" weather and guarded against with special care. In the next place, the three great cruisers were unaccompanied by "torpedo destroyers" and other lesser craft, which should have been patrolling all around them as an outer guard. And in the third place, when the first cruiser, the *Aboukir*, was torpedoed, the other two instead of fleeing, as their own safety demanded, closed in upon the spot as though all danger was over, and gallantly sought to rescue the *Aboukir's* survivors. They thus came almost to a standstill and offered themselves as helpless targets to the submarine. Such a performance was as foolhardy as it was heroic.

What followed is here told by the successful German commander. He was fêted, honored and promoted at home; but he soon afterward perished when commanding a less lucky U-boat against wiser foes. The little submarine with which he made his great coup was the *U-9;* the larger one with which he met his own destruction was the *U-29*.

The story of the sinking of the cruisers is also given by the senior surviving British officer of the *Cressy*, Commander Nicholson. He had held a subordinate rank on the *Cressy,* the last of the three cruisers to be destroyed, and he saw from her deck the entire catastrophe. Nearly fifteen hundred British seamen perished.

BY LIEUT. OTTO WEDDIGEN

I AM 32 years old and have been in the navy for years. For the last five years I have been attached to the submarine flotilla, and have been most interested in that branch of the navy. At the outbreak of the war our undersea boats were rendezvoused at a series of harbors on our coast of the North Sea.

Each of us felt and hoped that the Fatherland might be benefited by such individual efforts of ours as were possible at a time when our bigger sisters of the fleet were prohibited from activity. So we awaited commands from the Admiralty, ready for any undertaking that promised to do for the imperial navy what our brothers of the army were so gloriously accomplishing.

I was married at the home of my brother in Wilhelmshaven to my boyhood sweetheart, Miss Prete of Hamburg, on August 16th. Before that I had been steadily on duty with my boat, and I had to leave again the next day after my marriage. But both my bride and I wanted the ceremony to take place at the appointed time, and it did, although within twenty-four hours thereafter I had to go away on a venture that gave a good chance of making my new wife a widow. But she was as firm as I was that my first duty was to answer the call of our country, and she waved me away from the dock with good-luck wishes.

I set out from a North Sea port on one of the arms of the Kiel Canal and set my course in a southwesterly direction. Thus I was soon cruising off the coast of Holland. I had been lying in wait there only a few days before the morning of September 22nd arrived, the day on which I fell in with my quarry.

When I started from home the fact was kept quiet and a heavy sea helped to keep the secret, but when the action began the sun was bright and the water smooth—not the most favorable conditions for submarine work.

I had sighted several ships during my passage, but they were not what I was seeking. English torpedo boats came within my reach, but I felt there was bigger game further on, so on I went. I traveled on the surface except when we sighted vessels, and then I submerged, not even showing my periscope, except when it was necessary to take bearings. It was ten minutes after 6 on the morning of last Tuesday when I caught sight of one of the big cruisers of the enemy.

I was then eighteen sea miles northwest of the Hook of Holland. I had then traveled considerably more than 200 miles from my base. My boat was one of an old type, but she had been built on honor, and she was behaving beautifully. I had been going ahead partly submerged, with about five feet of my periscope showing. Almost immediately I caught sight of the first cruiser and two others. I submerged completely and laid my course so as to bring up in the center of the trio, which held a sort of triangular formation. I could see their gray-black sides riding high over the water.

When I first sighted them they were near enough for torpedo work, but I wanted to make my aim sure, so I went down and in on them. I had taken the position of the three ships before submerging, and I succeeded in getting another flash through my periscope before I began action. I soon reached what I regarded as a good shooting point.

Then I loosed one of my torpedoes at the middle ship. I was then about twelve feet under water, and got the shot off in good shape, my men handling the boat as if she had been a skiff. I climbed to the surface to get a sight through my tube of the effect, and discovered that the shot had gone straight and true, striking the ship, which I later learned was the *Aboukir,* under one of her magazines, which in exploding helped the torpedo's work of destruction.

There were a fountain of water, a burst of smoke, a flash of fire, and part of the cruiser rose in the air. Then I heard a roar and felt reverberations sent through the water by the detonation. She had been broken apart, and sank in a few minutes. The *Aboukir* had been stricken in a vital spot and by an unseen force; that made the blow all the greater.

Her crew were brave, and even with death staring them in the face kept to their posts, ready to handle their useless guns, for I submerged at once. But I had stayed on top long enough to see the other cruisers, which I learned were the *Cressy* and the *Hogue,* turn and steam full speed to their dying sister, whose plight they could not understand, unless it had been due to an accident.

The ships came on a mission of inquiry and rescue, for many of the *Aboukir's* crew were now in the water, the order having been given, "Each man for himself."

But soon the other two English cruisers learned what had brought about the destruction so suddenly.

As I reached my torpedo depth I sent a second charge at the nearest of the oncoming vessels, which was the *Hogue.* The English were playing my game, for I had scarcely to move out of my position, which was a great aid, since it helped to keep me from detection.

On board my little boat the spirit of the German Navy was to be seen in its best form. With enthusiasm every man held himself in check and gave attention to the work in hand.

The attack on the *Hogue* went true. But this time I did not have the advantageous aid of having the torpedo detonate under the magazine, so for twenty minutes the *Hogue* lay wounded and helpless on the surface before she heaved, half turned over and sank.

But this time, the third cruiser knew of course that the enemy was upon her and she sought as best she could to defend herself. She loosed her torpedo defense batteries on boats, starboard and port, and stood her ground as if more anxious to help the many sailors who were in the water than to save herself. In common with the method of defending herself against a submarine attack, she steamed in a zigzag course, and this made it necessary for me to hold my torpedoes until I could lay a true course for them, which also made it necessary for me to get nearer to the *Cressy.* I had come to the surface for a view and saw how wildly the fire was being sent from the ship. Small wonder that was when they did not know where to shoot, although one shot went unpleasantly near us.

When I got within suitable range I sent away my third attack. This time I sent a second torpedo after the first to make the strike doubly certain. My crew were aiming like sharpshooters and both torpedoes went to their bull's-eye. My luck was with me again, for the enemy was made useless and at once began sinking by her head. Then she careened far over, but all the while her men stayed at the guns looking for their invisible foe. They were brave and true to their country's sea traditions. Then she eventually suffered a boiler explosion and completely turned turtle. With her keel uppermost she floated until the air got out from under her and then she sank with a loud sound, as if from a creature in pain.

The whole affair had taken less than one hour from the time of shooting off the first torpedo until the *Cressy* went to the bottom. Not one of the three had been able to use any of its big guns. I knew the wireless of the three cruisers had been calling for aid. I was still quite able to defend myself, but I knew that news of the disaster would call many English submarines and torpedo boat destroyers, so, having done my appointed work, I set my course for home.

My surmise was right, for before I got very far some British cruisers and destroyers were on the spot, and the destroyers took up the chase. I kept under water most of the way, but managed to get off a wireless to the German fleet that I was heading homeward and being pursued. I hoped to entice the enemy, by allowing them now and then a glimpse of me, into the zone in which they might be exposed to capture or destruction by German warships, but, although their destroyers saw me plainly at dusk on the 22nd and made a final effort to stop me, they abandoned the attempt, as it was taking them too far from safety and needlessly exposing them to attack from our fleet and submarines.

How much they feared our submarines and how wide was the agitation caused by good little *U-9* is shown by the

English reports that a whole flotilla of German submarines had attacked the cruisers and that this flotilla had approached under cover of the flag of Holland.

These reports were absolutely untrue. *U-9* was the only submarine on deck, and she flew the flag she still flies—the German naval ensign—which I hope to keep forever as a glorious memento and as an inspiration for devotion to the Fatherland.

I reached the home port on the afternoon of the 23rd, and on the 24th went to Wilhelmshaven, to find that news of my effort had become public. My wife, dry eyed when I went away, met me with tears. Then I learned that my little vessel and her brave crew had won the plaudit of the Kaiser, who conferred upon each of my coworkers the Iron Cross of the second class and upon me the Iron Cross of the first and second classes.

BY COMMANDER BERTRAM W. L. NICHOLSON

Sir: I have the honor to submit the following report in connection with the sinking of H. M. S. *Cressy,* in company with H. M. S. *Aboukir* and *Hogue,* on the morning of the 22nd of September, while on patrol duty:

The *Aboukir* was struck at about 6.25 a. m. on the starboard beam. The *Hogue* and *Cressy* closed and took up a position, the *Hogue* ahead of the *Aboukir,* and the *Cressy* about 400 yards on her port beam. As soon as it was seen that the *Aboukir* was in danger of sinking all the boats were sent away from the *Cressy,* and a picket boat was hoisted out without steam up. When cutters full of the *Aboukir's* men were returning to the *Cressy* the *Hogue* was struck, apparently under the aft 9.2 magazine, as a very heavy explosion took place immediately. Almost directly after the *Hogue* was hit we observed a periscope on our port bow about 300 yards off.

Fire was immediately opened and the engines were put full speed ahead with the intention of running her down. Our gunner, Mr. Dougherty, positively asserts that he hit the periscope and that the submarine sank. An officer who was standing alongside the gunner thinks that the shell struck only floating timber, of which there was much about, but it was evidently the impression of the men on deck, who cheered and clapped heartily, that the submarine had been hit. This submarine did not fire a torpedo at the *Cressy*.

Capt. Johnson then maneuvered the ship so as to render assistance to the crews of the *Hogue* and *Aboukir*. About five minutes later another periscope was seen on our starboard quarter and fire was opened. The track of the torpedo she fired at a range of 500 to 600 yards was plainly visible and it struck us on the starboard side just before the after-bridge.

The ship listed about 10 degrees to the starboard and remained steady. The time was 7.15 a. m. All the water-tight doors, deadlights and scuttles had been securely closed before the torpedo struck the ship. All the mess stools and table shores, and all available timber below and on deck, had been previously got up and thrown over side for the saving of life.

A second torpedo fired by the same submarine missed and passed about 10 feet astern. About a quarter of an hour after the first torpedo had hit, a third torpedo fired from a submarine just before the starboard beam hit us under the No. 5 boiler room. The time was 7.30 a. m. The ship then began to heel rapidly, and finally turned keel up, remaining so for about twenty minutes before she finally sank, at 7.55 a. m.

A large number of men were saved by casting adrift on Pattern 3 target. The steam pinnace floated off her clutches, but filled and sank.

The second torpedo which struck the *Cressy* passed over the sinking hull of the *Aboukir,* narrowly missing it. It is possible that the same submarine fired all three torpedoes at the *Cressy*.

The conduct of the crew was excellent throughout. I have already remarked on the bravery displayed by Capt. Phillips, master of the trawler *L. T. Coriander,* and his crew, who picked up 156 officers and men.

The report of the Admiralty of Commander Reginald A. Norton, late of H. M. S. *Hogue,* follows:

Commander Norton's Report

I have the honor to report as follows concerning the sinking of the *Hogue, Aboukir,* and *Cressy:* Between 6.15 and 6.30 a. m., H. M. S. *Aboukir* was struck by a torpedo. The *Hogue* closed on the *Aboukir* and I received orders to hoist out the launch, turn out and prepare all boats, and unlash all timber on the upper deck.

Two lifeboats were sent to the *Aboukir,* but before the launch could get away the *Hogue* was struck on the starboard side amidships by two torpedoes at intervals of ten to twenty seconds. The ship at once began to heel to starboard. After ordering the men to provide themselves with wood, hammocks, etc., and to get into the boats on the booms and take off their clothes, I went, by Capt. Nicholson's [1] direction, to ascertain the damage done in the engine room. The artificer engineer informed me that the water was over the engine room gratings.

While endeavoring to return to the bridge the water burst open the starboard entry port doors and the ship heeled rapidly. I told the men in the port battery to jump overboard, as the launch was close alongside, and soon afterward the ship lurched heavily to starboard.

I clung to a ringbolt for some time, but eventually was dropped on to the deck, and a huge wave washed me away. I climbed up the ship's side and again was washed off. Eventually, after swimming about from various overladen pieces of wreckage, I was picked up by a cutter from the *Hogue,* Coxswain L. S. Marks, which pulled about for some hours, picking up men and discharging them to our picket boat and steam pinnace and to the Dutch steamers *Flora* and *Titan,* and rescued, in this way, Commander Sells of the *Aboukir,* Engineer Commander Stokes (with legs broken), Fleet Paymaster Eldred, and about 120 others.

Finally, about 11 a. m., when we could find no more men in the water, we were picked up by the *Lucifer,* which proceeded to the *Titan* and took off from her all our men except about twenty who were too ill to be moved.

---

[1] This officer had been in command of the *Hogue.* He is not the Commander Nicholson of the *Cressy* who makes the report.

A Lowestoft trawler and the two Dutch ships *Flora* and *Titan* were extraordinarily kind, clothing and feeding our men. My boat's crew, consisting mainly of Royal Navy Reserve men, pulled and behaved remarkably well. I particularly wish to mention Petty Officer Halton, who, by encouraging the men in the water near me, undoubtedly saved many lives.

Lieut. Commander Phillips-Wolley, after hoisting out the launch, asked me if we should try to hoist out another boat, and endeavored to do so. The last I saw of him was on the after-bridge, doing well.

Lieut. Commander Tillard was picked up by a launch. He got up a cutter's crew and saved many lives, as did Midshipman Cazalet in the *Cressy's* gig. Lieut. Chichester turned out the whaler very quickly.

A Dutch sailing trawler sailed close by, but went off without rendering any assistance, although we signaled to her from the *Hogue* to close after we were struck.

The *Aboukir* appeared to me to take about thirty-five minutes to sink, floating bottom up for about five minutes. The *Hogue* turned turtle very quickly—in about five minutes—and floated bottom up for several minutes. A dense black smoke was seen in the starboard battery, whether from coal or torpedo cordite I could not say. The upper deck was not blown up, and only one other small explosion occurred and we heeled over.

The *Cressy* I watched heel over from the cutter. She heeled over to starboard very slowly, dense black smoke issuing from her when she attained an angle of about 90 degrees, and she took a long time from this angle till she floated bottom up with the starboard screw slightly out of water. I consider it was thirty-five to forty-five minutes from the time she was struck till she was bottom up.

All the men on the *Hogue* behaved extraordinarily well, obeying orders even when in the water swimming for their lives, and I witnessed many cases of great self-sacrifice and gallantry.

I have the honor to submit that I may be appointed to another ship as soon as I can get a kit.

CAPTURE OF ANTWERP

GERMANY ALMOST COMPLETES THE CONQUEST OF BELGIUM

OCTOBER 9TH

SIR A. CONAN DOYLE   WINSTON CHURCHILL
COMMANDER DE GERLACHE DE GOMMERY
GENERAL VON FALKENHAYN   GUSTAV FELLER

With the failure of their first rush to destroy France, the Germans returned to their smaller triumph over Belgium, and proceeded to complete its conquest. They had seized Brussels, the capital, but had ignored the western region along the seacoast with its great seaport metropolis, Antwerp. Now, Antwerp had been long famous for its fortifications. It was known as "the impregnable fortress." Could it stand against the Austro-German howitzers? The Allies were at least sufficiently hopeful to encourage the Belgians to make the attempt; and British marines were sent to their aid.

With the marines, since this held something of the nature of a forlorn hope, went the British cabinet official responsible for sending them, Mr. Winston Churchill. As the effort failed, there was much condemnation of it later; so we here present the story of the siege by one of Mr. Churchill's critics, Sir Arthur Conan Doyle, the famous author and writer of the most popular British history of the war. We then give Churchill's own story.

The spirit of the siege, however, as Belgians saw it, is but little expressed by these Britishers. They give only the facts. So for the heart and meaning and tragedy of it all, we turn to the Belgian soldier and statesmen, De Gerlache. The German view is then given by the chief of the "High Staff" Falkenhayn who succeeded Moltke in the general command, and by the popular historian, Feller.

BY SIR A. CONAN DOYLE

IT was at this period that a great change came over both the object and the locality of the operations. This change depended upon two events which occurred far to the north, and reacted upon the great armies locked in the long grapple of the Aisne. The first of these controlling circumstances was that, by the movement of the old troops and the addition of new ones, each army had sought to turn the flank of the other in the north, until the whole center of gravity of the

304

war was transferred to that region. A new French army under General Castelnau, whose fine defense of Nancy had put him in the front of French leaders, had appeared on the extreme left wing of the Allies, only to be countered by fresh bodies of Germans, until the ever-extending line lengthened out to the manufacturing districts of Lens and Lille, where amid pit-shafts and slag-heaps the cavalry of the French and the Germans tried desperately to get round each other's flank. The other factor was the fall of Antwerp, which released very large bodies of Germans, who were flooding over western Belgium, and, with the help of great new levies from Germany, carrying the war to the sand-dunes of the coast. The operations which brought about this great change open up a new chapter in the history of the war.

The Belgians, after the evacuation of Brussels in August, had withdrawn their army into the widespread fortress of Antwerp, from which they made frequent sallies upon the Germans who were garrisoning their country. Great activity was shown and several small successes were gained, which had the useful effect of detaining two corps which might have been employed upon the Aisne. Eventually, towards the end of September, the Germans turned their attention seriously to the reduction of the city, with a well-founded confidence that no modern forts could resist the impact of their enormous artillery. They drove the garrison within the lines, and early in October opened a bombardment upon the outer forts with such results that it was evidently only a matter of days before they would fall and the fine old city be faced with the alternative of surrender or destruction. The Spanish fury of Parma's pikemen would be a small thing compared to the *furor Teutonicus* working its evil deliberate will upon town-hall or cathedral, with the aid of fire-disc, petrol-spray, or other products of Kultur.

The main problem before the Allies, if the town could not be saved, was to insure that the Belgian army should be extricated and that nothing of military value which could be destroyed should be left to the invaders. No troops were available for a rescue, for the French and British old formations were already engaged, while the new ones were not yet ready for action. In these circumstances, a resolution was come to by the British leaders which was bold to the verge of rashness and so chivalrous as to be almost quixotic. It was determined to send out at the shortest notice a naval division, one brigade of which consisted of marines, troops who are second to none in the country's service, while the other two brigades were young amateur sailor volunteers, most of whom had only been under arms for a few weeks. It was an extraordinary experiment, as testing how far the average sport-loving, healthy-minded young Briton needs only his equipment to turn him into a soldier who, in spite of all rawness and inefficiency, can still affect the course of a campaign. This strange force, one-third veterans and two-thirds practically civilians, was hurried across to do what it could for the failing town, and to demonstrate to Belgium how real was the sympathy which prompted us to send all that we had. A reënforcement of a very different quality was dispatched a few days later in the shape of the Seventh Division of the Regular Army, with the Third Division of Cavalry. These fine troops were too late, however, to save the city, and soon found themselves in a position where it needed all their hardihood to save themselves.

The Marine Brigade of the Naval Division under General Paris was dispatched from England in the early morning and reached Antwerp during the night of October 3rd. They were about 2,000 in number. Early next morning they were out in the trenches, relieving some weary Belgians. The Germans were already within the outer enceinte and drawing close to the inner. For forty-eight hours they held the line in the face of heavy shelling. The cover was good and the losses were not heavy. At the end of that time the Belgian troops, who had been a good deal worn by their heroic exertions, were unable to sustain the German pressure, and evacuated the trenches on the flank of the British line. The brigade then fell back to a reserve position in front of the town.

On the night of the 5th the two other brigades of the division, numbering some 5,000 amateur sailors, arrived in Antwerp, and the whole force assembled on the new line of defense. Mr. Winston Churchill showed his gallantry as a man, and his indiscretion as a high official, whose life was of great value to his country by accompanying the force from England.

The bombardment was now very heavy, and the town was on fire in several places. The equipment of the British left much to be desired, and their trenches were as indifferent as their training. Nonetheless they played the man and lived up to the traditions of that great service upon whose threshold they stood. For three days these men, who a few weeks before had been anything from schoolmasters to tram-conductors, held their perilous post. They were very raw, but they possessed a great asset in their officers, who were usually men of long service. But neither the lads of the naval brigades nor the war-worn and much-enduring Belgians could stop the mouths of those inexorable guns. On the 8th it was clear that the forts could no longer be held. The British task had been to maintain the trenches which connected the forts with each other, but if the forts went it was clear that the trenches must be outflanked and untenable. The situation, therefore, was hopeless, and all that remained was to save the garrison and leave as little as possible for the victors. Some thirty or forty German merchant ships in the harbor were sunk and the great petrol tanks were set on fire. By the light of the flames the Belgians and British forces made their way successfully out of the town, and the good service rendered later by our Allies upon the Yser and elsewhere is the best justification of the policy which made us strain every nerve in order to do everything which could have a moral or material effect upon them in their darkest hour. Had the British been able to get away unscathed, the whole operation might have been reviewed with equanimity if not with satisfaction, but, unhappily, a grave misfortune, arising rather from bad luck than from the opposition of the enemy, came upon the retreating brigades, so that very many of our young sailors after their one week of crowded life came to the end of their active service for the war.

On leaving Antwerp it had been necessary to strike to

the north in order to avoid a large detachment of the enemy who were said to be upon the line of the retreat. The boundary between Holland and Belgium is at this point very intricate, with no clear line of demarcation, and a long column of British somnambulists, staggering along in the dark after so many days in which they had for the most part never enjoyed two consecutive hours of sleep, wandered over the fatal line and found themselves in firm but kindly Dutch custody for the rest of the war. Some fell into the hands of the enemy, but the great majority were interned. These men belonged chiefly to three battalions of the 1st Brigade. The 2nd Brigade, with one battalion of the 1st, and the greater part of the Marines, made their way to the trains at St. Gilles-Waes, and were able to reach Ostend in safety. The remaining battalion of Marines, with a number of stragglers of the other brigades, were cut off at Morbede by the Germans, and about half of them were taken, while the rest fought their way through in the darkness and joined their comrades. The total losses of the British in the whole misadventure from first to last were about 2,500 men—a high price, and yet not too high when weighed against the results of their presence at Antwerp. On October 10th the Germans under General Von Beseler occupied the city. Mr. Powell, who was present, testifies that 60,000 marched into the town, and that they were all troops of the active army.

BY WINSTON S. CHURCHILL

The project of sending a relieving army to the aid of Antwerp did not originate with me. It originated with Lord Kitchener and the French Government. I was not concerned or consulted in the arrangements until they had advanced a long way; and until large bodies of troops were actually moving or under orders to move.

On the night of October 2, 1914, at midnight I was summoned to a conference at Lord Kitchener's house. I then learned, what to some extent I knew from the telegrams— first, that plans for sending a relieving army to the aid of Antwerp were already far advanced and were being concerted between Lord Kitchener and the French Government, that they had not yet reached a point where definite offers and promises could be made to the Belgian Government, and that, meanwhile, that afternoon the Belgian Government had telegraphed its decision to evacuate the city with the field army and to withdraw from the fort and practically to abandon the defense.

We were all extremely distressed at this; it seemed that at the moment when aid was available everything was going to be thrown away for the sake of three or four days' continued resistance. In these circumstances I offered—and I do not regret it a bit—to proceed to Antwerp at once, to tell the Belgian Government what was being done, to ascertain the situation on the spot, and to see in what way the defense could be prolonged until a relieving force could be established. My colleagues accepted this offer on my part, and I crossed the Channel at once.

The next day, having consulted with the Belgian Government and with the British Staff officers who were at Antwerp watching the progress of the operations, I made a telegraphic proposal. I had to be extremely careful not to say anything on behalf of the British Government which would encourage the Belgians to resistance in the hopes of getting help we could not afterward make good. The proposal which I made may be briefly stated. It is all set out in the telegrams, and some day will be made public. It is as follows: The Belgians were to continue the resistance to the utmost limit of their power. The British and French Governments were to say within three days definitely whether they could send a relieving force or not, and what the dimensions of that force would be. In the event of their not being able to send a relieving force the British Government were to send in any case to Ghent and other points on the line of retreat British troops sufficient to insure the safe retirement of the Belgian field army, so that the Belgian field army would not be compromised through continuing the resistance on the Antwerp fortress line. Incidentally, we were to aid and encourage the defense of Antwerp by the sending of naval guns, naval brigades, and any other minor measures likely to enable the defenders to hold out the necessary number of days. This proposal I made subject to confirmation on both sides. Nothing was settled until both Governments accepted. The proposal was accepted by both Governments. I was informed by telegraph that a relieving army would be sent, its dimensions and composition were sent to me for communication to the Belgians, and I was told to do everything possible to maintain the defense meanwhile. This I did without regard to consequences in any direction.

I am not going to describe the military events which are well known; but I think it is a great mistake to regard Lord Kitchener's efforts to relieve Antwerp—in which I played a subsidiary though important part—as an event which led only to misfortune.

I believe that military history will hold that the consequences conduced extremely to the advantage of the Allies in the west. The great battle which began on the Aisne was spreading day by day more and more toward the sea. Sir John French's army was coming into line and beginning the operations of the battle of Armentières, which developed into the great battle of Ypres, and everything was in flux.

The prolongation of the resistance of Antwerp, even by only two or three days, detained great German forces in the vicinity of the fortress. The sudden and audacious arrival of a fresh British division and a British cavalry division at Ghent and elsewhere baffled the cautious German staff and led it to apprehend that a large army was arriving from the sea. At any rate, their advance proceeded in a halting manner, although opposed by weak forces, and I believe it will be demonstrated in history—certainly it is the opinion of many highly competent military officers at the present time —that the whole of this enterprise, the moving of those British troops and the French troops who were in association with them, though it did not save Antwerp, had the effect of causing the great battle to be fought on the line of the Yser instead of twenty or thirty miles further south. If that is so, the losses which were incurred by our naval division, luckily not very heavy in life, will certainly have been well expended in the general interest.

BY COMMANDANT DE GERLACHE DE GOMMERY

In Antwerp, where for weeks the heart of Belgium had been throbbing, preparations were being made for a desperate resistance.

To facilitate the defense the dykes of the Scheldt, the Rupel, and the Nèthe had been opened at several points, and in this way a large area of low-lying land had been inundated. Within a radius of many miles the Belgians had blown up luxurious country houses, ancient châteaux, charming villas, farms and windmills, and—which was an even more painful sacrifice—the thousands of superb trees, which were the only ornament of this level region, were felled.

Trenches had been dug and works of all kinds had been constructed. The armament of the forts had been completed and improved, as far as was possible, by means of cannon sent from France by way of Ostend.

Two armored trains, veritable moving fortresses, had been built in the Cockerill works at Hoboken-lez-Anvers; they were armed with British naval guns of 4.7 inches caliber.

On the other hand, as the Scheldt had remained open to merchant vessels, and as all sorts of provisions had been arriving in abundance, the city was secured against the rigors of a long siege.

But how many things we had to think of; what anxieties were ours, from which our powerful enemies were exempt, and what distressing problems we had to solve!

Measures had to be taken to preserve from the risks of a possible bombardment the most valuable of the paintings which adorned the churches, the museums, and certain private houses. The "Descent from the Cross," the "Assumption of the Virgin," and other masterpieces of Rubens, the "Entombment of Christ," by Matsys, the "Temptation of St. Martin," by De Vos, and a number of no less inestimable treasures were transferred to places of safety.

The metallic funds of the National Bank and the blocks used in printing paper money were sent to England.

All German prisoners were also sent to England and the Belgian wounded were gradually transferred to Ostend and other places on the coast.

A further complication: homeless refugees were arriving in ever-increasing numbers from the surrounding country. It was not possible to allow them to remain more than three or four days in Antwerp, and it was therefore necessary to facilitate their exodus toward the coast or to Holland or England.

On the 26th and 27th of September the Germans made fresh demonstrations in the direction of Termonde, obviously with the intention of crossing the Scheldt at this point.

On the 26th they encountered at Andeghem (some two or three miles to the southwest of Termonde) a small body of Belgian infantry, which, although it had no artillery to support it, resisted them heroically until the arrival of re-enforcements, which put the Germans to flight in the direction of Alost.

The battle of Lebbeke was fought on the following day under similar conditions: the Belgians were at first weak in numbers, but resisted valiantly despite heavy losses; then re-enforcements arrived, and the Germans finally scattered toward Maxenzele and Merchtem.

On the 28th heavy siege howitzers, coming from Maubeuge, German and Austrian, went into action, and thenceforth the *tempo* of events was accelerated. These terrible guns, which nothing could resist, were installed—as we afterwards discovered—upon concrete foundations prepared for that purpose long before the invasion of our too confiding country. Their fire was in the first place directed against the Waelhem and Wavre-Sainte-Catherine forts.

On the 29th the Wavre-Sainte-Catherine fort was already reduced to silence; by 6 o'clock in the evening the survivors of its valiant garrison were forced to evacuate the works.

The German fire was then concentrated upon the Waelhem, Koningshoyckt, and Lierre forts.

On the 30th the great reservoirs at Waelhem, which supplied Antwerp and the suburbs, were damaged by shells, and the water supply was seriously jeopardized. The Wael-hem fort held out as long as possible, and when all that was left of its brave garrison at last abandoned it, it was only a heap of ruins.

It became evident that the intrenched camp of Antwerp —contrary to the ideas generally entertained—would not prove invulnerable. The supreme command foresaw the moment approaching when the army would be forced to abandon the fortress in order to avoid a surrender *en masse*. It was decided to transfer the base of operations westward to Ostend, and immediately the work of removal began : the transport of wounded, of sanitary material, of army corps depots, of the recruits of the new levy, as well as the corps of volunteers, who were as yet untrained, the army service corps, and more besides than I can tell.

Antwerp lies wholly on the right bank of the Scheldt, and there is no bridge to connect it with the left bank, whence a railway runs to Gand and Ostend. For freight of an awkward nature, which would not allow of transshipment, it was therefore necessary to make use of the line which crosses the river by the Tamise railway bridge—some 12 miles upstream—and which crosses the Rupel at Willebroeck —that is, within range of the enemy's guns. But the rail-way precautions were so well conceived that trains were able to run every night—of course with all lights extin-guished—as late as the 7th of October.

The forts of Koningshoyckt and Lierre were silenced in turn on the 2nd of October. The Belgian infantry fell back beyond the Nèthe, blowing up the bridges across that river (26).

On this day General de Guise, Commander-in-Chief of the fortress of Antwerp, published the following proclama-tion addressed to the people of Antwerp :—

"I consider that it is my duty to inform the population inhabiting the territory of the fortress that the siege of the latter has for some days past entered upon an acute phase.

"As is proved by military history, in the course of a siege the fortified city itself may be exposed to the effects of the besieging artillery. Thus, in the present campaign,

the fortified cities of Liege and Namur have been subjected
to the early stages of bombardment.   Aware of the patriotic
sentiments of the valiant population of Antwerp, I am certain that it will maintain the calm and composure of which
it has given so many proofs since the commencement of hostilities, and that it will thus assist me to accomplish the great
task which has fallen to my lot."

That same day—the 2nd of October—a Taube flew over
Antwerp, dropping numerous copies of a strange bilingual
proclamation, of which the more significant passages are
here translated :—

BRUSSELS, *October* 1, 1914.

BELGIAN SOLDIERS!

Your blood and your whole salvation—you are not giving them to your beloved country at all ; on the contrary, you
are serving only the interests of Russia, a country which
only desires to increase its already enormous power, and
above all the interest of England, whose perfidious avarice
has given birth to this cruel and unprecedented war.   From
the outset your newspapers, paid from French and English
sources, have never ceased to deceive you, to tell you nothing
but lies about the causes of the war and about the battles
which have ensued, and this is still happening every day.

Each day of resistance makes you suffer irreparable
losses, while after the capitulation of Antwerp you will be
free from all anxiety.

Belgian soldiers, you have fought enough for the interests of the Russian princes, and for those of the capital-
ists of perfidious Albion.   Your situation is one to despair of.

If you desire to rejoin your wives and children, if you
desire to return to your work, in a word, if you want peace,
put an end to this useless struggle, which will only end in
your ruin.   Then you will quickly have all the benefits of a
fortunate and perfect peace.

VON BESELER,
Commander-in-Chief of the besieging Army.

Need I say that there was not one "Belgian soldier," nor one inhabitant of the besieged city, who did not read this impudent message with disdain?

The outer forts once demolished, the German artillery was able to approach the Nèthe. On the 2nd of October German shells fell on the village of Waerloos and set it on fire. On the 4th Contich was shelled and burned.

Under cover of their guns, which were so superior to ours in number, and, above all, in range, the Germans tried first to cross the Nèthe by Waelhem; but the Belgian infantry, intrenched upon the opposite bank, offered a brilliant resistance, and they were forced to transfer their efforts to Duffel and Lierre.

At Lierre our enemies came into conflict with the English. England had sent us some reënforcements: a brigade of marine infantry and two naval brigades, or some 7,000 men in all. Seven thousand men: it was not much; yet this scanty help meant to our exhausted troops, which were completely worn out, a material assistance, and, above all, an inestimable moral support.

Ah! if the left bank of the Scheldt had been ours all the way to the sea, how much more favorable the situation would have been! Our noble river would have been open to the warships of the Allies, which could have ascended it as far as Antwerp and beyond, and if a few gunboats of light draught, but powerfully armed, had been able to enter the Rupel and the Nèthe, these two rivers would have been really impassable, and our "national fortress" would have been absolutely impregnable.

On the 4th of October the Communal Council unanimously voted a resolution which expressed to the Government and the military authorities "the unshakable desire of the population to see the defense of the fortified position of Antwerp continued to the end, without regard to anything but the national defensive and without considering the dangers incurred by private persons or property."

The civil population of Belgium was truly admirable! Careless of danger, it thought only of the national defensive! And you must remember that, in order to facilitate the defense of Antwerp, it had been necessary within a radius of no less than twelve miles to raze to the ground hundreds of buildings, and that the officers who superintended these operations had the satisfaction of reporting that they did not hear a complaint—not a single complaint!

Now what the Belgians themselves had not thought it necessary to demolish was being fired by the German shells, and they accepted the sacrifice with the same composed resignation "without regard to anything but the national defensive." It mattered little that the countryside which had formerly been so pleasant and cheerful was being transformed into a desert so long as it still remained Belgian soil!

However, the situation grew worse from hour to hour.

Shrapnel fell without intermission on the Belgian and English trenches; the hail of fire was infernal.

On the 6th of October, about 4 o'clock in the morning, the Germans succeeded in crossing the Nèthe. The defenders of Antwerp had to fall back to the forts of the inner defenses. And the circle of steel and fire grew ever closer and closer. Soon there would be nothing for it but to seek to evade its embrace and save all that could be saved.

General de Guise warned the population of Antwerp that the bombardment of the city was imminent, and urged all who could do so to leave without delay.

Early on the 7th the members of the Government, the legations, and the officials of the Central Administration left by water for Ostend.

That morning the local newspapers openly admitted the gravity of the situation. But they suffered no loss of dignity. "Whatever fresh sacrifice the salvation of the country requires of us, we accept it." This, in substance, was what they said: "Belgium will emerge the greater for her trials." But the Belgian newspapers of Antwerp had been issued for the last time.

On the afternoon of Friday, the 9th of October, the Germans entered the great commercial city, for whose conquest they had schemed and prepared for a number of years.

"They showed by their attitude," said an ocular witness, "that they were by no means comfortable in their minds.

The deep silence which hung over the city made them uneasy. They carried their rifles handy, ready to fire as they went forward."

Their booty must have caused them some disillusion. Before its cautious retreat the Belgian army had destroyed all it could not carry away; a number of forts were blown up; the bridge of boats was destroyed; the German merchant vessels seized at the commencement of hostilities were sunk or rendered unnavigable; and the great petroleum reservoirs were fired. In a word, they had destroyed all they could, and had in every way done their best to reduce the significance of the German victory to a minimum.

The retreat from Antwerp was covered and masked until the last moment, not only by the fire of the second ring of forts and by that of a few field batteries, but also by the Belgian and British detachments which courageously occupied the trenches between Contich and the Scheldt through the whole of the 8th.

Unhappily, despite the admirable order which presided during this henceforth famous retreat, several thousands of men avoided surrender only by entering Holland. A portion of our fortress troops was also forced to retire into Dutch territory in order not to surrender to the Germans.

As for the total of the material losses experienced by the nation in Antwerp and the district, it may be estimated at £40,000,000. But what matter these losses, and those, at least five times as great, which the country had suffered during the past two months!—what matter all our grief and mourning even, if honor was saved!

Moreover, the King—the soul of our resistance—and the bulk of his valiant legions had succeeded in gaining Ostend, where the Government was already installed.

BY GENERAL VON FALKENHAYN

German Chief-of-Staff as successor to General Von Moltke

Great Headquarters, October 10th.

After a siege of only twelve days, Antwerp has fallen into our hands. On September 28th the first shot was fired against the forts of the outer lines. On October 1st the

CAPTURE OF ANTWERP

first forts were taken by storm, on October 6th and 7th the strongly embanked Nethe intrenchments, for the most part four hundred meters wide, were overcome. On October 7th the bombardment of the town was announced in accordance with the Hague agreement. As the commandant declared that he would be answerable for the bombardment, it began at midnight from October 7th to 8th. At the same time the attack upon the inner forts began.

Early in the morning of October 9th the forts of the inner lines were taken, and on the afternoon of October 9th the city could be occupied without serious resistance. The probably very strong garrison had at first defended itself very bravely. But as it finally did not feel itself equal to the assault of our infantry and the marine division, as well as to the effectiveness of our powerful artillery, it had fled in complete disorganization.

Among the garrison there was also an English marine-brigade which had just lately arrived. According to English newspaper reports it was to form the backbone of the defense. The degree of disorganization of the English and Belgian troops is indicated by the fact that the negotiations for the surrender had to be carried on with the mayor—as no military authorities were to be found. The complete surrender was confirmed on October 10th by the chief-of-staff of the hitherto existing government of Antwerp. The last forts, which had not as yet surrendered, were occupied by our troops. The number of prisoners cannot yet be estimated. Many Belgian and English soldiers have fled to Holland, where they will be interned. Vast supplies of all kinds have been captured.

BY GUSTAVE FELLER

A semi-authoritative narrative issued to the German public

If the Belgians had at first believed that Antwerp was impregnable, they began to doubt it at the fall of Liege. The entire wealthy population fled from Antwerp, so that the mob had a chance to make free of the city unhindered. A large part of the Belgian army, about twenty thousand strong, had its camps surrounding the town.

In order to frustrate an attempt of German troops to force a crossing of the Scheldt at Termonde, the army defending Antwerp made a grand sortie on September 27th. Three times the Germans succeeded in repulsing the Belgian troops. On both sides strong detachments of artillery and many machine guns were active. The Belgians had effected a lodgment in the village of Edeghem, which was set on fire. Although the Germans were in the minority, this second sortie from Antwerp also completely failed.

After our 42-centimeter guns and the Austrian motor batteries had been set up in their proper positions, the bombardment of the three forts, Waelhem, St. Cathérine, and Wavre, began on the afternoon of September 28th. On September 29th the bombardment was continued. At times the three forts completely disappeared in the clouds of smoke which were caused by the explosion of the German bomb-shells. Now and then a shell fell into the forts of Liezele and Breendonk. Our troops from Turnhout also advanced, and the shelling of the outer forts of Antwerp began from Heyst op den Berg. On September 30th two of the forts, that had been subjected to our firing, were destroyed. At Fort Waelhem the Germans blew up the powder-magazine, destroyed the water-works, and occupied the advance positions. In the night from September 30th to October 1st the Germans bombarded the fortifications the whole night long. At half-past three a Zeppelin again appeared above the fortifications, hurled bombs, and spread not a little terror.

On October 2nd a "Taube" appeared above Antwerp and much damage was done during its pursuit. Some of the shells aimed at the "Taube" fell back into the streets and wounded and killed several people. One shell crashed through the roof of a house without exploding. The "Taube" scattered proclamations in French and Flemish signed by General Von Beseler, in which the soldiers were told that they were being deceived by the French and English and that the Russian victories were an invention of the Belgian press. Already on October 3rd the situation of Antwerp was considered very critical. The outer belt of forts had fallen, and the spirit of the people was very much depressed. The Commandant of the fortification issued a proclamation which cautioned the population to preserve order. The Belgian troops withdrew to the inner line of forts, and it was feared that the Germans would cut off the water-supply.

On October 4th the Belgian Government made all preparations to leave the city by water, and to transfer their residence to London. The inner works were under the bombardment of the heavy artillery, which was at a distance of only 18 kilometers from the most important constructions. The city of Lanaeken on the Dutch border was also occupied by the Germans. During the night of October 4th the cannonading ceased.

On October 5th an official Belgian communication made it known that reënforcements, by means of which the resisting power of the city had been increased, had reached Antwerp; but that the population should be advised that the fate of the country and, therefore, of Antwerp, was being at that very moment decided on the Aisne, and that the Allies, under these conditions, would have to avoid too great a reduction of their forces; that the garrison of Antwerp was, moreover, strong enough. Furthermore, the Commandant of Antwerp made known that every citizen was free to leave the city, but that he could not return as long as the siege lasted.

Because of the successful destruction of the aqueduct by our troops, the city was without drinking-water from the beginning of the month. So the danger of an epidemic in the poorer quarters of the town constantly drew nearer. On October 6th our troops succeeded in crossing the Nethe after the artillery had fought long and hard against the fortifications. The Germans were operating in the triangle Lierre-Puers-Antwerp, and had pioneers swim to the opposite shore. They succeeded in reaching it after repeated efforts and by means of great exertion. After the Nethe had been crossed, the heavy artillery was placed on the other shore and put into operation. Heavy infantry attacks followed the cannonading, combined with flank attacks on Fort Puers. The Belgians several times blew up the pontoons laid across the Nethe, but in defiance of death the pioneers made new crossings over the river.

In accordance with Article XXVI of the Hague Agreement concerning the laws of war on land, General Von Beseler, the Commander of the beleaguering army of Antwerp, on the afternoon of October 7th, through the mediation of the accredited representatives of neutral States at Brussels, acquainted the municipal authorities of the approaching bombardment. At midnight it began.

In the meantime, the arrival of the English auxiliaries had quieted the citizens very much. For three days a continuous procession of English troops had passed through the city. They were received and greeted by the population with enthusiasm; moreover, several omnibuses from London, still showing their colored advertisements, were there. The inhabitants of Antwerp probably overrated the number of English troops at thirty to forty thousand, as they always marched in a circle and thus gave the impression of being a sheer endless procession. Others from neutral countries also considered the given number to be exaggerated.

The proclamation of the Commandant, Lieutenant-General de Guise, to the mayors of the parishes which lay within the fortifications, was as follows:

"I have the honor to make known to the inhabitants that the heavy cannonading of the township of Antwerp and its environs is inevitable. The threat of bombardment or the carrying out of this threat will have no influence on the duration of the defense, which will be continued to the last. Persons who wish to escape the effects of the firing must depart as quickly as possible in the northern or northeastern direction."

The commander of the German troops already in the beginning of October had presented to the Commandant of Antwerp the request to point out to him the buildings which on account of housing works of art or for other reasons (hospitals, churches, etc.) should be spared in a bombardment. An attempt was actually made to avoid the buildings thus pointed out, but it was inevitable that now and then a projectile strayed and hit an undesired goal. At least we had done our part to avoid carrying on warfare in a barbarous fashion.

As already stated, the shelling began on October 7th, at midnight, and lasted throughout the night. On the following morning Antwerp was aflame in several places. It was rumored that we had set on fire the Georges Barracks, the petroleum tanks, and the munition depots. As it turned out later, however, the fire had been started by the English and Belgians themselves.

One of the refugees gave a vivid description of the first effects of the cannonading: "A tremendous humming and singing rent the air. The people who had been living in cellars for several days, and who had made these sound-proof by means of mattresses, rushed out of the houses as if crazed. The unfortunates ran aimlessly through the deserted streets; no one paid any attention to them. Many got into burning street-cars and became victims of the terrible panic which could no longer be controlled. In many places one met English divisions at the head of which were carried black flags with a skull drawn on them in white. I was told that it had fallen to their lot to defend the forts to the last man, and to let themselves be blown up.

"The Scheldt presented a terrible sight. It was reddened with blood. Bodies were being washed up onto the land in vast numbers. The deserters for a second time escaped from the prisons and escaped to Holland. The air was filled with a yellowish mist which extended over a distance of seven kilometers. In the station terrible scenes were enacted. Almost forty thousand people were waiting to depart. The dreadful detonations caused a panic; hundreds were trampled down; and then it was learned that the train service had been discontinued because of lack of trainmen."

As is substantiated also by the report of the first shelling of the city of Antwerp, the commander of the English troops had taken command of the defense of the town. The mayor wished to capitulate soon after the starting of the artillery attack, but the English commandant would not permit this. That the Belgians fought with the valor of despair must be laid to the English. The latter knew well enough what it signified if Germany came into the possession of Antwerp. On that account the instructions from London were to hold the city by all means. To be sure, the troops of the English and Belgians were fitted neither in numbers nor ability to fulfill their great task. It was even said that absolutely untrained English troops, who in part had never had a gun in their hands, had been sent to Antwerp. With such material for its defending troops, the fate of the city was sealed from the very start. The Englishmen had the will but not the strength to perform the obligation imposed upon them; the Germans, on the other hand, under the leadership of the well-known strategist and expert on fortifications, General Von Beseler, not only were fully determined to take Antwerp, but also had the means and the ability to do so.

Eye-witnesses reported that the cannon sometimes thundered ten shots to the minute and that the red glow in the sky was constantly expanding, a sign that always more parts of the town had caught on fire. As if out of a hell, the inhabitants fled from the town. At the Scheldt the petroleum tanks were burning and were making the whole surrounding country bright as day in the dead of night.

King Albert and his consort, as was reported from Antwerp, wished to remain in the town. But they were persuaded that it was useless and could become calamitous for the country if they remained in the city any longer. If the king should be wounded or captured, this would be worse for the independence of Belgium and for the resisting powers of the Belgian army than if even Antwerp itself fell. So the royal pair left the town in an automobile.

BATTLE OF THE YSER

BELGIUM OPENS HER DYKES TO SAVE A FRAGMENT OF HER TERRITORY

OCTOBER 16TH-30TH

CARTON DE WIART   MARSHAL JOFFRE
GENERAL VON FALKENHAYN

The Yser is Belgium's triumph. She had fought repeatedly, heroically, but always against such overwhelming numbers that defeat was inevitable. On the Yser she fought and won. So again we turn to a Belgian patriot for our chief story of the fight. M. De Wiart was Belgium's Minister of Justice in 1914. Later he headed the Belgian commission sent to the United States to enlist her aid.

The flooding of the Yser valley by which the Germans were finally stopped has naturally recalled the desperate war of an earlier century when Holland maintained her freedom by opening her dykes and flooding a large portion of her territory. The Belgian sacrifice was made on a much smaller scale; only a few square miles along the lower Yser River were inundated. Yet the results were most important. Behind the defense of this flood the Belgians were enabled to maintain their line of battle through all the War. The German invasion never reached along the coast-line beyond the Yser. The invaders were compelled to shift their attack to a point further inland; and there they met the rugged British defense around Ypres. The German narrative of the head of the High Staff, General Falkenhayn, makes this evident.

Thus the flooding of the Yser led to the long-fought battle of Ypres. Indeed, the two contests are often spoken of as one, and called the Battle of Flanders. Marshal Joffre's official account of the double battle is here given as showing the larger strategy that connected its two parts. Supreme in command over all this defensive region was the French general, Foch, already famed as the hero of the first battle of Nancy, and of the Marne. But neither French nor British played the main rôle at the Yser. True, some eight thousand French marines fought there with splendid valor, and the British warships along the coast did their part in bombarding the advancing Germans on the shore; but the main action was always in the hands of the Belgians themselves, the remnant which had escaped from Antwerp and a dozen earlier fights.

BY CARTON DE WIART
An Address Originally Delivered in London in June, 1915

LESS than a year ago the region of the Yser was assuredly one of the most peaceful and one of the happiest countries under God's sun. A country of rich pastures, intersected by ditches and canals, sown with towns and villages. Here and there, hidden in the verdure, were low, white farmhouses capped by red tiles. Rows of tall poplars, bent by the sea-winds, denote the course followed by the roads. A few thick-set towers, rustic steeples, and adorable belfries, of sculptured lace-like stone, recalled the old traditions—religious, corporative, communal, and artistic—which are still dear to the meditative and industrious Flemish race. Along the western horizon ran the pleasant girdle of the dunes, hiding the fashionable sea-fronts of La Panne, Saint-Idesbald, Coxyde.

To-day you must picture to yourself a bare, sinister plain, on which falls a rain of bombs and shells and shrapnel. The soil is broken by heavy traffic, plowed up by projectiles, watered with blood. Here and there the inundations have produced great sheets of water, whence emerge the ruins of farmhouses, and on which all sorts of rubbish is floating, and often corpses. And on this soil, from October 16, 1914, without respite, without interruption, men have been fighting and destroying and slaughtering one another.

While the 7th Division of the British troops, which had just disembarked in Flanders, fell back by way of Thourout toward Ypres, and a brigade of French Marine Fusiliers, which was sent to cover the retreat from Antwerp, and behaved so admirably at Quatrecht, fell back upon Dixmude, what was left of the Belgian army reformed itself hastily on the Yser, between Nieuport and Dixmude, and once more faced the enemy.

For the Germans had been swiftly diverted in considerable numbers from the approaches of Antwerp to West Flanders, in the hope of turning the left wing of the Allies and reaching Calais.

Reaching the Yser on the 15th of October, the Belgian army was attacked on the following day. On this day, indeed, the Germans endeavored to dislodge the French Marine Fusiliers, who had no artillery, from Dixmude; it was the Belgian artillery, so renowned for the skill of its gun-layers and the efficiency of its fire, which supported the French. On the 17th German shells were falling on the

whole line of the advanced Belgian positions between Dixmude and the sea. These attacks were the prelude to a terrible battle, which, lasting from the 18th to the 30th of October, was to make the heroic defense of the Yser by the Belgian army forever renowned in history.

On the 18th the Germans, after a desperate struggle, succeeded in carrying the advanced positions of Keyem and
Mannekensvere; but a brilliant attack by the Belgian army
recovered Keyem the same night.

On the 19th the intensity of the struggle was redoubled
along the entire front. The Kaiser had ordered his troops
to break through, cost what it might. Three times the German hordes were repulsed. Nevertheless, in their furious
impetuosity the Germans succeeded in carrying the advanced position of Beerst, while that of Keyem held out.

The center of the Belgian army was the object of violent and repeated attacks. It was then that our staff, in
order to diminish the pressure on the center, directed the
French Marine Fusiliers and a Belgian division to make a
sally from Dixmude, delivering a counter-attack on the
Beerst-Vladsloo front. On the evening of the 19th we
held Vladsloo and the outskirts of Beerst, and were threatening the flank of the enemy army. But it was learned that
important German reënforcements were arriving from the
direction of Roulers, and we withdrew. Keyem was thus
reoccupied by the Germans.

The 20th was marked by a violent bombardment of our
positions.

At Nieuport the Germans captured the Bamburg farm.
We retook it the same evening; after a fresh assault the
Germans dislodged us yet again. The same day, at Dix-
mude, two German attacks were repelled.

On the 21st, in the morning, a fresh attempt to carry
Dixmude; and another check. The Germans commenced a
formidable general offensive. In the afternoon their attacks once again spent themselves upon Schoorbakke and
Dixmude; they failed before the tenacity of our troops.

From the sea the British Fleet, which had come to our
rescue, enfiladed the German forces with the murderous fire

of its guns. But our enemies are courageous, and they sacrificed themselves with the fury of despair. On the 22nd of October, after a terrible bombardment, they succeeded at night in setting foot upon the left bank of the Yser at Tervaete; but we drove them into the river.

So many repeated attacks, and extremely violent attacks, delivered by a numerous and a desperate enemy would have got the upper hand of an army less brave than ours. French reënforcements had been promised us. Our men knew this, and they held out. But these reënforcements were long in coming. On the 23rd of October the first French reënforcements arrived on our left, and on the 24th the six Belgian divisions were supported by one French division and a few battalions of Territorials. On the night of the 23rd a furious attack upon Dixmude was repelled by the Marine Fusiliers (whose heroism will forever remain legendary, and with justice) and a couple of Belgian regiments. This was the sixth time that the German army had attacked Dixmude within a week, and at each of these repeated assaults there were frightful hand-to-hand combats and hecatombs of dead; and each time our valiant soldiers remained masters of the field.

The area conquered by the Germans on the 23rd, lying within the bend of the Yser between Schoorbakke and Tervaete, was violently bombarded and recaptured. Here it was that a notebook was found on a German corpse in which an officer of the 22nd Reserve Corps recorded the dreadful moral and physical sufferings endured in that hell of bullets and fire and blood; companies reduced to half their strength, units mixed together, the officers nearly all killed, famine and thirst and a sense of the uselessness of all efforts against our redoubtable little army: such was the balance-sheet on the German side.

Yet the Kaiser's troops seemed to rise out of the ground. Fresh reënforcements came to fill the frightful gaps made by our fire and our bayonet attacks. Foot by foot the Belgian army defended the soil lying between the left bank of the Yser and the railway from Nieuport to Dixmude, behind which it organized a new line of defense.

It was then that the Belgians, in this pitiless conflict, summoned to their aid a terrible and invincible assistant: the inundation of low-lying lands. The canals in the valley of the Yser spilled their water into the fields. The water rose and streamed along the German trenches; while on the left bank, where the level of the soil was higher, the Belgians heroically defended their positions. The Germans, threatened with death by drowning, rushed forward in a terrible offensive, seeking to break our lines, to conquer the dry land. In this unprecedented attempt they succeeded, on the 30th of October, in capturing one of our points of support, the village of Ramscappelle; but this essential position was immediately recaptured by two Belgian divisions and a few French battalions. This was the *coup de grâce*. On the 31st, decimated, dejected, defeated, the Germans abandoned their project of crossing the Yser; they retreated, abandoning guns and mortars engulfed in mire, enormous quantities of weapons, thousands of corpses, and many wounded.

In this epic struggle the Belgians, who numbered 60,000, lost a fourth part of their effectives; but they killed and wounded more Germans than there were soldiers in the Belgian army; they had covered the left wing of the Allies, and shattered the German effort which had threatened Dunkirk and Calais.

This long and heroic resistance of the Belgian army enabled the Franco-British forces to establish a solid front to the south, and thus to form a barrier upon which was shattered all the German attacks delivered during the great battle which took place in the neighborhood of Ypres at the end of October and during the first half of September, 1914.

"It was not a fresh army which confronted the Germans on the Yser," very justly remarked Colonel Repington in the *Times* of December 9, 1914. "It was the remnant of an army, war-worn and weak in numbers. For two months and a half the Belgians at Liege, Namur, Louvain, Haelen, Aerschot, Malines, Termonde, and Antwerp had confronted the Germans almost alone, and it was only the shattered, but still unconquered, remains of the field army which drew up behind the Yser after the retreat from the Scheldt.

"In this fine defense, which did honor to all the troops and commanders engaged in it, the Belgians performed a signal service to the Allied cause."

As a matter of fact, our enemies had other advantages over us than those conferred upon them by numerical superiority and the enthusiasm of their advance: they were connected with their base by our splendid network of railways, which they had had plenty of time to repair; their supply services could be organized at leisure in Belgium, which was still a wealthy country, and for the evacuation of their wounded they had at their disposal the excellent, capacious, and very numerous hospitals which we had installed at a short distance from one another at Bruges, Ostend, and all along the coast. Our exhausted troops had no base at all; and not only could they not count upon any immediate reënforcement, but their supply services had not had time, after their hasty retreat, to install or to reorganize themselves; and lastly, to fill the cup of misfortune, they could rely only upon distant hospitals, situated out of the country.

Compare the opposing forces, then, and their means of action; then add to the account, on the one side—I need not tell you which—contempt and continual disregard for all the laws and rules of humanity and honor, and, on the other side, an absolute and religious respect for the same, and you will, I firmly believe, be amazed and full of admiration for the "remnant, shattered but still unconquered," of this tiny Belgian army, which checked, on the banks of the Yser, the formidable and all-powerful German army.

BY MARSHAL JOFFRE

On leaving Antwerp on October 9th the Belgian army, which was covered by 8,000 British bluejackets and 6,000 French bluejackets, at first intended to retire as far as to the north of Calais, but afterwards determined to make a stand in Belgian territory. Unfortunately, the condition of the Belgian troops, exhausted by a struggle of more than three months, did not allow any immediate hopes to be based upon them. This situation weighed on our plans and delayed their execution.

On the 16th we made progress to the east of Ypres. On the 18th our cavalry even reached Roulers and Corte-mark. But it was now evident that, in view of the continual reënforcing of the German right, our left was not capable of maintaining the advantages obtained during the previous few days. To attain our end and make our front inviolable a fresh effort was necessary. That effort was immediately made by the dispatch to the north of the Lys of considerable French forces, which formed the French army of Belgium.

The French army of Belgium consisted, to begin with, of two territorial divisions, four divisions of cavalry, and a naval brigade. Directly after its constitution it was strengthened by elements from other points on the front whose arrival extended from October 27th to November 11th. These reënforcements were equivalent altogether in value to five army corps, a division of cavalry, a territorial division, and sixteen regiments of cavalry, plus sixty pieces of heavy artillery.

Thus was completed the strategic maneuver defined by the instructions of the General in Chief of September 11th and developed during the five following weeks with the ampleness we have just seen. The movements of troops carried out during this period were methodically combined with the pursuit of operations, both defensive and offensive, from the Oise to the North Sea.

On October 22nd our left, bounded six weeks earlier by the Noyon district, rested on Nieuport, thanks to the successive deployment of five fresh armies—three French armies, the British army, and the Belgian army.

Thus the coördination decided upon by the General in Chief attained its end. The barrier was established. It remained to maintain it against the enemy's offensive. That was the object and the result of the battle of Flanders, October 22nd to November 15th.

The German attack in Flanders was conducted strategically and tactically with remarkable energy. The complete and indisputable defeat in which it resulted is therefore significant.

The forces of which the enemy disposed for this operation between the sea and the Lys comprised:

(1) The entire Fourth Army, commanded by the Duke of Wurtemberg, consisting of one naval division, one division of Ersatz Reserve (men who had received no training before the war), which was liberated by the fall of Antwerp; the Twenty-second, Twenty-third, Twenty-sixth and Twenty-seventh Reserve Corps, and the Forty-eighth Division belonging to the Twenty-fourth Reserve Corps.

(2) A portion of another army under General von Fabeck, consisting of the Fifteenth Corps, two Bavarian corps and three (unspecified) divisions.

(3) Part of the Sixth Army under the command of the Crown Prince of Bavaria. This army, more than a third of which took part in the battle of Flanders, comprised the Nineteenth Army Corps, portions of the Thirteenth Corps and the Eighteenth Reserve Corps, the Seventh and Fourteenth Corps, the First Bavarian Reserve Corps, the Guards, and the Fourth Army Corps.

(4) Four highly mobile cavalry corps prepared and supported the action of the troops enumerated above. Everything possible had been done to fortify the morale of the troops. At the beginning of October the Crown Prince of Bavaria in a proclamation had exhorted his soldiers "to make the decisive effort against the French left wing," and "to settle thus the fate of the great battle which has lasted for weeks."

On October 28th, Prince Rupprecht of Bavaria declared in an army order that his troops "had just been fighting under very difficult conditions," and he added: "It is our business now not to let the struggle with our most detested enemy drag on longer. The decisive blow is still to be struck." On October 30th, General von Deimling, commanding the Fifteenth Army Corps (belonging to General von Fabeck's command), issued an order declaring that "the thrust against Ypres will be of decisive importance." It

should be noted also that the Emperor proceeded in person
to Thielt and Courtrai to exalt by his presence the ardor of
his troops. Finally, at the close of October, the entire German press incessantly proclaimed the importance of the
"Battle of Calais." It is superfluous to add that events in
Poland explain in a large measure the passionate resolve of
the German General Staff to obtain a decision in the Western theater of operations at all costs. This decision would
be obtained if our left were pierced or driven in. To reach
Calais, that is, to break our left; to carry Ypres, that is, to
cut it in half; through both points to menace the communications and supplies of the British expeditionary corps, perhaps even to threaten Britain in her island—such was the
German plan in the Battle of Flanders. It was a plan that
could not be executed.

On October 23rd the Belgians along the railway line
from Nieuport to Dixmude were strengthened by a French
division. Dixmude was occupied by our marines (fusiliers
marins). During the subsequent day our forces along the
railway developed a significant resistance against an enemy superior in number and backed by heavy artillery. On
the 29th the inundations effected between the canal and the
railway line spread along our front. On the 30th we recaptured Ramscapelle, the only point on the railway which Belgians had lost. On the 1st and 2nd of November the enemy bombarded Furnes, but began to show signs of weariness. On the 2nd he evacuated the ground between the
Yser and the railway, abandoning cannon, dead and
wounded. On the 3rd our troops were able to reënter the
Dixmude district. The success achieved by the enemy at
Dixmude at this juncture was without fruit. They succeeded in taking the town. They could not debouch from
it. The coastal attack had thus proved a total failure.

Since then it has never been renewed. The Battle of Calais, so noisily announced by the German press, amounted to a decided reverse for the Germans.

The enemy had now begun an attack more important than its predecessor, in view of the numbers engaged in it. This attack was intended as a renewal to the south of the effort which had just been shattered in the north. Instead of turning our flank on the coast, it was now sought to drive in the right of our northern army under the shock of powerful masses. This was the Battle of Ypres.

In order to understand this long, desperate, and furious battle, we must hark back a few days in point of time. At the moment when our cavalry reached Roulers and Cortemark (October 28th) our territorial divisions from Dunkirk, under General Biden, had occupied and organized a defensive position at Ypres. It was a point d'appui, enabling us to prepare and maintain our connections with the Belgian army. From October 23rd two British and French army corps were in occupation of this position, which was to be the base of their forward march in the direction of Roulers-Menin. The delays already explained and the strength of the forces brought up by the enemy soon brought to a standstill our progress along the line Poelcapelle, Paschendaele, Zandvorde, and Gheluvelt. But in spite of the stoppage here, Ypres was solidly covered, and the connections of all the Allied forces were established. Against the line thus formed the German attack was hurled from October 25th to November 13th, to the north, the east, and the south of Ypres. From October 26th on the attacks were renewed daily with extraordinary violence, obliging us to employ our reënforcements at the most threatened points as soon as they came up. Thus, on October 31st, we were obliged to send supports to the British cavalry, then to the two British corps between which the cavalry formed the connecting link, and finally to intercalate between these two corps a force equivalent to two army corps. Between October 30th and November 6th Ypres was several times in danger. The British lost Zandvorde, Gheluvelt, Messines, and Wytschaete. The front of the Allies, thus contracted, was all the more difficult to defend; but defended it was without a recoil.

The arrival of three French divisions in our line enabled us to resume from the 4th to the 8th a vigorous offensive. On the 10th and 11th this offensive, brought up against fresh and sharper German attacks, was checked. Before it could be renewed the arrival of fresh reënforcements had to be awaited, which were dispatched to the north on November 12th. By the 14th our troops had again begun to progress, barring the road to Ypres against the German attacks, and inflicting on the enemy, who advanced in massed formation, losses which were especially terrible in consequence of the fact that the French and British artillery had crowded nearly 300 guns on to these few kilometers of front.

Thus the main mass of the Germans sustained the same defeat as the detachments operating further to the north along the coast. The support which, according to the idea of the German General Staff, the attack on Ypres was to render to the coastal attack, was as futile as that attack itself had been.

During the second half of November the enemy, exhausted and having lost in the Battle of Ypres alone more than 150,000 men, did not attempt to renew his effort, but confined himself to an intermittent cannonade. We, on the contrary, achieved appreciable progress to the north and south of Ypres, and insured definitely by a powerful defensive organization of the position the inviolability of our front.

BY GENERAL VON FALKENHAYN

In Flanders the enemy's attempts at envelopment were repulsed at the end of September and the beginning of October, but the German enveloping movement was not realized. This had been prevented by the superiority of the French network of railways. Although very considerable forces had been employed meanwhile, as, for instance, the bulk of the Second Army from the Rheims area, the Sixth Army, which had hitherto been employed in Lorraine, and strong cavalry detachments, which were pushed forward in a wide circle round the northern wing, the German front did not progress beyond a line west of Roye, west of Bapaume, and west of Lille. The coast on which the right flank was to rest, and from which it was hoped to obstruct England's Channel traffic, effectively attack the Island itself, and turn the French flank, was not reached.

In order to compel this end, a new Fourth Army was formed in Belgium towards the middle of October out of three divisions of the besieging troops from Antwerp, who had been set free by the fall of the fortress on the 9th of the month after a siege of barely twelve days, and four army corps from Germany which had just become fit for service, under the command of General Duke Albert of Würtemberg, with Colonel Ilse as Chief of Staff. It was ordered to advance against the Yser sector with its right flank resting on the sea. At the same time from the Sixth Army an attacking group concentrated north of Lille, the former right wing of the German front in Flanders, was to attack straight ahead west of Lille.

The prize to be won was worth the stake. Strong French and English forces had already reached the Yser during the first ten days of October—the English had been withdrawn altogether from the old front near Rheims— and were trying to get into touch on the eastern bank with the Belgian divisions which were retreating from Antwerp. Our forces had not been sufficient to prevent the withdrawal of these troops before the fall of the fortress. Although the Belgians were in an extremely miserable condition they would soon be able to attack again if supported by English or French formations. There was no doubt about the resolute offensive intentions of the English and the French. Not only had the danger that the Germans would be finally cut off from the Belgian coast again become acute, but also the danger of an effective encirclement of the right wing. They both had to be removed unconditionally. If this, at least, was not done, then the drastic action against England and her sea traffic with submarines, aeroplanes and airships, which was being prepared as a reply to England's war of starvation, was impossible in their present stage of development. It was also questionable in certain circumstances whether the occupied territory in Northern France and Western Belgium was to be held; the loss of it would necessarily have led to evil results.

If, on the other hand, the German Army succeeded in throwing the enemy back across the Yser sector and in following him, it could expect to force a favorable change in the whole situation on the Western front after the supplies of troops and ammunition had been meanwhile replenished.

The enemy's offensive was completely broken. He was thrown back almost everywhere either to, or across, the Yser, and a firm connection was established between the coast at Nieuport and the previous German right wing near Lille, thus forming a front from the Swiss frontier to the sea. That which had to be attained under any circumstances, if the war was to be carried on with any hopeful prospects, was attained. Several times it seemed as though it only needed perseverance in the offensive to obtain a complete success—how near we actually were to it has since been made sufficiently plain. At the time, however, our movement came to a standstill.

Inundations, skilfully managed by the Belgians, put an end to the attack of the German right wing, which was making good progress and bore the main pressure. The young army corps further south fought with incomparable enthusiasm and unexcelled heroism. The disadvantages of their urgent and hasty formation and training, and the fact that they were led by older and for the most part retired officers, as others were not to be had, naturally made themselves felt. In particular there were deficiencies in the new field-artillery formations, a fact that was emphasized all the more strongly by the shortage of ammunition. Nor was the leadership entirely satisfactory. At the beginning of November, G. H. Q. could not conceal from itself that a further thorough-going success was no longer to be obtained here, particularly in the inundated area, in the face of an opponent who was continually growing stronger.

YPRES: THE STRUGGLE FOR THE CHANNEL PORTS

GERMANY ALMOST REVERSES THE DECISION OF THE MARNE

OCTOBER 26TH-NOVEMBER 15TH

FRENCH ANNIVERSARY REVIEW
A. N. HILDITCH   COL. E. D. SWINTON
GUSTAV FELLER

Ypres is, or tragically was, an ancient and long celebrated Belgian city on the upper waters of the little Yser River. The mighty contest which spread over all this region during the autumn of 1914 is treated by Marshal Joffre in our preceding article as a single battle, the far-spread "Battle of Flanders." The Germans also looked on it as a whole and called it the Battle for Calais, or for the Channel Ports, at which they aimed. To the Britons, however, Ypres stands out alone from all the rest. To them Ypres soon became the center and symbol of the entire war. This was the portion of the defense line assigned them by their own request when their troops came northward from the Aisne. Mons, where they had begun their fighting in the first August days of retreat, is not far from Ypres, to whose shell shattered ruins they held doggedly through all the years of war.

Here lay those "Flanders fields" which were to be so richly stained with Europe's bravest blood. For the Germans selected the Ypres "salient" as their main point of attack. Again and again they strove to break the British line. The "battles of Ypres" became too numerous to count.

None of the contests of later years, however, equaled in intensity the first one, here described, the "battle for Calais." This was the supreme effort of the Germans to "reverse the decision of the Marne." Twice in the course of their month-long attack they almost achieved their purpose; and these two occasions, on October 31st and November 11th, are made the main themes of the following account. The first narrative is a popular eulogy on Britain's aid to France, delivered in a great Paris newspaper on the anniversary of October 31st. The other two narratives are by Britons, justly proud of their victory. Mr. Hilditch describes in detail the fighting of October 31st. Col. Swinton, the celebrated "Eye-Witness" of all the early British fighting, depicts the November 11th assault. The reader should also turn back to the preceding article for Marshal Joffre's account of the larger action, which included the struggle at Ypres.

C. F. H.

BY THE EDITORS OF THE "PARIS MAIL"

IF it is ever permissible to speculate shudderingly on what might have been if certain events had or had not happened, it is clearly justifiable to declare that at 2 o'clock on October 31, 1914, the fate of Europe was decided. It was the crucial hour of that heroic day. It is the hinge upon which the future history of the world turns.

To-day we celebrate the triumphal but bloody anniversary of the first battle of Ypres. We have lived through vivid, valorous months and years, we have watched battle after battle, terrible, intense, full-fraught with significance; and we have not even yet, in the vortex of events, realized how supreme was the crisis through which we passed three years ago, and how frightfully our fate trembled in the balance. There should be, in those who understood the peril of that great afternoon, a spirit of profound thanksgiving, incandescent in the glow of mighty memories.

As in all the big moments of history, it was an accident, a providence if you will, that turned the faltering scale. Lord French, Sir Douglas Haig, and General Gough, in earnest, anxious consultation in the château at Ypres, had taken all their dispositions, had done all that the high command could do. They could only trust in the traditional bravery of the British soldier to stay the overwhelming German masses—a mere 150,000 men against over half a million. They were tired, perturbed, but borne up by unconquerable faith, and their brains were as alert as ever. The Yser was in the rear of the thin British line. Retreat threatened irreparable disaster. If the line broke the Germans would roll up the Allies, would menace Paris more desperately than before, and, above all, the Channel ports would be laid bare. Messengers followed each other in hot haste, the telephone brought its burden of news from all parts of the field, and the generals must have felt the icy breath of fear touch their ardent faith.

For the line did break. The day was lost. Disaster had arrived. Against such odds, what could mortal man do? The gallant General Lomax was wounded at Gheluvelt, and the 1st Division recoiled, shattered. The breach was made. The whole front must give. The reserves? There were no reserves. Every man was fighting, and men were falling everywhere. Gheluvelt was, then, the grave of civilization.

But then a wonderful thing happened. Destiny changed its face. There occurred, as so often in the annals of our empire, at the exact second when the clock of doom was about to strike, the Miracle. Brig. Gen. Charles Fitz-Clarence, whose name cannot be too highly honored (alas! that he perished splendidly at the head of his men a few days later), had shown himself many times to be a soldier of mettle. Thrice he had earned the V. C. in beleaguered Mafeking. He was as skillful as he was courageous, a soldier with the true genius of a soldier. In the press and confusion of the moment he saw in a flash the débâcle that was imminent. The 2nd Worcesters were there. They were not under his command. But what mattered ceremony in such a moment? He gave his orders to Major Hankey, and the Worcesters flew forward to the rescue. It was not a question of hours. A minute more or less would have made all the difference. The Worcesters came up in time. The 1st Division rallied. Gheluvelt was retaken. The line was repaired. The day was retrieved. The Channel ports were saved. Liberty lived again in a civilized world.

For consider the problem which had faced Field Marshal French in those latter doubtful days of October. The Germans, foiled in their sweep on Paris, had begun their dash to the sea. Their object was plain; their military strategy was simple, bold, and apparently conclusive. If the Marne had destroyed their first plan, their second was even greater. If they swung down on the northern coast of France—and what could stop them?—they would dominate the Channel and cut off the prospect of further British reënforcements. Think of the course the war would have pursued without the Channel ports in Allied hands. How many millions of men and of shells have since passed safely across that narrow strip of sea? With that door to France barred, the task of Britain would have been immeasurably harder. But without looking far into the future, Germany might reasonably expect to outflank the Allies, to deal a decisive blow which would end the war, to possess (in the alternative) a jumping-off place from which to invade England.

The Germans rushed west; the Allies pushed northward to interpose a barrier against this flood of armed barbarians. Joffre thrust out his forces to La Bassée, leaving Lord French and his troops in the center. But French, with the sure knowledge that the place of the British regiments was on the left flank, nearest the coast, a post of danger, a post of honor, and a post of vital importance to Great Britain since the control of the Channel was essential to the glorious little island with the glorious little army, came to an understanding with the French commander and distributed his men accordingly beyond La Bassée.

The position toward the end of the month was roughly as follows: Sir Horace Smith-Dorrien and the 2nd Corps were fighting and incurring enormous losses between La Bassée and Aubers; Sir William Pulteney was with the 3rd Corps east of Armentières to the Bois Grenier (French cavalry filling up the gap); Sir Edmund Allenby and the Cavalry Corps were on the left, on the eastern side of the Messines-Wytschaete Ridge; while to the north lay the 4th Corps (which included the 7th Division and the 3rd Cavalry Division), under Sir Henry Rawlinson, panting after its efforts in covering the retreat of the Belgians from Antwerp and in attempting to take the bridge at Menin, on the Lys.

There remained Sir Douglas Haig and the 1st Corps, who came up from the Aisne on October 19th, and were on the Belgian frontier. The question for Lord French was how to employ them. To strengthen his hard-pressed troops, already too extended? Or to fill up the empty sector between General Rawlinson and the Belgian army, then on the Yser?

The dilemma was dreadful; the risk in either event was huge. The British commander did not shrink from the danger. Coolly, deliberately, he took his desperate decision to defend at all costs the unprotected portion of the line. Haig planted himself from Zonnebeke to St. Julien, and from St. Julien to Bixschoote, and the epic period of the first battle of Ypres began. British battalions "disappeared." Two thousand three hundred men and forty-four officers were left to the 7th Division, which a few days earlier numbered 12,000 men and 400 officers. But if the losses were terrific the performances of the little band against crushing forces were prodigious.

The climax of the furious battle was reached on October 31st, and the culminating hour was that between 2 o'clock and 3 o'clock. It was then that the German hordes seemed for a moment to have triumphed, it was then that the stroke of genius of General Fitz Clarence sent the right men to the right point at the right time. The peril passed; the line steadied; and thereafter all the declamation of the Kaiser, all the assaults of the Prussian Guards, could not shake the deathless army that fought its greatest fight on the Flanders battlefield for the keys of France and of England.

BY A. NEVILLE HILDITCH

"Perhaps the most important and decisive attacks (except that of the Prussian Guard on November 11th) made against the 1st Corps during the whole of its arduous experiences in the neighborhood of Ypres took place on October 31st. . . . I was present with Sir Douglas Haig at Hooge between two and three o'clock on this day, when the 1st Division were retiring. I regard it as the most critical moment in the whole of this great battle. The rally of the 1st Division and the recapture of the village of Gheluvelt at such a time were fraught with momentous consequences."— SIR JOHN FRENCH, in his dispatch dated November 20th.

The line of trenches which stretches from the sea at Nieuport to the Swiss frontier runs, in its course through Flanders, not through Ypres, but in a distinct curve around it. At the end of October, 1914, the east abutment of this salient was formed by a trench-line crossing the Menin road east of Zonnebeke, of Gheluvelt, and of Zandvoorde, the salient curving back west on either flank, the southern "reëntrant" from **Zandvoorde**, the northern from Zonnebeke. The German attacks upon Ypres during the first period of their assault, from October 20th to November 17th, took three directions, and had two objects: upon the northern and southern reëntrants in an effort to break through and to cut off from the city the British defending the easterly part of the salient; and against the east abutment itself in a direct attempt to drive the defenders back westwards through the city. The first attacks, October 21st-3rd, were made against the northern reëntrant in the neighborhood of Bixschoote, held partly by British and partly by French, and against the east abutment in the neighborhood of Becelaere, defended wholly by British. After its successful repulse the French relieved the British of part of their northern reëntrant front. A few days later, on October 29th, the Germans commenced a series of fierce and unremitting assaults upon the eastern line of the salient, and upon the southern reëntrant in the neighborhood of Hollebeke and Messines, where the London Scottish, the first Territorials to join battle with the enemy, won honor by a famous charge.

Southeast of Ypres runs a canal to Comines. The Ypres-Moorslede road, passing through Zonnebeke, proceeds in a northeasterly direction, and the angle between this and the canal is bisected by the Ypres-Menin road, with the villages Hooge and Gheluvelt upon its line. The rough quadrilateral formed by this angle and by lines joining Zonnebeke to Kruiseik, and Kruiseik to the canal near Hollebeke, constituted, during the final days of October, the area covered by the British 1st Corps, to which were attached the 7th Infantry Division and the 3rd Cavalry Division. It is an area broken by numerous ridges and small hills, and covered by many woods. It has become an area of depopulated villages, of naked ruins, of shattered bridges, of fields of trampled crops, of improvised graveyards where the sods lie fresh and rough upon close-packed and numberless graves; an area where cattle wander uncared for, where farmsteads lie open to the sky, with pigs and fowls roaming wild over scenes of waste and disorder.

It was this area that Sir Douglas Haig, by a line of trenches stretching from Zonnebeke round the woods to the crossroads a mile east of Gheluvelt, over the fields to Kruiseik Hill, and westwards along the ridge of Zandvoorde to the château east of the village, was called upon to defend. He took over this position on October 27th. Two days later there burst upon his front the opening phases of a storm of unprecedented force and fury.

For a while it was the turn of the British. Machine guns, massed at various points, were brought to bear on the enemy with terrible effect. The Germans, dashing boldly forward across the open, fell in such numbers that wounded and dead piled themselves into heaps. Nevertheless, the enemy continued to advance in force, and heavy fighting went on for several hours. At length parts of the British line were penetrated, and some trenches were occupied, among them those of the Gordon Highlanders and the Yorkshire Regiment, who, however, recovered their ground by gallant charges. Sir Douglas Haig was informed that a portion of his front line had been forced back. The center of attack was the Menin road; upon the right of this road lay the 7th Division and the 3rd Cavalry Division, upon the left the 1st Division and, farther on, the 2nd Division. The general counter-attacked, nearly the whole of his forces being involved. The 7th Division, supported on its right by the cavalry, advanced upon Kruiseik, where trenches had been lost, and upon the German front from there to the Gheluvelt crossroads, while the 1st Corps struck at the opposing lines east of the Polygone Wood, on the other side of the road. But the enemy resisted stubbornly, and it was two o'clock before signs of their giving way offered encouragement to the British. The latter pressed their assault, and, as the day advanced, the issue of the struggle became decisive. Kruiseik Hill was recaptured. Most of the line to the north of the Menin road was recovered, and in some places advanced, the enemy retaining possession at one point alone. By nightfall the position was much the same as upon the previous evening.

Rain had begun to fall heavily at about six o'clock, and

the night, without a moon to throw a ray of comfort to the men in the sodden trenches, was as black as pitch. A terrific thunderstorm broke; and heaven's artillery, perhaps to show Heaven's anger, for a while silenced the artillery of man. Soon, however, the Germans, taking advantage of the conditions, emerged from the darkness and fell upon the British lines at several points. They were repulsed, but considerable fighting occurred throughout the night upon the Menin road. It gradually lessened until, shortly after daylight, a tremendous artillery fire was opened upon the cavalrymen defending the Zandvoorde ridge.

The 3rd Cavalry Division was commanded by Major-General the Hon. Julian Byng. It consisted of the 6th Brigade, containing the "Fighting Tenth" Hussars, the 1st Dragoons, the 3rd Dragoon Guards; and of the 7th Brigade, containing the 1st and 2nd Life Guards and the Royal Horse Guards. It had accompanied General Sir Henry Rawlinson in his operations around Ghent and Antwerp, and, as became the reputations of the regiments it included, had fought gallantly and suffered heavily in the severe fighting which had been necessary to stave off the German advance upon Ypres until supports arrived. The praise later bestowed upon the cavalry by Sir John French for the way in which they took turns in the trenches in the absence of reënforcements on no occasion more justified itself than upon the morning of October 30th. Kavanagh's 7th Brigade occupied the front line upon the Zandvoorde ridge, with Makins's 6th Brigade as reserves in the rear.

The Hussars and Dragoons were bombarded heavily, yet showed no sign of weakness. But at length many of the trenches were completely blown in, one troop being buried alive. Zandvoorde was shelled, whole houses lifting momentarily, it seemed, into the air, and falling, masses of pulverized masonry and débris, amid the roar of great explosions, and with columns of black smoke streaming upwards from their ruins for a hundred feet. The cannonade became so violent and the casualties so great after a while that Byng was compelled to withdraw. All the battles in his Egyptian campaigns put together could not form a shrieking inferno such as this. He moved back his division a mile or more as far as Klein Zillebeke. The Germans made a rapid advance, and took possession of the Zandvoorde ridge.

The German Emperor and his General Staff had grasped the importance of this northern area of war. Calais had become their great objective. The deadlock into which the situation was threatening to develop could hardly be regarded by them with complacency. Their troops had first attempted to break the Allied line between Nieuport and Dixmude, where the Belgian army, the 42nd French Division under General Grosetti, and the 7,000 Breton marines of Admiral Ronarc'h, held the line. Fierce fighting had followed, and supreme courage had been shown on both sides. It is said that, upon one occasion, the gigantic and genial Grosetti sat in an armchair for two hours near the ruined church of Pervyse, exposed to a rain of shell, as an encouragement to his men. The German assault had finally been repelled by the opening of the sluices and the flooding of the dunes.

Ypres had thus become now the gate to Calais, and the vital importance of its capture was repeatedly urged by Berlin upon the German generals in Belgium. Fifteen army corps and four cavalry corps, under the Crown Prince of Bavaria, the Duke of Wurtemberg, General von Fabeck, and General von Deimling, were assembled there. If the Germans, by the weight of overwhelming numbers, could hack their way through the British line, could seize Ypres, could push on with all speed through the gap, the whole Allied line would be thrown back, the French and Belgians to the north of the city would be threatened with envelopment, and the way to Dunkirk and Calais would be open. The hated English in their snug island across the narrow seas would realize with fear and trembling that the army of Germany was almost within sight of their shores. Northern France would lie practically defenseless before the conquering hosts of the Rhine. Von Deimling, with the 2nd Bavarian and the 13th, 14th, and 15th Army Corps, lay immediately to the east of Ypres, and theirs would be the privilege of taking the city. But von Deimling knew the difficulty of attempting, as he had been attempting for many days with disheartening failure, to pierce that obstinate British line. The latter was composed of tried and well-trained troops: his own forces were made up mainly of new and reserve formations, though he had, it was true, several great advantages. He could mass his men at a point for purposes of offensive by reason of his great numerical superiority. The immensely powerful armament of siege artillery which had wrought the destruction of Antwerp had been moved westwards to the support of the troops attacking Ypres.

In this connection, however, there was a consideration which gunners must bear carefully in mind. The Kaiser in person was coming to the scene. His Imperial Majesty specially desired to be present when Ypres was taken, and to have the peculiar satisfaction of viewing the discomfiture of the British. It was fitting that the War Lord of the Fatherland should be among the first to enter in triumph the last city of Belgium in hostile hands, and should return thanks on the spot for the complete deliverance of so fair and so rich a land from the lawless tendencies of a progressive democracy to the influence of the rule of "kultur." But it certainly must not be a deserted and gutted mass of ruins from which he would proclaim with befitting ceremony and splendor, as it was said he desired to do, the annexation of the country. Artillerymen must therefore place special restraints upon their soldierly zeal, and must see to it that no shell fell upon the city, save at strategical points. After the visitation of the Emperor, indeed, in order to secure discipline amongst the populace, or if, by any chance, the attack failed, the imposing old medieval buildings, the magnificent Cloth Hall, with its frescoes and its statuary, the Cathedral of St. Martin, with its paintings, its pulpit of rich Baroque carving, its gorgeous rose window, its altar of Carrara marble, might then, perhaps, be given over to destruction. But at present German hands must be stayed. The artillery must busy themselves in earnest upon the enemy's lines, for it wanted but one day to the end of

October, and the Kaiser had considered it specially desirable that the city should be won within the month. The morrow should see the final great assault, delivered with irresistible force: and the morrow would decide whether glory or dishonor, the price of failure before the Emperor's eyes, would be the portion of von Deimling and his army.

No sooner had the sun risen on the fateful last day of October than Haig's battle-line stirred into life. The rumbling of distant cannon soon became as insistent, the discharges of neighboring guns as violent, as ever. His line had, indeed, changed considerably during the preceding twenty-four hours, and now stretched in a curve from Zonnebeke around Gheluvelt to the bend of the canal. At the latter point, on the extreme right, lay General Moussy with the French troops who had come up as reënforcements on the previous evening. Moussy, in accordance with Sir John French's instructions, moved forward early in the morning to attack the enemy. After a preliminary bombardment he left his trenches and advanced across the open. The French ranks were scattered by shrapnel and rent by a fierce rifle and machine gun fire. It soon became obvious that the Germans were massed very thickly in front. Moussy was brought to a complete standstill, but was able, in spite of heavy shelling, accompanied by infantry attacks, to maintain his ground.

Meanwhile, Byng was mustering his 3rd Cavalry Division, then acting as reserves, near Hooge. It was a few minutes after eight o'clock upon a gray, murky, autumn morning. As the division transport was moving out of Zillebeke, the headquarters, many shells began to drop upon the village. Violent explosions shattered every windowpane in the place, and many buildings were devastated. The transport successfully cleared the danger zone, however, after suffering some inevitable losses. In about an hour's time a message was brought to General Byng: Allenby's cavalry corps on the other side of the canal was being heavily attacked again, and was sorely in need of assistance. The 7th Brigade were immediately dispatched, rode off as fast as the wooded country rendered possible, and were

placed on the left of Allenby's line, which they held till nightfall. Some time later the 6th Brigade received a further
message that sent them galloping down the Menin road to
Veldhoek. The line of the 1st Division had been broken,
and Gheluvelt was in the hands of the enemy.

Troops of the 3rd Brigade, under Brigadier-General
Landon, had been defending the village. On their right lay
General Capper's 7th Division, on their left more troops of
the 3rd and 1st Brigades. It was not long after daybreak
when artillery thundering just south of Gheluvelt betokened
the advance and assault of Moussy. Presently the cannonading spread to where the 3rd Brigade was posted. An
artillery bombardment was maintained for some time, until
the advance of German infantry along the Menin road
brought about sharp hand-to-hand fighting in the neighborhood of the famous crossroads just east of the village. The
struggle for some hours swayed to and fro in attack and
counter-attack. The booming of guns, the shells soaring
overhead, the explosions, the crackling of rifles in the woods,
the deep droning note of aëroplanes, formed a medley of
sound nerve-shattering to the spectator, but unheeded by
the combatants in deadly warfare of point-blank rifle-shot,
of bayonet or sword.

At length, however, the German assault began suddenly
to develop. British counter-attacks could make no headway.
Great forces of the enemy swarmed forward, following the
direction of the Menin road, and within a short time, in
spite of desperate resistance, at some places swept over the
trenches like a tide. The Coldstream Guards were cut up
terribly: the Royal West Surreys, driven in on both flanks,
were nearly surrounded, and lost their colonel. In the village itself the Welsh Regiment could hardly hold their
own. The line was broken, and the danger was great.

But Lomax and his 1st Division had been through the
retreat from Mons, and knew the secrets of orderly and
timely retirement which, even while dissolution threatened,
would wrest victory from their foes. Each regiment had
a record that for retreat had precedents, but for rout none:
and each upheld that record upon this day. Lomax extri-

cated his two brigades, hard pressed, and retired westwards from Gheluvelt. The 6th Cavalry Brigade came galloping down to their support. Other reserves there were none to spare, for every portion of Sir Douglas Haig's line was now engaged, and south of the Menin road the 7th Division and the 2nd Brigade, on General Moussy's left, were being heavily shelled. Meanwhile, the Germans had swept forward, and had taken possession of Gheluvelt. As their advance threatened the left wing of the 7th Division, retirement became imperative, and Capper drew back on his flank, though not without loss.

The Royal Scots Fusiliers, of the 21st Brigade, had, upon the retirement of the 1st Division, remained doggedly in their trenches. The Germans began to close round their rear. Brigadier-General Watts, upon receiving orders to retreat, tried to telephone to Colonel Baird-Smith, the battalion commander, but the wire had been cut by shrapnel. Two orderlies were dispatched, who, however, met death or wounds upon the way, and Baird-Smith, receiving no instructions to withdraw, held his ground. For a long time the Royal Scots made a gallant but unavailing stand, fighting, hemmed in on all sides, desperately to the end. It is recorded that, when later, with a few survivors, Baird-Smith had been taken off as a prisoner, a German general came up and congratulated him, with words expressing wonder how his men had held out so long. Meanwhile, the retirement of the rest of the brigade had been conducted successfully. No sooner, however, had Capper extricated and secured his left wing than masses of German infantry began to assail desperately his right.

It was now well after noon. The 1st Division was still struggling hard to maintain ground, but was being driven back slowly by overwhelming numbers of the enemy. A desperate conflict raged for a long time in the Polygone Wood. To Lomax, and to Monro of the 2nd Division, the seriousness of the position was apparent. The messages that flashed continually along the wires to their headquarters at Hooge spoke always of tremendous odds and of inevitable retirement. The air, even around the general's headquarters, was alive with shell and shrapnel.

Shortly before two o'clock the building was struck. Whether spy or aëroplane signaled the range to the German artillery, that range was effectually mastered, and shells began to fall upon the headquarters with deadly accuracy. Plans, maps, and papers were scattered amid the débris. Lomax was wounded, struck by a fragment of shell, and six staff officers, three of the 1st and three of the 2nd Division, fell, killed outright. Monro, dazed by the shock, staggered about in the smoke and fumes, and fell unconscious. Orderlies and ambulance men hastened up. Brigadier-General Landon for a time assumed command of the 1st Division, attacks upon whose front were still being pressed as violently as ever. Fighting was raging fiercely in the woods of Veldhoek, scarred and torn by shrapnel. But so severe was the pressure that the British were forced steadily back.

Meanwhile, the enemy had been assailing the right of the 7th Division, constituted by the 22nd Brigade, holding a line in the neighborhood of Klein Zillebeke. On this day between Capper's 7th Division and the French under Moussy were the 2nd and 4th Brigades, under Major-General Bulfin. Beneath a hail of exploding shells, of bursting shrapnel, of whistling bullets, the British held their ground for some time, but at length the 22nd Brigade was forced back. General Capper, however, had brought up his reserve battalions to this right flank, and he hurried them forward to restore the line. Before they came into action, Bulfin realized that his left flank, the 2nd Brigade, which had touched the right of the 22nd Brigade, was exposed to the enfilade fire of the enemy bursting through the gap. His line lay upon a ridge, and he could not fight upon two fronts: he was therefore forced to withdraw. Meanwhile, Capper's counter-attack, after a sharp action in which several machine guns were captured, had proved successful, and thus the right of the 7th Division advanced as the left of the 2nd Brigade retired. The former troops, regaining their old trenches, found their right wing exposed. The

Germans, however, were not pressing their attack so heavily, and the British were able to maintain the recovered ground. But the gap formed between Bulfin and Capper had enabled large bodies of the enemy to penetrate into the heavily wooded ground east of Zillebeke and in Moussy's rear. One large force, a battalion strong, soon began to advance upon the village of Zillebeke itself.

It was now after two o'clock, and the Commander-in-Chief himself, alive to the grave danger of the position, had come upon the scene. Haig's center was being driven in: his right wing was hard pressed, and one portion had withdrawn: large numbers of the enemy had penetrated into the woods in the rear, and were, did they but know it, within reach of Sir John French himself at Hooge. There were no reserves available to relieve this perilous situation. The shadows of disaster seemed to be gathering thickly around. But there was one chance, however slender, of retrieving the day. Though the right and center were being hotly attacked, the left was only slightly engaged. A thick column of the enemy had torn its way through the center and pressed on. If troops on the left, comparatively fresh, could strike hard at the right flank of that protruding column, if they could cut through it, could recapture Gheluvelt, could check the advance of the enemy, large forces of the latter would be surrounded, their offensive would be broken, and time, if only a breathing-space, would be gained in which to reform the scattered lines, and to seek reënforcements from the French. Those scattered British lines were, indeed, in need of reforming. In the stress of counter-attack, of continual retirement, of fierce hand-to-hand fighting, many units had become inextricably mixed, and at some threatened points officers had had to collect and throw into the fighting whatever men they could, regardless of regiment or brigade. English, Scottish, Irish, or Welsh would be jumbled hopelessly together in the same trench under the orders of some unknown subaltern: or a brigadier might at one time find himself in command of a few companies, at another time in control of a division. A little while later, at about half-past two, General Lomax, who had, in spite of his wound, resumed command of the 1st Division, reported to Hooge that he was again moving back, and that the enemy were coming on in great strength.

Von Deimling had reason to congratulate himself now on being almost in sight of complete success. His objective seemed within easy reach. His men were swarming on, and the British were going back. He could already look forward to honors more to be desired even than the Iron Cross, distributed as it was rather too lavishly among fellow generals much less worthy than himself, and to imperial congratulations for a victory won before the War Lord's eyes. Germany might mourn great losses: but the name and the fame of von Deimling would resound from the Vistula to the Rhine.

But now came a change. The French under General Moussy had discovered the presence in their rear of large bodies of the enemy, and Moussy was soon informed that one detachment was making for Zillebeke. The French general was in great straits, for every available man he had was already in the fighting line. He sent back for reënforcements, but in vain. Finally, forming a desperate resolve, he ordered the corporal of his escort to collect whatever men he could, whether armed or unarmed, no matter what their business. Moussy had seen eight campaigns during nearly sixty years of life, and if this was to be his last he intended that France should not be able to reproach his name with neglect of any possible expedient that might avert the threatened disaster. The corporal and his men scoured the immediate countryside and appealed to every man they met with. Cooks in the bivouac and Army Service Corps men, hewers of wood and drawers of water, were requisitioned for the enterprise, and paraded, mostly, it is said, without arms, to the number of some 250, before the general. The 65 Cuirassiers of his escort were dismounted. Their gleaming breastplates and helmets with flowing mane, their high cavalry boots and their sabers, set off effectually the motley appearance of their ill-equipped comrades. Moussy guided his detachment stealthily towards Zillebeke, and caught the Germans, a battalion strong, by surprise.

The French swept forward shouting, led by the general and his corporal, and the demoralized Germans fled before them as Englishmen had once fled before the camp-followers of Bruce at Bannockburn. They retired to the woods in disorder.

Now came the Briton's turn. The right wing of the 2nd Division and part of the 1st Division advanced rapidly from the north, and fell upon Gheluvelt and the German right flank. There was a series of fierce bayonet charges, with the Worcesters to the fore. The regiment which Wellington had named the best in the army gained laurels now equally as honorable as those which had drawn such praise in the Peninsular campaigns. Closely supported by the 42nd Artillery Brigade and the Oxfordshire Light Infantry, the Worcesters, led by Major Hankey, rushed down upon Gheluvelt under a very heavy fusillade. They forced the Germans out of the Château and its grounds at the point of the bayonet, and fierce fighting followed in the streets. But the issue was never in doubt, and the enemy were soon driven headlong from the village.

At other points the counter-attack was equally successful. The 1st Division rallied, in accordance with orders, on the line of the woods east of where the Menin road bent round towards Ypres, and here stood their ground stubbornly, until presently the expected enfilade fire from the north checked assaults upon their front. The Germans were now in danger of being cut off by the capture of Gheluvelt, and the British attack from the north had prevailed. Everywhere the enemy's offensive was broken and his discomfited infantry forced to withdraw. The 7th Division followed in their wake almost as far as its original line, where it entrenched, while the 1st Division advanced and reëstablished connection on the left. The menace of the enemy in the woods between Hooge and Klein Zillebeke was at once dealt with. Two regiments of Makins's 6th Cavalry Brigade, in eight squadrons, were sent in this direction, and had a short but most successful engagement. Advancing with dash and vigor, some mounted, others dismounted, they took the enemy by surprise, and killed and wounded large numbers.

The woods having been cleared effectually, the cavalry occupied the gap between the 7th Division and the 2nd Brigade. The line was now quite restored, and the crisis was over. Long and terrible had been the struggle, and those who survived it could justifiably feel that hardly any other conflict in the war had been more desperately fought, or had had issues more momentous in the balance.

BY COL. E. D. SWINTON

Wednesday, the 11th of November, was another day of desperate fighting. As day broke the Germans opened fire on our trenches to the north and south of the road from Menin to Ypres. This was probably the most furious artillery fire which they have yet employed against us.

A few hours later they followed this by an infantry assault in force. This attack was carried out by the First and Fourth brigades of the Guard Corps, which, as we now know from prisoners, have been sent for to make a supreme effort to capture Ypres, since that task had proved too heavy for the infantry of the line.

As the attackers surged forward they were met by our frontal fire, and since they were moving diagonally across part of our front they were also attacked on the flank by artillery, rifles, and machine guns. Though their casualties before they reached our line must have been enormous, such was their resolution and the momentum of the mass that in spite of the splendid resistance of our troops they succeeded in breaking through our line in three places near the road. They penetrated some distance into the woods behind our trenches, but were counter-attacked again, enfiladed by machine guns and driven back to their line of trenches, a certain portion of which they succeeded in holding, in spite of our efforts to expel them.

What their total losses must have been during this advance may be gauged to some extent from the fact that the number of dead left in the woods behind our line alone amounted to 700.

A simultaneous effort made to the south, a part of the same operation although not carried out by the Guard Corps, failed entirely, for when the attacking infantry massed in the woods close to our line, our guns opened on them with such effect that they did not push the assault home.

As generally happens in operations in wooded country, the fighting to a great extent was carried on at close quarters. It was most desperate and confused. Scattered bodies of the enemy who had penetrated into the woods in the rear of our position could neither go backward nor forward, and were nearly all killed or captured.

The portion of the line to the southeast of Ypres held by us was heavily shelled, but did not undergo any very serious infantry attack. That occupied by the French, however, was both bombarded and fiercely assaulted. On the rest of our front, save for the usual bombardment, all was comparatively quiet.

On the right one of our trenches was mined and then abandoned. As soon as it was occupied by the enemy the charges were fired and several Germans were blown to pieces.

Thursday, November 12th, was marked by a partial lull in the fighting all along our line. To the north a German force which had crossed the Yser and intrenched on the left bank was annihilated by a night attack with the bayonet, executed by the French. Slightly to the south the enemy was forced back for three-quarters of a mile. Immediately on our left the French were strongly attacked and driven back a short distance, our extreme left having to conform to this movement. Our allies soon recovered the ground they had lost, however, and this enabled us to advance also.

To the southeast of Ypres the enemy's snipers were very active. On our center and right the enemy's bombardment was maintained, but nothing worthy of special note occurred.

The fact that on this day the advance against our line in front of Ypres was not pushed home after such an effort as that of Wednesday tends to show that for the moment the attacking troops had had enough.

Although the failure of this great attack by the Guard Corps to accomplish their object cannot be described as a decisive event, it possibly marks the culmination if not the close of the second stage in the attempt to capture Ypres, and it is not without significance. It has also a dramatic interest of its own. Having once definitely failed to achieve this object by means of the sheer weight of numbers, and having done their best to wear us down, the Germans brought in fresh picked troops to carry the Ypres salient by an assault from the north, the south and the east. That the Guard Corps should have been selected to act against the eastern edge of the salient may be taken as proof of the necessity felt by the Germans to gain this point in the line.

Their dogged perseverance in pursuance of their objective claims wholehearted admiration. The failure of one great attack, heralded as it was by an impassioned appeal to the troops made in the presence of the Emperor himself, but carried out by partially trained men, was only the signal for another desperate effort in which the place of honor was assigned to the corps d'élite of the German army.

It must be admitted that the Guard Corps has retained that reputation for courage and contempt of death which it earned in 1870, when Emperor William I., after the battle of Gravelotte, wrote: "My Guard has found its grave in front of St. Privat," and the swarms of men who came up bravely to the British rifles in the woods around Ypres repeated the tactics of forty-four years ago when their dense columns, toiling up the slopes of St. Privat, melted away under the fire of the French.

BY GUSTAV FELLER

This was the fullest and most widespread German account of the fighting, as given to the German people.

On October 15th a desperate struggle developed in the neighborhood of Ypres and Courtrai, where the German divisions from Antwerp bore with the greatest vehemence on the extreme left wing of the French in order to form a junction between the western wing of the Germans in Belgium and their right wing in France. Our troops pushed forward victoriously at Ypres. In the struggles, which were very bitter near Lille, the enemy on this day (October 22nd) retreated slowly along the whole front. As the territory was partly flooded, our troops could advance but slowly, yet on October 24th the Yser-Ypres canal was crossed by the Germans after stubborn fighting. In spite of the reënforcements which the English received, our troops were able to press onward east and northeast of Ypres and to capture about five hundred Englishmen, among whom were a colonel and twenty-eight officers. On the same day the English squadron, which had taken part in the battle from the sea, had to retreat because several ships had been severely damaged. On October 26th, Poperinghe, west of Ypres, was occupied by our troops. Poperinghe is situated on the line Ypres-Hazebrouck, ten kilometers west of Ypres. The distance between Poperinghe and the French frontier is only five kilometers.

On October 29th the Germans crossed the Yser canal not only near Dixmude but also farther south in the direction of Warneton and Armentières. On the same day violent bayonet attacks developed near Dixmude until finally the incredibly strong intrenchments of the French and English were taken. Everywhere the Germans forced their way onward, even though their advance was a slow one. Several fortified positions of the enemy were taken on October 29th near Lille and three hundred men captured and four cannon taken as booty. On October 30th our army in Belgium took Ramscapelle and Bixschoote. Zandvoorde, Hollebecke, and Wenbecke were also taken by storm. On October 31st our troops pushed their way forward successfully at Ypres and with losses on the side of the English.

There is something strange about the battles in Flanders, in the way in which they started about the middle of October and dragged on for months. It is a desperate struggle of the English and French with the Germans, and the Belgians do not take very much part. The French here sacrificed themselves to no purpose for the English, who were most of all bent upon hindering the advance of the Germans toward Calais and thus preventing the possibility of a German descent upon hallowed English soil. For this reason the contest was so desperate, the struggle for every inch of land so fierce, that we were also forced to exert our strength to the utmost in order to wrest the victory from the foe.

For a long time our enemies labored under the delusion that by their union they formed a mighty barrier to cut off our progress, and that we would eventually have to lose all the advantages which we had gained since the beginning of the War. This hope was also based on the assumption that Germany had but little capital and would be starved out in a short time if England should cut off the supplies. But when we had conquered Belgium after a scant two and a half months and had reached the Belgian coast, anxious care filled the hearts of our enemy, and in the struggle for existence or non-existence, the courage of despair awoke. The anxiety increased all the more as the Russians did not seem to be in any hurry to enter Berlin triumphantly, and the hope that the Russian friend would help had gradually to be abandoned.

In conjunction with the battles in Flanders, which had reached a sort of culmination around the end of October and the beginning of November, there occurred the combat on the coast near Middelkerke. It lasted for three days and the English squadron which was pressing hard upon the German army was repulsed. Seven of the English ships commanded by Admiral Hood were put out of commission by the German field artillery. One of them sank soon afterwards.

In our further advance upon Ypres more territory was gained; and on November 2nd Messines fell into our hands. Opposite the right wing of the German army Hindus were now fighting, not however in closed ranks, but scattered along the whole English front.

On November 3rd, the following report on the battles in Flanders was sent out from the Great Headquarters: "The floods south of Nieuport make all operations in that region impossible. Landed property is for a long time ruined. In some places the water is over a man's height. Our troops have withdrawn from the flooded district without the loss of man, horse, cannon, or vehicle. Our attacks upon Ypres are progressing. Over 2,300 soldiers, for the most part Englishmen, were made captive and several machine guns taken."

From the fact that the German troops could withdraw without any losses, it can be gathered that the German intelligence service, which was carried on by airships and flying-machines, measured up to expectations. One must know Belgium, especially the country surrounding Nieuport, to be able to picture what happened. The country is perfectly level. Numerous canals and drains traverse the region, high dikes keep the sea from overflowing the flat country, which is in part lower than the water-level at high tide. The French and English opened the lockage of the Yser-Ypres canal along the coast and put the land under water.

A fierce struggle had long been going on around the base, Ypres, on the aforementioned canal. The capture of 2,300 Englishmen and the taking of machine guns was, under the conditions described above, quite a success. The report, according to which the thundering of the German cannon could be heard across the canal at Dover, bore witness to the violence of the struggles. A tense excitement took possession of the population of Dover.

We also pressed onward near Ypres and southwest of Lille. There was especially hard fighting in the triangle—Dixmude, Rousselaere, and Ypres—and over a thousand Frenchmen were taken prisoner near Ypres. The shelling of Arras was begun with the greatest intensity. The whole population fled. Only the officials remained behind. The conflicts around Arras were also carried on with the greatest animosity. The bombshells struck the town in great numbers and changed houses to heaps of ruins. German flyers circled over the region.

On November 8th and 9th our troops took about 1,000 prisoners (French, colored folk, and English), in spite of strong resistance, and also captured several machine guns. A reversed attack which the enemy undertook from Nieuport in the evening failed completely. On November 11th, after severe fighting, which lasted for several days, our soldiers were able to drive their opponents out of St. Eloi, lying to the south of Ypres; about a thousand prisoners and six machine guns came into our possession.

In these battles it was especially our young volunteer

regiments that stormed the hostile positions, defying death and singing "The Watch on the Rhine." Thus, on November 11th, near Langemark, the first lines of the enemy positions were stormed by these brave ones and two thousand of the French infantry of the line were captured.

A further heroic exploit of our troops was announced to us on November 11th. Dixmude was stormed and we advanced across the canal. The ground around Ypres, especially in the northern part, perhaps as far as Merckhem, is a network of canals, which form numerous small divisions. The most important of these drains is the Yser-Ypres canal, and it forms a greater hindrance with its high flood-dikes and its broad water surface than the Nethe segment south of Antwerp. These canal defenses are now triumphantly in our hands.

The bombardment of Ypres began on November 7th. An eye-witness gave the following vivid description of it: "The Germans have been bombarding Ypres with their heavy cannon. The city is burning, and a large part is laid waste; no lives have been lost, as the city had been evacuated. The flames quickly spread, owing to a strong northeast wind; and soon the western part was nothing but a blazing pile of ruins. Ten to twelve bombshells fell every minute. The tower of the cathedral of St. Martin has been partly destroyed, and in the northern part, where there are many fine old houses, much damage has been done. German flyers are hovering over the city and throwing bombs.

Finally, on the night from November 11th-12th, our troops entered Ypres. During the raging storm they had succeeded in advancing to the trenches of the Allies without being noticed. There violent struggles ensued, during which continually new masses of German troops appeared. The ranks of the Allies were pierced and the hot conflict was continued in Ypres, where the bayonet played the leading part. Here eleven hundred more men were taken prisoners, and Ypres is ours.[1]

---

[1] In the fighting of November 11th some German troops did reach to Ypres, but they were driven back at once, and Ypres was never in German hands.

CANADA RUSHES TO BRITAIN'S AID

THE LARGEST ARMADA THAT HAD EVER CROSSED THE ATLANTIC

OCTOBER-DECEMBER

SIR MAX AITKEN

Britain's successes in the Great War were very largely due to the loyalty with which her colonies upheld her. And the first of these to rush to her aid was her great American colony, Canada. The story of how eagerly and wholeheartedly that aid was given is here told by a distinguished member of Parliament, Sir Max Aitken.

Germany, in discounting the importance of Britain's entry into the War, had hoped much from the discontent of the colonies. She had counted on the colonials as being subject races, bitter of heart as she by her severity had made her own subject races. She was amazed to find that in Canada, Australia, South Africa, New Zealand, and even in India and Egypt, men looked upon the motherland as a real mother, to be loved and aided and protected. In nothing indeed has the Briton's greatness shone more great than in the steadfast loyalty he had won from all his empire. Not by force but by fair and generous dealing had he bound the colonials to his cause.

As to the extent of Canada's aid, that mounted with the years to something like half a million men. The first Canadian fleet that carried soldiers to Britain brought 33,000 men, and no such number had ever crossed the Atlantic in a body before. Even the famous armada with which General Howe had come to conquer the colonies in the American Revolution had been of smaller size. The United States fleets of the later war years of course far exceeded this; but for the moment the Canadian armada was the superlative in intercontinental transport, a record by which to measure the colony's loyalty and devotion.

BY SIR MAX AITKEN

WAR came upon us without warning, like a thunderbolt from a clear sky. Our people were essentially non-military, fearing no aggression from a peace-loving neighbor, and ignorant of the imminence of German aggression. Yet, in seven weeks, Canada created the first apparatus of war. In seven weeks we assembled an army which, a few months later, was to save Calais on the battlefield of Langemarck. As a demonstration of practical loyalty the exertions of Canada were only equaled by Australia and New Zealand. As an example of administration rising to an emergency, the effort has never been surpassed in military history.

When the British ultimatum to Germany demanding the recognition of the neutrality of Belgium expired, the Canadian Government decided to raise an Expeditionary Force. As this news flashed across the Dominion, the fires of patriotism, which had been smoldering, burst into flame in every province. Parliament was in vacation, but the Prime Minister returned from the West and summoned his Cabinet. The Minister of Militia was already at work in his office, for the proposal of the Canadian Government to raise 20,000 men had been accepted by the British Government.

Within two months of the outbreak of war between Great Britain and Germany, the Dominion of Canada concentrated, armed, and sent to Europe an Expeditionary Force of 33,000 men. A voluntary army, the first complete Canadian Division ever assembled, with more than half a Reserve Division, this force was by far the greatest body of soldiers that had ever crossed the Atlantic at one time. It comprised cavalry, artillery, infantry, engineers, signalers, supply and ammunition columns, field ambulances and hospital staffs, provided with all the apparatus required for the handling and treatment of the wounded; it carried its own complement of rifles, machine guns, field guns, and heavy artillery, and a store of ammunition.

It was not the first time that Canadians had taken up arms in defense of Imperial interests. In the Crimean War, Canadians fought in the ranks of the British army. The Indian Mutiny saw the old Prince of Wales' Royal Canadian Regiment at Gibraltar and at Malta. More than 7,000 Canadians fought for England in the South African War. But now the Empire was to be tested to its foundations. The Minister of Militia, Major-General the Hon. Sir Sam Hughes, K.C.B., acted with the promptness and energy for which he was already famous in the Dominion. In less than a month the Government, which had asked for 20,000 men, found almost 40,000 at its disposal, and the Minister of Militia deemed it necessary to issue orders that no more recruits be enrolled for the first contingent.

Thus did Canada answer the call. From the workshops and the offices of her cities, from the lumber camps of her forests, from the vast wheatfields of the West, from the farms and orchards of the East, from the slopes of the Rockies, from the shores of Hudson Bay, from the mining valleys of British Columbia, from the banks of the Yukon, from the reaches of the St. Lawrence, the manhood of Canada hurried to arms.

No mere jackboot militarism inspired them. They sought neither the glory of conquest nor the rape of freedom, nor the loot of sacked cities. No selfish ideal led them to leave their homes and exchange the ease and comforts of civil life for the sufferings of war and the risk of death. They came forward, free men and unconstrained, with a simple resolve to lay down their lives, if need be, in defense of the Empire—their Empire, too—the very existence of which, as they swiftly saw, was menaced by the most formidable military combination which had ever sprung to arms. The first contingent was born partly of the glory of adventure but more of the spirit of self-sacrifice; and this spirit, in its turn, was born of the deepest emotions of the Canadian people—its love of Country, of Liberty, and of Right.

The Government, in deciding to raise a contingent for service in Europe, were carrying out the national will, and when Parliament entered upon its special session, some days after the declaration of War, unanimity prevailed. The Prime Minister spoke for all parties when he declared that Canada stood "shoulder to shoulder with Britain and the other British Dominions in this quarrel." Sir Wilfrid Laurier spoke of the "double honor" of Canadians of French descent in the opportunity of "taking their place to-day in the ranks of the Canadian Army to fight for the cause of the allied nations." The Government announced its further intention of raising a sum of fifty millions of dollars for war purposes.

As soon as the policy of the Government had been ratified, General Hughes devised and ordered the establishment of the largest camp that had ever been seen on Canadian soil. The site at Valcartier was well chosen. It lay some sixteen miles to the west of Quebec, within a day's march of the gathering transports. The soil was, in the main, light and sandy, and a river of pure water was available. Yet the work of adapting this virgin soil to military purposes was enormous, and the transformation, effected within a fort-night by an army of engineers and workers, a remarkable triumph of applied science. Roads were made, drains laid down, a water supply with miles of pipes installed, electric lighting furnished from Quebec, and incinerators built for the destruction of dry refuse. A sanitary system, second to none that any camp has seen, was instituted. Every company had its own bathing place and shower baths; every cookhouse its own supply of water. Troughs of drinking-water, for horses, filled automatically, so that there was neither shortage nor waste. The standing crops were gar-nered, trees cut down and their roots torn up. A line of rifle targets 3½ miles long—the largest rifle range in the world—was constructed. Three miles of sidings were run out from the wayside station, and a camp telephone ex-change was quickly put in working order.

Camp and army leaped to life in the same hours. Within four days of the opening of the camp, nearly 6,000 men had arrived in it. A week later the number was 25,000. In those August days all roads led to Valcartier, and the railways rose to the occasion, gathering the first Division to the rendezvous, from every corner of the country, in great trains, each of which carried and fed 600 men.

The assembling force comprised elements from every phase of Canadian life. There were those whose names were known throughout the land. There were men who had fought at Paardeburg—some of them "very barely" within the age limit of 45. One, who had retired from a colonelcy of a regiment, offered to serve as a private, so anxious was he to go. He was more than satisfied when he received a majority. Another, who had spent his fifteenth birthday as a bugler in South Africa, has since celebrated his third war birthday in the Flemish trenches.

The original intention of the authorities was to send to England a Division, consisting of the regular complement of three infantry brigades; but, on September 1st, General Hughes announced at the camp that a fourth brigade would be formed, to be used as drafts to supply the war wastage in the other three.   Towards the end of the month the Government decided to send all four brigades over together. "The total reënforcements for the first year of a great war," said Sir Robert Borden in announcing his decision, "are estimated at from 60 to 70 per cent.   If the reserve depots necessary for supplying such reënforcements were established in Canada, eight or ten weeks might elapse before they could reach the front. . . . For these reasons, as well as others, we deemed it advisable that the reserves shall be kept on hand in Great Britain, as the force at the front must continually be kept at full strength, and that without the slightest unnecessary delay."

While the new army underwent its preliminary training at Valcartier, there were other preparations of every kind to be made.   The cloth mills of Montreal began to hum with the manufacture of khaki, which the needles of a great army of tailors converted into uniforms, greatcoats and cloaks. The Ordnance Department equipped the host with the Ross rifle—a Canadian-made arm.   Regiments were shuffled and reshuffled into battalions; battalions into brigades.   The whole force was inoculated against typhoid.   There were stores to manufacture and to accumulate; a fleet of transports to assemble; a thousand small cogs in the machine to be nicely adjusted.

Early in September, the whole First Division was reviewed by the Governor-General in a torrential downpour of rain; and again, towards the end of the month, a few days before embarkation, the Duke of Connaught (accompanied by the Duchess and the Princess Patricia) took the salute at Valcartier from the first army of Canada.   At this final review the contingent was fittingly led past the saluting base by the man whose name, more than any one other, will be linked in history with the First Canadian Division. General Hughes had cause to be proud of the 33,000 men who marched past that day, fully armed and fully equipped, well within two months of the declaration of war in Europe.

The feat of raising such a force is all the more remarkable when one considers that, with the exception of the Princess Patricia's Light Infantry, the overwhelming majority of the men who volunteered for the Great War were civilians, without previous experience or training. The "Princess Pats," as that already famous regiment is now commonly called, was the only one that consisted almost entirely of old soldiers.

The Governor-General's review over, news from the camp came fitfully. The censor was at work, and the public guessed rightly that the division was on the move. Through the darkness and the rain and the mud of the night of September 23rd-24th, the guns crawled down the sixteen miles of valley that brought them to Quebec at daybreak, the men drenched, but happy in the knowledge that they were at last off to the war. The weather was so bad that the infantry, instead of marching, were brought down in a long succession of heavy trains. The embarkation of horses, men, guns and wagons was completed in less than three days. And so the First Canadian Division, with its Reserves, sailed away down the St. Lawrence, in a fleet of Atlantic liners such as the mighty gateway of Canada had never before borne on her bosom.

The fleet assembled in Gaspé Basin, on the coast of Quebec, where the warships which were to convoy it across the Atlantic awaited it. On October 3rd the transports steamed out of Gaspé Bay. The voyage was uneventful if rather long, the fleet entering Plymouth Sound on the evening of October 14th. So strict had been the censorship that the arrival of the Canadian Armada was quite unexpected by the people of Plymouth and Devonport; but no sooner had the word gone forth that the Canadian transports had arrived, than the townsfolk flocked to the waterside, to cheer and sing, and cheer again.

No one was allowed on board the transports, but, when on the succeeding days the troops were landed and marched through the streets, they received a welcome which they will never forget. Hundreds of the men had relatives and friends who were anxious to catch a glimpse of them at the docks, but access was refused. The only exception made throughout the various disembarkations was in the case of the late Field-Marshal Lord Roberts.

Lieut.-General Alderson had been appointed to the command of the contingent, and visited the commanding officers before the work of disembarkation began.

The Canadian Division, the Princess Patricia's Canadian Light Infantry, and the Newfoundland Regiment occupied camps on Salisbury Plain at Bustard, West Down South, West Down North, Pond Farm, Lark Hill, and Sling Plantation. Here the Canadians remained until their departure for France. Here, in the mud and cold and rain of those four dismal months, they worked and lived and displayed that spirit of endurance, courage, and willingness which has since proclaimed them to the world as troops of the finest quality. On the sodden grazing lands, in the fog and mud of the battalion lines, in the dripping tents and crowded, reeking huts, the men of Canada gave promise of the great spirit they possessed, and their officers saw it and were proud.

Lord Roberts visited the Division soon after its arrival in England. It was the last public appearance of this great soldier in England, and the following are the principal points in his speech to the Canadian troops:—

"We have arrived at the most critical moment of our history, and you have generously come to help us in our hour of need.

"Three months ago we found ourselves involved in this war, a war not of our own seeking, but one which those who have studied Germany's literature and Germany's aspirations, knew was a war which we should inevitably have to deal with sooner or later. The prompt resolve of Canada to give us such valuable assistance, has touched us deeply. That

resolve has been quickened into action in a marvelously
short space of time, under the excellent organizing and
driving power of your Minister of Militia—my friend,
Major-General Hughes.

"We are fighting a nation which looks upon the British
Empire as a barrier to her development, and has, in consequence, long contemplated our overthrow and humiliation.
To attain that end she has manufactured a magnificent fighting machine, and is straining every nerve to gain victory.

"It is only by the most determined efforts that we can
defeat her."

The King paid his first visit to our troops early in No-
vember. His Majesty was accompanied by Field-Marshals
Lords Roberts and Kitchener, Sir George Perley, Member
of the Canadian Cabinet in charge of the office of the High
Commissioner in London, and Sir Richard McBride, Prime
Minister of British Columbia.

The Princess Patricia's Canadian Light Infantry left
Salisbury Plain early in December and joined the 27th British Division. The regiment was brigaded with the 3rd
King's Royal Rifles, 4th King's Royal Rifles, 4th Rifle Brigade, and 2nd King's Shropshire Light Infantry.

The King again visited the Canadian troops on February 4, 1915; and on the following day a Division composed
of three infantry brigades, three artillery brigades, ammunition column, divisional engineers, divisional mounted
troops, and divisional train, marched off Salisbury Plain
and entrained for their port of embarkation under the command of Lieut.-General Alderson.

The 6th, 9th, 11th, 12th, and 17th Battalions were left
in England as the Base Brigade of the Division. These battalions were formed later into the Canadian Training De-
pot; later still, together with reënforcements from Canada,
into the Canadian Training Division, under the command
of Brigadier-General J. C. MacDougall.

Such, in its principal commands, was the army which
left Canada for the Great Adventure. It carried with it,
and it left behind, high hopes. It was certain that no men

of finer physique or higher courage could be found anywhere in any theater of this immense struggle. But there were some—and these neither faint-hearted nor unpatriotic—who recalled with anxiety the scientific organization and the tireless patience with which Germany had set herself to create the most superb military instrument which the world has ever seen. And they may have been forgiven if they asked themselves:

"Can civilians, however brave and intelligent, be made in a few months the equals of those inspired veterans who are swarming in triumph over the battlefields of Europe?"

"Can generals, and staffs, and officers be improvised, able to compete with the scientific output of the most scientific General Staff which has ever conceived and carried out military operations?"

These were formidable questions, and even a bold man might have shrunk from a confident answer. The story of Canada in Flanders, however inadequately told, will make it unnecessary ever to ask them again.

GERMANY LOSES HER AFRICAN POSSESSIONS

GENERAL BOTHA HOLDS SOUTH AFRICA LOYAL TO BRITAIN

OCTOBER-DECEMBER

FRANK A. MUMBY   DR. OTTO KARSTEDT

Canada's position in the War was different from that of South Africa. In Africa there were German colonies; so the world war spread wide over the African continent, and the French and British there were too busy fighting their own Germans to be able to send prompt aid to Europe.

The large German colonies in Africa numbered four. The most important was German East Africa, with a population of over seven millions, a vast tract that bordered on the Indian Ocean and spread inland so far that a force of several hundred men might easily lie hidden in its depths for many months. Indeed, not until 1917 were the last Germans in its forests compelled to surrender. The other German colonies made briefer resistance. The largest was South West Africa, on the lower Atlantic coast, vast in size but almost empty of population because of the German wars against the natives. Kamerun, or the Cameroons as English speaking peoples have called the region, is a big and fairly well peopled district on the west coast in the dense equatorial region north of the Congo, almost half of it having just been acquired from France in 1911. Togoland, the smallest but perhaps most prosperous of the German possessions, lies not far to the west of Kamerun. How each of these was fought for and conquered is told here by a noted British publicist and by the German authority appointed to review this matter for his government.

Germany, however, counted not on these huge but almost wholly savage regions to maintain her power in Africa. She looked more hopefully to the smaller but far more thickly settled Boer states. These had been conquered by the British only after the long and hard fought Boer War of 1902, and had then in 1909 joined the British colonies of Natal, Cape Colony, etc., in the Union of South Africa. Naturally Germany assumed that this union was forced, and that the Boers hated it. She made the further assumption that at a mere shadow of help from her they would rise in revolt, even though facing almost sure defeat.

To some slight extent Germany was right; a few Boers did revolt, as the following story tells. As a whole, however, the Boers stood by the British. So fairly had they been dealt with in the South African Union that a dozen years of peace had been enough to cement the ties of a genuine brotherhood. The Boers were of Dutch ancestry and

370

thus almost as near of race to the English as to the Germans. Moreover, their most trusted leader, General Botha, had become Prime
Minister of the Union. The amazing faith placed in him by both
Britons and Boers is shown by his having risen to this remarkable
rule over the very people who had defeated him. That trust he fully
justified by the way he now held South Africa together, choked off
rebellion, and then led the way to the defeat of the Germans in their
own colonies. All Africa, except for the inaccessible regions of East
Africa, was lost to Germany in the first few months of the Great War.

C. F. H.

BY FRANK A. MUMBY

A GLANCE at the map will show that, with Germany's
scattered colonies in Africa upon the outbreak of the
war in August, 1914, hostilities were inevitable in many
places at once. Togoland—the smallest of her African possessions, but the only German colony which succeeded in
paying its way—was the first to fall, thanks largely to the
pluck and enterprise of Captain F. C. Bryant of the Royal
Artillery—holding the temporary rank of lieutenant-colonel
—senior officer of the Gold Coast Station. Without waiting for orders, Colonel Bryant crossed the frontier into Togoland on August 7th with a small detachment of the Gold
Coast Regiment of the West African Frontier Force, in
motor-cars, and seized Lome, the coast town and capital,
without opposition. The Germans fell back towards Kamina, 100 miles inland, where their wireless station was
situated—powerful enough to work direct to Berlin—but
hotly contested the British advance from the coast. Colonel
Bryant had placed himself in communication with the
French officer commanding in Dahomey, on the other side
of Togoland, and a small but extremely useful French
force was soon coöperating with the British on their right
flank. The Germans destroyed the bridges, cut all communications, and fortified themselves with trenches and elec-
trified wire entanglements. But the Allies were not to be
denied. They gradually forced the enemy back on Kamina,
though the fighting was so fierce that in one engagement
alone the British lost 17 per cent. of their total. At length,
on August 26th, the German governor, regarding the position at Kamina as hopeless, destroyed the wireless station

and sent a flag of truce, offering, if given all the honors of war, to capitulate, stipulating for certain terms. Colonel Bryant replied that as the Germans were not in a position to ask for terms they must surrender unconditionally. He added, however, that Britons always respected private property, and that there would be as little interference as possible with the trade of the country, as well as with the private interests of firms. Thereupon the German authorities surrendered unconditionally, and on August 27, 1914, the Allied Forces entered Kamina, after a little campaign which deserves an honorable place in the history of this worldwide war. The roll of honor—eight British and French officers and non-commissioned officers killed and wounded, and sixty-six killed and wounded among the native troops—was shared about equally by the Allies.

Britain and France also coöperated in dealing with the German Cameroons, the capital of which was the next to fall. This success, however, was only an incident in a campaign of an infinitely more arduous nature than that in Togoland. One of the British columns invading the German colony under the command of Major P. Maclear, Royal Dublin Fusiliers and Nigeria Regiment, crossed the frontier on August 25, 1914, and after meeting with some resistance and capturing one of the German forts at Garua, was so heavily counter-attacked that it was compelled to retreat into British territory with the loss of Maclear and four other officers killed, and four officers wounded, besides considerable casualties among the native troops.

Meanwhile another British column reconnoitering from Ikom, in the southern province of Nigeria, after meeting with slight resistance, had, on August 25th, occupied Nsanakang, 5 miles over the German frontier. A third British force from Calabar crossed the Akwa Jafe River, which here forms the Anglo-German boundary, on August 29th, and seized Archibong, on the road to Rio del Rey, without experiencing any loss. On September 6th, however, the garrison which had been left in Nsanakang was suddenly attacked at 2 a. m. by the enemy, who had received strong reenforcements. This attack was repulsed, but a second one, made at 5 a. m., proved successful after a stubborn resistance.

While these events were taking place on land, the British cruiser *Cumberland* and the gunboat *Dwarf,* with a French cruiser, had reconnoitered the mouth of the Cameroon River and its approaches to Duala. Towards the middle of September a desperate attempt was made by the Germans to blow up the *Dwarf* with an infernal machine. Two nights later she was again attacked, this time by the German merchant-ship *Nachtigal,* the only result of which was that the *Nachtigal* herself was wrecked in making a fruitless attempt to ram the gunboat. Other assaults on the *Dwarf* were made in German launches, but were defeated in every instance by the gallant British crew. The *Cumberland* also distinguished herself by her capture of no fewer than nine German liners off the Cameroon River, where doubtless they had taken shelter upon the outbreak of war. The German gunboat *Soden* was also captured, and commissioned at once. On September 24th, French troops from Libreville attacked Ukoko, in Corisco Bay, attended by the French warship *Surprise.* The German forces were driven back, and the German armed auxiliaries *Khios* and *Itolo* sunk by the *Surprise.* Three days later, following upon a bombardment by His Majesty's ships, the towns of Duala and Bonaberi surrendered unconditionally to an Anglo-French force under the command of Brigadier-General C. M. Dobell, escorted by two cruisers.

The Germans had considered Duala impregnable, and were taken completely by surprise by the rapidity with which the Allies forced their way up the river, over every obstacle in the shape of mines and sunken ships which had been placed in their path. "We had set fire to the Governor's yacht and bombarded half the town," wrote a British officer on General Dobell's staff, "before they realized we were there! All was done so quietly and quickly." The enemy destroyed their wireless station and instruments before surrendering the place. Several hundred German prisoners were captured, while the casualties upon our side amounted to one naval signalman and four natives wounded. The Allied forces, pressing their advantage, succeeded in driving back the Germans in the three directions in which they retreated from Duala. In a brilliant action on October 6th the French forced the passage of the Japoma bridge to the east of Duala with a loss of two natives killed, and four Europeans and eight natives wounded.

On October 8th an attack was made up the Wuri River on Jabassi with a naval and military force commanded by Brevet-Colonel E. H. Gorges, Commandant of the West African Regiment. Although this was repulsed, a second attack, on October 14th, was successful, Jabassi being occupied and ten Europeans being captured. Another force, commanded by Captain Heywood, of the Royal Artillery and Nigerian Regiment, attacked the enemy near Susa, on the railway which runs north from Bonaberi, and defeated him, with the loss of one officer killed and twenty-seven native soldiers killed, wounded, and missing. Faced in the north by a column of the Nigeria Regiment, which had occupied the district round Mora, the German forces withdrew to the south.

On the other side of the continent the Germans took the initiative, well aware that for the time being at least they held the advantage in the matter of military strength. The white population of between 5,000 and 6,000 in German East Africa consisted chiefly of Germans of fighting age, while, in addition, their native infantry and police forces numbered together about 2,000. Army reservists from other parts of the world had reënforced the troops before the outbreak of war. Thus the Germans in East Africa, well provided as they were with ordinary guns, as well as with a number of machine guns, constituted at once a formidable force. Ordinarily Britain did not keep more troops in these African possessions than were necessary for the maintenance of order, our military policy being based on concentration; but with the outbreak of hostilities the normal garrison of both the British East Africa and Uganda Protectorates was strengthened as soon as possible by strong reënforcements from India, as well as by mounted and unmounted volunteers raised locally. The normal force consisted of native police and the East African Rifles, which, although not so numerous as the German garrison, was, in Lord Crewe's words, "extremely efficient and well officered." Our unofficial population of East Africa responded to the call to arms with a readiness which called forth a public tribute of thanks from the Secretary of State for the Colonies. Well for our prestige that it was so, for the reenforcements were forestalled by various attempts on the part of the enemy to raid British territory. One party of invaders made a dash to blow up the Uganda Railway near Maungu, but this was frustrated before any damage was done, and all the German dynamite and outfit dispatched for the purpose were captured. Other efforts were made during September, 1914, to raid British territory across the boundary of the East Africa Protectorate, but all were repulsed, save the occupation of one unimportant frontier station on the border by a small party of the enemy, whose entry it was not at the time convenient to oppose.

On September 6th there was a hot engagement to the west of Tsavo—famous for its man-eating lions—between a British force, composed partly of Indian troops and partly of King's African Rifles, and a strong force of the enemy. The Germans brought Maxim guns into action, which the Punjabis made a gallant effort to rush with the bayonet. In the end, after being severely handled, the enemy were beaten back, though not without some losses on our side.

Two days later the scene of action changed to the Nyasaland border, where the main British force advanced to repel a German column some 400 strong, including fifty Europeans, which had crossed the frontier. Successfully evading the British, the invaders, at sunrise on September 9, 1914, attacked Karonga, the town at the north end of Lake Nyasa, which is the starting point for Tanganyika. The town was defended by only one officer, fifty African Rifles and police, and eight civilians, but they kept the enemy at bay for three hours, when one of the columns from the main British force arrived on the scene and saved the situation. The Governor of Nyasaland reported that "the enemy fought with great determination, and had to be dislodged by repeated bayonet charges; but they were ultimately driven towards Songwe. The British force," he added, "was too exhausted to pursue"; but it succeeded in capturing two field and two machine guns, besides inflicting heavy losses among the German officers—seven killed and two wounded and captured—and rank and file. The British loss among the whites was four killed and seven wounded. This action was typical of various other engagements along the Anglo-German frontiers of East Africa during the month of September, 1914, the raiders in nearly every case being soundly beaten and forced to retire.

One of many plucky deeds was the repulse of a German force nearly 200 strong, with a couple of Maxim guns, between the Magadi railway and the frontier, by a squadron of the East Africa Mounted Rifles, only thirty in number, commanded by Captain Chapman. After an hour's severe fighting in thick bush country the Germans were thoroughly beaten, retiring hastily towards Longido. Their casualties are said to have been thirty-three (eleven dead), and in the hurry of their retreat they left behind them many loads. Twelve of the gallant thirty British were killed and wounded.

In addition to the British, a Belgian force from the Congo also operated with success against the Germans in the region between Lakes Tanganyika and Victoria Nyanza.

While these things were happening during the early months of the war in the Cameroons and East Africa, the sternest campaign of all in this continent was beginning on the southwest coast, where Nachtigal had first hoisted the flag of Germany on colonial soil. Here the British campaign was undertaken by the Union Government of South Africa, with General Botha in command. The number of the enemy was estimated at 10,000 mounted infantry and artillery, all admirably trained and equipped, besides a camel corps of 500. Blockhouses were dotted about the country, well armed, and connected with each other by telephone, and with the capital, Windhoek, by wireless and underground telegraph. Roads and railways had been planned for "The

Day" when British South Africa was to be invaded, while emissaries were ever at work across the frontier to play upon the prejudices and ambitions of the remaining irreconcilables among the Boers. The partial success of these plots necessarily interfered with the development of the British campaign in German territory.

When the news that Britain had declared war resounded through the Empire, it was not surprising that South Africa, notwithstanding the magnificent spirit of the vast majority of both Boers and British, found herself face to face with danger from within as well as from without. In certain parts the old canker of racial hatred was still smoldering, and German agents had been indefatigable in their efforts to keep this alive, in accordance with the secret service system of Pan-Germanism. These agents were specially busy in the country districts, where news from the outside world filtered through for the most part by word of mouth, colored by the prejudices or hidden designs of the speaker. In the towns and more populated districts the people had means of reading and judging for themselves, and for the most part, in Britain's hour of need, demonstrated their wholehearted loyalty to the Empire at once. The sudden outbreak of world-wide war, however, was so unexpected that it found South Africa as a whole unprepared, vaguely and anxiously wondering what would happen now that national problems which might have been solved by time without serious disturbance—or, on the other hand, have become more dangerous with insidious growth—had of necessity to be brought up for immediate solution.

Above and beyond all other problems was that of the relation of South Africa to the Empire. That section of the Government which had mustered under the leadership of General Hertzog—and whose members came in consequence to be known as the Hertzogites—was in a very decided minority, but it held strongly to the view that South Africa had no concern in the destinies of the British Empire as a whole, maintaining that, in the event of a European War involving Great Britain, South Africa should have the right to claim absolute neutrality. On that account, and on personal grounds of animosity towards General Botha and other leaders of the Government—personal feeling playing no small part in the grave crisis which ensued—General Hertzog left the Cabinet and gathered round him what came to be known as the neutrality party, the ultimate aim of which, there could be little doubt, was complete South African independence. What would have been the fate of this party had the Empire's call to arms not brought matters so suddenly and unexpectedly to a head it would be idle to speculate, but the outbreak of hostilities in Europe also meant the declaration of war between the rivals in South Africa. General Botha threw down the gauntlet to the neutrality party at once, and the real friends and the real foes of the Empire were forced to declare themselves. To that extent, therefore, the Great War was a blessing in disguise. An open wound is better than a cancerous growth.

A splendid stand was made by General Botha and his colleagues. In their address of unswerving loyalty to His Majesty, promising to defend the Union and coöperate with the Imperial Government to maintain the security and integrity of the Empire, they carried the day in Parliament with an overwhelming majority of ninety-two against twelve. Nine of the minority were members for the Orange Free State, including General Hertzog himself, who proposed an abortive amendment, which, while promising to support all measures of defense necessary to resist any invasion of Union territory, declared that an attack on German territory in South Africa "would be in conflict with the interests of the Union and of the Empire."

Defeated in Parliament, the opponents of the Union Government proceeded to more drastic steps. General Christian Beyers, Commandant-General of the Defense Force, handed in his resignation on September 15th, and published a manifesto which plainly showed his implacable hatred of Great Britain and the dangerous tendency of the revolt. Beyers's action was much more serious than the subsequent treachery of De Wet, who, though a power to be reckoned with in the Free State, had not the same high reputation as a leader among the rest of his compatriots as his slippery achievements in the last war had won for him in Great Britain.

Both Beyers and De Wet had signed the treaty of Vereeniging, which ended the Boer War of 1899-1902, though among the last to give in. Beyers, after a time, had apparently become so loyal in his allegiance that in 1907 he was appointed Speaker of the Transvaal Legislative Assembly, and subsequently accepted the post of Commandant of the Union Defense Force. His loyalty was unsuspected up to the last. As General Smuts, the Minister of Defense, pointed out, in reply to the ex-Commandant-General's manifesto, Beyers had given no hint to the Union Government of his contemplated resignation when discussing the very expedition to German Southwest Africa which he afterwards opposed. He had himself been largely responsible for the plan of operations to be adopted, and, indeed, had been regarded as the future Commander-in-Chief of the British Campaign.

On the very day on which Beyers handed in his resignation in Pretoria he met General De la Rey, whose old allegiance to Botha and patriarchal influence with his people made his attitude at this time of supreme importance. The possible fruits of that meeting remain unknown, for it was while the two generals were on their way by motor-car, that very evening, to address a demonstration at Lichtenburg in opposition to the Government, that De la Rey, as the car was passing through Johannesburg, was accidentally shot dead. It happened that the police were hunting at the time some desperate bandits, who were known to be escaping through the district in a motor-car. Beyers and De la Rey dashed through Johannesburg without responding to the challenge of the police patrol, with the result that the car was fired on, and De la Rey, to the grief of the whole country, was killed on the spot.

As soon as Beyers's betrayal was revealed it was natural that the public should recall his cordial meeting with the German Emperor in 1912. But until the actual event they did not suppose that this accomplished lawyer Boer, who had been born and educated in the old Cape Colony, was capable of extreme treachery. A self-styled prophet named Vanrensburg, who acquired a certain influence in the Transvaal, had, however, preached that the Dutch Republics would be reëstablished with De Wet and Beyers as presidents, and the words had fallen on fruitful soil.

It was on October 13, 1914, that the Union Government publicly announced that rebellion was in the land. Europe had been at war for nine weeks. During about half that period, or ever since the resignation of General Beyers as Commandant-General of the Union Defense Force, the Government and General Botha had well-founded suspicions that something was wrong with their forces in the northwest of the Cape Province, which were under the command of Lieutenant-Colonel Maritz. To Solomon Gerhardus Maritz the British yoke had never been congenial. He was a Cape rebel in the Boer War of 1899-1902, a man of strong character, noted for the speed and endurance with which he conducted guerrilla fighting. But he had now undertaken a forlorn hope.

Maritz had a force of Germans under him, besides his own rebel commando, and had dispatched to German Southwest Africa all those of his officers and men who were unwilling to join the Germans. From the enemy also he boasted that he had ample guns, rifles, ammunition, and money. Maritz temporarily occupied Keimoes and Kakamas. Affecting to be still a commandant of the Defense Force, he disarmed the inhabitants of the latter place on the plea that he required the rifles to arm a force against the German border. Here, too, he hoisted the Vierkleur, the flag of the old Transvaal Republic, though presently it was displaced by the German flag. A few days later he sent in an order to Colonel Brits to evacuate Upington, and, receiving no answer, declared his intention to attack it. The plan, however, was frustrated. On the same day a squadron of the Imperial Light Horse rounded up seventy-one of the rebels; and next day the Imperial Light Horse and Enslin's Horse (the latter composed of Dutch burghers of the Transvaal) brought in fifty more, who had surrendered.

At five o'clock on the morning of October 22nd, Maritz

attacked Keimoes, a town between Kakamas and Upington on the northern bank of the Orange River. At first he was supposed to have over 1,000 men, including several hundred Germans, with eight guns and four machine guns, but later evidence showed the force to be almost entirely German. Keimoes was held by 150 Union men until reënforcements arrived, when the enemy was driven back, leaving two dead and removing their wounded. One of four officers captured was the German Count von Schwerin. Maritz himself was shot through the knee-cap. The Union casualties were eight wounded. The rebels retiring on Kakamas, Colonel Brits, after a forced night march, arrived at the outskirts of that town at dawn on October 24th, and surprised them with a vigorous attack. A portion of the rebel force defended for about an hour and then retreated. Colonel Brits entered the town without opposition, but, his horses being done up after the heavy march, he was unable to pursue Maritz. The rebels retreated westward towards Schuit Drift, leaving tents standing, and abandoning a large quantity of stores and ammunition. On the following two days Colonel Van de Venter engaged and defeated at Calvinia a portion of Maritz's force which had left Kakamas about a week before.

Since the outbreak of the revolt there had been a stream of willing captives. Twenty-four rebels surrendered to Colonel Van de Venter's scouts at Brandolei and 100 to Captain Vermaas at Onderste Doorns without any fighting. It was clear that Maritz's men, the younger of whom he held together by threats of the sjambok, had repented their allegiance. Many, on surrendering, volunteered for active service. Others sent messages expressing intention to escape and join the Union forces. Maritz himself, who was said to be at loggerheads with the Germans, offered to surrender on terms, but the offer was contemptuously ignored. On October 27th Colonel Brits met and defeated a portion of his force at Schuit Drift. Colonel Alberts, who arrived at Truerfontein on October 29th, sent a reconnoitering force out under Commandant de Villiers. They met a strong rebel commando with white flags on their rifles. On the

Union commandant's approach the rebels attacked and captured 110 of his men. But these were not to wait long for release. The rebels advanced from two points against Colonel Alberts, who easily defeated them, and chased them for 20 miles. The rebels scattered over a front of 5 miles, leaving carts, bicycles, etc. Their losses were 13 killed, 36 wounded, 240 captured. From Kenhardt at the same time Colonel Commanding Celliers announced the capture of rebel leaders, including Maritz's adjutant, Major Ben Coetzee. Colonel Brits was now able to report that the invasion of the Cape Province was finally broken. He had defeated the combined rebel and German force at Schuit Drift.

After his complete defeat at Kakamas, Maritz fled into German territory. Meanwhile a more sinister complexion was given to the rebellion by developments in the northern districts of the Orange Free State and western districts of the Transvaal. On October 27th the Government announced the discovery that General De Wet and General Beyers respectively were heading movements there. Armed rebellious commandoes were already in existence. The town of Heilbron had been seized and the officials of the Government made prisoners. At Reitz a train had been stopped and armed citizens of the Defense Force taken from it and disarmed.

Christian De Wet was known to be no ardent lover of the British, but his utterances since the war, when he had been General Commander-in-Chief of the Orange Free State Forces, had been marked by a loyal tone apparently sincere. One of the most striking of these utterances was made in 1909, when, as Minister of Agriculture for the Orange River Colony, he addressed a gathering of farmers near Bloemfontein. At the end of the meeting the audience sang the *"Volkslied,"* De Wet joining in. "That is quite right," he said; "it is our old hymn. But now, as we are British subjects and loyal men, we must also sing 'God save the King' "—which they did with equal heartiness, De Wet leading the singing. This was quite in the spirit of the counsel to the nation with which he had closed his book on the war between Boer and Briton: "Be loyal to the new

Government! Loyalty pays best in the end. Loyalty alone is worthy of a nation which has shed its blood for freedom."

General Botha's attitude on the outbreak of the revolt was one of calm and dignified strength. He himself assumed command of the operations. Accepting a standard presented by the ladies of the Transvaal on October 22nd, he said that he could not break his oath whatever happened; that he would do everything in his power to prevent further bloodshed; and that it would be the happiest day for him when South Africa was restored to peace. Early on October 27th General Botha started from Rustenburg, west of Pretoria, to round up Beyers's rebels. In a few hours he came in touch with them, and drove them in headlong rout, capturing eighty fully armed. Fighting took place towards the end of the day's pursuit. One of Botha's men and several of Beyers's were wounded.

But it was in the Free State that the chief danger-spot lay. The affected districts were Heilbron, Vrede, Lindley, Reitz, and Bethlehem. Near Lindley, De Wet destroyed the railway in several parts. He detached a body of rebels to loot Harrismith, but was tackled at Doornberg (November 7th) by the Government forces, though not in sufficient strength, under Commandant F. R. Cronje. In this fight De Wet's son Daniel was killed. De Wet and his men behaved like brigands in the towns they occupied. At Winburg they stole everything they could lay hands on in the shops—even dolls, hats, and rolls of velvet—and at the shop of Mr. Wright (the Mayor) De Wet struck in the eye an assistant who answered his demand for petrol by saying there was none. De Wet acted as if demented. He had suffered two slight paralytic strokes a year or so before. His most childish exhibition was at Vrede (October 29th). By his order on that occasion the magistrate was dragged in view of the inhabitants to the monument in front of the Dutch Church, where the rebel general made a speech. After referring to the "miserable pestilential English," he said: "King Edward VII. promised to protect us, but he failed to do so, and allowed a magistrate to be placed over us." De Wet then bitterly accused the magistrate of having fined him 5 shillings for beating a native with a small shepherd's whip. "You pleaded guilty," interjected the magistrate. From this incident General Smuts, Minister of Defense, wittily characterized the rebellion as "the five-shilling rebellion." De Wet at Vrede also spoke of the invasion of German Southwest Africa as a dastardly act of robbery, and added that "the ungodly policy" of General Botha had gone on long enough.

These were but the fulminations of a desperate man. Dutch and British in the Union had at the outset held meetings and rallied to the side of General Botha, and the failure of the rebellion was sure, though the difficulties of the country and its vast area prolonged the resistance. De Wet had induced many to join him in the belief that there would be no fighting. The whole Free State, he represented, was rising; the Government would do nothing. On November 12th, in the Mushroom Valley, these illusions were shattered. De Wet was caught napping, being actually in bed when General Botha opened a fierce attack. Colonel Myburgh and Colonel T. Smuts were associated with the Commandant-General, while Colonel Brand coöperated from Hoenderkop. The result was complete defeat and rout of the rebel force, over twenty of whom were killed and a large number wounded. Of the prisoners taken 255 were European and 27 native. Prisoners De Wet had taken, including Senator Stuart and the magistrate at Winburg, were recaptured and released by Colonel Brand. The Union losses were three killed, twenty-four wounded.

Two of De Wet's sons surrendered to a special Justice of the Peace on November 21st. The same night De Wet crossed the Vaal River into the Transvaal. He was pursued by Commandant du Toit in a motor-car, but escaped with four followers only. Joining a small commando which had been secretly forming in the Schweizer Reneke district, he started westward, and on November 25th crossed the railway near Devondale siding, 18 miles north of Vryburg. From Vryburg Colonel Brits advanced in hot pursuit, aided by a motor-car contingent from Witwatersrand. On the 27th fifty of De Wet's force were captured at Kommandant Spruit. The leader had left this party the day before and trekked west. But he was at the end of his tether. His actual capture was effected by Colonel Jordaan.

The final drama in the misguided movement which had led to their being engaged in civil war was also the most tragic. By the time Beyers was engaged by Commandant Sarel Du Toit at Reitgat on the Zandspruit on December 7th he had only seventy men left. But he inflicted loss and escaped again. The rebels split up, Beyers's party, about thirty strong, being pursued by Commandant Botha to Klerkstroom. Captain Ruys and Veldtkornet Denecker crossed from Maquissi, and at sunrise on the 8th met a small band of rebels on the Zandspruit, and drove them towards the Vaal River. On the banks of the Vaal a sharp engagement took place, lasting fifteen minutes. During the fight Beyers and others galloped to the river and tried to cross. They were fired on. Beyers fell from his horse, but managed to grasp by the tail another horse, and was swimming back to the Free State side. He drifted down the swollen stream, calling for help. A branch was thrown towards him, but it was of no avail. Fighting was still in progress. Soon he disappeared under water. His field-glasses and his revolver were found; also his horse, which had been killed. The body was recovered at Vliegekraal, not far from the spot where he was seen to sink. The same day that Beyers died saw the unconditional surrender of the rebel General Wessels with over 1,200 men; within the next fortnight Wolmarans and John Pretorius were captured.

In a manifesto on December 9th General Botha announced that "this senseless rebellion" was practically at an end, and counseled a spirit of tolerance and forbearance, and merciful oblivion. "Our next duty," he concluded, "is to make it impossible for German Southwest Africa to be again used in the future as a secure base from which to threaten the peace and liberties of the Union. I hope and trust the people will deal with this danger as energetically as they have dealt with the internal rebellion."

BY DR. OTTO KARSTEDT

The defense of the German colonies, particularly those in Africa, was rendered more difficult chiefly by the fact that it was impossible, from the moment the war began, to supply the protectorates with the requisite amount of munitions of war. Only to German East Africa was it possible to send a single vessel in 1915 and again in 1916. In consequence of the English blockade the defenders were dependant exclusively upon the stores which were there at the outbreak of the war. Soon there was a lack of the most urgent necessities, such as medicines, ammunition, clothing, etc. Nevertheless in the economic sphere splendid achievements were recorded in the colonies. Success was obtained in Kamerun as in German East Africa in acquiring the so essential quinine and utilizing it. Even gunpowder was produced from the raw material of the country. Old cannons used for firing salutes were converted by means of the most primitive materials into field pieces, and, auxiliary troops were equipped with the breachloaders which the natives possessed.

The Germans of Southwest Africa, in view of their slender force and the long boundary line, everywhere menaced, maintained a waiting attitude. The Union, because of the indications of a rising on the part of the Boers under Delarey and Dewet, was likewise retarded in the decision as to definite action, so that the whole month of August passed quietly. Only on September 15th did the English make an attack on the German station Ramensdrift, on the Orange River. In order to draw larger bodies of enemy troops into the trap the Germans purposely withdrew toward the north. This stratagem succeeded, and, on September 26th, 300 Englishmen were cut off at Sandfontein and forced to surrender after a hard fight.

Thereupon our opponent desisted for the moment from pushing his attacks from the south and transferred his energies to the attack from Lüderitzbuch, where, protected by warships, he began to land 8,000 men on September 9th. In consequence, the German troop had been transferred to Aus, between Lüderitzbucht and Keetmanshoop. There it established a strong position from which, later on, it was not ousted, but permitted to march out.

The English, for the time, confined themselves to the repeated bombardment of Swakopmund. To push forward from Lüderitzbucht had not been possible for them. Not until December 16th, 1914, after the Boer rebellion had been put down, did the English, presenting a broad front, advance from Lüderitzbucht. On December 24th, ships appeared before Walfish Bay, which formerly had been occupied by the Germans. Great numbers of troops were landed, and Botha who, in the meantime, had assumed the leadership, began the construction of a road from here to Swakopmund. In consequence, the position in the south near Aus became entirely untenable, if the troop did not wish to expose itself to the danger of being torn in two. The whole southern part of the colony was therefore evacuated, and all cattle, material, etc., were transported north. The situation became the more difficult in view of the fact that the natives, instigated by England, had risen and were devastating the country, robbing and murdering everywhere.

Proceeding from the Swakopmund base the enemy, about the middle of February, 1915, attacked the camps of the coast guard company at Felseneck. To screen the retrograde movement, a new position had been occupied between Otavibahn and Swakopmund. At the end of February, the enemy attacked this with superior forces, and succeeded, by reason of his abundant means of transportation, in cutting off a part of the position and compelling it to surrender. The attack against the other part of the position failed. Nevertheless it had to be vacated; so that our opponent had practically overcome the Namib circle from Swakopmund. Windhuk was now directly endangered, and the leaders of the troop therefore resolved to abandon the capital and withdraw farther toward the north. All material, etc., was sent to Tsumeb. Botha, meanwhile, continued pushing his may along the railroad, so that on May 4th, 1915, he could occupy Karibib. Negotiations for an armistice had led to no result.

Botha now advanced in three columns against the last
German positions in the north, whose predicament was the
greater in view of the fact that they had been compelled to
relinquish their last advantage, the Otavi railroad. Botha,
with 15,000 men, advanced to Otavi, and thence to Otavi-
fonstein, where he attacked a part of the troop with a vastly
superior force. In order not to be cut off, the Germans retreated fighting. The right wing of the enemy, 4,000
strong, advanced from Okahandja over Waterberg to Tsumeb. Here also the Germans had to abandon the cover of
their position in order to avoid being surrounded, the more
so because they no longer had any artillery. Thereafter it
was inevitable that they would be forced by hunger to surrender. The governor therefore entered into negotiations
with Botha, which resulted in the capitulation of the remainder of the troop, consisting of 3,400 men, on May 9th,
1915.

For an attack on German East Africa England had collected a large number of troops from India, which on November 2nd, 1914, made an attack, organized on a large
scale, on Tanga, the terminus of the Usambara railroad.
Despite the great preponderance of numbers on the English
side, the defence, under General von Lettow-Vorbeck, not
only repulsed the attack, but compelled the enemy to retreat
to his ships, leaving behind many killed and wounded, and
a large quantity of very welcome material. An attack
simultaneously planned by the English to proceed from
across the border of British East Africa, failed on November 3rd, the enemy sustaining heavy losses. By the end of
1914 the whole protectorate had been freed from the enemy.

In January, 1915, the English undertook a new attack
on a large scale against Tanga, this time proceeding from
Mombosa. This also was repulsed at Jassini in severe
battles which took place on January 18th and 19th.

Less fortunate were the German attacks directed against
British East Africa, although skirmishing parties repeatedly
succeeded in penetrating as far as the Uganda railroad and
in destroying parts of it. Indeed, a grand English attack
which took place in the middle of July and was directed

against the region of the Kilimanjaro, proved unsuccessful. The English could only temporarily occupy Bukoba on Lake Victoria and partly destroy it.

These numerous failures which had their effect on the prestige of England in Africa, had engendered a sentiment in England which forced the adoption of the most vigorous measures in East Africa. The leadership of the English was entrusted to General Smuts; that of the Belgians, to General Tombeur. On March 28, 1916, Smuts began his advance with two strong divisions against the chief German position under General von Lettow-Vorbeck, lying between Taveta and Rombo on Kilimanjaro. By passing around its left wing, the attacker compelled the defence to fall back on the Kitovo mountains. The great superiority in numbers of the English, with the aid of the most modern military equipment, and above all, of cavalry, compelled the defenders to retreat ever farther toward the coast. At the same time Smuts sent cavalry through the steppe toward Kondora-Irangi, which place was occupied on April 20th. His own advance, in consequence of losses and sickness and because of a number of successful German counter-attacks, was temporarily halted at West Usambara. On the 7th of July, however, he was able to advance again along the Pangani and the Usambara mountains and occupy Tanga, from which place he conducted operations along the coast. At the same time the troop which had occupied Kondora-Irangi pushed onward toward the south and, on July 29th, had reached the Midland railroad at Dodoma. Swerving to the right, it occupied Morogoro on August 26th, so that, in consequence, Daressalam became untenable. On September 4th, it was abandoned to the English, who, advancing along the coast toward the south, had previously taken Pangani and Bagamoyo.

Simultaneously with the English, the Belgians had taken up the offensive from the west and northwest; and, despite the obstinate resistance of a small German troop, they succeeded in occupying the entire west and northwest of the colony. They entered Tabora on September 19th, 1916.

At the same time English troops, which had been landed in Muanga, were also put in march toward Tabora.

Contrary to expectation, the defenders of the north-western part of the colony and Tabora, who were under the command of General Wahle, succeeded in uniting with General von Lettow-Vorbeck in the south of the colony, although they had frequently been surrounded by the English.

When, in the fall of 1916, all the places along the coast, as well as all the railroads, had been lost, the defense of German East Africa was ended. The rest was a war in the bush which was made against the small troop of von Lettow-Vorbeck, which had been cut off from all supplies. The condition of von Lettow-Vorbeck was practically analagous to that of a hunted animal, for the ring about him was completely closed, the Portuguese also having meanwhile declared war. Forced farther and farther to the south, where he even succeeded in striking a decisive blow against the Portuguese, clearing the colony of them, he, on December 1916, again broke through the circle of his pursuers toward the south and into Portuguese territory. A succession of sharp and successful blows followed, which, however, could not avert the inevitable conclusion of the struggle. At times von Lettow-Vorbeck could penetrate for a distance of 300 kilometres into Portuguese East Africa. In the fall of 1918 he had entered Rhodesia and had occupied Kassama, in the northeastern part of that province. From here he wished to proceed to Broken Hill. Following the provisions of the armistice, von Lettow-Vorbeck, on November 15th, laid down his arms, with 30 officers, 125 other Europeans, and 1,165 colored troops, 1 field piece, 24 machine, and 14 lighter guns. A heroic struggle without a parallel had terminated; even the enemy not withholding his praise. von Lettow-Vorbeck remained unconquerable. His achievements in an unequal struggle and his talent for organization place him forever in the front rank of our military leaders.

TURKEY DECLARES WAR

SHE SEEKS TO DRAW ALL MOHAMMEDANS INTO A "HOLY WAR"

OCTOBER 29TH

PROF. STEPHEN DUGGAN   TALAAT PASHA
SULTAN MEHMED   ESSAD EFFENDI, SHEIK-UL-ISLAM

A previous section has told how Turkey was drawn somewhat into the power of Germany by joining her in the trick of the pretended purchase of the German warships *Goeben* and *Breslau*. Germany now used these same ships for another stratagem which dragged Turkey into an open partnership in the War. The German admiral who had remained in command of the *Goeben* took his ship onward to the Black Sea and there deliberately attacked the Russians. Turkey was compelled either to punish him or accept the responsibility for his deed. The former she could not do, so she assumed the quarrel as her own. Following the German pattern, she declared that her ships had been the ones attacked and had gloriously "defended" themselves. The proclamation of the Turkish Sultan is here given, explaining his country's entrance into the War as he wanted his people to regard it—or rather, since the Sultan was a mere figure-head, these are the explanations of Talaat and Enver, the two Pashas who led the dominant Turkish party, the "Young Turks."

Then follows a still more interesting document, the FETVA, or church proclamation, announcing that this was a Holy War of all Mohammedans against the Christians. It was this Fetva that the Allies feared more than Turkey herself; for the Fetva might easily have roused against Britain her enormous Mohammedan populations in India and in Egypt. These, however, were soon convinced that there was nothing really religious about the Turkish call to arms, and that both the Sultan and the Sheik were really the helpless tools of the young Turks. The form of a Fetva is peculiar. It consists of a series of questions and their answers, the questions being drawn up so as to describe conditions and then ask if a certain course should be adopted in consequence. These questions are presented to an assembly of the chief dignitaries of the church, and after consultation they answer yes or no to each question. Questions and answers are then proclaimed to the "faithful."

To offset the distorted view of events thus presented here by the words of both Sheik and Sultan, we preface them by a neutral account of Turkey's real position. This article by Professor Duggan, a foremost American authority on the Balkans, was published in 1916.

A still more interesting review of the situation is that here given from the memoirs of Talaat Pasha. He, as chief executive of the "Young Turk" party was the real leader of Turkey throughout the War, directing her councils while Enver Pasha directed her armies. When Talaat was assassinated in 1921, he left behind some memoirs, which he opened with the words, "All I tell here is true, but not all of the truth." His family have allowed the publication of only a small part of these most illuminative memoirs, including the portion here given.

BY STEPHEN DUGGAN

A T the outbreak of hostilities between the Central Powers and the Triple Entente, all the Balkan states except Serbia proclaimed their neutrality. This was not done with the intention of maintaining neutrality. All of them had had their lust for territory whetted by war, and each now adopted a policy of "watchful waiting," of waiting for the propitious moment when it could enter the war and secure the greatest return in territory for the least expenditure in men and treasure. Each of the Balkan capitals became the scene of an intense diplomatic struggle between the representatives of the Central Powers and of the Triple Entente. The struggle was characterized first by the manner in which the fortunes of both groups of combatants rose and fell at the Balkan capitals in accordance with their success and failure on the battlefield, and second, by the amazing blunders of the Entente diplomacy. At the beginning of the war, Greece and Rumania leaned to the Triple Entente, whereas Turkey and Bulgaria favored the Central Powers; still, the aid of none of them was to be determined by sympathy, but by the greatest *quid pro quo*.

The war was but a week old when Turkey called to the colors all men between the ages of twenty-five and forty-five. The Young Turks in control of the government were determined to profit territorially by the European struggle, and it was practically a foregone conclusion upon which side Turkey would take her stand. Though England had once been willing to fight for the maintenance of the Ottoman Empire, that status was no longer vital to her, since she had secured the control of Egypt and thereby safeguarded the route to India. Moreover, she was now allied to Russia, whose traditional policy was to secure an early demise of the Sick Man. But the chief reason why Turkey was almost sure to side with the Central Powers was that whereas the Entente could offer only the maintenance of Turkey's territorial integrity in return for neutrality, the Central Powers could offer territorial aggrandizement in return for assistance. Early in August, Sir L. Mallet, the British ambassador, assured the Porte that the Entente would guarantee the *status quo,* were Turkey to remain neutral. At the same time the German ambassador was promising the restoration of Egypt to Turkey in return for Turkish alignment with the Central Powers.

Events moved rapidly and favorably for the Central Powers. As soon as war broke out, Great Britain laid an embargo on the two warships that had just been completed in British shipyards for the Turkish Government, and this action gave the greatest offense at Constantinople. On August 10th the German warships *Goeben* and *Breslau* escaped from the Entente fleets in the Mediterranean and arrived at the Golden Horn. International law required that they either be compelled to put out to sea or be dismantled and interned. Instead, the Porte shortly announced that the Government had bought both vessels from Germany. It afterwards informed Great Britain that the action was necessary to Turkey's defense because of Great Britain's unfriendly seizure of the two vessels under construction for Turkey in British shipyards. Moreover, in defiance of protests from the Entente powers, the German crews, engineers and gunners, instead of being sent home, were retained as parts of the Turkish navy.

As early as August 29th, Sir L. Mallet informed Sir Edward Grey: "There are grounds for thinking that the Germans are urging the Turks to send the *Goeben* and the *Breslau* into the Black Sea, where, they would argue, they had a right to go as Turkish ships. The Germans would count upon Russian warships attacking them, and war would ensue, seemingly provoked by Russia." Exactly two months later, on October 29th, the event predicted took place. Meanwhile, on September 10th, the Young Turks determined to take advantage of a divided Europe to denounce the Capitulations, viz., the treaties with foreign powers which limited the sovereignty of Turkey by granting to the nationals of the foreign powers privileges denied to native citizens. As Turkish legal administration is so corrupt that domicile and business in Turkey for foreigners would be impossible without the Capitulations, this action was received with strong protest by the United States and some of the other foreign powers.

In the meantime, a vigorous propaganda was carried on by German agents in Constantinople to influence public opinion. The subsidized press was bitterly anti-Entente, and published roseate reports of the German victories. As early as August 28th, Mr. Cheetham, the British agent at Cairo, telegraphed to Sir Edward Grey that Ottoman forces were mobilizing in the direction of the Red Sea and that Ottoman emissaries were stirring up feeling in Egypt against Great Britain. On September 28th, the Entente received a severe blow when the Porte notified the powers that the Dardanelles were closed. But the failure of the German advance upon Paris, and the great defeat of the Austro-Hungarians in Galicia had a calming influence upon the Turkish jingoes, and official neutrality was maintained. The Germans in Constantinople were determined, however, that Turkey should enter the war on the side of the Central Powers. The stakes were too high to admit of defeat. The extreme forbearance displayed by the British and French in the face of Turkish duplicity and insolence was due to their fear of the consequences that a rupture with Turkey might have upon their Mohammedan possessions. The Germans, on the other hand, hoped for a Holy War. The entrance of Turkey into the war upon the side of the Central Powers would keep a British army in Egypt to maintain the safety of the Suez Canal and to prevent any uprising. It would also detain a Russian army in Asia to withstand a Turkish advance into Russian Transcaucasia. On October 29th, Turkish naval vessels commanded by German officers suddenly bombarded several Russian Black Sea ports, including Odessa.

The following day, the Turkish minister of marine assured the British ambassador that the attack had not been ordered by the Government. This explanation did not placate Russia, which announced that it considered these hostile acts as inaugurating a war by Turkey upon Russia. Russia had no such reasons as England and France for patience with Turkey. The closing of the Dardanelles had already brought great distress to southern Russia, from which exports of wheat and oil had been rendered almost impossible.

In accordance with the Pact of London of September 5, 1914, whereby Great Britain, France and Russia converted the Entente into an alliance and informed the world that they would present a united front against their enemies and not conclude peace until their common purpose had been accomplished, Great Britain and France declared war upon Turkey, November 5th.

BY TALAAT PASHA
From his Memoirs in 1921

After the disasters of Turkey in 1913, she was left without a friend among the European nations. Russia then began a series of exactions, and Britain abandoned us to Russia. In this strait Germany alone assisted us, and by her protection enabled us to escape or at least postpone the Russian demands. This amiable attitude on the part of Germany encouraged us to suggest to the German Ambassador at the Porte that we might enter a permanent alliance with Germany. But while the ambassador seemed most favorable to this, the Berlin government was not. It answered in effect that Turkey was too weak, and that an alliance at the moment would be detrimental to both governments. This, in fact, explains our failure to find an ally anywhere. The European powers wished only for powerful allies, who could help rather than be a burden.

In June, 1914, however, we were surprised by an approach from the German government, which suggested that the project for an alliance be again considered. As we were in the same unhappy isolation as before, there seemed no reason for refusing this proposal. The alliance was discussed in a series of meetings with the German ambassador [Wangenheim], and agreement proved easy. A preliminary document was then prepared and signed, outlining the main points of the alliance, which was to be both military and political.

Just afterward there followed the series of events which culminated in the World War. We realized that Germany's change of attitude toward us must be due to her having foreseen some such warfare; but we still thought the alliance would benefit us. No European power would have welcomed us without expecting something valuable in return.

During the opening months of the War our position was very difficult. Practically we were already allied with Germany, and every day the German and Austrian ambassadors came to me urging our immediate entrance into the War. It would have been easy to have evaded them by pointing out that Italy, though a member of their alliance, had not joined them, or by showing that in invading Belgium, Germany had ignored her own signature to an alliance. But we were unwilling to break away completely from the partnership we had so anxiously sought and so much valued. So we told the Teutons we would gladly join them as soon as possible, but that to do so while Bulgaria remained undecided would be as dangerous for them as for us. Constantinople was wholly unprotected against a Bulgarian army. Since the Bulgars hated the Serbs, Germany should be able to persuade Bulgaria to join our alliance. Then, but not till then, Turkey could make good her agreement to fight in aid of Germany.

This logical answer enabled us to delay entering the War. So we waited and watched the course of events. Germany next urged us to conduct our own negotiations with Bulgaria; and as we could not well refuse this, Halil Bey and I went in person to Sofia. There, after many conferences with the Bulgarian leaders, we realized that they dared not act for fear of Rumania. If Rumania joined Russia, the combined armies could at once overwhelm Bulgaria; hence the latter could promise us nothing unless we could guarantee her against a Rumanian attack. For this reason we left Sofia and proceeded to Bucharest. There we became convinced after many conferences that Rumania was really determined on a strict neutrality. Radoslavoff, the Bulgarian premier, asked us to get a written promise of this neutrality; but Bratianu, the Rumanian premier, refused this.   He said that such a written contract would be unneutral, but that he could assure me by word of mouth that even if Bulgaria attacked Serbia, Rumania would continue neutral.   This promise seemed to Radoslavoff valuable but insufficient.   So we returned unsuccessful to Constantinople.

I am unaware how much the Entente statesmen knew of our efforts in Sofia and Bucharest; but after this expedition matters at Constantinople drifted on as vaguely as before.   The Germans and Austrians continued trying to trick us into the War, and the Entente tried to avoid each quarrel.   We played only for delay, which became constantly more difficult.   The German sailors in the city were very hard to control; and the number of German officials increased every day.   German influence grew always stronger.

Then came the Black Sea affair.   Our German admiral, Souchon, deliberately took our best Turkish ships [the *Goeben* and others] and bombarded the Russian fleet and some of the Russian cities.   We were generally supposed to have sanctioned this; and during the War I let this impression stand, rather than quarrel with the Germans.   Now that I am no longer at the head of affairs, I want it positively known that our Ministry knew nothing of the intended attack.   Neither I nor any other official authorized it.   On the contrary, we were much upset by it.   All the Cabinet members were very angry; we held a hurried meeting, and several of them resigned in protest.   The rest of us agreed to try to smooth the matter over.

The Russian ambassador at once sent us a vigorous protest.   So did the French and British representatives.   The latter two, however, were still hopeful of peace, and proposed that we make our innocence clear by dismissing our German admiral and sailors, and becoming strictly neutral.   We could not prolong this absurd situation.   To satisfy the Entente by a public repudiation of Admiral Souchon would have meant the loss of our German alliance forever. We held another anxious Cabinet meeting, the important one at which war was decided on.

My own position was that while much annoyed at the Black Sea affair, I nevertheless continued to believe that we should join with Germany. The Entente could give us nothing but the renewal of promises, so often broken, to preserve to us our present territory. Hence there was nothing to be gained by joining them. Moreover, if we refused aid to our German allies now in the time of their need, they would naturally refuse to help us if they were victorious. If we stayed neutral, whichever side won would surely punish Turkey for not having joined them, and would satisfy their territorial ambitions at our expense. As my country's leader, I surely could not lead her into such a hopeless situation. Therefore, I favored fighting on the side of Germany. The time of our entering was a lesser matter, though I would have preferred waiting for a more propitious moment.

During our Cabinet discussion news was brought us of an increased gathering of Russian troops upon our Caucasian frontier. The antagonism between the two armies there was already serious. So I advised that we accept the Black Sea affair as our own, put as good a front upon it as we could, and declare war against the Entente. A majority of the remaining Cabinet members supported me, and the conditions proposed by the French and British ambassadors were refused. Turkey openly joined the Teuton cause.

BY SULTAN MEHMED
Proclamation

To my army! To my navy!

Immediately after the war between the Great Powers began, I called you to arms in order to be able in case of trouble to protect the existence of empire and country from any assault on the part of our enemies, who are only awaiting the chance to attack us suddenly and unexpectedly as they have always done.

While we were thus in a state of armed neutrality, a part of the Russian fleet, which was going to lay mines at the entrance of the straits of the Black Sea, suddenly opened fire against a squadron of our own fleet at the time engaged in maneuvers.

While we were expecting reparation from Russia for this unjustified attack, contrary to international law, the empire just named, as well as its allies, recalled their ambassadors and severed diplomatic relations with our country.

The fleets of England and France have bombarded the straits of the Dardanelles, and the British fleet has shelled the harbor of Akbah on the Red Sea. In the face of such successive proofs of wanton hostility we have been forced to abandon the peaceful attitude for which we always strove, and now in common with our allies, Germany and Austria, we turn to arms in order to safeguard our lawful interests.

The Russian Empire during the last three hundred years has caused our country to suffer many losses in territory, and when we finally arose to that sentiment of awakening and regeneration which would increase our national welfare and our power, the Russian Empire made every effort to destroy our attempts, either with war or with numerous machinations and intrigues. Russia, England, and France never for a moment ceased harboring ill-will against our Caliphate, to which millions of Mussulmans, suffering under the tyranny of foreign dominations, are religiously and whole-heartedly devoted, and it was always these powers that started every misfortune that came upon us.

Therefore, in this mighty struggle which now we are undertaking, we once for all will put an end to the attacks made from one side against the Caliphate, and from the other against the existence of our country.

The wounds inflicted, with the help of the Almighty, by my fleet in the Black Sea, and by my army in the Dardanelles, in Akbah, and on the Caucasian frontiers against our enemies, have strengthened in us the conviction that our sacred struggle for a right cause will triumph. The fact, moreover, that to-day the countries and armies of our enemies are being crushed under the heels of our allies is a good sign, making our conviction as regards final success still stronger.

My heroes! My soldiers! In this sacred war and struggle, which we began against the enemies who have undermined our religion and our holy fatherland, never for a single moment cease from strenuous effort and from self-abnegation.

Throw yourselves against the enemy as lions, bearing in mind that the very existence of our empire, and of 300,000,000 Moslems whom I have summoned by sacred Fetva to a supreme struggle, depend on your victory.

The hearty wishes and prayers of 300,000,000 innocent and tortured faithful. whose faces are turned in ecstasy and devotion to the Lord of the universe in the mosques and the shrine of the Kaabah, are with you.

My children! My soldiers! No army in the history of the world was ever honored with a duty as sacred and as great as is yours. By fulfilling it, show that you are the worthy descendants of the Ottoman Armies that in the past made the world tremble, and make it impossible for any foe of our faith and country to tread on our ground, and disturb the peace of the sacred soil of Yemen, where the inspiring tomb of our prophet lies. Prove beyond doubt to the enemies of the country that there exist an Ottoman army and navy which know how to defend their faith, their country and their military honor, and how to defy death for their sovereign!

Right and loyalty are on our side, and hatred and tyranny on the side of our enemies, and therefore there is no doubt that the Divine help and assistance of the just God and the moral support of our glorious Prophet will be on our side to encourage us. I feel convinced that from this struggle we shall emerge as an empire that has made good the losses of the past and is once more glorious and powerful.

Do not forget that you are brothers in arms of the strongest and bravest armies of the world, with whom we now are fighting shoulder to shoulder. Let those of you who are to die a martyr's death be messengers of victory to those who have gone before us, and let the victory be sacred and the sword be sharp of those of you who are to remain in life.

MEHMED-RESHAD.

BY THE SHEIK-UL-ISLAM
Fetva

If several enemies unite against Islam, if the countries of Islam are sacked, if the Moslem populations are massacred or made captive; and if in this case the Padishah in conformity with the sacred words of the Koran proclaims the Holy War, is participation in this war a duty for all Moslems, old and young, cavalry and infantry? Must the Mohammedans of all countries of Islam hasten with their bodies and possessions to the *Djat?* [Jehad, Holy War.]

Answer: "Yes."

The Moslem subjects of Russia, of France, of England and of all the countries that side with them in their land and sea attacks dealt against the Caliphate for the purpose of annihilating Islam, must these subjects, too, take part in the Holy War against the respective governments from which they depend?

Answer: "Yes."

Those who at a time when all Moslems are summoned to fight, avoid the struggle and refuse to join in the Holy War, are they exposed to the wrath of God, to great misfortunes, and to the deserved punishment?

Answer: "Yes."

If the Moslem subjects of the said countries should take up arms against the government of Islam, would they commit an unpardonable sin, even if they had been driven to the war by threats of extermination uttered against themselves and their families?

Answer: "Yes."

The Moslems who in the present war are under England, France, Russia, Serbia, Montenegro and those who give aid to these countries by waging war against Germany and Austria, allies of Turkey, do they deserve to be punished by the wrath of God as being the cause of harm and damage to the Caliphate and to Islam?

Answer: "Yes."

THE CAPTURE OF TSING-TAU

JAPAN EXPELS GERMANY FROM THE FAR EAST

NOVEMBER 7TH

COUNT OKUMA   BARON KATO
A. N. HILDITCH   ADMIRAL SCHLIEPER

One by one the outer nations were drawn into the terrible circle of
the War. We have seen how Turkey entered unwillingly, foolishly,
driven by a reckless adventurer. Japan went in deliberately, we
might almost say gladly. She had long been in alliance with Britain;
she desired the friendship of Democracy throughout the world; and
she had bitter reason for resentment against Germany, which had been
foremost in depriving her of her spoils of victory over Russia and
China in the earlier wars. She was only too eager for so excellent an
opportunity of driving Germany out of the Far East.

She did this, with some small British and Australian aid, as thoroughly as Britain and France were expelling Germany from Africa.
Thus in the first months of the War Germany lost on the Pacific and
in Africa an empire which she had been forty years in building and
which had placed her high among world empires.

Japan's main effort was directed against Germany's stronghold in
the East, the fortified port of Tsing-tau, the center of the district of
Kiao-chau, from which the Germans ruled most of the Chinese province of Shantung. This much disputed region had been wrested from
China by the Germans as compensation for the murder of two German
missionaries deep in unknown China. Tsing-tau had been developed
into a great fortress well able to withstand a siege.

Japan's reasons for entering the War are here presented by her
leading statesmen at the time, Count Okuma, the Prime Minister, and
Baron Kato, the Minister of Foreign Affairs. Then follows a sym-
pathetic sketch of her work at Tsing-tau by one of her British allies.
The section closes with the passionate German picture of Admiral
Schlieper.

BY COUNT OKUMA

The following "ultimatum" of the Japanese Government was delivered to Berlin on August 15th.

We consider it highly important and necessary in the
present situation to take measures to remove the causes of all
disturbance of peace in the Far East, and to safeguard general interests as contemplated in the Agreement of Alliance
between Japan and Great Britain.

402

In order to secure firm and enduring peace in Eastern Asia, the establishment of which is the aim of the said Agreement, the Imperial Japanese Government sincerely believes it to be its duty to give advice to the Imperial German Government to carry out the following two propositions:

(1) Withdraw immediately from Japanese and Chinese waters the German men-o'-war and armed vessels of all kinds, and to disarm at once those which cannot be withdrawn.

(2) To deliver on a date not later than September 15th, to the Imperial Japanese authorities, without condition or compensation, the entire leased territory of Kiao-chau, with a view to the eventual restoration of the same to China.

The Imperial Japanese Government announces at the same time that in the event of its not receiving, by noon on August 23rd, an answer from the Imperial German Government signifying unconditional acceptance of the above advice offered by the Imperial Japanese Government, Japan will be compelled to take such action as it may deem necessary to meet the situation.

BY BARON KATO

Early in August the British Government asked the Imperial Government for assistance under the terms of the Anglo-Japanese Alliance. German men-of-war and armed vessels were prowling around the seas of Eastern Asia, menacing our commerce and that of our ally, while Kiao-Chau was carrying out operations apparently for the purpose of constituting a base for warlike operations in Eastern Asia. Grave anxiety was thus felt for the maintenance of peace in the Far East.

As all are aware, the agreement and alliance between Japan and Great Britain has for its object the consolidation and maintenance of general peace in Eastern Asia and the maintenance of the independence and integrity of China as well as the principle of equal opportunities for commerce and industry for all nations in that country, and the maintenance and defense respectively of territorial rights and special interests of contracting parties in Eastern Asia. Therefore, inasmuch as we were asked by our ally for assistance at a time when commerce in Eastern Asia, which Japan and Great Britain regard alike as one of their special interests, is subjected to a constant menace, Japan, who regards that alliance as a guiding principle of her foreign policy, could not but comply to the request to do her part.

Germany's possession of a base for powerful activities in one corner of the Far East was not only a serious obstacle to the maintenance of permanent peace but also threatened the immediate interests of the Japanese Empire. The Japanese Government therefore resolved to comply with the British request and if necessary to open hostilities against Germany. After the Imperial sanction had been obtained I communicated this resolution to the British Government and a full and frank exchange of views between the two governments followed and it was finally agreed between them to take such measures as were necessary to protect the general interests contemplated in the agreement and the alliance. Japan had no desire or inclination to become involved in the present conflict, only she believed she owed it to herself to be faithful to the alliance and to strengthen its foundation by insuring permanent peace in the East and protecting the special interests of the two allied Powers.

Desiring, however, to solve the situation by pacific means, the Imperial Government on August 15th gave the following advice to the German Government. [Here the Minister quoted the text of the Japanese ultimatum.] Until the last moment of the time allowed, namely, until August 23rd, the Imperial Government received no answer and in consequence the Imperial rescript declaring war was issued the next day.

With Austria-Hungary, as she had only the most limited interests in the Far East, Japan desired to maintain peaceful relations as long as possible. At the same time it appeared that Austria-Hungary also desired to avoid complications. In fact, as soon as Japan and Germany entered into a state of war, Austria-Hungary asked for the consent and good offices of the Imperial Government to permit the *Kaiserin Elizabeth,* the only Austrian man-of-war in the Far East likely to force a state of war, to go to Shanghai and there to disarm. I was about to communicate to the Austrian Ambassador the fact that Great Britain and Japan did not entertain any objections to the disarming of the *Kaiserin Elizabeth,* when suddenly on August 27th the Austrian Ambassador informed me that in consideration of Japan's action against Germany his Government instructed him to leave his post, and diplomatic relations were broken off.

When the relations of Japan and Germany reached the point of rupture the Imperial Government asked the American Government if in case of need it would be good enough to undertake the protection of Japanese subjects and interests in Germany. This request the American Government promptly complied with and subsequently upon the rupture of diplomatic relations between Japan and Austria-Hungary the Imperial Government again appealed for American protection for Japanese subjects and interests in Austria-Hungary, when the American Government gave the same willing consent. I desire to avail myself of this opportunity to give expression to the sincere appreciation of the Imperial Government of the courtesy so kindly extended by the American Government.

While regretting that Japan has been compelled to take up arms against Germany, I am happy to believe that the army and navy of our illustrious sovereign will not fail to show the same loyalty and valor which distinguished them in the past, so that all may be blessed by early restoration of peace.

BY A. NEVILLE HILDITCH

Before the outbreak of hostilities with Great Britain, Vice-Admiral the Graf von Spee, who commanded the German Pacific squadron, had steamed away from Tsing-tau with most of his ships. To use Tsing-tau as a naval base while engaging in commerce-raiding seemed a sound and a practicable plan, since the British and Australian naval forces, though superior, were hardly strong enough simul-

taneously to blockade the harbor and to search the seas.
The plan was, however, rendered impossible by the Japanese ultimatum, and the Admiral, after having lingered
for some weeks in the Western Pacific, departed for other
seas and other adventures. Such was the result of Japan's
action, and thus dangerous were the tactics that Japan's
action had frustrated. For Tsing-tau, situated upon one of
the two peninsulas, divided by two miles of waterway, inclosing the bay of Kiao-chau, with its safe and spacious
anchorage for vessels of any size, constituted one of the
most important naval bases on the Chinese coast. It had,
indeed, been described as the key to northern China.

Dominating the eastern coast of the Shantung peninsula,
the port of Tsing-tau formed the center of the semicircular
area known as Kiao-chau, extending on a radius of 32 miles
around the shores of the bay, with a population of 60,000.
This area was, under the Chinese-German agreement as to
Tsing-tau, influenced and controlled by Germany, though
not strictly subject to her, and regarded as neutral territory. Its surface was mainly mountainous and bare, though
the lowlands were well cultivated, but in parts it was rich in
mineral wealth, large but undeveloped supplies of coal being
present. In winter the port, connected to the junction of
Tsi-nan by a German-built railway, was the natural outlet
for the trade of northern China. The heights which surrounded the bay offered admirable sites for fortification,
while the land approaches to Tsing-tau were guarded by
formidable defenses stretched across its peninsula. In many
quarters the stronghold was regarded as a second Port
Arthur. The Germans had paid particular attention to defense, so much so, indeed, that over five-sixths of the white
inhabitants were engaged in military occupations. Five
thousand German marines constituted the normal garrison,
though the outbreak of war in August called about a thousand more men—volunteers, reservists, and sailors—to the
colors. The complement of the *Kaiserin Elizabeth,* an Austrian cruiser sheltering in the harbor, left for Tientsin,
having received orders to disarm their ship, but returned in
time to join the defenders. The garrison was amply pro-

visioned for five or six months, and well provided with weapons, stores, and munitions. Most of the German ships off the Chinese coast at the outbreak of war, indeed, had made immediately for Tsing-tau, and discharged upon its wharves many thousand tons of cargo. When war with Japan became inevitable, therefore, the defenders could anticipate a successful resistance, provided the expected instantaneous victories in Europe materialized.

On Friday evening, August 21st, at roll-call, the Governor, Captain Meyer-Waldeck, read out a message from the German Emperor exhorting the garrison to defend the town to their utmost, and to do their "duty to the last."

Vice-Admiral Sadakichi Kato, who commanded the Japanese attacking squadron, immediately upon arrival took measures to protect himself against danger from mines. Seven islets clustering round the mouth of Kiao-chau Bay were occupied, to form a convenient local naval base, while mine-sweepers swept the surrounding seas. No less than a thousand mines were taken from the water. A blockade of the whole Kiao-chau coast was declared, as commencing August 27th, and war vessels patrolled the shores, some seventy miles long. Action soon began, and continued during ensuing days, with shells that at intervals screamed towards the town. Kato was awaiting the approach by land of a coöperating army, which had now disembarked on the northern coast of the Shantung peninsula, about 150 miles due north of Tsing-tau.

The landing was effected on September 2nd, without hindrance or opposition on the part of the Chinese. The Government, following the precedent of the Russo-Japanese War, immediately published a declaration refusing to hold itself responsible for the obligations of strict neutrality in areas that formed, within Lung-kow, Lai-chau, and the neighborhood of Kiao-chau Bay, passageways essential to the belligerent troops. It was, of course, incumbent upon the Powers involved to respect Chinese property and administrative rights. Japan, therefore, was permitted to make use of the main roads to transport an army to the rear of Tsing-tau. The forces landed composed a division numbering 23,000, and commanded by Lieutenant-General Mitsuomi Kamio. An advance guard was sent forward without delay, but soon found its way rendered impassable by torrential floods which at this time swept down upon and devastated the province of Shantung, bridges, roads, an'd even villages being submerged and destroyed, with great loss of life, largely owing to Chinese official incompetence. The Japanese, after covering 20 kilometers in two days, reached a stream so swollen that crossing was impossible. The artillery had to return to Lung-kow.

About September 18th, after hostile patrols had been driven away from the shore by the fire of destroyers, Japanese artillery and troops were landed at Laoshan Bay, north of Tsing-tau, just within the leased territory. A small British force was also sent to the Tsing-tau area to coöperate with General Kamio.

The enemy at all points fell back, and the advance upon the town continued. The Japanese drew their lines across the neck of the narrow peninsula upon which Tsing-tau stands. There were indications that the main forces were now in contact. The only obstacle, but a formidable one, between the invaders and the forts themselves was constituted by the dominating height of Prince Heinrich Hill, from whose crest, rising some five miles from the town, all the forts could be bombarded. General Kamio estimated that three days of fighting would be required for its capture: it was as all-important to the defense as to the attack, and was sure to be strongly held. The forts themselves, of the latest type, were elaborately constructed, and equipped with concrete and steel cupolas, mounting high caliber pieces. They commanded both landward and seaward approaches to the town, those nearest the invading Japanese being situated upon, and named, Moltke Berg, Bismarck Berg, and Iltis Berg. Earth redoubts and trenches between formed the German line of defense. Plans for the most considerable engagement, the assault of Prince Heinrich Hill, that had so far taken place, to begin on Sunday, September 27th, were made by the Japanese general. It developed more speedily than had been expected. German artillery opened a terrific cannonade upon the Japanese lines, while three warships shelled the attacking right wing from the bay. The German fire was heavy and accurate. Japanese warships and aëroplanes, and also the British battleship *Triumph,* however, created a diversion that relieved the assaulting forces. Two of the forts were shelled from the sea, and suffered serious injury. During the morning of the 28th the Germans withdrew from Prince Heinrich Hill, leaving fifty of their number and four machine guns in Japanese hands, and many dead upon the slopes. The Japanese casualties numbered 150. By noon the whole position was in the attackers' hands, and the beleaguered town, visible from the height, was now face to face with siege. German officers who knew all the points, weak and strong, of the defenses, could not but realize their inability to withstand the siege guns which Japan would sooner or later bring to the attack. But the heavy artillery was yet far away. A month was to elapse before the pieces could be dragged across the difficult country, and emplaced in prepared positions on Prince Heinrich Hill.

At one o'clock on October 12th, Captain Meyer-Waldeck, the Governor of Tsing-tau, received a joint wireless message from the commanders of the besieging troops and the blockading squadron, offering a safe escort out of the town to Tientsin of neutrals and non-combatants. He at once assented. Delegates met next day at ten o'clock to discuss details, and on the 15th the American consul, accompanied by German women and children and Chinese subjects, left the town. It is recorded that, before reopening bombardment after the departure of the non-combatants, the Japanese, ever polite, signaled, "Are you now quite ready, gentlemen?" For reply a German sniper, taking careful but faulty aim, sent a bullet which removed three out of the eleven hairs of the signalman's mustache.

On November 2nd the Austrian cruiser *Kaiserin Elizabeth,* which had, with the German gunboats still afloat, been engaging vigorously in the fighting, sank, having probably been blown up deliberately, and the floating dock also disappeared. Iltis Fort, moreover, was silenced, two guns be-

ing smashed and ammunition giving out, and Japanese infantry advanced and captured an eminence in German hands.
On another ridge, however, hard by the silenced fort, some
German naval gunners carried out a ruse which saved for
the present both their position and their battery, composed
of naval 9-centimeter pieces, which were exposed dangerously to fire from sea and land.   Lieutenant von Trendel, in
command, during the night constructed wooden models of
cannon, which he placed in position 200 yards from his real
guns.   Next morning he exploded powder near by, and drew
the fire of the besiegers, attracted by the flashes, upon the
dummies.

That day the wireless and electric power stations were
wrecked, and large attacking forces crept further forward,
despite severe fire, and entrenched closer to the enemy's
lines.   In the evening and night the latter showed special
activity, star rockets and other fireworks being used to
illumine the opposing positions, which were heavily fusil-
laded.   A German night attack was delivered, but was repulsed.   Next day, the 4th, and on the two following days,
progress was maintained.   The Allied trenches were pushed
forward until they were right up to and almost half round
the nearest German forts.   Many casualties were suffered,
but the German fire was kept down by the Japanese guns,
whose accuracy was remarkable.   The weather conditions
were unfavorable, high winds and heavy rains prevailing,
and the troops in the trenches had to endure hard privations.
So effective was the bombardment, however, that during
November 5th and 6th plans were prepared for the final
assault.

Early in the morning of November 6th the airman von
Pluschow flew away across Kiao-chau Bay, and did not return.   He escaped with the Governor's last dispatches into
Chinese territory, where his machine was interned.   That
day and night saw no cessation of the firing, the guns of
the defenders still roaring at intervals.   About an hour after
midnight the first impulse of the general attack took effect.
While a particularly heavy artillery fire kept the Germans
in their bombproof shelters, the central redoubt of the first

line of defense, which had been badly shattered by the bombardment, was rushed by a storming party headed by General Yoshimi Yamada. Engineers had in the darkness sapped right up to the barbed-wire entanglements, which being cut, provided way for the infantry, who, while part held the enemy in front, rushed the redoubt on both flanks. Two hundred prisoners were taken, and the Japanese flag was hoisted. The besiegers were through the German line, but the position had to be consolidated, or disaster would follow. Danger from the flank was, however, soon obviated by advances in other parts of the line. Just after five o'clock a battery on Shao-tan Hill was captured; half an hour later another battery in Tao-tung-chien redoubt was taken, and Fort Chung-shan-wa, the base of the German right wing, fell. The shadows were still dense, and the final phase of the siege, viewed from Prince Heinrich Hill, presented a sight brilliant with many flashes and flaming fireworks, and a sound dominated by the thunder of the batteries.

At dawn Japanese and British were closing in, and were tensely awaiting the final assault. It was never made. Soon after seven o'clock a welcome sight relaxed the tension of the troops, torn, dirty, and weary, calling forth cheers from the British, and shouts of "Banzai!" from the Japanese. The campaign was over: Tsing-tau had fallen. White flags were fluttering from the forts.

That evening delegates from the two armies met and signed the terms of capitulation, which were unconditional. Honors of war were accorded the defenders, the Governor and his officers being permitted to retain their swords. The Allies marched into the town, and on November 10th the garrison was formally transferred. Over 4,000 Germans were sent to Japan as prisoners, and large quantities of war material were confiscated. The Japanese casualties numbered 236 killed and 1,282 wounded; the British, 12 killed and 53 wounded. On November 16th the Allies formally took possession of Tsing-tau; and a memorial service was held for the dead.

BY REAR-ADMIRAL SCHLIEPER

"We guarantee performance of our duty—to the last!"
A solemn heritage have these words become, these words
which the governor, naval Captain Meyer-Waldeck, just
managed to have transmitted by telegraph to his Commander-
in-Chief, from far-away Kiau-chau as a characteristic German pledge. Each one of us here in the Fatherland, clearly
realizing that the message voiced much bitter tragedy, was
grateful in his inmost soul to the brave man. Those of us,
however, who had been permitted to witness that which out
yonder had been undertaken and developed with enthusiasm
and flaming love of country, will to-day, on the morning
of November 8th, have felt especially sorrowful when they
read these words: "Tsing-tau has fallen!"

The flags were yet waving in celebration of the German
naval victory along the coast of Chili off Coronel—and already there comes in the quick succession of events the solemn tidings of the end of an heroic struggle, which was
maintained on a rocky height against gigantic odds. We
saw it coming—and yet our thoughts rebelled against the
accomplished fact, our whole being revolted against so much
baseness and deceit which a dual alliance, consisting of our
white cousins and of wily yellow Asiatics, had instigated
against German possessions. A sudden pang may flash
through us when we view so much German blood spilled,
but at the same moment our hearts should beat in fervent
gratitude for our heroes of Tsing-tau.

For seventeen years the German flag waved above yonder
rocky post. When in the nineties the awakening of the
Asiatic East steadily progressed, when a slit-eyed island folk
became always more desirous of mastering everything considered European, the time had come for Germany to get a
foothold in order to be able to maintain her "place in the
sun." The commanders of our naval military forces had
long had their orders for this reason to look around; and
when the murder of two German missionaries in Shantung
demanded energetic action, Admiral von Diedrichs, with the
landing troops of the ships under his command, occupied the

Chinese barracks on the northern cape of the bay of Kiau-chau.   On the same day he raised the German flag in spite of the vehement protests of the Chinese general who was stationed there.   On March 6, 1898, China agreed to a lease which should run for ninety-nine years, by which the bay of Kiau-chau, and a territory, in accordance with her wishes, was ceded to Germany.

Thereupon, by sending a division, consisting of ships and marines and detachments of sailor-artillery, care was taken that the new possession received augmented protection. After the barracks and dwellings had been first of all thoroughly cleansed for weeks—as a brother-officer wrote to me at the time—German Kultur could placidly make its entrance in Tsing-tau and the surrounding country.   And this came to pass.   With what love and care, with what pride and desire to create, the work was carried on in our far distant Kiau-chau, this pen is not capable of describing.   But one could easily follow it up in the monographs and plans published annually by the Imperial naval office.   It has been my privi-lege to visit many of our colonies and for a long time, but nowhere did I meet such a beneficent joy in creating as in Tsing-tau.   Every one wished to accomplish great things, and to emulate the other workers.   Everything was per-meated with German thought and German soundness.   There it was demonstrated to foreigners, to those who have now stolen it from us.   The German can colonize, even if he has pursued it only in recent years.

Seventeen years under the German flag!   How every-thing developed during that time!   German hydraulic archi-tecture and energy called into existence an extensive harbor Lighthouses, casting their beams far and wide, were erected on points and steep ridges.   One villa after another arose, not pretentious and obtrusive, no, rather tasteful and snug. Soon whistled the locomotive; the powerful step of our splen-did marine artillery resounded on the well-cared-for new roads.   Where once upon a time bleak rocks stood out promi-nently against the sky, the green of German afforesting soon covered the bare surfaces.   Everything was furthered—even the annual stream of guests, who, coming especially from

Shanghai, disported themselves on the beach of Tsing-tau. The governors, Truppel and Jaeschke, shaped a territory which a Meyer-Waldeck with his faithful followers was to defend to the knife in the past months.

Yes, everything flourished in Kiau-chau; but for this very reason, desire, greed, always came nearer and wished to taste, no, not to taste, to possess the whole of it. The opportunity for highway robbery could not have been more favorable. The World War had been enkindled—so quickly help yourself, for Germania has her hands full at home. Therefore act quickly; for we'll never gain our object more easily, and our white colleague there under the Union Jack, who always acts as if he were so superior but who really fears us yellow folks out here, he is fighting on our side, wants to crush his cousin with us. So quickly send an ultimatum to Germany, an insolent one to be sure, what does that matter. "Near is my shirt, but nearer is my skin"; and our colleague, John Bull, he would so much like it.

A disdainful rejection was the answer of Germania— and then Meyer-Waldeck drew his sword! "War! War!" was reëchoed in the region of Tsing-tau, "war against a fine pair of brothers! So let it be: we shall fight to the last drop of blood."

And how they did fight! Nothing came of the desire to present the fall of Tsing-tau as a birthday present to the Mikado on October 31st, as the Japanese had planned. There was bitter fighting. The enemy often sustained bloody repulses. The warships, including the *Kaiserin Elizabeth,* of the Austro-Hungarian navy, valiantly assisted. The *Kaiserin Elizabeth* wanted at all events to fight with us, to conquer, or—to sink. Then on September 28th, Tsing-tau was completely cut off by land; the situation steadily became more serious. From far and near the compatriots had hastened there—they would not desert their dear Tsing-tau at such a critical time. On September 27th combined Japanese and English forces had advanced to the Litsun River. In the ensuing engagements they left one hundred and fifty dead and wounded on the place of combat.

On October 14th two German forts fell after a heavy

bombardment on the part of the hostile warships. But the German guns answered smartly. A 20-centimeter projectile strikes the deck of the English man-of-war *Triumph* and causes heavy damage. In the meantime the German torpedo-boat *S-90* has destroyed the Japanese cruiser *Takashiho* in a bold attack. What does it matter that it had later on to sacrifice itself, as it would otherwise have fallen the prey of a large hostile superior force! It was able to save its crew.

The odds steadily increase, the glances toward the German eagle become more covetous, as the latter, bleeding from many wounds, stakes his all to keep what he has acquired, but which under his protection only too readily has stirred up the envy of others, even as this despicable trait of our opponents is the real reason for the World War.

A dreary, melancholy, gray November day without! Gone is the decoration of flags and the rejoicing of the day of Coronel! Everything in its time! To-day the throb of our hearts belongs to you heroes out yonder, our whole mood, our whole sentiment; for you have fought as German heroes have never been better able to do.

But we here at home, we will continually repeat it to our children: Do not forget November 7, 1914: do not forget to pay back those yellow Asiatics, who had learned so much from us, for the great wrong they have done to us, stirred up though they were by the petty English mercenary spirit! My pen refuses to go on! But one thing more I should like to attest to: Of a truth, ye heroes—ye dead, ye mortally wounded ones and ye survivors—ye did your duty to the last!

FAILURE OF THE GREAT ATTACK ON WARSAW

POLAND IS GROUND BETWEEN THE MILLSTONES

NOVEMBER 19TH-DECEMBER 6TH

GRANVILLE FORTESCUE   MARSHAL VON HINDENBURG
PRINCESS L. BARIATINSKY

We have seen that the first stage of the War on the Russian front had found the Germans with but a thin line of defense, and the Austrians numerous but enfeebled by the discontent of their subject peoples, and hence incapable of holding their own against the sturdy Russians and their able generals. After the fall of the Austrian power at Lemberg, it became necessary for the Germans to save their exhausted ally from invasion and destruction. General Hindenburg did this by a sudden bold advance against Warsaw, the capital of Poland. The Russian forces delayed their advance in Austria to rush to Warsaw's defense, and Hindenburg withdrew quickly to safety.

In mid-November, however, Hindenburg began a far different advance on Warsaw, one of the most determined, bloodiest, and long continued battles of the War. This was distinctly a major operation of the year, ranking with the huge battles of Lemberg and Ypres if not with that of the Marne.

Hindenburg won a great battle at Lodz, but was ultimately beaten back, and Warsaw for the time was saved. The cost to Poland itself was terrible. The Germans as they withdrew deliberately laid everything waste, so that the territory should no longer be of any value in supporting the enemy. What this military performance meant in terms of human misery to the Poles is immeasurable and unspeakable. Belgium never suffered as Poland did.

The Polish and Russian outlook on this tragedy is here given by the well-known Russian writer and philanthropist, Princess Bariatinsky. The details of the campaign are told by an eye-witness, the British observer with the Russian troops. The German side is given by its chief commander. Indeed, it was for his services in this campaign that Hindenburg was raised to the highest military rank and became Marshal Hindenburg.

BY GRANVILLE FORTESCUE

IN the study of this campaign we must always bear in mind that the Germans lay great stress on what I can only describe as sensational coups. Their point of view is

416

that the capture of a point such as Paris or Calais has a distinct psychological effect, in addition to the actual strategical results obtained. For this reason Von Hindenburg now suddenly became obsessed with a longing to capture Warsaw. There were also political reasons to influence this decision.

According to the Kaiser's proclamation a new King was promised to the Poles, and it is conceivable that if the Germans were in occupation of Warsaw and held nine-tenths of Polish territory they would instal one of their satellites as the successor of the ancient line. This, therefore, brings us to the audacious counter-offensive planned by Von Hindenburg, and it must be conceded that the old warrior conceived and executed the maneuver in a highly effective way.

He had already by his sudden retreat to the Silesian frontier committed the bulk of the Russian forces to an attack on Cracow, and having more or less denuded central and northern Poland of the enemy, he prepared his dramatic counter-stroke. He knew what advantages he held in having the network of railroads in Silesia at his disposal, and he took full advantage of his superior mobility. The transference of numerous army corps from Southern Silesia to Thorn and the adjacent cities was of a piece with the German methods of railway organization. Undoubtedly Von Hindenburg was correctly informed of the weakness of the Russians in Central Poland. He also knew he would have to pay but little attention to his flanks if he marched his army boldly down the tongue of land between the Vistula and the Warta. Simultaneously with the main movement from Thorn the Germans commenced an extraordinary counter-offensive from Vielun. The adventures of these two corps under the command of General François, a German Huguenot, form one of the most remarkable incidents of the campaign.

He fought his way directly eastwards through the Russian army which was now being brought rapidly back to Warsaw to check Von Hindenburg's disclosed offensive between the Vistula and the Warta. South of Lodz General François's two corps, reduced by hard fighting to a corps and a half, was practically surrounded. It will be remembered at the time how the official *communiqués* from Petrograd announced the surrounding and capture of an entire German army corps. This desirable consummation was, however, not brought about, to the great annoyance of the Russian General Staff.

I know from a German officer who served with this little army that they wandered round for six days in a circle, finding themselves everywhere blocked by superior Russian forces. Fortunately for them, at the last moment a gap was discovered. This gap was supposed to have been stopped by General Rennenkampf, who had a corps and a half at his disposal. This old Manchurian veteran went forward at forced marches with half a corps, leaving the task of bringing up the main body to his second in command. He seized a position which closed the gap, but unfortunately his second in command failed him. The reënforcements did not come up in time, and the Germans, driven desperate by their terrible position, cut their way through Rennenkampf's slender force, made good their escape after suffering heavy losses in men and material, and eventually joined hands with Von Hindenburg. Rennenkampf was in consequence relieved of his command, as well as his second in command, but it would seem as if the fates had dealt unkindly with the old veteran.

During all this time Russky was trying to make a half-wheel to throw his army across the line defending Warsaw, which he had now grasped was Von Hindenburg's real objective. An isolated Russian division which held Plock was eaten up by the Germans, and it was only extraordinary exertions on the part of the Russians that enabled Russky finally to occupy and intrench the line of the Bzura and Rawka.

There was a very sharp encounter at the junction of the railroads east of Lodz. Lodz itself was probably one of the most stupendous battles in the history of the world. The Germans had six corps engaged and the Russians eight, but not all the eight were present at the early fighting. It would be idle to try to give a detailed account of the movements of both armies, the front covered being so enormous. The compilation of the orders given during the battle would alone be a stupendous task. As a net result of the fighting and the terrific slaughter, the Russians were obliged to evacuate the city of Lodz and to fall back on Warsaw and the line of the Bzura. Before the main army took up this position there was a heavy rearguard action in Lovitz. In speaking of rearguard actions, it must be remembered that the term is no longer used in its former sense. In modern warfare whole corps cover the retirement of an army, and engage in actions which, as far as numbers of men and guns are concerned, equal some of the greatest battles of the Napoleonic era.

After the evacuation of Lodz we find the Russians safely entrenched along the line of the Bzura, which is the natural defense of Warsaw. In the general retirement, however, one division had been left in an advanced position to the west of Sochaczew. The Germans launched twelve separate assaults on this isolated corps, which was endeavoring to retire over ground of exceeding difficulty. A great portion of the division fell into the hands of the enemy, and the Germans claim to have captured over 20,000 prisoners.

This was the last incident in Von Hindenburg's second great offensive against Warsaw. By this time that offensive had spent its force, and in the interval of comparative quiet which followed, the Russians seized the opportunity of regrouping their armies along the line which they held until they finally evacuated Poland.

While the operations slackened in North Poland, hostilities were continued without interruption in North Galicia. The Russian offensive had advanced so close to Cracow that it became imperative to relieve the pressure. The Germans, apparently having at their disposal an inexhaustible supply of reserves, sent forward an army to threaten Pietrokow. At the same time the Austrians made their counterattack across the southern passes of the Carpathians.

This move was extremely important, because the advance guard of the Russian army had entered Hungary by one of the passes further west. The Austrian counter-offensive was carried out with great skill, and compelled a change of front on the part of the Russians. It was at this time that the investment of Przemysl was first raised. The cordon of steel was withdrawn from the Galician city, and the Austrians were not slow to take advantage of their opportunity. The civil population was practically expelled, and reënforcements, as well as immense supplies of food and ammunition, were brought in.

Not only did Von Hindenburg's offensive alter the complexion of the military situation in Galicia, it also had a distinct bearing upon the operations in East Prussia. The Russian operations against the Masurian Lakes were completely disorganized. It was, therefore, decided to abandon the proposed offensive in East Prussia, and to make a strong line in front of Warsaw. All the Russian armies were drawn upon to coöperate in this new distribution. The line of defense decided upon formed a half circle from Novo Georgevitch to Radom. Roughly, the Russian line was bounded on two sides by the Vistula, with the Bzura, Rawka, and Pilitza also serving as formidable obstacles.

Now the Germans began another of their incomprehensible frontal offensives. The battles of the Bzura—the plural is used advisedly, because they extended over a period of two months—can be in a way likened to the campaigning along the Yser. I first visited the actual scene of conflict on December 22, 1914. At that time the Germans were directing their main offensive against Sochaczew and Bolimow.

At the latter point they achieved certain local successes. I read afterwards in American papers that the Germans claimed a tremendous victory, going so far as to grant the school children a holiday in honor of their success. It certainly did the school children no more harm than it did the Russians. In justice to the enemy, however, it must be admitted that they showed the sternest courage in face of most appalling conditions. Time and time again whole battalions would wade through the freezing waters of the Rawka to struggle out on the opposite bank, where the snow-covered entrenchments poured forth immediate destruction on those who survived the passage of the river.

Daylight fighting ceased very early in these operations, and most of the attacks were carried through at night. Of course, both sides kept up intermittent artillery and rifle fire during the day, but it was only under cover of darkness that troops could be formed for the notorious mass attacks. Often the Russians would allow large bodies of the Germans to reach their side of the river, only to close in on them from three sides and either annihilate or capture them.

Throughout this period the Germans were unable to bring up the heavy artillery, owing to the awful state of the roads. Most of these heavy guns were not German, but Austrian. Finally, Von Morgan, who commanded at Bolimow, managed to get up two of the famous 30.5 centimeter Austrian guns and commenced the bitter contest for the possession of Mogely farm.

At first the great shells disconcerted the Russians, but after a time they paid as little attention to them as they did to the smaller projectiles. The 30.5 centimeter shells would often make a crater eleven feet deep and forty paces in circumference. When they actually hit a trench, which fortunately was seldom, it ceased to exist, and the occupants disappeared, completely covered with earth, but after being dug out were often found but little hurt. Sometimes, however, they would suffer from concussion, which it often took two months to cure, although there would be no visible wound.

The Germans suffered severely from the cold. Forty prisoners captured in a counter-assault were brought into Guzow. A cart carrying two machine guns followed. But it was not the trophies of war but the men who interested me. Only about half had overcoats. And these were made of a thin, shoddy material that is about as much protection as paper against the Russian wind. When you know that the prison camps are all in distant, cold Siberia, try and think of the lot of prisoners. Yet for the moment the Germans were content. They were allowed to sleep. This is the boon that the man fresh from the trenches asks above all things. His days and nights have been one constant strain of alertness. His brain has been racked with the roar of cannon and his nerves frayed by the irregular bursting of shell. His mind is chaos. One thing he knows, he must fire and fire and fire. It does not matter if the gun barrel blister his fingers with its heat, never must it stop. That is the only way to hold back the line of wicked bayonets. When the bayonets come it is death or a Siberian prison camp. But when a soldier is once captured he feels that this responsibility of holding back the enemy is no longer his. He has failed. Well, he can sleep in peace now.

The fighting for the Bzura was a desperate, endless struggle. Days of see-saw battle found the Germans pressing the major part of their military might against the angle made by the Bzura and Rawka with the Pilitza River. Charge and counter-charge were the order of the day and night. Supermen, indeed, are these soldiers of the first line who stagger forward and back with repulse and attack.

BY FIELD MARSHAL VON HINDENBURG

The consideration that formed the basis of our new plan was this: In the existing situation, if we tried to deal purely frontally with the attack of the Russian Fourth Army, a battle against overwhelming Russian superiority would take the same course as that before Warsaw. It was not thus that Silesia would be saved from a hostile invasion. The problem of saving Silesia could only be solved by an offensive. Such an offensive against the front of a far superior enemy would simply be shattered to pieces. We had to find the way to his exposed, or merely slightly protected flank. The raising of my left hand explained what I meant at the first conference. If we felt for the enemy's northern wing in the region of Lodz, we must transfer to Thorn the forces to be employed in the attack.

We accordingly planned our new concentration between that fortress and Gnesen. In so doing we were putting a great distance between ourselves and the Austro-Hungarian left wing. Only comparatively weak German forces, including Woyrsch's exhausted Landwehr Corps, were to be left behind in the neighborhood of Czenstochau.

For our new concentration in the region of Thorn and Gnesen all the Allied forces in the East were distributed among three great groups. The first was formed by the Austro-Hungarian Army on both sides of the upper Vistula, the two others of our Eighth and Ninth Armies. We were not able to fill the gaps between the three groups with really good fighting troops. We had to put what were practically newly formed units into the sixty-mile gap between the Austrians and our Ninth Army. The offensive capacity of these troops was pretty low to start with, and yet we had to spread them out so much along the front of very superior Russian forces that to all intents and purposes they formed but a thin screen. From the point of view of numbers, the Russians had only to walk into Silesia to sweep away their resistance with ease and certainty. Between the Ninth Army at Thorn and the Eighth on the eastern frontier of East Prussia we had practically nothing but frontier guards reënforced by the garrisons of Thorn and Graudenz. Facing these troops was a strong Russian group of about four army corps north of Warsaw on the northern banks of the Vistula and the Narew. If this Russian group had been sent forward through Mlawa, the situation which had developed at the end of August before the Battle of Tannenberg would have been repeated. The line of retreat of the Eighth Army therefore appeared to be once more seriously threatened. From the critical situation in Silesia and East Prussia· we were to be released by the offensive of the Ninth Army in the direction of Lodz against the flank of the Russian main mass which was only weakly protected. It is obvious that if the attack of this army did not get home quickly, the enemy masses would concentrate upon it from all sides. The danger of this was all the greater because we were not numerically strong enough, nor were our troops good enough in quality, to pin down the Russian forces in the bend of the Vistula, as well as the enemy corps north of the middle Vistula, by strong holding attacks, or indeed mislead them for any considerable length of time. In spite of all this we intended to make our troops attack everywhere, but it would have been a dangerous error to expect too much from this.

Everything in the way of good storm troops had to be brought up to reënforce the Ninth Army. It was to deliver the decisive blow. However great was the threat to the Eighth Army, it had to give up two corps to the Ninth. Under these circumstances it was no longer possible to continue the defence of the recently freed province on the Russian side of the frontier; our lines had to be withdrawn to the Lake region and the Angerapp. This was not an easy decision. As the result of the measures of which I have spoken the total strength of the Ninth Army was brought up to about five and a half corps and five cavalry divisions. Two of the latter had come from the Western Front. In spite of our earnest representations Main Headquarters could not see their way to release further units from that side. At this moment they were still hoping for a favorable issue to the Battle of Ypres. The full extent and meaning of the difficulties of a war on two fronts were revealing themselves once more.

The lack of numbers on our side had again to be made good by speed and energy. I felt quite sure that in this respect the command and the troops would do everything that was humanly possible. By November 10th the Ninth Army was ready. On the 11th it was off, with its left wing along the Vistula and its right north of the Warta. It was high time, for news had reached us that the enemy also intended to take the offensive. An enemy wireless betrayed to us that the armies of the northwest front, in other words all the Russian armies from the Baltic to and including Poland, would start for a deep invasion of Germany on November 14th. We took the initiative out of the hands of the Russian Commander-in-Chief, and when he heard of our operation on the 13th he did not dare to venture on his great blow against Silesia, but threw in all the troops he could lay hands on to meet our attack. For the time being Silesia was thus saved, and the immediate purpose of our scheme was achieved. Would we be able to go one better and secure a great decision? The enemy's superiority was enormous at all points. Yet I hoped for great things!

In its rapid changes from attack to defence, enveloping to being enveloped, breaking through to being broken through, the "Battle of Lodz" reveals a most confusing picture on both sides. A picture which in its mounting ferocity exceeded all the battles that had previously been fought on the Eastern Front!

In conjunction with the Austro-Hungarians we succeeded in stemming the floods of half Asia.

Army Order at the Eastern Front, November 27, 1914

In the course of severe fighting lasting several days my troops have brought to a standstill the offensive of a numerically superior Russian army. [The Army Order reproduces a telegram from the Kaiser, in which the latter, after congratulating the commander on his new success and that of his troops, thanks him for protecting the eastern frontier. The Kaiser adds that he cannot better express his thanks than by promoting the General to the rank of Field Marshal.]

I am proud at having reached the highest military rank at the head of such troops. Your fighting spirit and perseverance have in a marvelous manner inflicted the greatest losses on the enemy. Over 60,000 prisoners, 150 guns and about 200 machine guns have fallen into our hands, but the enemy is not yet annihilated. Therefore, forward with God, for King and Fatherland, till the last Russian lies beaten at our feet. Hurrah!

BY PRINCESS BARIATINSKY

No wonder indeed that the Poles, who feel a fundamental unity among themselves in all three parts of Poland —Russian, Austrian and German—hate the German yoke with its hard, arrogant persistence and shrink with horror from a Germanized future; no wonder they turn to Russia with hope. The Germans who predominate in the Austro-German-Turkish Alliance—that true Triple Alliance of greed, ruthlessness, and barbarism—are the most implacable foes of Poland and will never voluntarily liberate their Polish subjects; whereas the victory of Russia means to the Poles the crushing of German militarism, the coöperation of Russia in a democratic Polish policy for the whole of Poland, and the elimination of the countless German colonists, who by hook and by crook have wormed their way into Russian Poland and are regarded by the Poles as their greatest enemies. On the other hand, the Poles, with a political prudence for which some would not give them credit, believe that this is a moment, not for settling old scores with Russia, but by coöperation with her for winning new rights and new responsibilities.

I, as a Russian woman, perhaps should not, and certainly would not, speak of the bad treatment of the Poles by Germany, because I know very well that Poland has suffered much from Russia in times past; but the feeling I have mentioned is that of the Poles themselves. Their future, as they see it, lies within the Russian Empire, as an autonomous, possibly a strongly federated state. Complete separation would ruin them economically and is not desired by the Polish democrats. But there is emphatically no desire to be joined to either of the Teutonic Empires. Even the Austrian rule, which nationally and ecclesiastically has been less oppressive than that of the Germans, is more odious to the Poles than their worst experience at the hands of Russia.

This is well shown by an open letter to the Emperor Francis Joseph, written by the recently deceased Theodore Eje-Milkovski, a Polish nationalist: "Your Majesty orders us to fight side by side with Prussianized Germans, who have always given examples of wild persecution of Poles. Can you imagine anything more shameful than this? The method—*divide et impera*—by means of which we were usually kept in dependence has wrought us enormous harm, having made us quarrel with the Ruthenians, who, like ourselves, are also an oppressed nation. Your fawnings on my compatriots were only to make out of them Austrians of Polish descent; nor did the mistakes of your statesmen and diplomatists at the time of the Balkan crisis bode us any good. Austria ought to think more about her own fate than to tempt youth with her promises which neither Austria nor Germany is able to fulfill. Austria would save herself if she would leave William II. to the fate he deserves."

With their characteristic political stupidity the Germans were blind to the Polish view of Poland. They thought they could cheat the Poles by a false cry of Revolution and all Poland would be on their side. Disappointed at being so wrong in their calculation, they have wreaked a terrible revenge upon Poland, with the result that every part they have touched is devastated. This has become a regular program. Whenever the Russians have had to abandon a district of Poland, in come the Germans bringing revolutionary proclamations. They have no success; enraged, they revenge themselves by murder, outrage, pillage, and fire. When they are driven back they destroy everything so as to hinder the advance of the Russians. This is repeated at different places, then at the same places over again, until the ruin of the country is complete. In some parts the invaders have been thrice, in others five times. The picture is one beyond description.

In Austrian Poland, known as Galicia, an added cause of misery was the financial crisis caused by the Austrian banks, from which the managers immediately decamped at the beginning of the war, carrying away all the money with them, thus spreading far and wide a state of destitution, aggravated by the fact that the Galician officials were left with their salaries unpaid. In the country districts in this part of Poland the harvests for several years have been bad, owing to excessive rain, and the war coming on top of this has produced complete agricultural ruin.

Imagine a front of 700 miles—Poland and Galicia together—and a hostile army invading it five times. The first great move towards Warsaw ended in the battle of Druskenike, at which the Germans were driven back and burned everything they did not steal. The second was by the fortress of Ossovetz; they were driven back again, destroying villages and towns on the way. The third came right up to Ivangorod. Again they were forced back, and again fire and pillage. The fourth move was against Sohachov on the Bzura, with the same result. The fifth, also repulsed, came by way of Gumin and Ossovetz. Since then the tide of battle has ebbed and flowed and ebbed again, and at the time of writing the Russian forces are slowly retiring temporarily, overweighted by superior numbers, so that once more the land is being overrun by the Austro-German hordes. The country through which the armies have passed and fought is absolutely desolate. Large towns have been practically destroyed; hundreds of villages and every hayrick in the country have gone up in flames. The Germans have carried off everything portable with them—the crops, food, fuel, oil, candles, soap, salt, warm clothes, boots, medicines. Churches have been robbed of money and jewelry. Livestock, of course, has disappeared; even the books and musical instruments have suffered the common fate, and in their rage of destruction the modern Huns have actually broken up the benches in the schoolrooms. Throughout a tract of country three times the size of Belgium, the first necessities of life are lacking, and it is no exaggeration to say that millions of people are starving and homeless. Most of the terrible excesses committed by the German troops in the Western theater, for which the German name will be forever execrated, have been repeated over and over again in Poland, in some cases in an aggravated form. I know authenticated instances of diabolical outrages on women, of soldiers blinded and disfigured by the use of sulphuric acid, and other cases quite as bad as any that were reported to Lord Bryce's English Committee of Investigation on German atrocities.

Apart from the enormous relief work undertaken by the private initiative of great societies and citizens' committees, the Russian Government has given ten million pounds to relieve the suffering of Poland; but in the gigantic flood of distress nothing can be sufficient. Warsaw, the capital of

Poland, that lovely town which expresses all the refined taste of the Poles, has been turned into a great home for the new class created by this revolutionary war—the refugees. In the most fashionable quarter of the city, the great Concert Hall in Chopin Street that a few months ago was the favorite resort of Warsaw society, is now a refugee shelter, where thousands bring the scraps of property they have saved from the general ruin, lucky even to have escaped with their lives. War mixes up all in the common misfortune, and here may be seen the once rich and the once poor, who are all now both penniless and homeless. This hall is a veritable vale of sorrows, but it leads out to a network of relief works that the Poles have built up since the beginning of the war. The appearance of a new social class, of an entirely new set of social conditions, has evoked a new form of public effort, which is full of most instructive lessons for social reformers. There has sprung into being a Citizens' Committee for the whole of Poland, with its office in Warsaw and sub-committees for each town or district, including all the representative men and women of Poland. These committees are purely voluntary, and the work they have done is invaluable. No one, least of all the Poles themselves, would have imagined that after years of exclusion from public life, the Poles would display such remarkable organizing ability as they have done on the Citizens' Committees.

The need of Poland not only calls forth in all parties in Russia sentiments of charity, but opens the way to an understanding of one of the problems set before us by the war. An influential Committee has been formed, under the name of "Petrograd to Poland," to assist in relieving distress. Forty-five trucks, equal in capacity to ninety English railway trucks, full of warm clothing and other necessaries, are dispatched twice a week to Warsaw for distribution; besides regular feeding trains run from the Polish centers into the country districts to feed the starving. A special deputation from the Committee accompanied the first trains to explain that these gifts were offered, not only in a spirit of pity, but as an expression of love that had long been felt.

KRAGUJEVATZ: SERBIA'S LAST VICTORY

THE RECONQUEST OF BELGRADE

DECEMBER 3RD-15TH

ROBERT LAFFAN   MME. MARINCOVICH
BULGARIAN OFFICIAL BULLETIN

Three times in 1914 did the Austrian forces invade Serbia, and three times were they decisively repulsed. Of the first invasion we have already told. The second was comparatively feeble and unimportant; but it is here described by Mr. Laffan along with the big third invasion. Mr. Laffan was a British religious worker in Serbia, who became a volunteer chaplain in the Serbian army, and as such saw the events which he describes.

This third Austrian invasion was at first successful, because the Serbian ammunition was almost exhausted. Hence the Serbs perforce retreated, abandoning their exposed capital, Belgrade. Then a store of ammunition reached them from their western allies; and in front of their arsenal town, Kragujevatz, they turned upon the Austrians and beat them completely. In this big and hard-fought battle there were perhaps three hundred thousand men on either side.

The Serbs now reëntered Belgrade(in triumph, led by their aged and valiant King Peter. Of this reëntry we are here told by a prominent Serbian lady who was present. The section is then closed by a contemptuous Bulgarian summary of the victory, to show the general Balkan attitude. The Bulgarians, ever in deadly hostility to the Serbs, were at heart as eager for Austrian victory as the Austrians themselves.

BY ROBERT LAFFAN

ON the heels of the retreating Austro-Hungarians the Serbs crossed the rivers and entered Bosnia and southern Hungary, while the Montenegrins pressed northwards into Herzegovina. It was an intoxicating moment. Not only had the Serbs defended the soil of free Serbia, but now they had swept out into the empire of their powerful adversary and appeared as deliverers amongst their subject brethren of the "Greater Serbia" that was to be. In many districts they found themselves in the midst of a pure Serbian and Orthodox population, which received them with demonstrations of welcome. Many were the sentences of death, imprisonment, or confiscation of property afterwards pronounced by various courts of the monarchy on its Serbian subjects for their reception of King Peter's army. But at the moment fortune seemed to smile on the Allied cause in eastern Europe. Though on the distant western front, the German rush was not yet definitely repulsed from the heart of France, in the east the Russians were unexpectedly successful and the Austro-Hungarian offensive in Poland had become a struggle for the defense of Galicia. In Bosnia the Serbs pressed on till they were encamped on the hills round Serajevo, and feasted their eyes on the beautiful city which they hoped soon to make their own.

But the Hapsburg monarchy was too powerful an adversary to be lightly attacked. Despite the Russian offensive Austro-Hungarian military pride could not submit to defeat at the hands of the despised "barbarians" of the Balkans. A second advance on Serbia was undertaken in September, and the Serbian army had to fall back and offer battle on its own ground. With them went a large number of Serbian families from Sirmia and Bosnia to avoid the natural penalties for having fraternized with their late invaders. These refugees, whose destitution was relieved by public subscriptions through the newspapers, constituted a serious drain on the slender resources of the country.

Yet the Austro-Hungarians were at first held on the western frontier of Serbia and were unable to advance far from the river banks where they were covered by the guns of their own monitors. At one point only did the new offensive seem likely to achieve success. Round Losnitza the Serbs had but a small force. Throwing their troops on this gap in the defense, the Austro-Hungarians steadily advanced during the middle of September. Suffering terrible losses owing to their attacks in close formation, but constantly replenishing their ranks with fresh troops, they pushed on towards Valyevo, which their general had promised to enter on September 20th. A moment of suspense ensued while the fate of central Serbia, and therefore of Belgrade, still heroically defying all assaults, hung in the balance.

Then a desperate fight at Rozhan turned the tide of invasion and the Austro-Hungarians were obliged to fall back on the Guchevo hills. Protected there by big guns on the Bosnian side of the Drina, they were able to beat off the Serbian attacks, and prepare for yet another effort.

During October there was desultory fighting along the frontiers. The Serbs attempted an invasion of Bosnia in order to compel their enemy to retire from Serbian soil. But the difficulties of supply and transport in that wild country were too formidable and the Serbian army too small to run the risk of detaching forces adequate to the task. Meanwhile the Serbian retirement from Sirmia enabled the Austro-Hungarians to continue their bombardment of Belgrade, which seemed likely to become completely wrecked.

In November the enemy launched their third and greatest invasion. General Potiorek, at the head of five army corps and two supplementary divisions, resumed the attack from the northwest. The situation was again critical. The Serbian troops were in the marshy plains between the Drina and the Save. The roads on which they depended for supplies had been broken up and rendered almost impassable by three months of war. The supply of ammunition was steadily dwindling. A withdrawal of the whole line was clearly necessary, despite the depressing effect of such strategy upon the army and the civil population. It was necessary to give the Austro-Hungarians a taste of the difficulties of the country. "All my strategy," said Voivoda Putnik in reference to this campaign, "consisted in placing between the enemy's fighting line and their impedimenta the Serbian national mud."

The decision was amply justified. Many of the Austro-Hungarian troops suffered terribly from hunger owing to the partial breakdown of their commissariat. Yet despite the geographical obstacles they continued to advance into Shumadia, supported by their numerous and powerful artillery. Driven from Rozhan, the Serbs abandoned Valyevo and retired to the hills that separate the valleys of the Kolubara and the Morava. The news of the fall of Valyevo was greeted with enthusiasm in Vienna, where it was supposed to indicate the collapse of the Serbian resistance. General Potiorek was decorated with a new order specially inaugurated in honor of his triumph.

But the Serbian army was still intact, though the dangers of the situation caused the General Staff to order the evacuation of Belgrade and a concentration to the south along the Rudnik range of mountains. At the beginning of December Serbia seemed to be at her last gasp. The Austro-Hungarians made their long-expected triumphal entry into Belgrade. Kragujevatz seemed certain to fall. The enemy moved large reënforcements into the lower Morava valley to make certain of Nish and so to cut off the Serbian retreat along the line of the railway. Worse still, the munitions were known to be almost exhausted; whole batteries were reduced to six rounds per gun. Worst of all was the moral effect of continued retreat. The Serbian peasant-soldier, seeing his familiar countryside in the possession of the enemy, began in many cases to lose confidence in superiors who would not offer battle. A little nation that had risen to renewed life after 400 years of death, and had struggled through endless difficulties towards liberty and unity, seemed on the brink of destruction. A more powerful and organized foe than any she had yet encountered had her by the throat. The nations of the West, still unprepared for war on the necessary scale, were unable to send forces to her support, nor could they have arrived in time had they been available. Serbia's doom was surely sealed. All her efforts were to end in submission to the empire which already misgoverned her co-nationals. All that the friends of Serbia could do was to avert their eyes in sorrow of heart while the death-blow was administered.

But at the moment when all seemed lost, relief came, and the Serbian army gathered itself together for a supreme effort. The news that supplies of ammunition were coming to the Serbs from her western allies must have leaked out. For a Bulgarian band descended from Strumitza one night at the end of November and succeeded in blowing up the railway bridge at the point where the frontier ran dangerously near the line. Fortunately they were too late. The munitions had already passed on their way northwards, and the Serbian High Command were preparing for their great stroke.

The aged king now appeared among his soldiers on the heights of Rudnik. The faint-hearted he invited to return to their homes. They should not be made to pay for their desertion should the coming fight be won. But the house of Karageorgevitch would conquer or die.

It was on December 3rd that the Serbs suddenly turned upon their enemy. General Mishitch, who had taken command of the First Army, now reported that he was confident of being able to break the opposing line. Moving forward even before he had received permission from Headquarters, he flung his force upon the astonished Austro-Hungarians. The Serbian gunners, masters of their science, poured such a pitiless rain of shells upon them that they believed the Serbs to have been in some wonderful way vastly reenforced. From every direction the Serbian infantry closed in on them, creeping over the hills and appearing suddenly from unlikely quarters. In the first three days of the fighting the Serbs took over 5,000 prisoners and the hillsides were strewn with the dead and wounded. The Austro-Hungarians fell back, hoping to re-form their shattered units. But they were given no respite. While they were continually attacked in front, a division under Colonel Angelkovitch moved rapidly through the mountains and planted itself between them and Valyevo. By this maneuver the Fifteenth Corps and part of the Sixteenth were cut off from their line of communication and had to make the best of their way by tracks and footpaths towards the Drina. Their retreat became a rout. Then the Serbs moved forward all along the line. Valyevo was recaptured after two hours' resistance, and the remaining Austro-Hungarian armies were driven northwards. As the disorder and confusion increased among the retreating enemy the fighting became a mere pursuit. In their haste to overtake the flying Austro-Hungarians the Serbs could not deal with the numerous prisoners who had surrendered. Convoys of several hundred were sent off into the interior with single guides to lead them. Finally no men could be spared, and the astonishing spectacle might be seen of long columns of prisoners marching across Serbia with no accompanying guard whatever. "Follow the telegraph wires and you'll come to Lazarevatz," they were told. To many towns of the interior the first news of victory was brought by these strange companies of unguarded prisoners.

On December 15th, thirteen days after they had left it, the Serbs were back in Belgrade. The soil of the mother country was again free from the invader. Seldom, since the time when Sennacherib's host melted away from the walls of Jerusalem, has there been so sudden and dramatic a change of fortune. In a fortnight the Serbs had been roused from despair by the iron will and swift decision of their leaders, and had hurled their opponents in headlong flight across the frontiers. Bravely had Serbia done her share of the common task of the Allies. Successive Austro-Hungarian armies had been shattered, and forces equal to the whole of Serbia's strength had been put out of action. When the Serbs came to count their spoils they found that they had captured close on 70,000 prisoners, 192 guns, 90,-000 rifles, 491 cartloads of ammunition and large supplies of other material of war. Truly the modern Serbian heroes had surpassed all the deeds of their forefathers. No enemy would again lightly attack the peasant-army that had rolled the pride of the Hapsburg empire in the dust.

Great were the rejoicings in Nish and Belgrade that Christmastide—the last that many thousands of Serbs were to spend in their own country. Well might they imagine that for the present their troubles were over and that their sorely tried nation was now to have a breathing-space of peace and quietness. Permanent peace they would not buy at the cost of abandoning France, Britain, and Russia; although Austria-Hungary now offered excellent terms, the Serbs felt themselves morally bound to the Allies, who had entered the war directly or indirectly on their account, despite the fact that the Powers of the Entente had not made (nor have yet made) any treaty with the Serbian Government. Peace did indeed reign in Serbia for many months;

but peace took her toll of suffering and death no less than war. By an irony of fate the very completeness of Serbia's victory brought upon her new and terrible misfortunes. Amongst the quantity of prisoners for whom at first adequate provision could not be made, were large numbers who had succumbed to disease amid the hardships of war. Scattered among the towns and villages of Serbia they soon began to spread the dreaded scourges of typhus and cholera. The trouble began in the west, in the districts of Uzhitze and Valyevo, where the line of the enemy's flight had remained littered with the dead bodies of men and animals. But the contagion spread rapidly across the country, and there were few means of arresting its progress. Since the outbreak of war Serbia had suffered from a shortage of doctors. Her medical students were accustomed to study at Vienna and other foreign universities, and in the summer 120 doctors and medical students, though non-combatants and therefore protected by international law had been interned in Austria-Hungary. Besides, strictness over hygiene is the result of a very developed material civilization and the Serbian peasantry had no idea of the measures necessary to combat the danger in their midst. In her agony Serbia sent an appeal to her allies, and soon medical units —British, French, Russian, American—were hurried out and set themselves with vigor to conquer the diseases. For four months they labored, many of the doctors, nurses, and orderlies falling victims to their devotion, and then they triumphed. By July, 1915, the typhus and the cholera were overcome, and Serbia was herself again, but with the loss of thousands of lives which she could ill spare.

BY MME. MARINCOVICH

Everybody knows the story of the deliverance of Belgrade; how the little Serbian army fell back for strategic reasons as the Austrians entered the city, but finally, after seventeen days of fighting without rest (for the Serbian army has had no reserves since the Turkish war), knit its forces together, marched 100 miles in three days, and drove the Austrians headlong out of the capital.

King Peter rode at the head of his army. Shrapnel from the Austrian guns was still bursting over the city. But the people were too much overjoyed to mind. They lined the sidewalks and threw flowers as the troops passed. The soldiers marched in close formation; the sprays clung to them, and they became a moving flower garden. The scream of an occasional shell was drowned in the cheers.

They are emotional people, these Serbians. And something told them that, even with death and desolation all about them, they had reason to be elated. A few hours before, the Austrians had been established in Belgrade, confident that they were there to stay for months, if not for years. Now they were fleeing headlong over the River Save, their commissariat jammed at the bridge, their fighting men in a rout.

So King Peter rode through the streets of the capital with his army, and came to the cathedral. The great church was locked, because the priests had left the city on errands of mercy. But a soldier went through a window and undid the portals. The King and his officers and some of the soldiers and as many of the people as could get in crowded into the cathedral. And, lacking some one to say mass, the King became a priest—which is an ancient function of Kings—and, as he knelt, the officers and soldiers and people knelt. There was a vast silence for a moment; and then, in every part of the church, a sobbing.

BULGARIAN OFFICIAL BULLETIN

The Austro-Hungarian action against Serbia seems to have failed. It goes without saying that the return of the Serbians to Belgrade does not mean yet that the handful of the starving and half-naked Serbian army has been victorious against its strong opponent.

The Serbian success, according to latest information, is due to means that are very little laudable in themselves.

The commander of the advance posts of the Austro-Hungarian army, being a native of Dalmatia, became intimate with the Serbians and committed an odious treason. He disclosed to them the dispositions of the Austro-Hungarian forces, and he himself, with the sections forming the guard, surrendered to the Serbians.

From the Austrian rearguard one part scattered to various villages, another was sleeping. They were not ready and, caught unexpectedly, were dispersed.

Austro-Hungarian prestige is severely wounded. The shameful treason shows how dangerous is the Pan-Serbian propaganda to the integrity of the Austrian Empire, when corruption has reached even the officers standing in high command.

The Austro-Hungarian General Staff, as we are informed, has already taken those measures imposed by the situation. The Generals, Frank and Potiorek, have been recalled and will be probably court-martialed. And it seems that the "brilliant" Serbian victories are the beginning of the end of the "Slav Belgium."

THE SEA FIGHTS IN THE SOUTHERN OCEAN

BRITAIN DRIVES THE GERMANS FROM THE HIGH SEAS

NOVEMBER 1ST AND DECEMBER 8TH

W. MACNEILE DIXON   REAR-ADMIRAL FOSS

When the War opened there were of course various German warships and auxiliary merchant ships scattered over the seas. Each one of these had a story of its own, before each one was ultimately caught and destroyed by Britain's pursuing fleet. These individual rovers did considerable damage to Allied shipping, the most successful of them being the *Emden,* whose career is a very Odyssey of the seas. In November she was caught and sunk in battle by the Australian cruiser *Sydney.* Next to the *Emden* in destructiveness was the *Prinz Eitel Friederich,* a swift and sumptuous passenger steamer converted into a raider. In March of 1915 she entered a United States port for safety and was there interned. During the later war she acted as a United States transport.

More dangerous than these scattered single ships was the Asiatic squadron of the Germans under Admiral Von Spee. He cruised through the Pacific to the southward, and off the coast of South America he encountered a much smaller and feebler British squadron. This daringly gave him battle on November 1st off the harbor of Coronel, and was defeated, almost destroyed.

This resulted in a second and much larger sea battle. Britain, knowing now where Von Spee's squadron was, sent against it a naval force as much superior to it as it had been to the tiny British ships at Coronel. This larger British squadron caught Von Spee off the Falkland Islands, which lie in the Atlantic close to the southern extremity of South America. Here on December 8th Von Spee's squadron was destroyed.

Professor W. Macneile Dixon, who here tells the story of both fights, is one of Scotland's most distinguished scholars. Admiral Foss is among Germany's most noted naval critics.

BY W. M. DIXON

THE presence of swift enemy cruisers on the ocean routes constituted indisputably the gravest danger to the trading and passenger vessels of the Alliance. Great Britain, therefore, whose shipping trade—three-quarters of the whole world's—was particularly exposed to heavy losses

from raiders, found herself called upon to police, and none
will call it an easy matter, all the waters under heaven, from
East to West and from pole to pole. A few days before the
outbreak of war, a nicely judged maneuver, Admiral von
Spee in command of the German fleet in China disappeared
into the ocean silences. For some time his movements remained a mystery but his ships were soon to be heard of.
Once at sea he detached from his squadron *Emden,* who
set about her work in the Indian seas, *Leipzig* and *Nürnberg,*
who sailed for the West Coast of America, and with his
more powerful vessels, *Scharnhorst* and *Gneisenau,* himself made haste to the Pacific. Raids on British merchant-
men had always formed part of the German scheme of naval
war, and great hopes were entertained of its success. Despite the size of her own fleet and the assistance admirably
rendered by her allies, Britain's necessities at home made
it impossible to spare immediately scores of vessels for
service in pursuing the raiders, and not until mischief
enough had been wrought were the hunters successful in
tracking and striking down their quarry. By means of
German traders, who found means even in war time to secure for him the necessary fuel, Von Spee renewed his supplies and kept his bunkers full of coal. Finally he effected
a strong concentration of five cruisers with attendant colliers at Valparaiso.

It was imperative in British interests that Von Spee's
career should as speedily as possible be cut short. What
forces were present in that area to accomplish this task?
They consisted of Admiral Craddock's squadron of three
armored ships, *Good Hope,* his flagship, *Monmouth,* and
Glasgow; the first-named a large cruiser capable of 23 knots'
speed, and armed with two 9.2-inch guns of an old pattern,
together with a secondary battery of sixteen 6-inch; *Monmouth* of equal speed carried no heavy guns, but had fourteen 6-inch weapons; *Glasgow,* a faster vessel, was but
weakly armed with two 6-inch guns. An armed liner of no
fighting value against warships, *Otranto,* accompanied the
cruisers, and *Canopus,* whose armament included four 12-
inch weapons, was on her way to join the squadron. Against

the German lighter cruisers, therefore, Craddock was well prepared, but should he encounter in addition *Scharnhorst* and *Gneisenau,* new and heavily armored ships carrying 8.2-inch guns of the newest style, his case was perilous. For two points must here be borne in mind; the first that the mere size of a gun is not sufficient to attest its destructive power, its age and pattern must also be considered; the second that 6-inch guns on the lower deck, such as were carried by *Good Hope* and *Monmouth,* may prove of little service in a heavy sea. There is no doubt the British Admiralty had anxieties about Craddock, recognized the danger in which he stood, and to meet it sent *Canopus* to strengthen him. But this ship, even had she arrived in time, could have brought with her no addition to his fighting strength. Modern actions are fought at high speed, and *Canopus,* built in 1899, was probably capable of no more than 15 knots. Her lameness saved her, and at a later date debarred her from any share in the Falkland Battle. During the whole period of her cruise she remained a negligible quantity. In defense of the British Admiralty it must be remembered that the war was still in its earliest stage, the new and splendid vessels since added to the navy not yet in commission, and the need in home waters imperative for an unquestionable superiority against the German High Seas Fleet, which might on any day or hour make its appearance in force. There the chief danger lay, and to detach powerful units for operations in the far seas appeared at the moment too risky a policy.

So the scales of fate descended against Admiral Craddock, who, sailing North from the Horn, on Sunday, November 1st, ran with his three cruisers into Von Spee's squadron of five, off Coronel, on the coast of Chili. It was an evil day, an angry gale rising, and a heavy sea already running with a prospect of worse. Five o'clock in the afternoon found the British Admiral, who signaled *Canopus,* still far to the South, "I am going to engage enemy now," steaming on a parallel course with the German fleet and distant from it about twelve miles. On sighting the British, Von Spee had shifted his helm, swung round to the south and drew in towards the high land. The weather had grown steadily worse and was now of the wildest, the wind of almost hurricane force, the evening drawing in as the great warships tore through the storm amid the throbbing of their own engines and the roar of furious seas, which poured in cataracts of foam over the plunging bows. The German Admiral's skillful maneuver in sheering under the mountainous coast gave him the advantage of position. His own vessels, hardly visible against the land, made a poor target for the English guns, his enemies were silhouetted in the last level rays of an angry sunset. Never was naval battle fought in the midst of such warring elements, or in such a theater of gloom. The frowning sky, the high and threatening coast, the shrieking gale and thundering seas matched well the raging guns and the feverish energies of men engaged in the mad orgy of battle. The decision came swiftly. Before ten minutes were past and after the third broadside *Monmouth* staggered out of the line, reeling and in flames. She struggled bravely back again only to receive more shattering wounds. Soon *Good Hope,* too, was aflame and out of control. Before the action had lasted three-quarters of an hour a terrifying explosion signaled her end. *Monmouth,* hardly more than a drifting wreck, answered *Glasgow's* signals for another half-hour. Then no answers came: she, too, was gone. The good German shooting—*Gneisenau* had several times won the Kaiser's prize for gunnery—and against a sharply defined target, the fact that their 8-inch guns threw a broadside of 3,300 pounds to which the reply from *Good Hope's* two 9-inchers was 760 pounds, and that the British 6-inch weapons, on their lower platforms, could do little in the seas that ran that day—were the decisive factors. Indeed, the British gunners, since they could not "spot" the fall of their shells, fired, for want of a better target, at the flashes of the German guns. No attempt at rescue appears to have been made. The sun had already set, and the weather, it is said, made it impossible. Boats could not be launched but lines and buoys from the vessels themselves might have had some success. We cannot tell. Nothing at least was

done, and not a soul of the sixteen hundred men aboard
the two British ships survived the battle. The unarmored
Glasgow, her sides rent by shells, made her best speed south
to join and warn *Canopus.*

Von Spee's victory was complete, but destiny had decreed for him a brief career. So resounding a blow against
the British fleet could not be suffered with impunity. It
was soon to be countered with a still fiercer buffet. But he
had secured for himself a name and fame in the annals of
the sea. He had won the first, and probably the last, of
German naval victories against the proudest of his country's
foes—Britain, not easily worsted or caught napping on her
native element. Nor can he himself have had any illusions in pondering that day's work for the Fatherland, splendid as it was. He foresaw clearly enough destruction
threaten him, that at no distant date he must join his gallant enemy in a sailor's grave. He made, however, the
best use of his time, and for several weeks hovered on the
trade routes of the South. Then difficulties of coaling, for
these increased with every week and month, drove him to
the Falklands, those treeless, rugged islands, where his coming had long been foreseen and dreaded by the little colony.
The plan to overpower the feeble defenses and to establish
there an easily defended German base had for some time occupied his mind. The promising move proved fatally unlucky, for he sailed straight into the lion's mouth.

The moment the news of Craddock's defeat reached
England, the Admiralty made an unhesitating and swift
decision; hardly twenty-four hours elapsed before the
avenging squadron sailed, and on December 7th Admiral
Sturdee arrived off the Falklands with seven vessels, which
included the battle cruisers *Invincible* and *Inflexible*. They
were to coal there and thereafter make search for Von
Spee. But he saved them the trouble, to his own chagrin
and the amazed delight of the British sailors. The very
morning after their arrival, punctual, as if on invitation, the
German ships obligingly appeared on the horizon. Sturdee's
squadron lay hidden behind the land and coaling quietly
proceeded while the unconscious Von Spee drew closer. By

nine o'clock *Gneisenau* and *Nürnberg* were within range and
Canopus fired a shot or two from the harbor over the pro-
jecting heights.   The two cruisers sheered off and waited
for their colleagues to join them.   The British were possibly in greater strength than they had reckoned.   Then, as
they opened the harbor mouth, they made the fatal discovery.   Not yet, however, did Von Spee immediately recognize the strength of the opposing force.   It was more
threatening than he had anticipated, but how threatening?
He waited and watched, nor guessed that ere the sun had
set, his fighting days would be done.   Then the British began to emerge.   First came the smaller ships, *Glasgow* and
Kent, and after them the battle-cruisers but shrouded in
smoke.   When it cleared a little the German Admiral saw
that only speed, if speed indeed availed, could help him.
He turned, and, before that menacing array, fled under full
steam to the East.

The weather offered a remarkable contrast to that in
which the battle off Coronel had been fought, for on this
December morning sunshine flooded the calm sea and the
breeze was light.   When the chase finally settled down the
rival fleets were within about twelve miles of each other,
and in view of the inhabitants of Port Stanley for about
two hours.   The British made no great haste, for the issues
were not in doubt.   All hands were piped to dinner as usual,
and time was even allowed for a smoke before Sturdee decided to close with the enemy.   Then under the peaceful
heaven the sleuth hounds stretched themselves on the course
that could only end in death.

The prospect of imminent action hardly at all disturbs
the routine of a British warship.   She is always prepared
and in fighting trim.   Every man on board knows exactly
what is required of him, and from the call of the bugle to
"Action Stations," till the whole tremendous machine is
working at its highest tension and prepared to hurl itself
upon the enemy hardly five minutes is required.   Watertight
doors and portholes are closed, woodwork thrown overboard, inflammable gear stowed and the men at quarters in

a few moments. Then the ship seems deserted for all the crew are behind armor.

As the Germans steamed away *Scharnhorst* was leading. About one o'clock Admiral Sturdee signaled "Open fire and engage enemy." Almost immediately, to increase their chances of escape, the three light cruisers left the German line and, dropping, it was thought, mines as they went, scattered to the south, followed at once by *Glasgow, Kent* and *Cornwall*. *Bristol* had already been detached to destroy Von Spee's attendant colliers. The battle thus resolved itself into a main and several subsidiary actions. Firing as they ran, *Gneisenau* and *Scharnhorst,* about two o'clock, changed course to the southeast. By three the battle was at its height, *Inflexible* engaging *Scharnhorst, Invincible,* Sturdee's flagship, *Gneisenau,* and it was clear that the German vessels were already receiving severe punishment. Outranged by the British, their return fire was almost negligible. At times a shell would cause a large hole to appear in *Scharnhorst's* side, "through which could be seen a dull red glow of flame," a very glimpse of the pit. Soon her masts and funnels went over the side—by four o'clock in a great cloud of smoke and steam she vanished with her entire crew. The pursuit of *Gneisenau* continued and made attempts at rescue impossible. Later on, about five o'clock, under the concentrated fire of the British cruisers she could do no more, turned over at first slowly, showing the men gathering on her side, and then like her unhappy consort, in a great burst of steam and smoke, her stern high in the air, plunged to the ocean depths.

Towards the end of the action, reports one of her surviving officers, one could not get along the upper deck as there was practically none left. "Nearly every man on the upper deck had been killed, all the guns were out of action, and one turret had been thrown bodily overboard by 12-inch lyddite shell. Both their engines were broken up and they had a fire in the after part of the ship. They would probably have had many more fires, but our shells striking the water near the ship sent up columns of water which kept on putting out the fires. The spouts of water sent up by our shells hitting the water near them went up as high again as their mastheads, probably about 300 feet." Half the *Gneisenau's* men were killed by shell fire before she went down. One German officer at least has no quarrel with fortune. The turret in which he stood was struck and there was no other survivor. He joined the crew of another gun and the same thing happened. He ran to still another gun station and a third shell disposed of that. While he was at work with a fourth gun the ship sank and, after over an hour's exposure in the icy water, he was picked up. Some men are surely born under a lucky star! The work of saving the survivors, floating "like a great patch of brown seaweed" on the surface, at once began, lines and buoys were thrown, all available boats swung out, and nearly two hundred men, including the captain, rescued from the icy water. Incredible as it may seem, these men expected to be shot and exhibited astonishment and delight when kindly treated. How little the Germans know of England and her sea tradition!

Meanwhile *Glasgow* pursuing *Leipzig* received about 5 o'clock a wireless message that the main battle was done. The German cruiser, already severely handled, fought on, however, very gallantly till 9 o'clock, when she, too, disappeared with all hands, save five officers and seven men picked up by the victor.

Another single combat, the most stirring, fiercest and most equal of all in this engagement, took place between *Kent* and *Nürnberg*, which had a knot greater speed than the British cruiser. The story is best told in the words of the *Kent's* captain. "It was a single ship action," he wrote, "as no other ship was in sight at the time. The chase commenced at noon and the action commenced at 5 p. m. After a sharp action, during which *Kent* was struck by the enemy's shell no less than thirty-five times, *Nürnberg* sank at 7.26 p. m.

"*Nürnberg* is a faster ship than *Kent,* but I appealed to the engineers and stokers to do all in their power to catch her and finely they responded to my appeal. The *Kent* went faster and faster until she was going 25 knots, more than a knot faster than she had ever been before. The enemy got nearer and nearer until at last she got within range of our guns. Soon *Kent's* shell began to fall thick and fast around her and she was struck many times till she was in flames. The enemy continued firing their guns until the ship was sinking, and as she sank below the surface some brave men on her quarter-deck were waving the German ensign. No sooner had she sunk than the *Kent's* men displayed the same zeal and activity in endeavoring to save life as they had done in fighting the ship. Boats were hastily repaired and lowered by men eagerly volunteering to help. Unfortunately the sea was rough and the water very cold, so we only succeeded in picking up twelve men, of whom five subsequently died."

Thus, then, in its various episodes the Battle of the Falkland Isles was fought and won. A crushing and decisive blow had been struck, but two German ships, *Prinz Eitel Friederich,* an armed liner, and *Dresden,* a light cruiser, had made their escape and were still at large in the Pacific. They, too, had to be dealt with. For some months longer they contrived to elude capture and to harass shipping on the Chilian coast. In March, however, *Eitel Friederich* came to the end of her resources, reached an American port and decided not to leave it. About the same time *Dresden* was rounded up by *Kent* and *Glasgow* at Juan Fernandez. She displayed little stomach for fighting and after a five-minutes' action hauled down her colors. The crew were taken on board the British ships. She had been badly damaged and set on fire. Finally the magazine exploded and she sank, the last of Von Spee's once able and menacing squadron.

BY ADMIRAL FOSS

The small protected cruiser *Emden* was at Tsingtau at the beginning of the war. She immediately left port, captured the Russian postal steamer *Rjaesan* and brought it into Tsingtau, where it was re-christened *Cormoran.* This ship, after extensive cruising, was interned at Guam.

The *Emden* then began her now famous cruise to the

South.   Passing through the Straits of Malacca, she sank there half a dozen large British steamers, the passengers and crews being sent on other vessels to Calcutta and Rangoon.   The *Emden* always knew how to evade the cruisers sent in pursuit of her.   On September 22, 1914, she destroyed the large petroleum tanks at Madras, disappearing in the darkness as quickly as she had come, when the forts opened fire on her.   Toward the end of September she sank four ships near Ceylon.   Of the vessels captured by her, she retained only the coaling ships.   Purposely she showed herself outside of Pondicherry, only to disappear again in the Arabian Sea.   She sank here five additional ships, and on October 20th set her course for a new scene of operations.   Passing between Sumatra and Java, she sank a large Japanese ship near Borneo on October 27th and again passed through the Straits of Malacca, where, at dawn of the 28th, she put into Penang, being camouflaged by reason of a fourth chimney.   She was believed to be the expected British cruiser *Yarmouth,* for which reason no alarm was given by the French torpedo boat *Mousquet,* which was here on guard.   The small Russian cruiser *Sheneshug,* which was lying in the harbor, was sunk, losing of her crew of 275, 1 officer and 88 men, 120 being wounded.   Thereupon the *Emden,* setting out to sea again and, on her way, throwing a few bombs into the petroleum tanks on shore, encountered outside the harbor the beforementioned French destroyer *Mousquet,* which she sank.   This attack naturally caused terror and consternation in India, whereas in England it had a sort of unique sporting interest, the commander of the *Emden,* Captain Müller, enjoying for a time a certain popularity there.

Early on the morning of November 9th the *Emden* put ashore a detachment of 3 officers and 40 men on one of the Cocos Islands, lying somewhat to the south of Sumatra, in order to destroy the wireless station and the cable to Australia and Madagascar. The *Emden,* however, had been recognized and the station had time to ask for assistance. Her call was caught by a transport conveying troops from

Australia to Colombo. This transport was accompanied by the cruisers *Sydney* and *Melbourne,* and the former was at once ordered to steam ahead with all possible speed. Before the *Emden* had time to take her detachment on board again, a battle ensued between the two ships. The unequal contest began at 40 minutes past nine and was at first favorable to the *Emden,* which struck her opponent ten times before she herself was hit. However, the first shots which reached her proved so effective that after half an hour the commander saw himself compelled to put his vessel on a coral reef, during the flight again scoring five hits against his pursuer. The foremast and smokestacks had been shot away, the steering gear damaged and the stern was in flames. After the *Emden* had run aground, the commander of the *Sydney* fired a few more shots which destroyed the engines, and then took up the pursuit of the *Emden's* coaling ship. On reaching the ship only the crew could be captured, the vessel itself having been sunk by opening the valves in the bottom of the ship. Subsequently the captain of the *Emden* surrendered in order to avoid further bloodshed, having lost 36 officers and 93 of his crew.

Therewith ended the successful career of the splendid ship. The vessels she had sunk aggregated 80,000 tons.

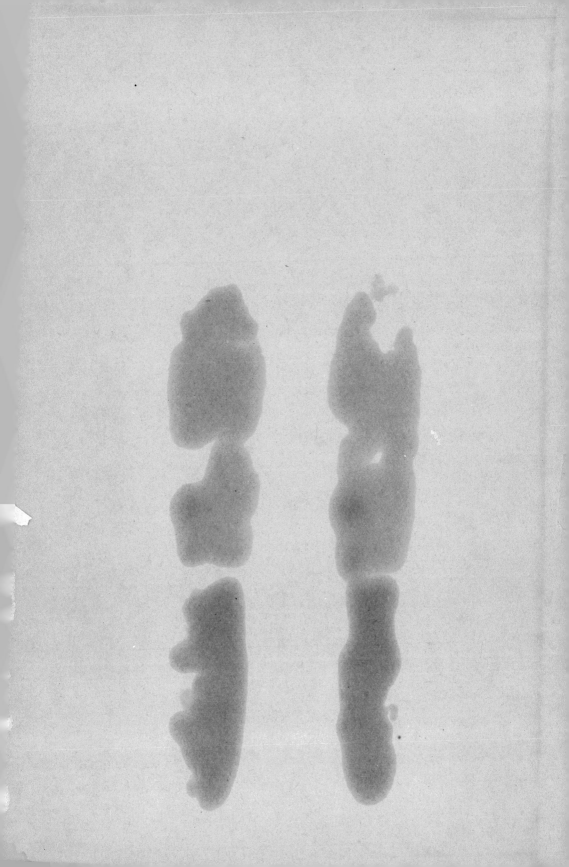